Mastering Visual Studio .NET

Mastering Visual Studio .NET

Ian Griffiths, Jon Flanders, and Chris Sells

O'REILLY®

Beijing · Cambridge · Farnham · Köln · Paris · Sebastopol · Taipei · Tokyo

Mastering Visual Studio .NET
by Ian Griffiths, Jon Flanders, and Chris Sells

Published by O'Reilly & Associates, Inc., 1005 Gravenstein Highway North, Sebastopol, CA 95472.

O'Reilly & Associates books may be purchased for educational, business, or sales promotional use. Online editions are also available for most titles (*safari.oreilly.com*). For more information, contact our corporate/institutional sales department: (800) 998-9938 or *corporate@oreilly.com*.

Editor:	Brian Jepson
Production Editor:	Sarah Sherman
Cover Designer:	Emma Colby
Interior Designer:	Bret Kerr

Printing History:

March 2003:	First Edition.

ISBN: 0-596-00360-9
[M]

Table of Contents

Preface . . . . **ix**

1. Solutions and Projects **1**
Solutions   1
Projects   7
Solutions, Projects, and Dependencies   17
Organizing Your Projects   30
Conclusion   36

2. Files **37**
Text Editor   37
HTML/XML Editor   48
CSS Editor   51
Design Views   52
Miscellaneous Editors   56
Changing Editors   56
Custom Build Tools   58
Conclusion   62

3. Debugging **63**
Starting the Debugger   63
Controlling Execution   72
Observing State   88
Debugging and Project Settings   97
Advanced Debugging Techniques   101
Conclusion   109

4. Web Projects **110**
   Web Project Templates   110
   Managed Web Projects   113
   Visual C++ Projects   122
   Conclusion   124

5. Databases **125**
   Server Explorer   126
   Database Diagram Designer   130
   Table Property Pages   133
   Table Designer   138
   Query and View Designer   139
   SQL Editor   146
   Database Projects   147
   Multiuser Issues   156
   Databases and .NET Projects   156
   Conclusion   166

6. Setup and Deployment **167**
   Windows Installer   167
   Setup Project Types   170
   The Installation Process   172
   Views   172
   Project Properties and Conditions   173
   User Interface View   174
   File System View   188
   File Types View   194
   Registry View   196
   Custom Actions   197
   Launch Conditions   205
   Cab Files   211
   Conclusion   211

7. Integrating Components with Visual Studio .NET **213**
   Basic Integration   213
   Simple Integration Attributes   216
   Custom Property Types   224
   Custom Component Designers   234
   Conclusion   249

8. Automation, Macros, and Add-ins **250**

The VS.NET Automation Object Model   251

Macros   263

Add-ins   274

Conclusion   286

9. Wizards **287**

Wizard Basics   287

The VS.NET Wizard Engine   293

Custom Wizard Engines   304

Conclusion   310

10. Visual Studio Integration Program **311**

Why VSIP?   312

Creating Custom Packages   318

Conclusion   324

A. Project Templates **325**

B. Project Item Templates **334**

C. Shortcut Key Guide **340**

D. Source Control Basics **356**

E. Solution and Project File Formats **367**

F. Text Editor Settings **372**

Index **385**

Preface

Just after they started building platforms that required development, Microsoft began building tools to perform that development. The authors of this book are personally familiar with *edit*, Programmer's Workbench, *windbg*, QuickC, QuickBasic, Visual C++, Visual Basic, Visual Interdev, Visual J++, and the general-purpose, all-time favorite, Notepad.

We've come a long way. This book is meant to provide the information that you need to get the most out of Microsoft's latest, and certainly greatest, integrated development environment (IDE): Visual Studio .NET (VS.NET). While the ".NET" portion of the name designates VS.NET's role in providing a full-featured IDE for all forms of .NET development, all of the major functions that Microsoft has provided in past IDEs are also supplied.

Audience

This book is for absolutely anyone doing development in Windows at all. If you're an MFC, C++, STL, ATL, COM, Win32, Visual Basic, C#, HTML, XML, ASP.NET, database, web application, web service, Windows Service, standalone client, or component programmer targeting Windows or the Windows variants (i.e., Windows CE or the PocketPC), VS.NET is calling your name, and this book was written for you.

This book is broken up into two major sections. The first section is about getting the most out of VS.NET as it comes out of the box, including the following topics:

- Solutions and projects
- Files and the various file editors
- Debugging
- Web projects
- Database projects
- Setup projects

The second section is about extending VS.NET, including the following:

- Integrating controls and components with VS.NET
- The VS.NET automation object model
- Macros and add-ins
- Custom wizards
- The Visual Studio Integration Program (VSIP)

We also provide a number of reference appendixes:

- Project types
- Project item types
- Keystroke shortcuts
- Source code control
- Solution and project file formats
- Text editor settings

Along the way, we go beyond what you'll read in the documentation to include using VS.NET in ways that the authors and the community at large have found to be useful.

Conventions

We use the following font conventions in this book:

Italic is used for:

- Pathnames, filenames, and program names
- Internet addresses, such as domain names and URLs
- New terms where they are defined

`Constant width` is used for:

- Command lines and options that should be typed verbatim
- Names and keywords in programs, including method names, variable names, and class names
- XML element tags

`Constant Width Bold` is used for:

- Marked lines of output in examples

`Constant Width Italic` is used for:

- Items that should be replaced by actual values

How to Contact Us

We have tested and verified the information in this book to the best of our ability, but you may find that features have changed (or even that we have made mistakes!). Please let us know about any errors you find, as well as your suggestions for future editions, by writing to:

O'Reilly & Associates, Inc.
1005 Gravenstein Highway North
Sebastopol, CA 95472
(800) 998-9938 (in the United States or Canada)
(707) 829-0515 (international/local)
(707) 829-0104 (fax)

To ask technical questions or comment on the book, send email to:

bookquestions@oreilly.com

We have a web site for the book, where we'll list examples, errata, and any plans for future editions. You can access this page at:

http://www.oreilly.com/catalog/mastvsnet/

For more information about this book and others, see the O'Reilly web site:

http://www.oreilly.com

Acknowledgments

All of the authors would like to thank the reviewers (Craig Andera, Peter Clark, Sam Gentile, Drew Marsh, Dan Moseley and his colleagues, Pierre Nallet, and Tomas Restrepo) and the editorial staff at O'Reilly & Associates, Inc. We'd also like to thank Microsoft for access to the Visual Studio Integration Package and for Visual Studio .NET itself, an amazing tool that made this book such a pleasure to write.

Ian Griffiths

I would like to thank Chris, Jon, and O'Reilly for getting me on board with the project and for their help and advice as the writing progressed. I would also like to thank everyone who gave up their free time to provide support and feedback, especially Glyn Griffiths and Matthew Adams. I would particularly like to thank Abigail Sawyer for her understanding and support during the rather intensive writing process.

http://staff.develop.com/igriffiths

Jon Flanders

I would like to thank Chris and O'Reilly (specifically John Osborne and Brian Jepson) for the opportunity to be involved in this book. I'd also like to thank Ian for being an excellent coauthor choice; without him, the book would not be the book that it is. I also want to thank Shannon Terra Ahern for giving me inspiration and input on this book and for being there while I was writing it.

jfland@develop.com

Chris Sells

First and foremost, as always, I'd like to thank my family for putting up with my odd work habits while contributing to this book. This book is dedicated to them. I'd also like to thank my coauthors, Ian and Jon, for putting their heart and soul into this book and for tolerating my endless comments and requests. Finally, I'd like to thank the readers who inspired this work in the first place. You make it all worthwhile.

http://www.sellsbrothers.com

CHAPTER 1

Solutions and Projects

The first product Microsoft ever built was a Basic interpreter for the Altair 8800 personal computer,* so they've had a lot of years to perfect their development tools. That time has not been wasted. Visual Studio .NET is the culmination of more than a decade of work on Visual C++, Visual Basic, Visual InterDev, and Visual J++. In this chapter, we will introduce the foundation of all VS.NET-based software development: solutions and projects. Everything that you do with VS.NET will revolve around these two concepts, so a sound understanding of these is central to making effective use of this tool.

To build anything with Visual Studio .NET, you need to use a solution, and that solution must contain at least one project. Solutions are the containers for all your work in VS.NET. A solution contains a project for each build output. (For example, if you want to build a DLL, an EXE, and an MSI Installer file, your solution will contain three projects.) Projects themselves contain source files. In this chapter, you will learn the ins and outs of solutions and projects and how to use them as effectively as possible.

Solutions

A solution contains a collection of projects, along with information on dependencies between those projects. The projects themselves contain files. This structure is illustrated in Figure 1-1. You can have as many projects as you like in a solution, but there can be only one solution open at a time in a particular instance of VS.NET. (You can, of course, open multiple solutions by running multiple instances of VS.NET.)

Solutions contain only projects—you cannot nest one solution inside another. However, projects can belong to multiple solutions, as Figure 1-2 shows, which gives you great flexibility for organizing your builds, particularly in large applications.

---

* See *http://www.microsoft.com/presspass/features/2000/Sept00/09-0525bookff75.asp*.

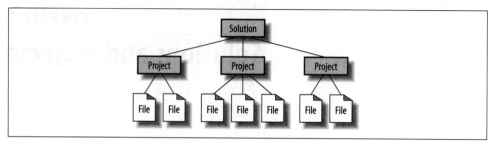

Figure 1-1. A solution, its projects, and their files

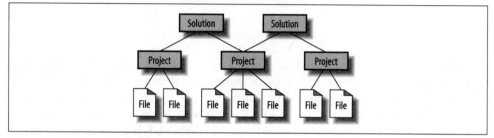

Figure 1-2. Projects that belong to multiple solutions

With Microsoft's previous generation of development tools, each language had its own integrated development environment. Now there is just one unified environment. In addition, there are no restrictions on the range of different project types any single solution can contain, so you can work on, say, an unmanaged C++ DLL in the same solution as a VB.NET Window Forms application, which can greatly simplify development, debugging, and deployment. But before we get too excited about that, let us see how to create a solution.

Creating a Solution

A new solution may be created in many ways in VS.NET. The simplest is to create a new project—by default, Visual Studio .NET will create a new solution with the same name as the project, placing the solution files* in the same directory as the project. Although this works fine for small projects, it isn't well suited to more complex applications. Since a solution is a container of projects, it does not make sense for the solution file to be inside the project directory. For multiproject solutions, having the directory structure reflect the solution structure usually makes more sense—it is best to have a directory that contains your solution file, with subdirectories for each individual project.

---

* Two files are typically created for each solution. The *.sln* file contains a complete description of the contents of the solution. The *.suo* file just contains information such as editor window positions and breakpoint settings. The *.suo* file is essentially dispensable since it is not required in order to build the projects in the solution; unlike *.sln* files, *.suo* files are not normally checked into source control.

Visual Studio .NET is happy to create this type of directory structure for you. When you create a new project by using the New Project dialog box (Ctrl-Shift-N), you can bring up additional options by clicking on the More button in the lower-lefthand corner of the dialog. These options are shown in Figure 1-3. (The More button turns into a Less button when the extra options are visible.) If you select the Create directory for Solution checkbox, Visual Studio .NET will not place the solution files in the same directory as the project. Instead, it will create a folder for your solution and inside this will create a second folder containing your project. The New Solution Name text box determines the name of both the solution and the solution folder. (You pick the project template you want to create as your first project and type its name in the Name text box as usual.)

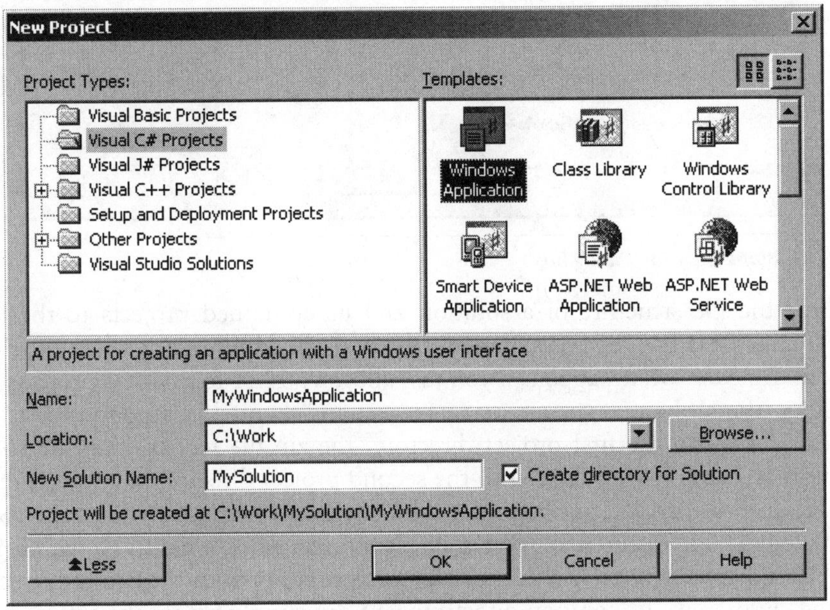

![New Project dialog box]

Figure 1-3. The New Project dialog box showing more options

You cannot select the Create directory for Solution option when creating a new ASP.NET project. With web projects, you will need to create a blank solution first in order to make your directory structure match your solution structure. To create a blank solution, use File→New→Blank Solution—this will show the New Project dialog box with the Blank Solution template selected (see Figure 1-4). You can use the Location text box to choose the path for this New Solution Name and the Name text box to give it a name. A folder with your chosen name will be created at the specified path, and a new solution file (with the same name as the folder) will be placed there.

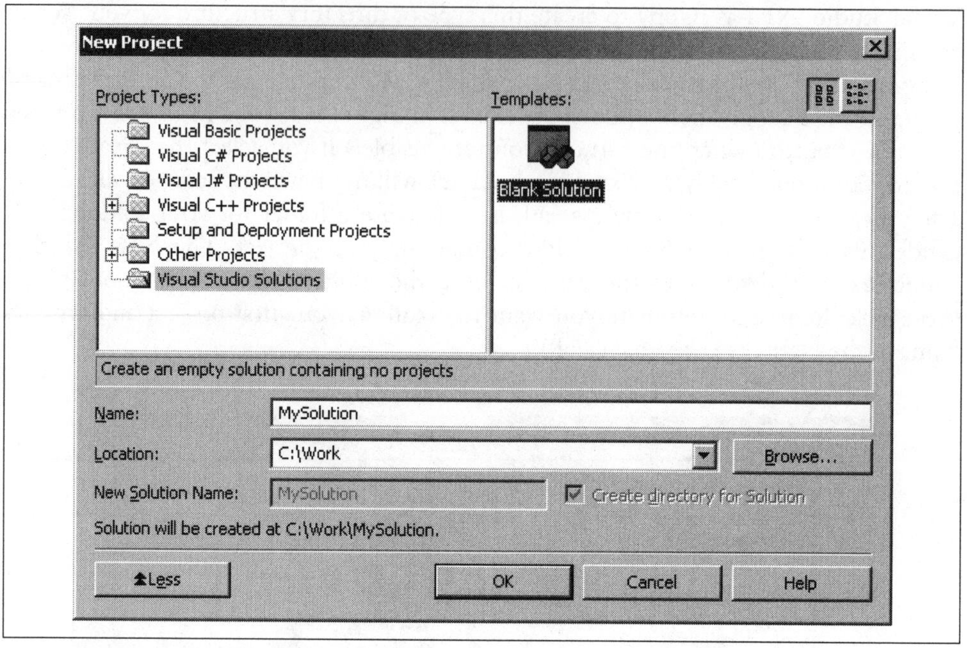

Figure 1-4. Blank Solution dialog box

Matching the file structure of a solution and its contained projects to the logical structure has the advantage of making it easier to put together a zip file of the whole solution. Consider what happens if you just allow VS.NET to put new projects in the default locations when you create a new project and then add a second project to the solution. If you zip the first project directory, the zip file will contain the solution file, but that solution file will refer to the second project directory. However, the second project directory will not be present in the zip file, because, by default, VS.NET will make it a peer of the first project directory instead of a child. However, if you make the directory structure reflect the logical structure, with the project directories all being children of the solution directory, you can simply zip up the solution directory, and the zip file will contain all of the projects that belong to the solution.

Figure 1-5 illustrates how the physical directory structure can reflect the logical structure of a project. Figure 1-6 shows how Visual Studio .NET will organize the directory structure if left to its own devices—the physical structure is less closely related to the logical structure. The solution file is located in an arbitrary project directory. (Specifically, it is in the first project that was created in the solution.) The project directories themselves may well be in the same directory as other, unrelated directories or files. So, to avoid the mess shown in Figure 1-6, be sure to check the Create directory for solution checkbox.

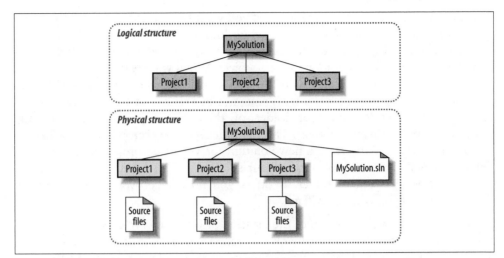

Figure 1-5. Solution structure and directory structure in harmony

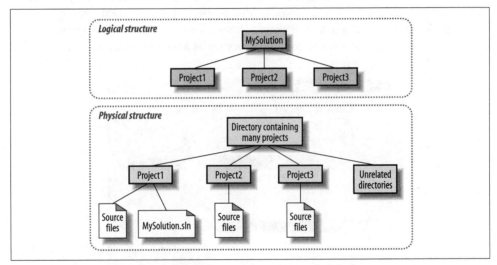

Figure 1-6. Solution structure and directory structure in discord (default)

Saving Web-Based Projects

By default, VS.NET creates all new solutions beneath the *Visual Studio Projects* folder inside of your *My Documents* folder.* However, it is a bad idea to put solutions that contain web-based projects here. Visual Studio .NET requires web projects to reside in a directory with Web Sharing enabled, and in Windows XP, you cannot turn on Web Sharing for directories underneath the *My Documents* folder.

---

* You can permanently change this default by going to Tools → Options, then going to Environment → Projects and Solutions and changing the path of the Visual Studio Projects text box.

A certain amount of planning is required if you want to keep control over where web projects end up, because although the default locations chosen by VS.NET for your files will work, they may not be the locations you were expecting, particularly if you let it create a new solution for a new web project. When you create a new web-based project, VS.NET communicates with the web server and checks to see whether an application already exists for the URL you specified. If not, it creates a new folder for the project under the root folder of the web server (which is usually %SystemDrive%\inetpub\wwwroot). The solution files, however, will be elsewhere— if you allow VS.NET to create a new solution for your web project (and it will by default), it will create a directory for your solution in the default location, underneath your *My Documents* folder. It offers you no choice over the location and doesn't even tell you where it will go!

If you want to remain in control of the location of your web projects and their solutions, you must first create a new blank solution. Then use Windows Explorer to create a folder for your web-based project inside of your solution folder. Enable web sharing on the new folder using the Web Sharing tab on the folder's property page, as shown in Figure 1-7. (You can get to the property page by right-clicking on the folder in Windows Explorer and selecting Properties.) Alternatively, you can use the IIS administration tool to set the new directory up as a web application.

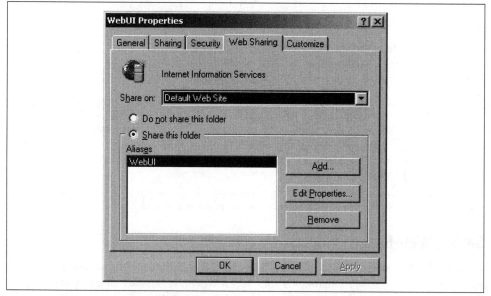

Figure 1-7. Web Sharing properties page

Once you have created the web shared folder, add a new web project to your solution. (Use File → Add Project → New Project. Alternatively, use the New Project dialog (Ctrl-Shift-N) but select the Add to Solution radio button—this will add the new project to your existing blank solution instead of creating a new solution.) You must specify the URL of the web share you created as the project location. This will cause Visual Studio .NET to use your existing web folder instead of creating a new one. When you create web projects in this way, all of the files needed for that web project and the solution that contains it are kept in one place rather than two.*

> When you create a folder that will contain a web-based project, you must make sure that the ASP.NET worker process will be able to access that folder. The ASP.NET worker process runs as the ASPNET user by default, so make sure that user account has permission to read and write files in that directory.

Projects

A project has two main jobs: to act as a container for our source files and to compile those files into some kind of component, typically either a Dynamic Link Library (DLL) or Windows Executable (EXE). We shall now run through the main types of projects supported by VS.NET.†

Project Types

Visual Studio .NET classifies projects by implementation language and then by project type in its New Project dialog box. However, many of the project types have a great deal in common despite using different languages, so although VS.NET 2003 Enterprise Edition lists more than 90 distinct types, most fall into one of six groups: managed local projects, managed web projects, Smart Device projects, unmanaged local projects, unmanaged web projects, and setup projects.

> Your copy of Visual Studio .NET may have even more project types—third-party add-ins can extend the list. You can also add your own project templates—see Chapter 9.

A *managed local project* will create a .NET assembly. *Managed web projects* do the same, but the project output is intended to be accessed by a client over a network connection, typically using either a browser or a web service proxy. Web projects are therefore always associated with a web application on a web server. And although managed web projects produce a .NET assembly just like a managed local project, with a web project, Visual Studio .NET will place the assembly on the web server as part of the build process.

---

* Of course, if your environment requires that you develop on a common web server rather than from your local machine, this will not be a viable solution, since the web project will be stored on another machine (the web server). In this case, Visual Studio .NET's default behavior for new web projects is perfectly reasonable, although it does make it impossible to keep the solution and all its projects in a single directory.

† Appendix A provides a complete list of project types. Some have been omitted from this chapter for brevity.

A web project can reside on either a remote web server or the web server on your local machine. Visual Studio .NET does not make any distinction between these two styles of development. However, if you use a remote server, you may need to modify its security settings in order to debug a web application successfully. See Chapter 3 for more information on debugging web applications.

Smart Device projects are available only in C# and VB.NET, and they build applications that target Pocket PCs and other mobile devices. These projects are not available with VS.NET 2002.

An *unmanaged local project* builds an unmanaged file (*.dll* or *.exe*). An *unmanaged web project* is the unmanaged counterpart of the managed web project type, in that its output will be deployed to and run from a web server.

Setup projects are used to create Windows Installer (*.msi*) files that can be used to deploy the final output of your solution.

Managed local

A managed local application could be written in C#, J#, VB.NET, or Managed C++ (MC++). VB.NET, C#, and J# all support the same local application types, which are shown in Table 1-1.

Table 1-1. C#, J#, and VB.NET managed local project templates

Project template	Project output	Type of file built
Windows Application	A Windows Forms application	Managed EXE
Class Library	An assembly to be used by other .NET assemblies	Managed DLL
Windows Control Library	An assembly containing at least one class derived from System.Windows.Forms.Control	Managed DLL
Web Control Library	An assembly containing at least one class derived from System.Web.UI.Control	Managed DLL
Console Application	A command-line application	Managed EXE
Windows Service	A Windows Service	Managed EXE
Empty Project	Any kind of .NET assembly	Managed EXE or DLL

Each of these project types builds a .NET assembly. You may be surprised to see the Web Control Library in this "local" category, but bear in mind that the distinguishing feature of a web project is that it is associated with a specific web application on a web server. Web Control Libraries can be used in any number of web applications but are not specifically associated with any one web application in particular. These projects simply produce a .NET DLL as their output, and this DLL will then typically be used by one or more web projects.

Managed C++ supports a subset of the project types available with C# and VB.NET. There is no MC++ Web Control Library project type, and on Visual Studio .NET 2002, the Windows Service, Windows Application, and Windows Control Library project types are also missing. The Visual Studio .NET designer does not support the use of Managed C++ to build Web Forms applications.

 Windows Forms applications were not supported in MC++ in VS. NET 2002 either, although it was technically possible to use the Managed C++ Application project type to build a Windows Forms application. This project type is really meant for building console applications, but if you didn't mind writing by hand all of the code that would normally be generated by the forms designer in C# and VB.NET projects, you could also use it to build Windows Forms applications. In VS.NET 2003, this is no longer necessary, as the Windows Forms Designer now supports MC++.

The MC++ project templates are in Table 1-2. Note that the names of these project types changed between VS.NET 2002 and VS.NET 2003, so both names are given in the table.

Table 1-2. MC++ managed local project templates

Project template	Project output	Type of file built
Console Application (.NET) (2003) MC++ Application (2002)	A command-line application (or a Windows Forms application, given sufficient determination)	Managed EXE
Class Library (.NET) (2003) MC++ Class Library (2002)	An assembly to be used by other .NET assemblies	Managed DLL
Empty Project (.NET) (2003) MC++ Empty Project (2002)	Any kind of .NET assembly	Managed EXE or managed DLL
Windows Forms Application (.NET) (2003 only)	A Windows Forms application	Managed EXE
Windows Forms Control Library (. NET) (2003 only)	An assembly containing at least one class derived from System.Windows.Forms.Control	Managed DLL
Windows Service (.NET) (2003 only)	A Windows Service	Managed EXE

Managed web-based

In a managed web-based project, the build output is copied to a web server and will run on that web server. (The web server can be either the one on your local machine or a remote server.) Of course, a web application typically needs more than just a compiled .NET assembly to run—there are usually files containing content such as *.css* and *.html* files, image files such as *.gif* or *.jpeg* files, and often files containing a mixture of code and content, such as *.aspx* files, that must be present on the server. So Visual Studio .NET does not just copy the compiled assembly to the web server—the entire project resides there.

Arguably, slightly too much resides on the web server. Visual Studio .NET uses a web project's associated web server folder as the canonical location for *all* project files, not just the ones that need to be there. So you will find all of your source files on the server along with the content and build output. This is because, conceptually, a web project doesn't store any of its files locally—the whole project lives on the web server. Source files are cached locally so that you can edit them and so that the compiler can compile them, but the permanent home of all project members and all build output is the web server.

If the prospect of storing the source for your web projects on the web server frightens you, don't worry—they need to be present on only development servers, not the live server. If you use a Setup and Deployment project to build an *.msi* file to install your project, only files needed by the web application to run will be included. So if you use this *.msi* to deploy the project on a server, the source files will not be installed. (Also, ASP.NET is configured not to serve out source files by default, so even on your development server, attempts to download the source using HTTP will fail.)

If you don't like *.msi* files, VS.NET is also able to perform the deployment itself directly. If you select a web project in the Solution Explorer and then select Project → Copy Project... from the main menu, VS. NET will show the Copy Project dialog. This allows you to copy a web project's files to another web server, and it provides you with the option to copy either all of the files or just the files the web application requires to run.

MC++ has only one project template in this group: ASP.NET Web Service (.NET). (VS.NET 2002 called this project type Managed C++ Web Service.) This project type is essentially the same as the VB.NET, J#, and C# ASP.NET Web Service project. All of the VB.NET, J#, and C# managed web-based projects are shown in Table 1-3.

Table 1-3. VB.NET, J#, and C# web-based projects

Project template	Project output	Output file types
ASP.NET Web Application	An ASP.NET Web Forms application	Managed DLL and web content files
ASP.NET Mobile Web Application (VS.NET 2003 only)	An ASP.NET Web Application intended to be viewed on Pocket PCs and other mobile devices	Managed DLL and web content files
ASP.NET Web Service	A web service	Managed DLL and web content files
Empty Web Project	Any C# or VB.NET web-based project	Managed DLL and web content files

An empty web project is useful if you want to build either an ASP.NET web application or web service, but you do not want the default options or files generated by VS.NET. (Of course, you could also write your own wizard to generate files that are more to your liking—see Chapter 9.)

Smart Device

Smart Device projects allow you to build applications that run on palmtop devices. These project types are not available on Visual Studio .NET 2002, and they target only C# and VB.NET. Each language lists just one Smart Device project. However, both the C# and VB.NET Smart Device projects open a wizard that allows you to target either the Pocket PC or the Windows CE platform, creating either a Windows Application, a Class Library, a Nongraphical Application, or an Empty Project. VS.NET ships with an emulator that enables you to test and run your applications on your PC without needing a real PDA. Detailed discussion of palmtop development is beyond the scope of this book. For more information on developing Windows Forms applications on the .NET Compact Framework, please see *Essential Windows Forms* (Addison-Wesley).

Unmanaged local

Unmanaged local projects build unmanaged executable files. These projects fall into three groups based upon the library used: Active Template Library (ATL) projects, Microsoft Foundation Class (MFC) projects, and straight Win32 projects. See Table 1-4.

Table 1-4. Unmanaged local projects

Library	Project template	Project output	Type of file built
ATL	ATL Project	An unmanaged executable that uses the ATL	DLL or EXE
MFC	ActiveX Control	An ActiveX Control built using MFC	DLL
MFC	Application	An MFC Windows Application	EXE
MFC	DLL	A DLL that uses MFC	DLL
MFC	ISAPI Extension	An ISAPI Extension DLL that uses MFC	DLL
Win32	Win32 Project	A simple Win32-based DLL or EXE	EXE or DLL

You may be surprised to see the MFC ISAPI Extension project listed as a local project, not a web project. But the defining feature of a web project is that it is associated with a particular web application on a server. MFC ISAPI Extension projects do not copy their build output to a web server—they work like any other local project. It is up to you to work out how to deploy the extension to a server.

Unmanaged web-based

Two ATL web-based projects, ATL Server Project and ATL Server Web Service, let you build web applications and web services, respectively. Both kinds of project build ISAPI extensions, using the ATL Server classes. (These classes were added to the ATL to coincide with the release of VS.NET.)

Like managed web-based projects, these projects connect directly to your web server and can contain other types of files than just the DLLs. To learn more about building unmanaged web-based projects with the ATL Server classes, see *ATL Internals*, Second Edition (Addison-Wesley).

Setup and deployment

The setup and deployment projects included in VS.NET allow you to create Microsoft Installer files (*.msi*) to deploy any VS.NET project. See Chapter 6 for more information about these projects.

Other project types

A few project types stand on their own, rather than fitting into any broad category. Database projects are described in Chapter 5. VS.NET Add-in projects are described in Chapter 8. Appendix A contains a complete list of all project types.

Adding Projects

Now that we have seen the available project types in VS.NET, let us see how to add projects to a solution. Adding projects is fairly simple—right-click on the solution in the Solution Explorer, and select Add → New Project to bring up the New Project dialog box, select the type of project you want, and then give it a name. You can also use Ctrl-Shift-N to bring up the New Project dialog box.

> If you use the Ctrl-Shift-N shortcut to add a new project to an existing solution, make sure you select the Add to Solution radio button. By default, the Close Solution button will be selected, which will close your solution and create a brand-new solution for the new project! You can avoid this entirely by using the context menu in the Solution Explorer as described earlier or with File → Add Project → New Project... from the main menu. Both menu options show the Add New Project dialog box, which is almost identical to the New Project dialog box, except it will never close an existing solution. Unfortunately, there is no keyboard shortcut for this dialog.

Figure 1-8 shows a typical example—a solution called WebManage containing three projects: a Class Library project named BusObj, an ASP.NET Web Application named WebUI, and a Windows Application named WinFormsUI. Figure 1-8 shows how this looks in the Solution Explorer.

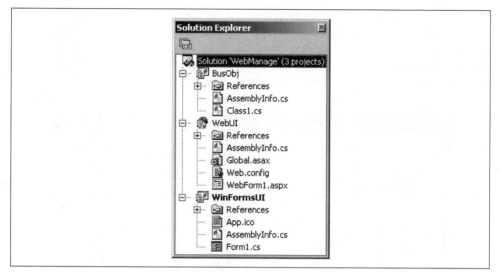

Figure 1-8. Multiple projects in the Solution Explorer

Managing files

Projects contain source files that will be compiled to produce the project's output. The following sections describe how to add new or existing files to a project and how to remove files from a project.

Adding a new file

You can add a new file to your project by right-clicking on the project in the Solution Explorer and selecting an item the Add submenu, which is shown in Figure 1-9. (The same choices are also available from the main Project menu.) The options these menus will offer depends upon the project type you are using (e.g., Add Web Form will be available only on web projects).

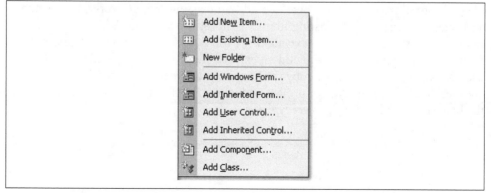

Figure 1-9. Adding a project item

The list of items offered on the menus is not comprehensive; it merely shows the most commonly used items. You can get the full list by selecting Add New Item (Ctrl-Shift-A), which will display the Add New Item dialog box, as shown in Figure 1-10. (See Appendix B for a list of the available items, and see Chapter 9 for more information about customizing the items and adding your own.)

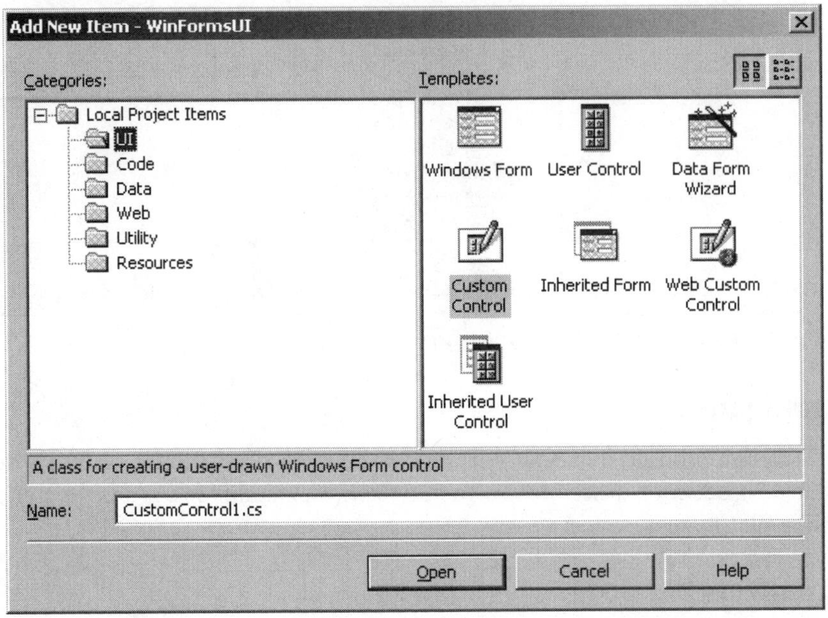

Figure 1-10. The Add New Item dialog box

Adding an existing file

Sometimes you will want to add an existing file to a project. For example, if you have downloaded some sample code from MSDN, you may want to add one of the sample's files to a project of your own. To add an existing file, go to the Project menu and select Project → Add Existing Item.... (Alternatively, select Add → Add Existing Item... from the project's context menu in the Solution Explorer. Or just use the Shift-Alt-A shortcut.) When you add an existing item, Visual Studio .NET will either use the existing file directly or copy the file into the project directory. The behavior it chooses depends on the type of project and where the file is located. Table 1-5 shows the behavior of the various project types.

Table 1-5. File management

Project or folder type	Behavior when adding existing items
Solution Items folder	Uses original
.NET Project (VB.NET, C# or J#)	Depends (see later), but usually makes copy
.NET Web Project (VB.NET, C# or J#)	Depends (see later), but usually makes copy
Visual C++ .NET	Uses original

With VB.NET, C#, and J# projects, if the file is already inside the project directory, no copy will be made. Otherwise, VS.NET will copy the file into the project directory.

If you would like to force VS.NET to use the original file when it would normally make a copy, you can choose to *link* the file instead. If you look at the Open button on the Add Existing Item dialog, you will see that it has a drop-down arrow on its right. If you click on this, it pops up a menu with a Link File option. If you select this option, VS.NET will add the original file to the project, even when it would otherwise have made a copy.

 The Link File option is not available on web projects. This restriction makes sense for local files—since the project resides on the web server, it would not make sense to allow links to files on a developer's local machine. With files already in the project directory on the web server, no copy will be made. Linking to a file in a different web directory is not supported.

Moving files between projects

If you wish to move a file between two projects in the same solution, you can simply use drag and drop in the Solution Explorer.

Removing or deleting a file

You can remove a file from a solution by highlighting it in the Solution Explorer and selecting Delete, either from the main Edit menu or from the file's context menu in the Solution Explorer. (You can also just press the Delete key.) For some project types, there will be a Remove option instead of a Delete option. Whether you see Remove or Delete will depend on the project type—VB.NET and C# projects offer Delete, everything else offers Remove. Either Delete or Remove will take the item out of the project's list of files, but Remove will leave the file in the directory, while Delete moves the file to the Recycle Bin.

Although C# and VB.NET projects provide the destructive Delete option instead of Remove, you may still remove an item from these project types nondestructively. Instead of selecting Delete, you can select Exclude from Project. (This is available both from the file's context menu and from the main Edit menu.) This takes the file out of the project but leaves the file in place on your hard drive—in other words, this does exactly what Remove does on other project types.

File properties

You can see a file's properties in the properties window by selecting the file in the Solution Explorer. (You can move the focus to the properties window by pressing the F4 key.) The properties shown will depend on the type of file and the type of project. Most files have very few properties, and the only properties common to all files regardless of type are Name and FullPath (those being the name of and path to the file). We will discuss type-specific file properties as we look at the individual file types in question.

Solution Items

Some files do not belong to any particular project in a solution. For example, you may have a solution that contains multiple web applications, all of which share a single Cascading Stylesheet (*.css*) file. You could arbitrarily pick one of the projects and make the file a member of it, but this does not accurately reflect how the file is used and could confuse other developers who use your code. Fortunately, you don't have to do this. Visual Studio .NET lets you add files to a solution without making them a member of any particular project. Such files are called *solution items*.

Solution items will not be compiled. Only files that belong to projects are compiled. Solution items are therefore typically some form of content or documentation.

You can add a solution item by selecting the Solution node in the Solution Explorer then using Add New Item (Ctrl-Shift-A) from the File menu to create a new solution item or Add Existing Item (Shift-Alt-A) to add an already existing file to the solution items. You can add any file type you like to a solution. Figure 1-11 shows how VS.NET displays solution items in the Solution Explorer.

If you use the Add New Item dialog box to create a new solution item, the new file will be created inside of your solution's folder. If you use the Add Existing Item dialog box, however, the items can live in any folder (i.e., you can add files that do not live in your solution folder). This is useful because it allows you to give yourself easy access to files in projects outside of your solution. Suppose you are writing a program that consumes a web service. It may be useful to have access to the WSDL file for that service. (A WSDL file is an XML file containing a detailed formal description

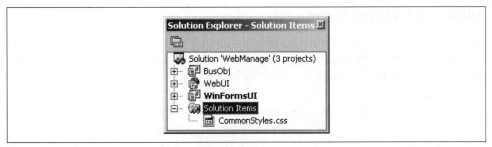

Figure 1-11. Solution items in the Solution Explorer

of the facilities offered by a web service.) This WSDL file will not be part of your client project—it will be supplied by the web service itself.* Although you can just go and find the file with the File Open dialog box every time you want to look at it, this gets old fast. You could also simply include the Web Service project in your solution, but that may slow down your load time and would also make it easier to modify and rebuild the project by accident. But if you just add the WSDL file to your solution as a solution item, it will be available in the Solution Explorer whenever you need it, without the need to include the project in the solution you are working on.

Miscellaneous Files

Visual Studio .NET will let you open and edit files that do not belong to any project and that are not solution items—you can open any file with File → Open or by dragging a file into VS.NET from Windows Explorer. This is useful because it allows you to edit files with a minimum of fuss. VS.NET calls these files miscellaneous files. You can get VS.NET to display all open miscellaneous files in the Solution Explorer. If you open the Options dialog box (Tools → Options) and expand the Environment folder, you will see a Documents item on the left. When you select this, one of the options presented on the right is "Show Miscellaneous Files in Solution Explorer." If you check this, any open files that do not belong to a project and are not listed in the Solution Items will appear in a folder labeled Miscellaneous Files in the Solution Explorer.

Solutions, Projects, and Dependencies

Remember that solutions do not just contain projects—they also hold information on the relationships between those projects. So once you have the projects you require in your solution, you must make sure Visual Studio .NET knows about the dependencies between them so that the projects will be built correctly. With .NET projects, this is done by setting up *references* from one project to another.

---

* By default, Web Service projects created by VS.NET do not contain a WSDL file, because the .NET Framework is able to generate these on the fly. However, because the WSDL can often be the basis of a contract between the web service provider and web service consumer, many web services hardcode the WSDL file into the project to make sure it doesn't change.

Adding References to Projects

All projects have a list of references, which is shown in the Solution Explorer directly beneath the project node. (See Figure 1-12.) Each item in this list represents a reference to some external component that your project uses.

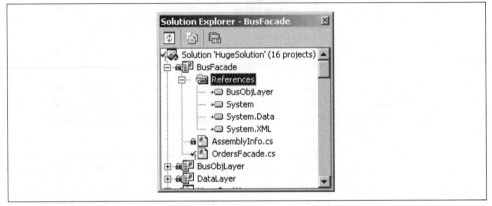

Figure 1-12. References

These external components can be .NET assemblies, COM components, or other projects within the same solution. With a .NET project, unless you add an external component to the References list, you will not be able to use that component's types in your project.

 With unmanaged C++ projects, you will add references only to other projects—you will not use the .NET or COM reference types. If your project depends on external C or C++ components, you will use the traditional ways of importing type definitions. (#include the header files and link in the *.lib* files.) For COM components, either #include the appropriate header files or use the #import directive on the relevant type library.

Adding a reference can serve up to four purposes:

- With .NET projects, it causes Visual Studio .NET to tell the compiler that your code uses the component, enabling you to use the types it contains—if you don't have the appropriate references in your project, you will get compiler errors complaining that a type or namespace cannot be found.

- If the component referred to is another project, Visual Studio .NET will infer dependency information from this and will use this information to work out the right order in which to build projects. (For example, if Project A has a reference to Project B, VS.NET will build Project B first, because it knows that Project A depends upon it.)

- Visual Studio .NET will copy the referenced component into the referencing project's build directory if necessary.

- VS.NET will load the type information contained in the referenced components and use it to provide IntelliSense—the pop-up lists of statement completion suggestions. (IntelliSense is described in more detail in the next chapter.) You can also browse the type information for all referenced components using the object browser. (This can be displayed with View → Object Browser, or Ctrl-Alt-J.)

 If you drag a component from the Toolbox onto a design surface such as a Windows Form or a Web Form, Visual Studio .NET will automatically add any necessary references to your project.

To add a reference to your project, right-click on it in the Solution Explorer and select Add Reference. (You can also select Add Reference from the context menu for the References node in the Solution Explorer.) This brings up the Add Reference dialog box, which is shown in Figure 1-13. There are three tabs on this dialog, one for .NET references, one for COM references, and one for Project references. The .NET tab and the COM tab enable you to add a reference to a .NET component and a COM component, respectively. Both present a list of installed components, but you can also use the Browse... button to import a specific component. The Project tab shows the projects in the solution that you can add as a Project reference. (Not all projects will be shown—for example, a project cannot have a reference to itself. Also, some project types do not produce output that can meaningfully be referenced from other projects—you cannot add a reference to a Database project or to a Setup and Deployment project.)

The COM tab simply lists all registered components on the local machine. .NET components provide VS.NET with more of a challenge, because, unlike COM components, .NET components do not need to be registered before they can be used, which makes it hard to build a complete list. VS.NET builds the list of available .NET components by looking in certain directories. By default, it looks in the install directory for the .NET Framework (*%SystemRoot%\Microsoft.NET\Framework\vX.X. XXXX*), but it will also look in any directories listed in a certain registry key.* So if you want extra components to be displayed in this dialog, add your own directories under that registry key.

The Copy Local property

Like most items in the Solution Explorer, references have properties that can be shown in the Properties pane (F4). Most of the properties are read-only and show details such

---

* *HKLM\Software\Microsoft\.NETFramework\AssemblyFolders.* Each directory should be specified as an *Assembly Folders* subkey whose (Default) value is set to the path.

![The Add Reference dialog box. A Windows dialog titled "Add Reference" with three tabs: .NET, COM, and Projects. The .NET tab shows a list of components with columns Component Name, Version, and Path.]

Component Name	Version	Path
Accessibility.dll	1.0.5000.0	C:\WINDOWS\Microsoft.NET\...
adodb	7.0.3300.0	C:\Program Files\Microsoft.N...
CRVsPackageLib	9.1.5000.0	C:\Program Files\Common Fil...
CRVsPackageLib	1.0.0.0	C:\Program Files\Common Fil...
CrystalDecisions.CrystalRepo...	9.1.5000.0	C:\Program Files\Common Fil...
CrystalDecisions.CrystalRepo...	9.1.3300.0	C:\Program Files\Common Fil...
CrystalDecisions.ReportSource	9.1.5000.0	C:\Program Files\Common Fil...
CrystalDecisions.ReportSource	9.1.3300.0	C:\Program Files\Common Fil...
CrystalDecisions.Shared	9.1.5000.0	C:\Program Files\Common Fil...
CrystalDecisions.Shared	9.1.3300.0	C:\Program Files\Common Fil...
CrystalDecisions.Web	9.1.5000.0	C:\Program Files\Common Fil...
CrystalDecisions.Web	9.1.3300.0	C:\Program Files\Common Fil...

Buttons: Browse..., Select

Selected Components:

Component Name	Type	Source

Buttons: Remove, OK, Cancel, Help

Figure 1-13. The Add Reference dialog box

as the path and version information. However, with a reference to a .NET component, you can change one property: the Copy Local property. If this is set to True, Visual Studio .NET will copy the component into the project's build directory.

The default setting for the Copy Local property depends on whether the reference is stored in the GAC (the Global Assembly Cache—the place where shared system components are stored). Such components are available to all applications without the need for copying files, so when you add a reference to a component that is in the GAC, Visual Studio .NET sets this property to false. For all other .NET component references, it will set this property to true.

The GAC is "global" only in the sense that the components it contains are available to all code on a particular machine. But just because there is a component in one machine's GAC doesn't mean that it is available everywhere. Be aware that when you reference a component in the GAC and then check the referring project into source control, it will not build when you download the project onto another machine if that machine's GAC does not contain the relevant component.

There is no formal mechanism for dealing with this in VS.NET. You may therefore want to consider establishing a procedure for putting nonstandard GAC components into source control, so that all developers will be able to get hold of them.

The behavior when the Copy Local flag is set to true is subtly different depending on whether the reference is to an external component or to another project in the solution. For external components, the copy is made when you create the reference. If the external component changes, or is even removed completely, Visual Studio .NET will not notice, and the project will carry on using the copy. If you care about the change, you must delete the reference and recreate it in order to get a new copy of the component. (Or you can just delete the copy from the build directory—this will cause VS.NET to make a new copy.) However, if the reference is to another project in the solution, VS.NET will make a new copy every time the project being referred to is rebuilt.

Project references are always preferable to external component references because of this automatic copy-on-build behavior. However, for third-party components, project references are not normally an option because you are unlikely to have the component's project file. (That would also require you to have the source.) However, third-party components tend not to change all that often, so the nonupdating nature of the references is less likely to be a problem.

Adding references to COM components

When you add a reference to a COM component in a .NET project, VS.NET will either find or create a .NET interop assembly. Interop assemblies are .NET wrapper components that enable a .NET project to use COM components. If there is a primary interop assembly registered on your system for the COM component, VS.NET will just use that. (Primary interop assemblies are wrapper assemblies generated with *tlbimp.exe* that are signed and distributed by the vendor of the COM component. Their purpose is to avoid a proliferation of wrappers by providing one definitive wrapper for a given COM component. VS.NET will look for primary interop assemblies in the GAC.) If no primary interop assembly is registered, VS.NET automatically creates a new interop assembly using the *tlbimp.exe* command-line tool and copies it into your build directory.

If you examine a COM reference after creating it, you will see that is really a reference to the interop assembly.

Adding references to other projects

With references to other projects, Visual Studio .NET automates two things: it automatically rebuilds dependent projects when necessary, and it automatically updates local copies after each change. For all other types of references, you are responsible for doing these jobs yourself.

Table 1-6 summarizes the behavior of the various types of references.

Table 1-6. Project reference types

Type of reference	IDE action	Versioning
Project	Copies the assembly to the build directory. Makes assembly available to the project.	When the referring project is built, VS.NET checks to see if the project being referred to also needs to be rebuilt. If it does, VS.NET will build it first and then copy the output to the referring project's build directory.
.NET, Copy Local = False	Makes assembly available to the project.	No copy is made, so if the original DLL is modified, the modified version will be used.
.NET, Copy Local = True	Copies the assembly to the build directory. Makes assembly available to the project.	A copy is made and will not be updated unless you explicitly remove and readd the reference.
COM	Uses primary interop assembly if available. Otherwise, uses the .NET *tlbimp.exe* tool to create an interop assembly. Adds reference to interop assembly.	If primary interop assembly used, behavior is the same as a .NET reference with Copy Local = False. If interop assembly generated by VS.NET, behavior is the same as .NET reference with Copy Local = True.

You should use project references whenever possible. It is technically possible to create a nonproject reference to the output of another project—you just add a new .NET reference and browse for the DLL. But you should avoid this because you lose all the advantages of a project reference. Project references make team development easier, since projects included in the same solution will be guaranteed to be present on each development machine (since these projects will be part of the checkin/checkout when working with the solution from source control). They also allows VS.NET to detect and disallow circular references.

Project Dependencies and Build Order

While adding a project reference automatically adds a dependency, you can also manage dependencies directly. Dependencies are solution-scoped properties that affect the build order of the projects in your solution. If Project A depends on Project B, VS.NET will always make sure Project B has been built before building Project A.

If you want to see the current build order, you can right-click on the solution in the Solution Explorer and select Project Build Order. This will show the Build Order tab of the Project Dependencies dialog as shown in Figure 1-14. The build order tab does not let you change the build order, because the build order is determined by the dependencies. You can view or edit your dependencies by clicking on the Dependencies tab (see Figure 1-15). Building the Solution

Once all of your references are in place, you can build your solution. The simplest way to do this is with Build → Build Solution (Ctrl-Shift-B). However, VS.NET offers many ways to build a solution, along with many ways to customize the build of a

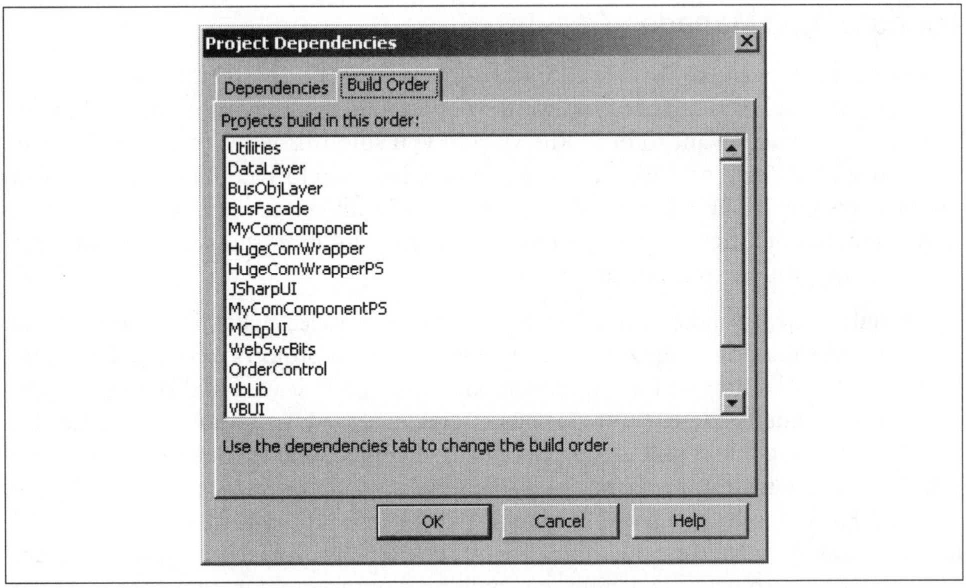

Figure 1-14. Build Order tab

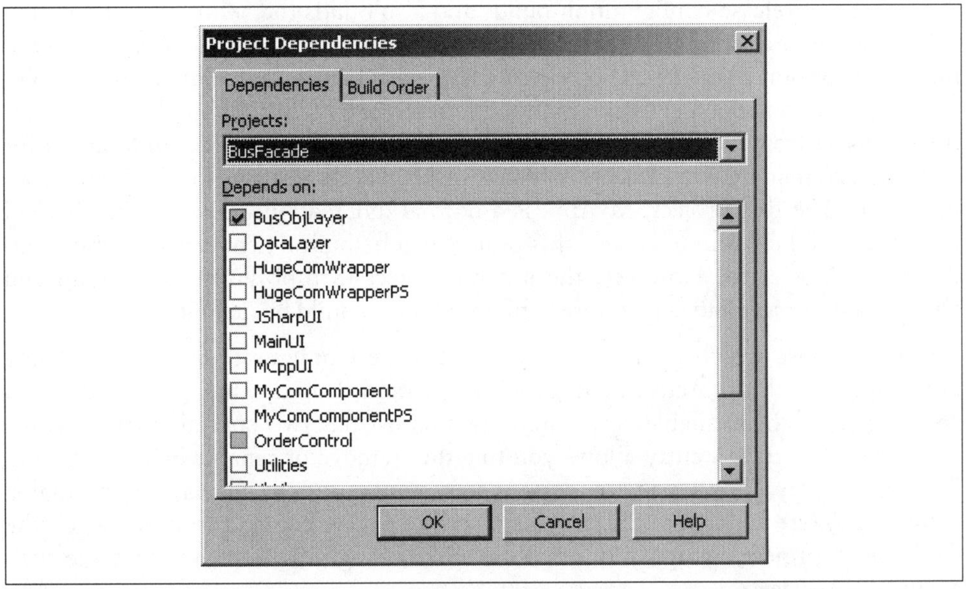

Figure 1-15. Dependencies tab

solution (e.g., the command line or the VS.NET object model). This section deals with the properties of solutions and projects that relate to builds, and also how to manually build projects and automate solution builds.

Configuration Manager

It is common to want to be able to build a given project in more than one way. For example, at development time, you want to build in debugging information, but you would not normally want to build the version you ship this way. You may also need to build special versions with extra logging enabled to help you diagnose a problem on a live system. To enable this, Visual Studio .NET allows projects and solutions to have a number of different *configurations*. Each configuration can specify its own settings for any property of any project.

By default, Visual Studio .NET creates Debug and Release configurations for all projects and solutions. The Debug configuration sets up projects to compile with full debugging information and no optimization, while the Release build does the opposite. You can modify these configurations or create new configurations as needed. For example, you might add unit testing code to your project that is compiled only in special unit test configurations. You can also create configurations that leave out certain projects. For example, Setup and Deployment projects take a fairly long time to build, but you usually want to build those only occasionally. In fact, a new Setup and Deployment project will, by default, be configured not to build in either the Debug or the Release configuration. So you might add a third configuration that builds everything that the Release configuration builds and also builds the Setup project.Solution configurations are set up using the Configuration Manager dialog box. You can get to the Configuration Manager dialog box by right-clicking on the solution in the Solution Explorer and selecting Configuration Manager or by selecting Build → Configuration Manager from the main menu. Figure 1-16 shows the Configuration Manager for a solution containing two projects, which is displaying the settings for the Debug configuration. The first project, MyApp, is a normal .NET application. As the checked box in its Build column indicates, this project will be built whenever the Debug configuration is selected. However, the second project (SetupMyApp) is a Setup and Deployment project and is therefore configured not to build by default.

You can choose which configuration's settings the Configuration Manager dialog box displays with the Active Solution Configuration drop-down list. In addition to showing all of the available configurations, this list has two special entries, <edit> and <new>. The <edit> entry allows you to either remove or rename a configuration. The <new> entry allows you to create a new configuration, displaying the dialog shown in Figure 1-17. We can use this to create a new configuration in which the deployment project, SetupMyApp, will be built, giving it an appropriate name such as InstallableRelease.

As well as allowing you to give your new configuration a name, the New Solution Configuration dialog box also allows you to select the configuration from which to copy settings. (The special <Default> entry shown in Figure 1-17 instructs Visual Studio .NET not to copy settings from any existing configuration, but to use default values instead.) In this case, when we just want to build an installable application, we would normally choose to copy settings from the Release configuration.

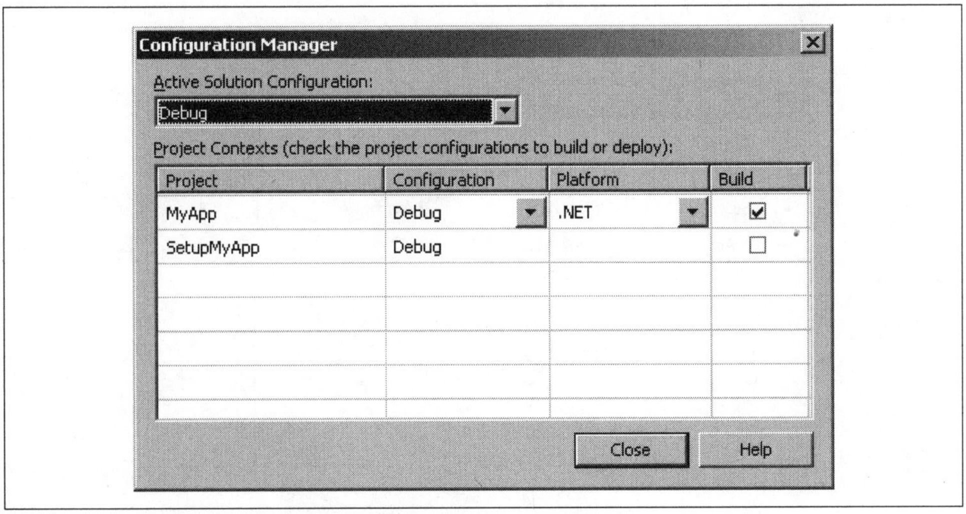

Figure 1-16. The Configuration Manager dialog box

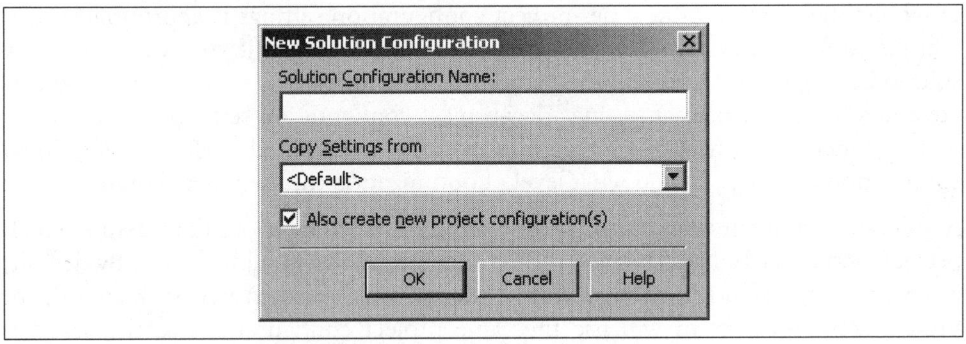

Figure 1-17. New Solution Configuration dialog box

The New Solution Configuration dialog box also has an "Also create new project configuration(s)" checkbox. This tells the IDE to create new configurations for each project—both projects and solutions can have per-configuration settings. If you are creating a new configuration merely to control which projects are built, this box should be unchecked. For example, in our InstallableRelease configuration, we will want the projects to be built with exactly the same settings as they use with the Release configuration, so there is no need to create new per-project settings.

Figure 1-18 shows a new configuration that was created without new project configurations. Notice that although the newly created InstallableRelease solution configuration is selected, each individual project's Configuration column shows that the project settings from the Release configuration are being used. The only difference between this solution configuration and the Release configuration shown in is that we are now building the setup project as well as the application—both items are checked in the Build column.

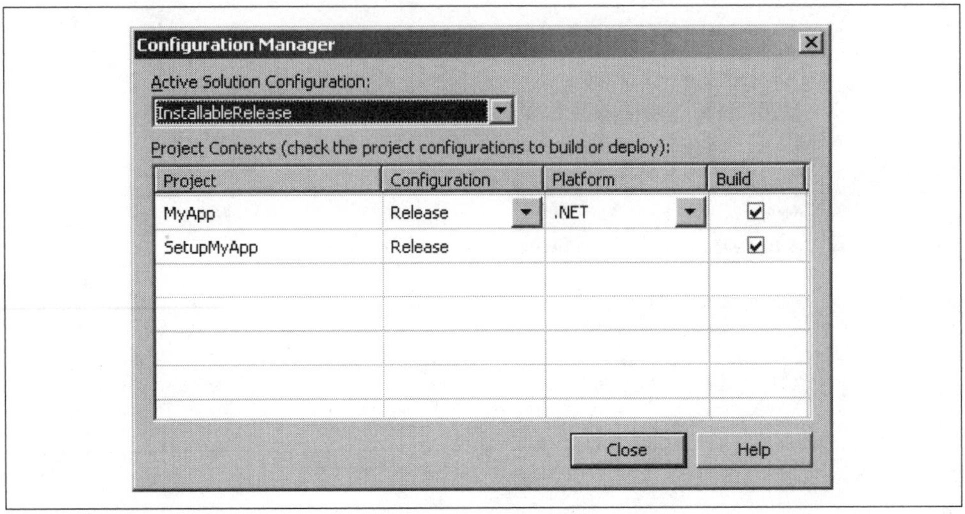

Figure 1-18. Including a setup project in a configuration

Disabling the creation of new per-project configuration settings is appropriate when you just want to control which projects are built. However, if you want your new solution configuration to build the projects in a different way, you will need to create a new set of per-project settings. Per-project configuration settings contain information such as whether debug information is required, which conditional compilation flags are set, and what level of optimization the compiler should use.

A solution's configuration information really does nothing more than define which projects should be built and which project configurations should be used. By default, a newly created solution configuration either will use its own newly created set of project configurations or will use the same project configurations as the solution configuration on which it was based, depending on whether the Create New Project Configurations checkbox was checked. However, it is possible to create a solution configuration that uses a different project configuration for each individual project. You could use this to create a special diagnostic build of an application in which all of the projects are built in their Release configurations with the exception of one troublesome component. Figure 1-19 shows how the Configuration Manager might look for this kind of configuration.

In this example, our solution has three projects. Figure 1-19 is showing a solution configuration called Diagnostic. It has chosen to build all three projects, but as the Configuration column shows, two will be built using Release settings, while the FlakeyComponent project is to be built with Debug settings.

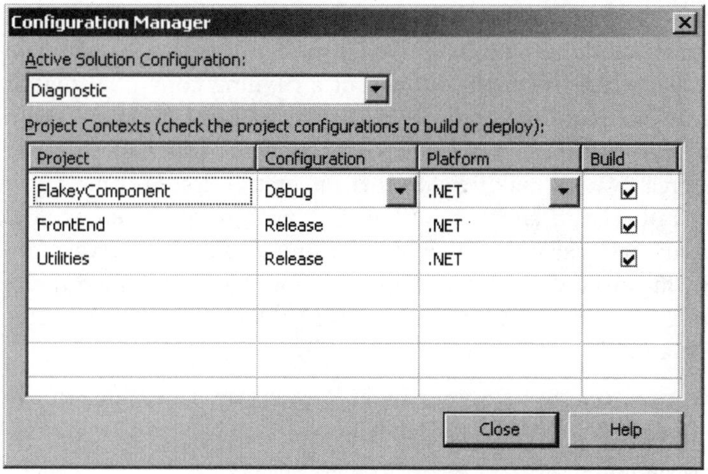

Figure 1-19. A solution using multiple project configurations

Manual Building

When you select Build → Build Solution (Ctrl-Shift-B), all of the out-of-date projects in the currently selected configuration are built. (A project is deemed out-of-date if any of its source files or any of the projects it depends upon have changed since it was last built.) To save time, you might sometimes want to override this and build only the project you are currently working on. Of course, you can create a configuration that builds only the projects you want, but there is a more direct approach if you want to rebuild just a single project. If you right-click the project you want to build in the Solution Explorer and select Build, VS.NET will build just that project and its dependencies. (If the project is selected in the Solution Explorer, you can also use Build → Build ProjectName from the main menu.)

Building occurs automatically for .NET projects when you start the debugger (F5). (With unmanaged projects, you will be asked if you want to rebuild if you change your project and attempt to run it without rebuilding it first.) Visual Studio .NET 2003 allows you to change how much is built for .NET projects—by default, it will build all projects (although if the projects have not been changed, this will be relatively quick, since the compilers will detect that nothing has changed). However, you can elect to have only the Startup project (the one that runs when you hit F5) rebuilt, along with any projects it depends on, rather than building everything in the solution. You can configure this in the Tools → Options dialog—under the Environment category, select the Projects and Solutions item, and check the "Only build startup project and dependencies on Run" checkbox.

Automated Building

So far, all the techniques we have looked at for building projects and solutions require a developer to be seated in front of a running copy of Visual Studio .NET. However, you may automate your builds, that is, launch a build without human intervention. For example, many development teams run a nightly build. (Nightly builds are a great way of making sure that integration issues come out of the woodwork sooner rather than later, as well as making sure that there is always a "latest version" to run tests against.) It would be unreasonable to expect some hapless employee to stay around until midnight every night just to launch the build (even if he were the last person to break the build), so the ability to start a build automatically is important.

The simplest way to automate your build is to create a *.bat* file with the following command line in it:

```
devenv /build Debug /out builderrors.log "MySolution.sln"
```

If this *.bat* file is placed in your solution directory, it will build the Debug configuration of the solution and send any errors to the *builderrors.log* file. In conjunction with the Windows "at" scheduling service, this is all you need to perform an automated, scheduled build. (This requires the *devenv* executable to be on the path, of course. Alternatively, you could hardcode the path into the batch file. The *devenv* executable lives inside the *Common7\IDE* subdirectory of the Visual Studio .NET installation directory.)

> There are two *devenv* executables: *devenv.exe* and *devenv.com*. Both work in much the same way, the only difference being that *devenv.com* is a console application, while *devenv.exe* is a Windows application. (In fact *devenv.exe* is the main Visual Studio .NET executable.) When running automated builds, the main difference is that if a single *.bat* file launches *devenv.exe* twice (e.g., to build two different configurations), both will run concurrently. (*devenv.exe* returns the console immediately, so the *.bat* file will not wait for the first to finish before starting the next.) But because *devenv.com* is a console application, the two tasks would run sequentially. If you do not specify the extension in the *.bat* file, *devenv.com* will be used.

You can pass other useful command-line switches to *devenv*. You can use the /rebuild switch to cause a clean and then a build or use /clean to clean out extraneous build files. You can also use the /project switch to build a specific project within a solution.

Using a simple batch file in conjunction with the Windows task scheduler to run your nightly build provides enough functionality for many solutions. In theory, you could further customize the build process using the automation model built into VS.NET (see Chapter 8 on macros). *devenv* provides the /command switch, which enables you to invoke any built-in command from the command line and to also invoke macros. Unfortunately, running macros in this way will have the unhelpful side effect of opening the Visual Studio .NET user interface and leaving it open even after the macro has finished. This means that, in practice, you cannot usefully invoke macros as part of an automated build. But, of course, you can always add extra lines to the *.bat* file to run other programs if you need to perform work not supported by VS.NET as part of your build.

External build tools

Many organizations do not use Visual Studio .NET to perform their automated builds, preferring command-line tools such as NAnt (*http://nant.sourceforge.net/*) and continuous integration managers such as Draco (*http://draconet.sourceforge.net*). However, this does not necessarily mean abandoning VS.NET altogether. It is common practice for individual developers to work with the VS.NET build systems on their own machine, with the external tools being used only on the build machines. To help make this easier, NAnt ships with a utility called SLiNgshoT that enables NAnt build files to be generated from VS.NET solutions and vice versa.

Build Events

You can instruct VS.NET to perform custom actions before or after a build occurs. (VS.NET 2002 supports Build Events only in C++ projects. VS.NET 2003 supports this feature in all languages other than VB.NET.) Build Events are used to run external tools as part of the build process. For example, ATL projects exploit this feature to run the COM component registration utility (*regsvr32.exe*) when a COM component is built.

In C# or J# projects, you can configure Build Events from the project property pages. (You can show these by selecting the project in the Solution Explorer and pressing Shift-F4 or by selecting Properties from the project's context menu.) In the panel on the left, expand the Common Properties folder and select the Build Events item, as shown in Figure 1-20.

The property grid shows three entries for Build Events. Two let you specify the custom actions to be invoked: one before the build starts and one after the build finishes. In both cases, you supply a command line to be executed as the custom action. The final property lets you select when to perform the post-build action. By default, it will be run only if the project builds successfully. However, as Figure 1-20 shows, you may also specify that the action Always occurs (i.e., it happens whether the build succeeds or not). You can also select "When the build updates the project output". This means that if the user rebuilds the solution, the action will be run only if VS. NET concludes that the project needs to be rebuilt (because it has changed).

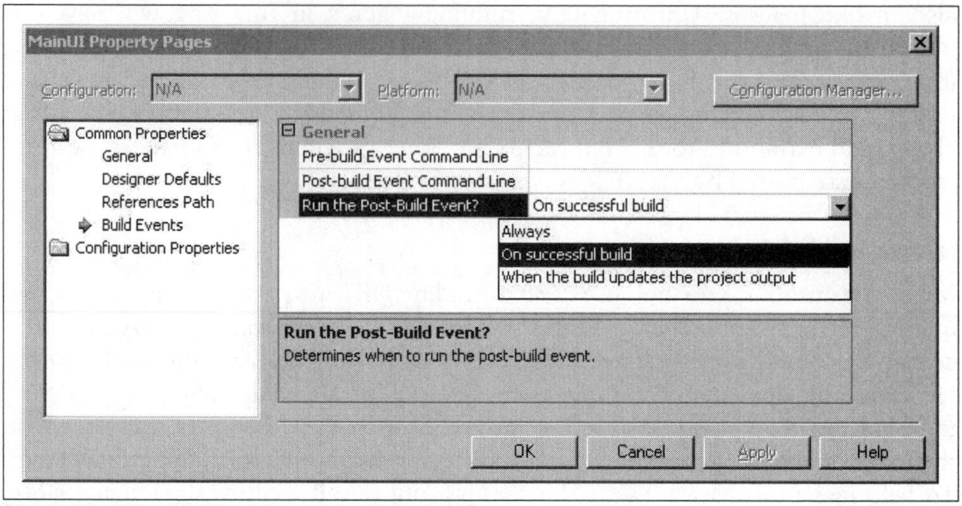

Figure 1-20. Build Events for C# and J# projects

C++ projects are built in a slightly different way from C# and J# projects, so Build Events work slightly differently. As before, they are configured with the project's property pages. But C++ projects categorize build settings slightly differently. Instead of a single Build Events item, there is a Build Events folder containing three items: Pre-Build Event, Pre-Link Event, and Post-Build Event. Each of these allows three properties to be configured, as Figure 1-21 shows.

As before, each Build Event can have a command line associated with it. The main difference with C++ projects is that there is an extra event: the Pre-Link Event. This occurs after compilation has finished but before linking occurs. Unlike with C# and J# projects, in a C++ project you have no choice about when the event occurs. The Pre-Link and Post-Build custom actions will be run whenever successful compilation and linking occurs. (And they will not be run if VS.NET determines that no changes have been made to the project.) Also, C++ projects allow a description for each event to be supplied. This text will be written to the Output window when the action is executed. The Excluded from Build option allows you to disable the custom action in specific configurations.

> Build Events work in the same way on both managed and unmanaged C++ projects.

Organizing Your Projects

Several different strategies are available when choosing a logical structure for your projects and solutions. So far, we have just used a single solution containing all of the projects that we are working on. (We also saw how to make sure that the physical structure of the solution on the filesystem matches the logical structure.)

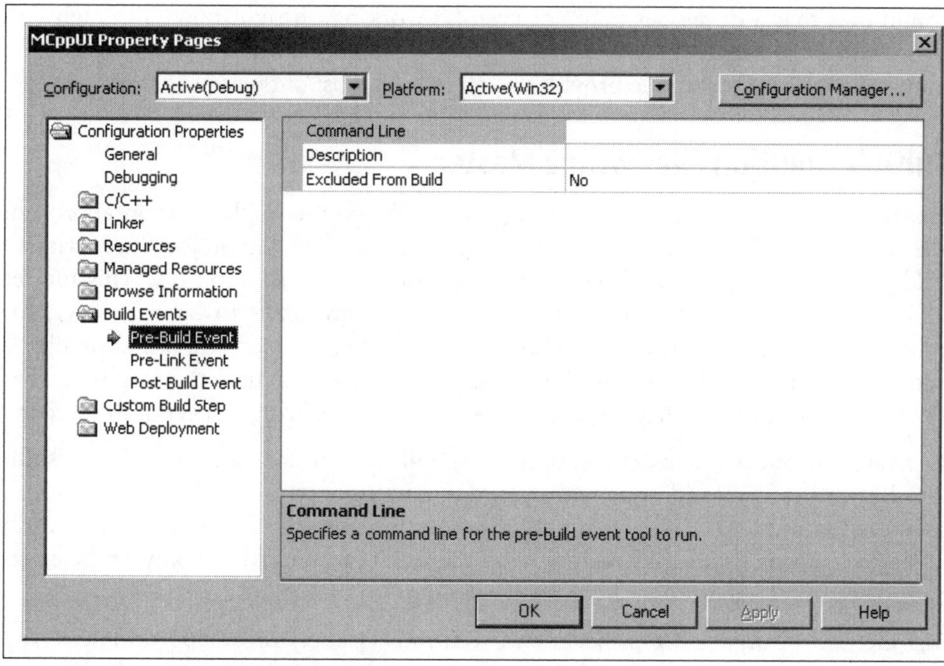

Figure 1-21. Build Events for C++ projects

But there are other options, and thinking about the structure of solution(s) and projects before you start to write code will potentially save you time in the end.

Remember that a project may belong to more than one solution. This gives us some flexibility in the way that we structure our projects. We will now examine the three basic ways to organize your solution(s) and projects and discuss their pros and cons.

Single Solution File

The easiest way to organize your projects is to put them all in a single solution—the approach we have used so far in this chapter. The main advantage of this style is its simplicity. This structure also makes automated builds simple, since only one solution will have to be built. The disadvantage is the lack of flexibility in a large project—any developers who wish to work on the solution will always have to have all of the solution's projects downloaded from the source control database.

Problems can arise as the number of projects in the system grows. Although VS.NET has no hard limit to the number of projects that can be added to a solution, at some point a solution with a large number of projects will become unwieldy. It can take a long time to open, since VS.NET will check the status of every project in the source control database. Large solutions will cause more memory to be consumed. Big solutions may also present logistical problems if multiple developers need to make changes to the solution files. Another potential problem is that as the solution gets bigger, the build time will tend to be unnecessarily high, as VS.NET may decide to rebuild files that a developer may not even be working on right now (although you can, of course, mitigate this by creating configurations that build only subsets of the solution). The next technique provides a solution to most of these problems.

Multiple Solution Files with a Master

The multiple-solution-with-master strategy is similar to the single-solution approach, in that there is still a single solution file that contains all of the projects necessary to build your system. The difference is that it is not the only solution file. This master solution file will be used whenever the entire solution needs to be built (e.g., for nightly or other automated builds). However, the master solution will not normally be used by developers in their day-to-day work. Instead, they will use other solutions that contain only the projects they require to work on some particular aspect of the system.

To create one of these smaller solutions, you will start by creating a new blank solution. But rather than adding new projects, you will select Add → Existing Project... from the solution's context menu in the Solution Explorer. (Or use File → Add Project → Existing Project... from the main menu.) You can add as many of the existing projects as you require.

This method of organizing projects and solutions is likely to be appropriate if you have a large number of projects (e.g., more than 10) and you want to make it easier for each developer to work on just one portion of the software. Using a solution that contains only the projects you need to work on has a number of advantages. It will reduce the amount of time it takes to open the solution, especially if the solution is in a revision control system. It will also reduce the amount of unwanted information displayed—the Solution Explorer, class view, and object browser will all be less cluttered and therefore easier to use.

> Although working with a subset of the projects will reduce the number of files that need to be retrieved from source control in order to begin work, developers are likely to need to get updates of more of the source tree before checking their changes back in. It would be a foolhardy developer who checks in changes without first making sure that those changes won't break the nightly build. And, of course, the only way to find out for certain whether your changes will pass the nightly build and any automated unit testing is to get an update of everything and perform a test build.
>
> Of course, if you are certain that your work won't affect certain other areas, you will probably get away without testing them yourself and just trusting to the automated processes. But do you really want to risk being the developer who broke the build?

Although this solution structure essentially builds on top of the single-solution approach, you will need a little planning to take advantage of it. You will not simply be able to pick arbitrary groups of projects and create new solutions for them—you will be restricted by the dependencies between the projects. For example, if your solution contains a UI project that uses a class library project, attempting to create a solution that contains only the UI project will not be successful—it will need a reference to the Class Library project in order to build. You should therefore try to keep the relationships between your components as simple as possible.*

File References Versus Project References

Of course, you could use a file reference instead of a project reference. This would enable the UI project to exist in a solution on its own. But there are problems with doing this:

- You must somehow get hold of a copy of the class library in order to add a file reference. (Of course, if you have a nightly build, there will always be a "most recent" version of the component somewhere on the network.)
- If the reference's Copy Local flag is set to true, you will need to delete and recreate the reference every time you wish to pick up a new version. (Alternatively, you can dig into the build directory and delete the copy, which will cause VS.NET to make a new copy.)
- If the reference's Copy Local is false, you will have to work out some way of making sure that the component can actually be found at runtime, since VS.NET will no longer copy it into the build directory. For COM components this is not a problem, as they are found through their registry entries, but for .NET components you will need to add a configuration file to tell the CLR where to find the components.

So you are usually better off with a project reference.

This style of solution structure introduces a new challenge. Now that there are multiple solutions, it will probably not be possible to make your filesystem structure match all of the solutions. For example, if we create solutions for working on a Windows Forms UI project and a Web Forms UI project, both of these solutions might need to contain the same Class Library project. Since a directory cannot be contained by multiple parent directories,† there is no single filesystem structure that

---

* Issues with VS.NET project references notwithstanding, it is good practice to minimize cross-component dependencies in order to simplify your build and test procedures. *Large-Scale C++ Software Design* (Addison-Wesley) provides excellent and extensive explanations of why this is so. Despite its title, many of the issues presented in this book are of interest to developers creating large software systems in any programming language.

† Strictly speaking, NTFS 5 reparse points do allow a directory to have multiple parents. However, even if all of your developers' machines have appropriate filesystems, your source control system almost certainly won't be able to deal with such a directory structure.

matches both solutions. The simplest way of dealing with this is to choose just one solution and make the filesystem match that. The obvious solution to choose for this is the master solution.

There will be some extra subdirectories in the master solution for this approach. Visual Studio .NET insists on giving each solution its own directory. (And although you can move *.sln* files after VS.NET creates them, it will insist on putting each in its own directory in your version control system, regardless of how you may have restructured the files on your local filesystem.) So there will be a directory for each secondary solution you create, containing just the solution files. The project files will be inside the project directories as before.

Projects inside of the master solution can then be contained by multiple different secondary solutions. This enables each developer to download and work with only those projects that are related to the part of the system she is currently working on. The only problems with this technique are the constraints imposed by use of project references and the fact that the master solution can become a bottleneck—anytime a new project is added, the master solution will need to be updated. (In software shops where people are in the habit of keeping files checked out for a long time, this can be a problem.) The final way of structuring your projects can get around both of these issues, although not without some inconvenience.

Multiple Solution Files with No Project References

If you want developers to have the maximum possible flexibility as to which projects they can download and work on, you could create one solution per project and have no master solution at all. The cost of this flexibility is that you have to deal with dependencies manually, because VS.NET has no way of representing cross-solution dependencies.

It is likely that some of your projects will depend upon other projects, but if they all live in their own solutions, you will have no way of representing this formally. You will have to use .NET file references instead of project references. This is inconvenient because you need to delete and recreate the references (or delete the copied component from the build directory) every time the component you are using changes. It also makes automated builds harder, since the build script will have to build multiple solutions, and it will also be responsible for getting the build order correct.

You may think that you could mitigate this by creating a master solution on top of this multisolution structure and adding the relevant project references to it. However, this will not work, because references are stored in *projects*, not in the *solution*, so if you add a project reference to a project, it doesn't matter what solution you happened to be using when you added the reference—you will have changed the project for everyone. Anyone who wanted to build the project would now be obliged to have a copy of the project on which it depends, defeating the whole purpose of this strategy.

However, although adding project references will not work, you could create a master solution and add explicit dependencies instead. (Remember that although implicit dependencies are inferred from project references, *explicit* dependencies are stored in the solution. So using explicit dependencies would not negate the benefit of being able to download any individual project in isolation.) This would make automated build scripts easier to create, but you would still be responsible for working out for yourself what the appropriate dependencies are. You also still need to recopy or recreate file references every time anything changes.

Choosing an Organizational Method

The simplest structure is the single-solution approach. Using this will mean that your solution's physical layout can easily match its logical structure, and you can always use project references to make sure that every project will be rebuilt and copied automatically when it needs to be. Choosing this structure as a starting point is almost always the right decision.

If the number of projects makes dealing with the solution too unwieldy, then you should consider migrating to the multiple-solution-with-master-solution structure. Your existing single solution will become your master solution, and you can add new solutions to partition your projects as required. When creating the new solutions, you will find that if you include a project that has a reference to another project, VS.NET will complain. (If you expand the project's References node in the Solution Explorer, you will see that the reference is still there but now has an exclamation mark in a yellow triangle over it.) You will need to add all referenced projects to the new solution in order to be able to build it.

If at all possible, you should always have a master solution—an organization with multiple solutions but no master should be chosen only as a last resort, as shown in Table 1-7. The advantages of more flexible partitioning rarely outweigh the disadvantages of not being able to use project references and the increased difficulty of automating builds.

Table 1-7. Solution organizational choices

Master solution	Advantages	Disadvantages
Single solution file	Simplest. Can use project references for other assemblies in the solution. Makes automated builds simple.	Might have to open more projects than you need. Rebuilds may take a long time unless you add solution configurations to build selected subsets.
Multiple solution files with master solution	Can still use master solution for automated builds. May be faster to work with a smaller set of projects than the whole. Can use project references.	More work to add new projects as you have to add them to multiple solutions. Cannot divide up master solution into arbitrary project groups—grouping is constrained by project references.
Multiple solution files with no project references	Adding new projects is easier (no sharing of projects between solutions). Can split your projects however you like.	Can't use project references across solutions, so dependencies must be managed by hand. Harder to automate the build of the entire system.

Conclusion

Projects and solutions are at the core of any work you do with Visual Studio .NET. Projects represent individual components or applications. Solutions are collections of related projects. Solutions can manage the dependencies between projects, ensuring that components are built in the correct order and copied into the right places. Of course, a solution and its projects would be of no use at all if they didn't contain source code of some kind, so in the next chapter we will look at the features in Visual Studio .NET designed to help you edit individual files.

CHAPTER 2

Files

In the last chapter, we examined solutions and projects in great detail without ever seeing any source code. However, the vast majority of the time you spend with Visual Studio .NET will involve writing code rather than configuring your solutions and projects. So we will now look at the features Visual Studio .NET offers to improve your productivity when editing files.

Text Editor

Visual Studio .NET provides a text editor that provides the basic source code editing facilities that are common to all languages. Each language service can extend the text editor to provide language-specific features. (See Chapter 10 for information about how language services extend VS.NET.) As well as supplying the basic text editing services, the editor also has hooks that allow language services to provide advanced features, such as IntelliSense and automatic formatting. Even though the exact way in which these services work is language-specific, the IDE provides the basic framework so that the behavior is as consistent as possible across languages.

You can configure the way the text editor behaves for each language. When a particular language takes advantage of a standard editor feature such as IntelliSense, you will be able to configure that feature's behavior either globally or, if you prefer, on a per-language basis. Most languages also have their own unique configuration options. You can edit all of these options by selecting Tools → Options and then selecting the Text Editor folder in the lefthand pane of the Options dialog box. As Figure 2-1 shows, you will see a list of supported languages. Appendix D describes all of the available options.

Visual Studio .NET provides many coding aids to make editing your source code easier. The following sections describe each of these features.

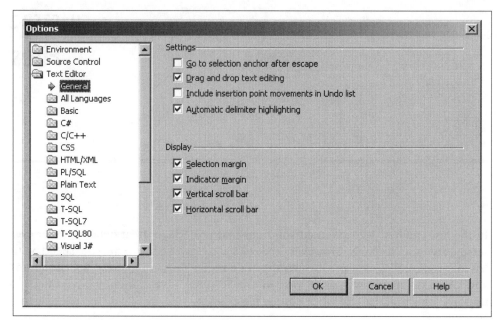

Figure 2-1. The Text Editor Options dialog box

IntelliSense

Visual Studio .NET provides a number of context-sensitive autocompletion features, collectively referred to as IntelliSense. VS.NET relies on the language service for the file you are editing to work out which symbols are in scope and uses this to show pop-up lists of suggestions, to show information in ToolTips or to autocomplete your text.

Four varieties of assistance are offered by IntelliSense. All of them can be invoked manually from the Edit → IntelliSense menu, but IntelliSense usually works automatically (unless you've disabled it). However, it can sometimes be useful to give it a kick, because in some situations, it doesn't operate automatically when you need it. (The most common example being when you want to bring up a list of members in scope at function scope. Many people use the trick of typing in this. to bring up a list of members, but it is easier to use the shortcuts once you know about them.) The four IntelliSense commands are:

List Members (Ctrl-J)

List Members displays a list of available members. The exact contents of the list are determined by the cursor position. If the cursor is placed after a variable name followed by a member access operator (. in VB.NET and C#, and either . or -> in C++), it will list the members of that variable's type. If the cursor is just on some whitespace inside a function, it will list all available variables, types, and members currently in scope.

You can find the member you want in the list by typing in the first few letters of the member until the member is highlighted or by selecting the member with the mouse or arrow keys. When available, VS.NET will display brief documentation for the currently selected item in a ToolTip next to the list. Once you have highlighted the member you would like to use, VS.NET can enter the member name into your code for you. Either double-click on the item or just type any character that would not be allowed in an identifier (e.g., any of (, ., ;, Space, or Enter). Alternatively, you can execute the Complete Word command (see later).

The List Members command executes automatically if you type in a variable name followed by the character for member access or object dereferencing (usually ., ->, or ::). However, the list will disappear if you start doing something else (e.g., you click to move the cursor elsewhere) so this shortcut is useful for bringing it back. Also, if you select the wrong item by accident, pressing Ctrl-J will reopen the list with your current selection highlighted, allowing you to move to the item you meant to select.

Parameter Info (Ctrl-Shift-Space)

This command displays the names and types of the parameters needed to call a method, along with the method's return type. This command works only if the cursor is inside the parentheses of a method call. (The command is invoked automatically when you type the open parenthesis for a method call.)

Quick Info (Ctrl-K, Ctrl-I)

The Quick Info command displays the complete declaration for any identifier in your code and, where available, a documentation summary. (This is the same information that will be shown if you move the mouse over an identifier and hover.) The declaration is displayed in a ToolTip-style box. If Quick Info is not autoenabled, hovering the mouse will not work, and you will need to execute this command manually to make the pop up display. (Even if Quick Info is autoenabled, it is still often useful to be able to invoke it without reaching for the mouse. You will also need to invoke the command manually if you need it while debugging—in debug mode, the default behavior when you hover over an item is to display its value instead of its quick info.)

Complete Word (Alt-Right Arrow or Ctrl-Space)

Complete Word will complete whatever symbol is currently selected in the IntelliSense member list. If the list is not currently open, IntelliSense will work out whether the letters typed so far unambiguously refer to a particular member. If they do, it will complete the member. If, however, the text already present is ambiguous (and the member list is not already open), it will display the member list. For example, if the text editor had the text `Console.W`, the `W` might be expanded to either `Write` or `WriteLine`. Since this is ambiguous, it will open the member list to let you choose the one you mean. If you have VS.NET 2003 and are using C# or J#, you can enable the "Preselect most frequently used members" option. (This setting can be found in the options dialog, which can be opened using Tools → Options. On the left of the dialog, expand the Text Editor category, and then under either C# or Visual J# select the Formatting item.) This will cause VS.NET to highlight the item you use most often. Otherwise, it will just choose the first matching item—Write in this case.

Some other autocompletion features are provided by the C# language service. Automatic skeleton insertion for interfaces and virtual methods is described later in this chapter (in the "Class View" section). Help is also provided with event handlers. (This feature is not available in VS.NET 2002.) If you write the += operator after an event member name (e.g., myButton.Click +=), a tooltip will appear offering to add code to create an appropriate delegate if you press Tab. If you go ahead and press the Tab key, it adds the appropriate code (e.g., new EventHandler(myButton_Click);). At this point a second tooltip will appear, offering to create a skeleton function whose signature matches the delegate and with a name matching its suggestion in the first completion. (So in this case, pressing Tab a second time would add a function called myButton_Click, with the correct signature for a Click event handler.)

C# Documentation

The C# programming language lets you put special comments in the source code that can be used to generate documentation. These comments must begin with three slashes instead of the normal two and must be in an XML-based format. The XML is typically converted into HTML-based documentation for your solution. However, the XML can also be used by IntelliSense to provide pop-up documentation for types and their members. It uses the summary element for this, so you should always keep that part fairly succinct. The following code snippet shows a typical example of this documentation:

```
/// <summary>
/// The main entry point for the application.
/// </summary>
[STAThread]
static void Main( )
```

If you type three slashes into the source editor in a C# file (or /**, which is the other way of indicating that a comment contains XML documentation), you will find that Visual Studio .NET automatically provides an XML skeleton for your documentation. This will always include a summary element, but if you put the comment before a method, VS.NET will also add elements for each parameter and for the return type. VS.NET also provides IntelliSense pop ups for the XML, telling you which elements are supported for the item you are documenting. (A complete description of the supported elements can be found in *C# in a Nutshell* (O'Reilly and Associates) and also in the C# Language Specification in the MSDN Library.)

IntelliSense will automatically use this documentation if it is present, but you must explicitly ask for HTML documentation to be built if you want it. You do this using Tools → Build Comment Web Pages.

The style of documentation produced by the Build Comment Web Pages menu item is different from the style used by VS.NET's own documentation. If you would like to generate documentation that looks similar to the documentation for the .NET Framework Class Libraries, you can download a free program from *http://ndoc. sourceforge.net.com* that will generate either HTML files or compiled help files that look just like the .NET documentation.

Beautifier

VS.NET can reformat the currently selected portion of a file. The exact behavior of this feature is controlled by the language service. This feature is not available for certain file types (such as text files).

To invoke this feature, first select the region of text you would like to reformat (if you want to reformat the entire file, use Ctrl-A or Edit → Select All). Then select Edit → Advanced → Format Selection (Ctrl-K, Ctrl-F). This will reformat the selected area. Most languages that support this feature allow the way in which reformatting occurs to be controlled—see Appendix F for details of the relevant settings.

Navigation Bar

A navigation bar is available for five different languages: C#, J#, C++, VB.NET, and HTML/XML. In C#, J#, and C++, the navigation bar is just a navigation aid—you can use it to navigate to specific type and member declarations. However, with VB.NET and HTML, the navigation bars have slightly more functionality.

The navigation bar allows you add event handlers in VB.NET and HTML files. If you are editing a class, form, or page that contains event sources, these will appear in the lefthand list. If you select one, the righthand list will show all of the events it provides. Selecting one of these adds a skeleton event handler.

The navigation bar is very fussy about the HTML structure. If your HTML is not clean, the navigation bar will not work correctly.

With VB.NET, the navigation bar also allows you to add new code as well as navigating to existing code. In VB.NET, if you select your class in the lefthand dropdown list, the righthand list will not only contain your class's members, it will also show some methods you have not yet implemented. The list will contain overridable methods from your base class, along with any members of interfaces your class implements. When you pick a method that you have not yet implemented, the editor adds a skeleton implementation (just the Sub or Function declaration and the corresponding End Sub or End Function).

Class View

The class view provides a way of navigating within a solution. You can display the class view with View → Class View (Ctrl-Shift-C). The class view shows a tree view of the types declared in your source files. In a multiproject solution, the types will be grouped by project.

When you expand a project in the class view, you will see all of the namespaces that the project defines, along with any classes that are in the default namespace. As you expand the tree view, you will see types and their members. If you double-click on any item in the tree, the cursor will go to its definition. You can also navigate in reverse—you can right-click in the text editor and select Synchronize Class View. This will show the Class View pane and will select the node corresponding to which-ever item the cursor was over.

In both C# and C++, you can also use the Class View pane to generate skeleton implementations for overridable members from base types, as well as for interface members. If you expand any type that you have defined, its first node will be labeled Bases and Interfaces. If you expand that node, you will see your class's base type, along with any interfaces that it implements. If you find an overridable member of the base type (or any member of an interface) that you would like to implement, you can right-click on that member and select Add → Override (Ctrl-Alt-Insert). This will add a skeleton for that member to your source file. You can also add skeletons for all members of an interface in one step: expand the Bases and Interfaces node, select the interface you require, right-click, and select Add → Implement Interface....

 Visual Studio .NET 2003 introduced new ways of generating skeleton implementations without using the class view. When you add an inter-face to the class's interface list in the text editor, a ToolTip appears offering to generate the stubs for you if you press the Tab key. And for overriding methods in the base class, simply typing in override any-where in the class will bring up an IntelliSense pop up showing all overridable methods—if you select one of these, VS.NET will gener-ate a skeleton implementation. But for VS.NET 2002, the class view is the only way to generate skeletons.

Another useful feature of the class view is that it can be customized. In a large project, there are likely to be a substantial number of classes. However, you may well be working with only a small subset of these at any given time. Rather than having to scroll through the tree to find the few classes you are interested in, you can create a new folder in the class view that contains just the items you wish to see. You create new folders with Project → New Folder. You can add as many folders as you like. Folders can contain types, namespaces, or even individual members—just drag them in there from their current place in the tree view. You can delete a type by highlight-ing it and pressing the Delete key. You can see an example of a custom folder con-taining a namespace, a type, and an individual member at the top of Figure 2-2.

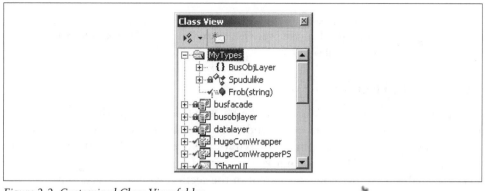

Figure 2-2. Customized Class View folder

Custom class view folders have no impact on the output of the solution—they merely change the way in which it is presented in VS.NET. Because of this, custom folder settings are not stored in the *.sln* file. Information that affects only the way in which VS.NET shows the project are typically held in per-user files, so custom folders settings are stored in the *.suo* file. This means that custom folders will not be saved into source control. (*.suo* files are not checked in by default, and it is not a good idea to check in user-specific IDE configuration files in any case.) You should therefore avoid relying on them to convey important information in team projects. (For example, do not rely on custom class view folders as part of your code documentation strategy.)

Navigation and Bookmarks

VS.NET provides a number of additional ways to navigate through your source code files. The View → Navigate Backward (CTRL+-) and View → Navigate Forward commands are like Undo and Redo commands for navigation—as you are moving from file to file, and within a file itself, the editor remembers your location when you execute certain commands. (Not all commands are remembered, as otherwise the editor would have to remember every single editing keystroke or command.) These commands include searches, Go To Line (Ctrl-G), Beginning of Document (Ctrl-Home), End of Document (Ctrl-End), Pasting Text, and Go To Definition commands.

Bookmarks provide another useful navigation aid. You can add a bookmark to any line of source code by placing the cursor on that line and selecting Edit → Bookmarks → Toggle Bookmark (Ctrl-K, Ctrl-K). It is easy to see when a line has been bookmarked, as there will be a visual marker in the indicator margin (unless you have turned the indicator margin off). You can then use the commands under Edit → Bookmarks to navigate back and forth between the different bookmarks you have placed in your source files, the most useful being Next Bookmark (Ctrl-K, Ctrl-N) and Previous Bookmark (Ctrl-K, Ctrl-P).

Bookmarks are saved when you close a solution. However, when you close an individual file, VS.NET discards any bookmarks you have placed in that file.

Outlining and Regions

The main language services (VB.NET, C#, J#, and C++) provide the text editor with outlining information for your source code. When outlining is enabled, VS.NET uses this to show markers in the lefthand margin of the text editor that delineate sections of your source code. The editor marks the start of a section by a minus (-) symbol inside a small square. It shows the extent of the section with a vertical gray line ending with a small horizontal tick.

Sections are frequently nested—a namespace will have a section, as will each class it contains and the members of those classes. In this case you will see the vertical gray line carrying on beyond the tick that marks the end of the nested section, as you can see in Figure 2-3 at the end of the section for the constructor.

These sections of code can be expanded and contracted, allowing you to hide sections of source code that you are not currently working on, thus making more effective use of your screen real estate. In Figure 2-3, you can see some sections of the source code that are hidden (like the using section) and some sections that are open (the code inside of the namespace declaration). When a section is hidden, it is represented by a plus (+) symbol in a square. The section can be unhidden by clicking on the +. Some text will be shown inside a box in the main part of the editor window next to the + to represent what is contained in the hidden section. The text shown will depend on the type of section—for example, in Figure 2-3, the using section appears as three periods, and the comment section appears as /**/. Hidden functions just show the function declaration. For #region sections (described later in this section), arbitrary text may be shown.

If you want to see the code contained in a hidden section without expanding it, you can hover the mouse over it. A ToolTip containing the hidden source code (or as much of the source code as will fit on the screen) will appear.

One of the hidden sections in Figure 2-3 appears as the text "Component Designer generated code". This is an example of a section created with the #region keyword. (This particular section was added, unsurprisingly, by the component designer.) The language service decides where the outline sections should be placed, and they are usually based upon language constructs. But in VB.NET, C#, and J#, you can add extra sections using the #region and #endregion keywords (#Region and #End Region in VB.NET). You can place a string next to the opening directive, and this will be displayed in the box when the outlined section is hidden. Figure 2-4 shows how the

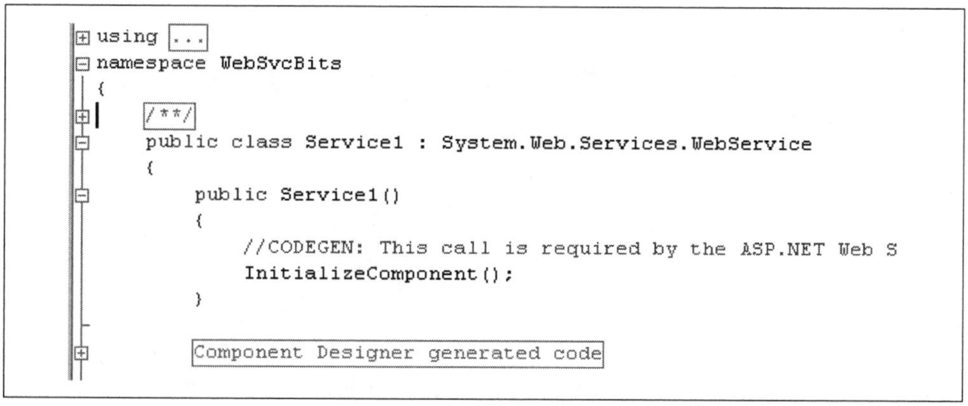

```
⊞ using ...
⊟ namespace WebSvcBits
  | {
⊞ |    /**/
⊟ |    public class Service1 : System.Web.Services.WebService
       {
⊟         public Service1()
          {
              //CODEGEN: This call is required by the ASP.NET Web S
              InitializeComponent();
          }

⊞         Component Designer generated code
```

Figure 2-3. Outlined sections of code

region at the bottom of Figure 2-3 looks when it is expanded—it is now clear how VS.NET knew what text to display when the section was hidden.

When a Visual Studio .NET designer generates code, it usually places it inside a #region directive. The main reason for this is that it discourages people from editing it by accident—regions are hidden by default. (You can change this default, though, as discussed in Appendix F.)

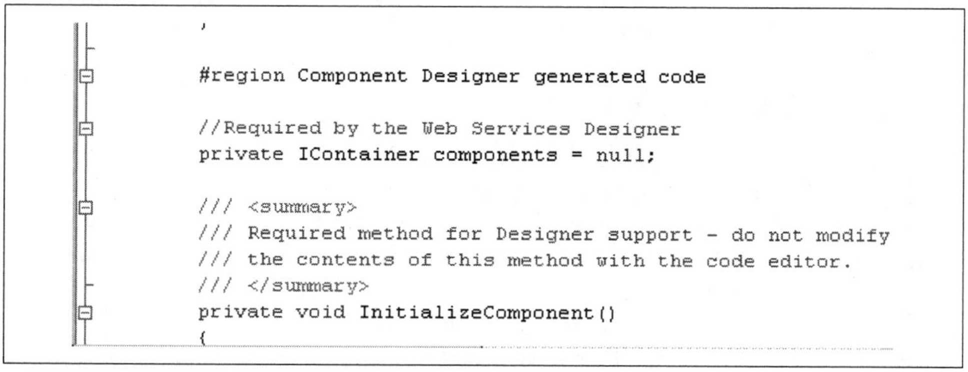

```
           ,
⊟          #region Component Designer generated code

⊟          //Required by the Web Services Designer
           private IContainer components = null;

⊟          /// <summary>
           /// Required method for Designer support - do not modify
           /// the contents of this method with the code editor.
           /// </summary>
⊟          private void InitializeComponent()
           {
```

Figure 2-4. The #region directive expanded

The commands for outlining are found under Edit → Outlining. The most useful command is Toggle Outlining Expansion (Ctrl-M, Ctrl-M)—if the cursor is inside a section that is not currently hidden, VS.NET will hide it. If the cursor is over a hidden section, VS.NET will expand it. Also, Collapse to Definitions (Ctrl-M, Ctrl-O) will hide all members, and Toggle All Outlining (Ctrl-M, Ctrl-L) will expand any collapsed sections in the file. If there are no collapsed sections in the file, it collapses everything.

Although C++ provides outlining, it is missing a few features. It does not support the #region directive. Also, if you turn outlining off for a C++ file, the only way to restore it is to close and reopen the file, whereas in C#, J#, and VB.NET you can simply use Edit → Outlining → Start Outlining. Also, with C#, J#, and VB.NET, you can have outlining turned off in the language setting for the text editor and still turn it back on for individual files (also using the Start Outlining command), but if you turn off outlining in the C++ settings, you cannot turn it back on for a single file.

Text and the Toolbox

The Toolbox (View → Toolbox) is used most often for visual editing (see the later section on designers, "Design Views"). But it can also be used as a place to keep useful chunks of text. You can select any section of source code, then drag the selection onto the Toolbox. (You can do this on any of the different tabs of the Toolbox—either the standard tabs or tabs you have added yourself.) Each time you do this, a new item will appear on the Toolbox. You can then move to another part of the same file or a different file and drag the item off the Toolbox and back into the editor where you would like it to be placed. This will create a copy of the original text. If you regularly need to insert pieces of boilerplate such as a standard comment header, this can be a great time-saver. To remove a text block from the Toolbox, right-click the text block and select Delete.

Clipboard Ring

Another section of the Toolbox that can be used for text editing is the Clipboard Ring tab. The clipboard ring holds the value of the last 12 copy or cut operations, and these are all displayed on the Clipboard Ring Toolbox tab. In fact, you don't need to use the Toolbox to take advantage of the clipboard ring—you can cycle through the items in the ring by pressing Ctrl-Shift-V until the text that you want appears in the text editor. Once you have found the item you want from the ring, it moves to the top of the ring. This means that if you want to paste it in again somewhere else, you only need to press Ctrl-V next time.

TaskList Comments

When you are editing a document, you may wish to leave comments in your code to remind yourself or others of work that still needs to be done. VS.NET can show a list of these kinds of comments along with their locations in the Task window—just select View → Show Tasks → Comment. By default, it will look for comments that start with either TODO, HACK, or UNDONE, but you can also add your own custom tokens to the list using the Options dialog (Tools → Options)—underneath the Environment folder, select the TaskList property page.

Each token has one of three priorities assigned to it (Low, Normal, or High). The priority controls a visual cue that is displayed in the TaskList window and determines the order in which items will be displayed. The built-in tokens are all Normal by default, but with the exception of the TODO token, you can change the priority for these and your own tokens with the TaskList property page.

The following source code shows some comments that use this feature. (In addition to using the three standard comments, this example uses two custom comments.)

```
//TODO:This code need optimizing
public void Slow( )
{
}
//HACK:This method is a kludge
public void BadCode( )
{
}
//UNDONE:Someone needs to finish this and it isn't me!
public void NotDone( )
{
}
//MANAGERSEZ:We need this method
public void Meaningless( )
{
}
//NOTTESTED:This code needs to be tested
public void Crash( )
{
}
```

This would produce a TaskList window like the one shown in Figure 2-5. Note that, by default, the TaskList shows only build errors. To enable the display of comments such as these, you must use the View → Show Tasks menu. These comments will be shown only if you select All or Comment.

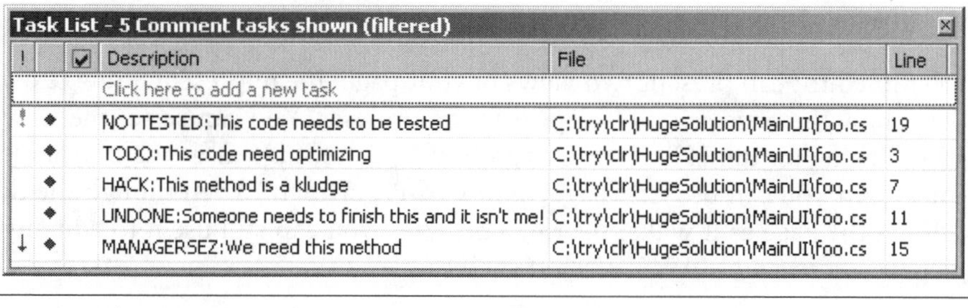

!	☑	Description	File	Line
		Click here to add a new task		
!	◆	NOTTESTED:This code needs to be tested	C:\try\clr\HugeSolution\MainUI\foo.cs	19
	◆	TODO:This code need optimizing	C:\try\clr\HugeSolution\MainUI\foo.cs	3
	◆	HACK:This method is a kludge	C:\try\clr\HugeSolution\MainUI\foo.cs	7
	◆	UNDONE:Someone needs to finish this and it isn't me!	C:\try\clr\HugeSolution\MainUI\foo.cs	11
↓	◆	MANAGERSEZ:We need this method	C:\try\clr\HugeSolution\MainUI\foo.cs	15

Task List – 5 Comment tasks shown (filtered)

Figure 2-5. TaskList window

If you double-click on a task in the TaskList window, it will bring you to the line of code containing the comment. You can also cycle forward and backward through your undone tasks by selecting View → Show Tasks → Next Task (Ctrl-Shift-F12) or View → Show Tasks → Previous Task, respectively.

HTML/XML Editor

The HTML/XML language service provides IntelliSense. For embedded client-side script in HTML, this works in much the same way as it does for any other programming language. And although the tags in HTML and XML documents do not constitute a programming language as such, VS.NET will still provide IntelliSense for tag and attribute names when it can.

HTML Script-Only View

The HTML navigation bar has two buttons on the right side. If you press the leftmost button, you can get a script-only view of your HTML—all of the HTML display elements will be hidden, leaving just the client-side script, as Figure 2-6 shows. If you select the rightmost button, nothing will be hidden.

Figure 2-6. HTML script-only editor view

HTML Views

The HTML editor can present two views of your page. It can present a raw text view, or it can show the page as it will appear in the browser. You can select the view you want by clicking on the HTML or Design button—they appear at the bottom left of the editor. (Or you can use Ctrl-PageUp or Ctrl-PageDown.) Even though the design view shows the page as it will appear in a browser, you can still use it to edit any text on the page—it provides WYSIWYG text editing.

Schemas, Validation, and IntelliSense

If you select View → Properties Window (F4) while in the XML or HTML editor, you will get a special property window that is different from the one you will see if you select the file in the Solution Explorer. The properties are different for HTML and XML files, but they do have one property in common: `targetSchema`. Visual Studio .NET uses this property to work out how to validate the document. It also uses it to determine which elements to display in IntelliSense member lists.

> With HTML files, if the cursor is inside a tag, the properties for that tag instead of the document properties will be shown. The `targetSchema` property is a document property, so if you want to see it, you must make sure that the cursor is not between the angle brackets of a tag.

Validation and IntelliSense get their type information from XML Schema Definition files for both XML and HTML files. These schemas are stored under the *\Common7\ Packages\schemas* folder in the VS.NET installation directory. (There are two subdirectories, *html* and *xml*.) The `targetSchema` property determines which of the schema files in these directories will be used, although the property works differently for HTML and XML files.

With HTML files, the `targetSchema` property has a drop-down list showing a variety of browser versions. For example, you can choose to restrict yourself to Version 3 browser features, or you can validate for Netscape 4.0. If you select a `targetSchema` using the Properties pane, VS.NET will add a `meta` tag to your document named `vs_ targetSchema` to indicate which schema is in use. (It stores the schema file's `targetNameSpace` in this tag, so if you want to add an extra schema of your own, simply make sure it has a unique `targetNameSpace`, and place it in the *html* directory along with the other schemas. You may also wish to add a `vs:friendlyname` attribute—VS.NET will display whatever string you put here in the drop-down list of schemas in the Properties panel.)

> Visual Studio .NET ignores the `!DOCTYPE`. If you select a schema for a down-level browser, you may want to change the `!DOCTYPE` to match— by default, it indicates HTML 4.0.

With XML files, validation is driven off the document element's namespace. Unfortunately, VS.NET ignores the standard `schemaLocation` and `noNamespaceSchemaLocation` attributes—a schema must be present in the *xml* schema directory in order to be used for IntelliSense and validation. Also, note that VS.NET cannot use a Document Type Definition (DTD) to provide validation or IntelliSense—it supports only schemas.

XML Data View

The XML editor can present a file's contents in an editable grid control. This allows you to put in element and attribute values without having to edit the XML document itself. Consider the following XML:

```
<?xml version="1.0" encoding="utf-8" ?>
<foo>
    <quuz quuzatt="World">
        <baz>Hello</baz>
    </quuz>
    <quuz quuzatt="Two">
        <baz>One</baz>
     </quuz>
</foo>
```

If you select the data view (by clicking on the Data button at the bottom left of the editor), it will display the grid as shown in Figure 2-7.

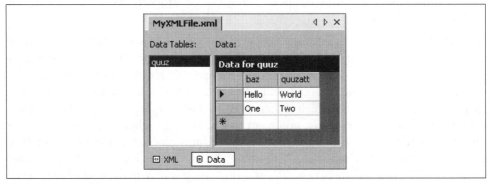

Figure 2-7. XML data view

XML Schema

When you are editing an XML schema document, as well as being able to edit the raw XML, a special schema view is available. This allows you to define element types visually. It also allows you to add relations between those elements. The Toolbox will present an XML Schema tab whenever you edit an XSD file, providing you with schema items that can be dragged onto the design view. The schema view can be selected by clicking on the Schema button at the bottom right of the editor. It is shown in Figure 2-8.

Visual Studio .NET can infer an XML schema from an XML file. When editing an XML file, the main menu will have an XML menu. If you select XML → Create Schema, Visual Studio .NET will create a schema (XSD file) based upon your XML document's structure and will add the new file to your project.

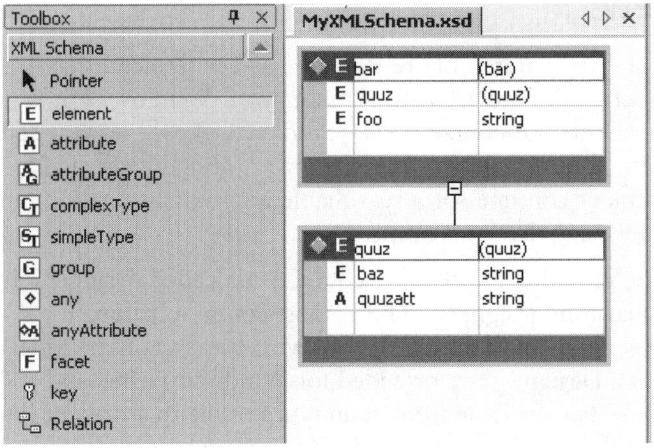

Figure 2-8. XML schema view

CSS Editor

The CSS Editor uses the normal text editor, but it also supplies a second, nontextual view. Whenever you are editing a CSS file, an extra tool window called CSS Outline will be available, presenting a tree view of the CSS file, as Figure 2-9 shows. By default, this view will be docked to the left of the screen, but since it is a tool window, you can dock it anywhere or undock it completely.

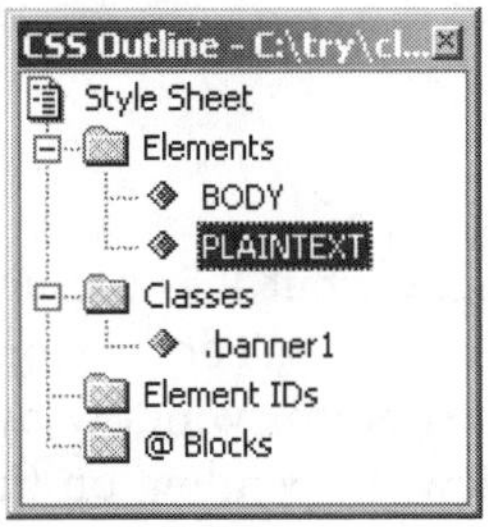

Figure 2-9. CSS Outline

There is also a visual code generator for CSS. When you select a CSS style in the text view, you can select Build Style... from the main Style menu or from the context menu. This will display a dialog that lets you edit the style visually. You can also select Styles → Style Rule to add a new style rule. You can preview your stylesheet by selecting View in Browser from the context menu. By default, this will show a test page that contains text with a variety of styles, but you can choose your own preview page by going to Styles → Select Preview Page.

Design Views

Certain types of .NET source file represent a user interface of some sort. The two most common examples are a C# file containing a Windows Forms Form class and an ASP.NET *.aspx* file. Of course, Visual Studio .NET will let you edit these files as text, but it is also able to provide a design view. A design view displays how the user interface will look at runtime (or a reasonable approximation of it) and allows it to be edited visually using drag and drop.

Design views are provided by software components called designers. It is possible to write your own custom designers. (This is most commonly done for Windows Forms controls, as described in Chapter 7.) However, the system provides a number of built-in designers. Designers are provided for Windows Forms and ASP.NET source files, but they are also available for certain types of file that are not intended for display. (For example, you can open a design view for any class that derives from System.ComponentModel.Component.)

> You can switch back and forth between the design view and the source view with keyboard shortcuts. If the source code view is visible, F7 will show the design view. If the design view is visible, Shift-F7 will show the source code view. You can also choose the view from the Solution Explorer—by default, it will show the design view when you double-click on a file, but the context menu allows you to choose the code view instead.

But before we can look at the design views themselves, we need to look at a closely related VS.NET feature, the Toolbox.

The Toolbox

The Toolbox itself is not a designer, but it is a crucial part of the VS.NET design-time architecture. The Toolbox (View → Toolbox or Ctrl-Alt-X) is a tabbed control that appears to the left of the text editor window by default. It contains items that can be dragged onto a design view. Depending on the file and view you are editing, the selection of tabs available in the Toolbox can change. (This is coordinated by the language service.) For example, if you are editing a Windows Forms source file, the Toolbox will show a list of controls, as Figure 2-10 shows.

Items from the Toolbox can be dragged onto the design view of your source file, and their properties can be set with the C# Properties pane. Design views support visual editing—you can resize and position controls with the mouse. However, the results of any visual editing that you perform are persisted to your source file as code. (See Chapter 7 for more details on design-time behavior.)

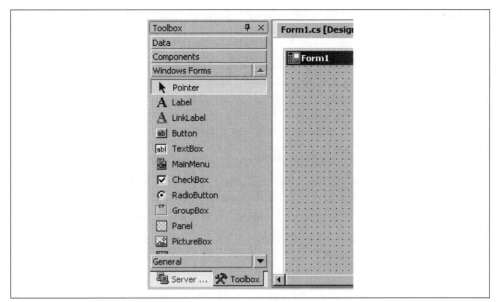

Figure 2-10. Toolbox in the Windows Forms design context

Nonvisual Components

Visual Studio .NET can present a design view for nonvisual components. (A component is any class that implements the IComponent interface, although most derive from Component.) For these classes, the design view cannot attempt to show how the component will look at runtime because the component is nonvisual. The design view just makes certain editing tasks easier.

The design view for nonvisual components just shows a *component tray*. This is an area showing all of the nonvisual components that are being used by the component you are editing. You can drag nonvisual components from the Toolbox into this tray. (In fact, *all* of the design views discussed in this section can show a component tray—if you drop a nonvisual component such as a timer onto a form, it will appear in the component tray instead of on the form itself.)

 Any editing you do with the design view of any component will modify the code in its InitializeComponent method. So your component must have an InitializeComponent method for the design view to be of any use. (Fortunately, most components do. If yours doesn't, add one, and call it from your constructor.)

You can select items in the component tray and edit their properties with the Properties pane (F4). If you double-click on the item, VS.NET will add a handler for its default event. In C#, J#, and MC++ projects, you can also use the Properties pane to handle nondefault events from these components: when you select a component in a design view (whether it is in the component tray or it is a visual component on a form), the Properties pane will have a button with a lightning bolt icon. This is the event button. If you press it, you will see a list of the events that the selected component provides. You can double-click any event in this list to make Visual Studio .NET add a handler for the event (or if a handler already exists, it will take you to the source code for the handler). Alternatively, you can select an event and then type in a name of a function. This will cause the designer to associate that event with the function (by hooking up a delegate), and if the named function doesn't yet exist, it will drop a skeleton implementation into the appropriate file.

In VB.NET, nondefault event handlers are hooked up using the navigation bar at the top of the editor. You select the event source from the left combo box, and then choose the event that you want to handle from the righthand combo box.

Windows Forms

The Windows Forms designer can provide a design view for any source file that contains a type derived from System.Windows.Forms.Control. If the type is derived from Form or UserControl (both of which derive from Control), the design view will be a representation of how the form or control will look at runtime. If the type is a custom control (i.e., it derives directly from Control) or is derived from some other control, the nonvisual design view described earlier will be used. (It is difficult for the designer to deduce how your custom or derived control will look from the code, so it doesn't even try.)

For forms and user controls, you will be able to drag controls from the Toolbox onto the form. You can also position and resize controls on the form with the mouse and edit their properties in the Properties panel.

Web Forms/HTML

The Web Forms designer is a little more complex than the Windows Forms editor. It provides visual editing of your source files in a similar way but involves two files—a single web form has both an *.aspx* file and a codebehind file. The codebehind file will be C#, J#, or VB.NET, but the user interface's appearance is defined by HTML in the *.aspx* file. The Web Forms designer therefore uses the HTML editor as the design view. The Web Forms designer is used for both *.aspx* files and ASP.NET user controls (*.ascx* files).

Although two files are associated with a web page, three different views are actually available. The source view (Shift-F7) is the C#, J#, or VB.NET codebehind page. But the design view (F7) can show either a visual representation of the page or the text in the *.aspx* file. You can flip between these two views of the *.aspx* file using the Design and HTML buttons at the bottom left of the design view editor or using either Ctrl-PageUp or Ctrl-PageDown.

HTML layout

Visual Studio .NET endeavors to make the Web Forms design view as faithful a representation of what the end user will see as possible. This is tricky, given the nature of HTML—it is a markup language and as such was originally designed to allow web browsers plenty of latitude in how they display a page. Graphic designers fought hard to wrest this flexibility away from the browser so that they could make sure that the page would look exactly how they wanted it to look on any browser (regardless of whether that was convenient for the end user or not). This resulted in additions to the HTML specification allowing the exact location of any element to be specified.

The Web Forms designer exploits this in order to make sure that the layout you choose at design time is followed as closely as possible at runtime. However, there are two reasons you might not want to exert this level of control.

First, you may decide that you don't in fact need to take complete control—the original HTML specification left control in the hands of the browser for a good reason: the browser knows how much space is available to display the page and knows what the user's preferences are for font sizes and colors. Unless you have a good reason for overriding the browser's decisions with respect to layout and formatting, it is probably best to respect the user's decisions. (If a user is accessing a web site from a mobile phone or a PDA, it would be frustrating for him to try and use a page that a graphic designer has decided requires an 800x600 pixel display.)

Second, although HTML gives you precise control over a web page's appearance in theory, the practice is a little different. Pages tend to come out slightly differently in different web browsers due to their diverse interpretations of the specifications. In extreme cases, a web page that attempts to take too much control may be unusable on certain web browsers.

Fortunately, you can discourage Visual Studio .NET from creating such control-freak web pages. HTML pages have a pageLayout property, which has two values: GridLayout and FlowLayout. FlowLayout is the default when you create an HTML document, and it allows the web browser to determine the exact layout of the page. However, new *.aspx* files default to GridLayout, in which the HTML designer uses absolute positioning (using a style attribute) to control the exact placement of every element on the page. Unless you really need this level of control, consider changing the setting to FlowLayout.

Server-side HTML elements

The elements on a web page are designed to be rendered by the browser on the client machine. However, it is sometimes useful for the code on the server to have access to these elements when the page is being generated in order to provide dynamic content. ASP.NET therefore supports the notion of server-side controls—elements that will ultimately be rendered by the user's browser but which are represented by an object on the web server while the page is being generated. Server-side code can modify element properties, such as the text or style dynamically.

The ASP.NET Web Forms controls (which are in the Web Forms tab of the Toolbox) are always server-side controls. You can also use standard HTML elements (these are in the HTML tab of the Toolbox). However, although HTML elements can run as server-side controls (i.e., you are not required to use the Web Forms controls just to get server-side objects), they don't by default. You must explicitly enable this behavior—it is off by default for efficiency reasons. You can make any HTML element a server-side control by right-clicking on it in the designer and selecting Run as Server Control. This adds the `runat="server"` attribute to the element and adds a corresponding declaration for that control in the codebehind file.

Web Services

ASP.NET Web Services have a design view, but it offers no special features. It is the same as the nonvisual component design view described earlier.

Miscellaneous Editors

In addition to the text editor and the specialized designers, a number of other editors are built into VS.NET. Editors are supplied for bitmaps, Win32 resource files, string resources, dialog resources, and version resources. VS.NET can also edit any binary file, as it supplies a hex/ASCII dump editor.

Changing Editors

When you open a file, Visual Studio .NET chooses which editor to use based on the file's extension. However, it is sometimes useful to edit that file with a different editor. For example, when you open an *.asmx* file, the default editor will let you edit only either the design view or the associated codebehind file. It will never show you the contents of the *.asmx* file itself. If you want to edit the *.asmx* file directly, you need to open it with the text editor. You can open any file in a project with the editor of your choice by selecting it in the Solution Explorer and then selecting View → Open With.... (You can also select Open With... from the file's context menu in the Solution Explorer.) This will display the dialog box shown in Figure 2-11.

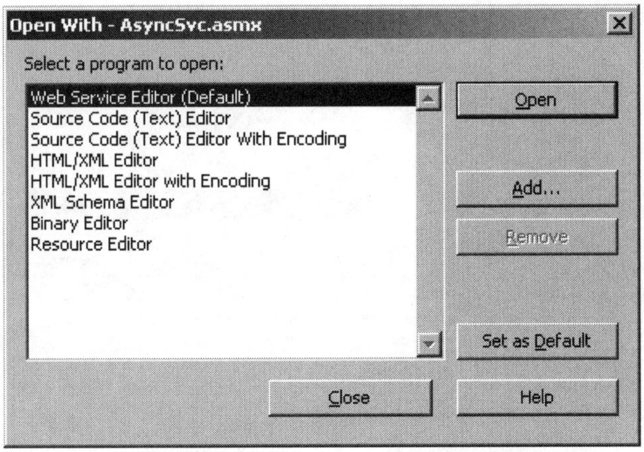

Figure 2-11. The Open With dialog box

From this dialog you can edit the file with any editor in the listbox. The editor with the (Default) tag after it is the default editor for the chosen document. You can change the default editor by selecting one from the list and clicking on the Set as Default button on the dialog box.

You can also use this dialog to add additional programs to the list of editors. Pressing the Add button displays a dialog box in which you can enter the path and name of an application. When you select that editor, VS.NET will spawn that application and pass the currently selected document to it.

Specifying an Encoding

The Visual Studio .NET text editor supports multiple character sets. Visual Studio .NET usually guesses which encoding should be used when opening files, but the Open With dialog box allows you to override its decision. As Figure 2-11 shows, some of the entries in the Open With list have the text "With Encoding" after them. If you select any of these, the Encoding dialog box (see Figure 2-12), which allows you select a specific encoding, will appear.

You can also choose an encoding when you save a document. If you select File → Save As, the Save File dialog box will appear. The Save button has a drop-down list, from which you can select Save with Encoding..., which will display the Advanced Save Options dialog box (see Figure 2-13). From this, you can choose an encoding scheme, and you can also select the way in which line endings are stored. (You can choose CR, LF, or CRLF.)

Figure 2-12. The Encoding selection dialog box

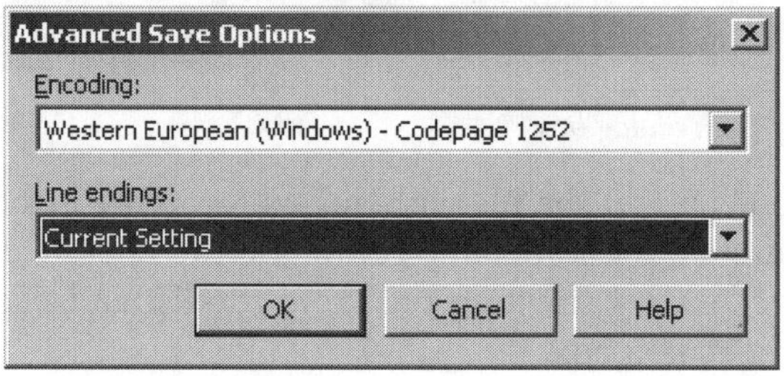

Figure 2-13. Advanced Save Options dialog box

Custom Build Tools

In C#, J#, and VB.NET projects, all source files have a Custom Tool property. This can be used to process a file at design time, optionally generating another file to be compiled into the project. The most common application of this in VS.NET projects is to generate a type-safe wrapper for the DataSet class from an XML schema file (*.xsd*). (See Chapter 5 for more information on type-safe DataSet wrappers.) However, this system is extensible, allowing you to add your own custom tools to generate code.

A custom tool is a COM component that VS.NET will run every time the source file changes and is saved. It must implement the IVsSingleFileGenerator COM interface. The main interesting method on this interface is Generate. VS.NET will call this each time the source file is saved, passing in the filename and the contents of the input file. The Generate method returns an array of bytes that will contain either C#, J#, or Visual Basic .NET source code, depending on the type of project. VS.NET saves these bytes to a file, which it compiles when the project is next built. (You can see this file in the Solution Explorer by pressing the Show All Files button.) Because the generated file is compiled as part of the project, IntelliSense will be available during development time for all of the types it defines.

While you could implement the IVsSingleFileGenerator COM interface directly, a managed base class provided in Visual Studio .NET 2002—Microsoft.VSDesigner. CodeGenerator.BaseCodeGeneratorWithSite—is much easier to use. To use it, just import the *Microsoft.VSDesigner.dll* assembly in the *Common7\IDE* directory of the VS.NET program directory. Your class must be decorated with the Guid attribute to determine its CLSID, but apart from that, the only thing you have to do is write the Generate method itself. The following code shows the implementation of a simple code generator.

```
[Guid("A0B5E5E9-3DF8-48bc-A6BA-E0DFD35C6237")]
public class MyGenerator : BaseCodeGeneratorWithSite
{
    public override byte[ ] GenerateCode(string file, string contents)
    {
        string code = "public class Foo { }";
        return System.Text.Encoding.ASCII.GetBytes(code);
    }
}
```

This particular example isn't very interesting—it always generates the same code and doesn't bother to examine its input. A more useful tool would generate code based on the input provided.

Once you've built your custom tool, it must be registered as a COM class. (You can do this by running the *regasm* command-line tool.) You must add certain keys to the registry to let Visual Studio .NET know about your custom tool. Figure 2-14 shows a typical example.

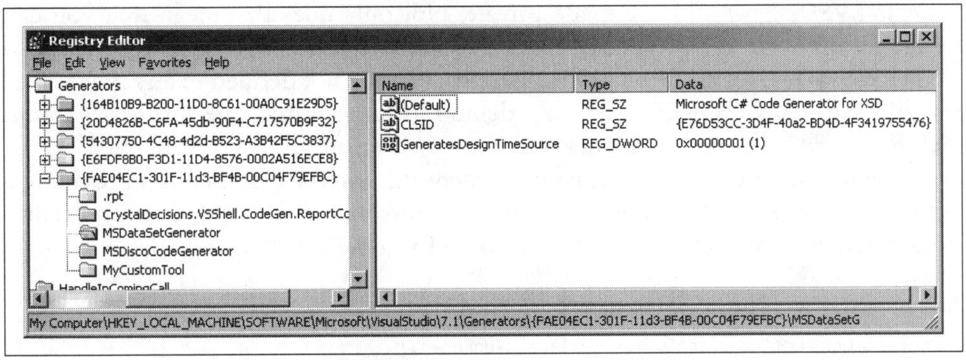

Figure 2-14. Custom tool registry entries

As you can see, you must add entries under this key:

```
HKEY_LOCAL_MACHINE\SOFTWARE\Microsoft\VisualStudio\7.1\Generators
```

(For VS.NET 2002, use 7.0 instead of 7.1.) Underneath here you will find several GUIDs. These are package IDs, which are listed in Table 2-1, and they determine which languages the custom tool will be available with. (See Chapter 10 for more information about VS.NET packages.) The example in Figure 2-14 shows a generator registered for C#.

Table 2-1. Package IDs used with custom tools

Package ID	Package
{FAE04EC1-301F-11d3-BF4B-00C04F79EFBC}	C#
{164B10B9-B200-11D0-8C61-00A0C91E29D5}	VB.NET
{E6FDF8B0-F3D1-11D4-8576-0002A516ECE8}	J#
{20D4826B-C6FA-45db-90F4-C717570B9F32}	Embedded C#
{54307750-4C48-4d2d-B523-A3B42F5C3837}	Embedded VB.NET

To add your own tool, create a new key underneath the relevant package. (So if your tool generates C#, place it under the C# package ID.) The name of the key will be the name the user types into the Custom Tool property in Visual Studio .NET. Set the key's default property to a string describing the tool. Next, add a string value called `CLSID`—this must contain the CLSID of your tool (as specified in its `Guid` attribute; you can generate a new GUID with Tools → Create GUID). Finally, add a DWORD value called `GeneratesDesignTimeSource`, and set it to 1—this tells VS.NET that the tool generates source code at design time and that it should be given the opportunity to do so every time the user saves the input file.

Once your custom tool has been registered, using it is just a matter of setting the relevant file's Custom Tool property. You can either set this manually or create a wizard that will do it for you programmatically. (See Chapter 9 for more information on Wizards.)

Unfortunately, with the release of Visual Studio .NET 2003, all of the types in *Microsoft.VSDesigner.dll* were made private. Not only does this mean that you can no longer derive from `BaseCodeGeneratorWithSite`, it also hides the implementation of the `IVsSingleFileGenerator` COM interface. (This is not defined in any type libraries that ship with VS.NET—the only definition for it is the one inside *Microsoft.VSDesigner.dll*.) This makes it tricky to write a custom tool in VS.NET 2003, as the documentation states that you must implement this interface despite not providing a definition. Fortunately, it doesn't make it impossible—the COM interface definitions you require are simple, and are shown in Example 2-1.

Example 2-1. Custom tool COM interface definitions

```
[InterfaceType(ComInterfaceType.InterfaceIsIUnknown)]
[Guid("3634494C-492F-4F91-8009-4541234E4E99")]
public interface IVsSingleFileGenerator
{
    [return:MarshalAs(UnmanagedType.BStr)]
    string GetDefaultExtension();
    void Generate([In, MarshalAs(UnmanagedType.LPWStr)] string wszInputFilePath,
        [In, MarshalAs(UnmanagedType.BStr)] string bstrInputFileContents,
        [In, MarshalAs(UnmanagedType.LPWStr)] string wszDefaultNamespace,
        out IntPtr pbstrOutputFileContents,
        [MarshalAs(UnmanagedType.U4)] out int pbstrOutputFileContentsSize,
```

Example 2-1. Custom tool COM interface definitions (continued)

```
        [In, MarshalAs(UnmanagedType.Interface)]
            IVsGeneratorProgress  pGenerateProgress);

}

[InterfaceType(ComInterfaceType.InterfaceIsIUnknown)]
[Guid("BED89B98-6EC9-43CB-B0A8-41D6E2D6669D")]
public interface IVsGeneratorProgress
{
    [return:MarshalAs(UnmanagedType.U4)]
    void GeneratorError(
        [In, MarshalAs(UnmanagedType.Bool)] bool fWarning,
        [In, MarshalAs(UnmanagedType.U4)] int dwLevel,
        [In, MarshalAs(UnmanagedType.BStr)] string bstrError,
        [In, MarshalAs(UnmanagedType.U4)] int dwLine,
        [In, MarshalAs(UnmanagedType.U4)] int dwColumn);

    [return:MarshalAs(UnmanagedType.U4)]
    void Progress(
        [In, MarshalAs(UnmanagedType.U4)] int nComplete,
        [In, MarshalAs(UnmanagedType.U4)] int nTotal);
}
```

You can then implement the `IVsSingleFileGenerator` directly. This is slightly more work than it was under VS.NET 2002, because we must now deal with the interop issues that were previously handled by the `BaseCodeGeneratorWithSite` base class. But this it not too onerous, as shown in Example 2-2.

Example 2-2. Implementing IVsSingleFileGenerator by hand

```
[Guid("A0B5E5E9-3DF8-48bc-A6BA-E0DFD35C6237")]
public class MyCustomTool : IVsSingleFileGenerator
{
    public byte[] GenerateCode(string file, string contents)
    {
        string code = "public class Foo { }";
        return System.Text.Encoding.ASCII.GetBytes(code);
    }

    public void Generate(string wszInputFilePath,
        string bstrInputFileContents, string wszDefaultNamespace,
        out IntPtr pbstrOutputFileContents, out int pbstrOutputFileContentsSize,
        IVsGeneratorProgress pGenerateProgress)
    {
        pbstrOutputFileContents = new IntPtr ();
        pbstrOutputFileContentsSize = 0;

        if (bstrInputFileContents == null)
            throw new ArgumentNullException();

        byte[] codeBytes = GenerateCode(wszInputFilePath, bstrInputFileContents);
```

Example 2-2. Implementing IVsSingleFileGenerator by hand (continued)

```
        int len = codeBytes.Length;
        pbstrOutputFileContents = Marshal.AllocCoTaskMem(len);
        pbstrOutputFileContentsSize = len;

        Marshal.Copy(codeBytes, 0, pbstrOutputFileContents, len);

    }

    public string GetDefaultExtension()
    {
        return ".cs";
    }
}
```

As you can see, the GenerateCode method here looks exactly the same as before—we have simply had to supply our own implementation of IVsSingleFileGenerator. This custom tool will work in both VS.NET 2002 and VS.NET 2003.

Although the BaseCodeGeneratorWithSite class was made private with the release of VS.NET 2003, you can still use this class if you want to, instead of using the code in Example 2-1 and Example 2-2. Microsoft has mad the source code for this class available for download at *http://www.gotdotnet.com/userarea/keywordsrch.aspx?keyword=BaseCodeGeneratorWithSite*.

Conclusion

Visual Studio .NET provides basic text editing facilities that are shared by all of the languages in the IDE. It can also provide advanced facilities, such as IntelliSense and automatic formatting when appropriate. Certain specific file types also have their own editors, such as the WYSIWYG HTML editor. Furthermore, certain types of source files can be viewed through the editor or through a design view, such as the Windows Forms designer.

So now that we have looked at all of the facilities required to write code—solutions, projects, and file editors—the next step will be to find the inevitable bugs in our code. So in the next chapter we will focus on the debugging features of Visual Studio .NET.

CHAPTER 3

Debugging

Faulty code has been with us since the dawn of computing. The first general-purpose stored-program computer to become fully operational was the EDSAC,* built at England's University of Cambridge. Maurice Wilkes was in charge of this project and recalls that while writing the computer's first real application, "the realization came over me with full force that a good part of the remainder of my life was going to be spent in finding errors in my own programs." If his 126-line program running within the confines of the EDSAC's 2-kilobyte memory capacity proved so difficult to debug, then what hope can there be for modern computer systems, which are many orders of magnitude more complex? Fortunately, debugging technology has improved since the 1940s.

Visual Studio .NET moves the state of the art of debugging forward. As you would expect, it provides all of the features we now consider mandatory in a debugging tool—source-level debugging, single-stepping, breakpoints, and variable watches. It also has many new and powerful features. Multiprocess and multihost applications can now be debugged from a single session. Multilanguage projects are supported. A single debugging session can deal seamlessly with code written in radically different technologies such as managed code, native code, and T-SQL. Web applications can now be debugged with ease.

Starting the Debugger

The debugger's job is to allow us to examine a running program's behavior so that we can pinpoint faulty code. In order to debug a program, Visual Studio .NET must *attach* to that program as the debugger, meaning that it takes control of the

---

* ENIAC was completed first, but unlike all modern computers, it was unable to execute code out of its own storage—programs were quite literally hardwired. The Manchester Baby was the first computer with a "stored-program" facility ever to execute a program, but EDSAC was the first to execute production code for real applications.

Debugging and Behavior Changes

Debugging is notoriously susceptible to the observer's paradox: you cannot examine anything without changing it. Ideally, the act of attaching a debugger would not change a program's behavior at all. In practice, most developers are familiar with the phenomenon in which faulty programs stop misbehaving the moment the debugger is attached. The two main reasons for this are:

- Compilers need to generate slightly different (and less efficient) code than normal in order to allow debuggers to work, which can cause subtle changes in program behavior.

- Attaching a debugger often changes the speed of execution (radically so if you single-step a thread or halt it with a breakpoint). Software systems are usually highly dynamic entities, so changing the speed at which they run often changes the observable behavior.

Visual Studio .NET is able to debug release builds, albeit with reduced functionality, which can avoid the first problem. However, with .NET applications, attaching the debugger can change the JIT compiler's behavior, so in some cases there are no simple solutions to these problems. (Running debug builds in your production systems can sometimes remove the symptoms of such a problem, but it is hardly a solution. At best, it is an emergency stopgap.) Visual Studio .NET attempts to tread lightly in debugging sessions, but inevitably you will come across the occasional *heisenbug*—a bug that vanishes as soon as you try to look at it (with apologies to Werner Heisenberg and his Uncertainty Principle). At this point, you must abandon the debugger and resort to the time-honored techniques that have served us well since the 1940s: painstaking detective work, deep thought, trial and error, printf (or its spiritual successors such as Debug.WriteLine), and copious supplies of caffeine.

program's execution. Once attached, a debugger can stop and start any thread, and it can examine the program's state. In fact, VS.NET goes beyond simple observation and allows us to modify the state and even the flow of execution.

A program can be attached to in three ways: launching the program from within Visual Studio .NET, attaching to an existing process, and just-in-time (JIT) debugging.

Launching to Debug

The simplest way to attach Visual Studio .NET's debugger to a program is to start the program using Debug → Start (F5). The program will start to execute as normal, but the development environment will change its appearance somewhat. VS.NET remembers two versions of your window and toolbar layouts, one for normal editing and one for debugging. This is useful, not only because you tend to need different tool windows open when debugging, but also because it makes it easy to tell that a debug session is in progress simply by looking at the screen layout.

When VS.NET is debugging, you will be able to suspend the debuggee's execution either by setting breakpoints (as described later) or with Debug → Break All (Ctrl-Alt-Break). The debugging session will end when the target program exits. Alternatively, you can ask Visual Studio .NET to stop debugging. You can use either Debug → Stop Debugging (Shift-F5), which will abort the program, or Debug → Detach All, which leaves the program running. (ASP.NET applications continue running whichever you use.)

Attaching to a Running Process

You do not need to launch the program from within Visual Studio .NET in order to debug it: it is possible to attach to a program that is already running. Debug → Processes... displays the dialog shown in Figure 3-1, allowing you to select a process to which to attach.

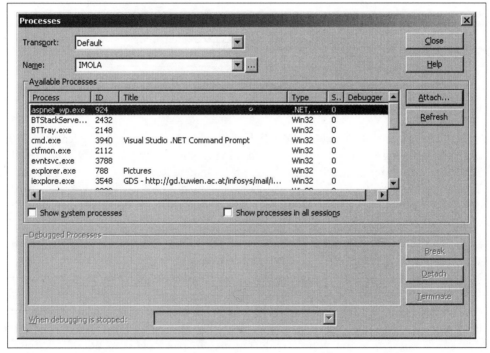

Figure 3-1. Attaching the debugger to a running process

By default, this dialog will show the processes running in the interactive user's session on the local machine. The Name field allows you to choose a different machine. (See the "Cross-Machine Debugging" section, later in this chapter, for more information on remote debugging.) Two checkboxes allow you to display system processes and processes running in other user sessions (for multiuser systems such as Windows XP and Terminal Services), but for most applications, the default filtered list will show everything you need to see.

If you select a process from the list and click the Attach... button, the dialog shown in Figure 3-2 will appear.

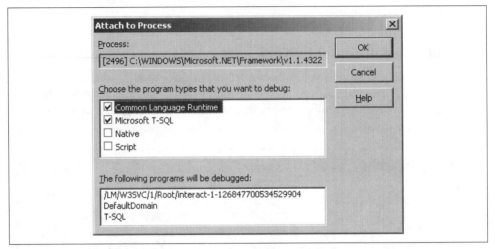

Figure 3-2. Specifying program types

This illustrates one of Visual Studio .NET's most interesting debugging features. Not only can it debug radically different technologies such as managed .NET code and SQL Server-stored procedures (the Common Language Runtime(CLR) and Microsoft T-SQL options, respectively), it is capable of managing all of these within a single debugging session. This means that if a C# program connects to a database and executes a stored procedure, Visual Studio .NET will let you step through both the C# code and the stored procedure in the same debugging session.

Visual Studio .NET supports four different "program types." These are CLR (.NET), T-SQL (SQL Server 2000 stored procedures), Native (classic Win32), and Script (COM scripting—e.g., classic ASP or client-side script in a web application). You can choose almost any combination of these whenever you attach to a process; the only limitation is that Native and Script are mutually exclusive. However, you should select only the types that you actually require. In particular, do not select Native unless you need it. Native programs are classic Win32 executables, and if you select this mode, you may not be able to detach the debugger without terminating the process. (Under Windows XP this problem will not occur—you will normally be able to detach nondestructively. But under Windows NT 4.0 or Windows 2000, unless you have installed the DbgProxy service, detaching from a native session will end the process.) Also, be aware that debugging with both native and CLR modes enabled tends to be rather slow.

The bottom half of the Attach to Process dialog box shows which programs will be debugged if you proceed. This is useful because it shows which program types are currently running in your selected process. Figure 3-2 shows a typical list for the ASP.NET worker process, and we can see that it is using the .NET runtime—two AppDomains are shown. DefaultDomain is ASP.NET's main AppDomain, but because ASP.NET isolates each web application in its own AppDomain, we can see a second, the /LM/W3SVC entry, listed here. Also note that there is a T-SQL entry in the list, which tells us that this process is connected to a SQL Server database. Compare this to Figure 3-3, which shows the same dialog for a command prompt process. The CLR, T-SQL and Script program types have all been selected, but the list of programs that will be debugged is empty, indicating that the process is not in fact using any of these program types. (You will still be allowed to attach Visual Studio .NET—it will simply assume that the specified program types are not in use yet but will be at some point in the process's future.)

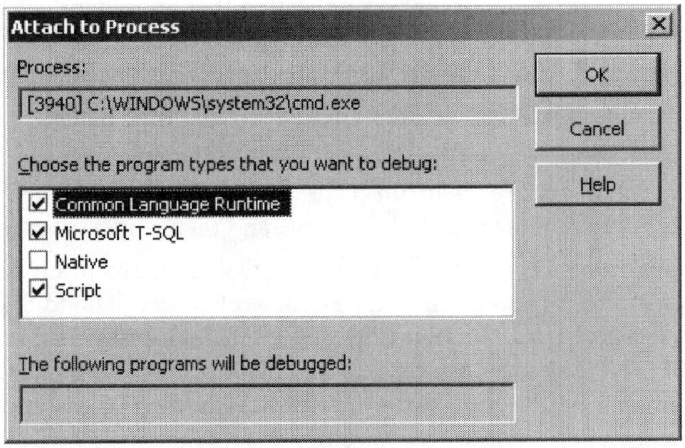

Figure 3-3. Inappropriate program type choices

Once you have chosen the program type(s) and clicked OK, VS.NET will return to the Processes dialog. Before you close it, you have the option to configure the default behavior when stopping the debugger—the combo box at the bottom of the window lets you choose between terminating the process and just detaching.

Just-in-Time Debugging

The final way of attaching Visual Studio .NET to a process is the mechanism known as just-in-time debugging.* This feature of Windows is designed to allow debuggers

---

* Do not confuse JIT debugging with .NET JIT compilation—JIT stands for the same thing in both cases, but these are different concepts.

to be attached to programs that have failed. When a program exhibits some fatally erroneous behavior, such as throwing an unhandled exception, Windows will run the JIT debugging handler specified in the registry (see the "Just-in-Time Debugging Registry Settings" sidebar). On systems with Visual Studio .NET installed, this will result in the dialog shown in Figure 3-4 being displayed.

Just-in-Time Debugging Registry Settings

.Net applications amd classic Win32 applications use slightly different mechanisms to find and attach a debugger just-in-time. If a .NET application throws an unhandled exception, the .NET Framework will run whichever program is registered in the `DbgManagedDebugger` value under the `HKEY_LOCAL_MACHINE\SOFTWARE\Microsoft\.NETFramework` key. It will also use the `DbgJITDebugLaunchSetting` value under the same key to determine exactly how to handle the exception.

0: it will bring up a simple message box indicating that an unhandled exception was thrown, allowing the user to terminateor debug the application by clicking on OK or Cancel, respectively. Clicking Cancel then runs the program specified in the registry.

2: the message box is bypassed, and the program is run immediately.

1: no dialog is shown and the JIT handler will not be executed—instead, the program's unhandled exception handler will run. (The default handler supplied by the .NET runtime prints an exception trace to the console and then exits.)

ASP.NET and Windows Forms applications have their own exception-handling mechanisma that will usually prevent the .NET Framework's default handler from running, so that these registry settings do not normally affect such programs. In web applications, the ASP.NET unhandled exception handler will display the appropriate error page as determined by the *web.config* file. With Windows Forms applications, any exception thrown during normal message processing (i.e., after `Application.Run` has been called) will be trapped by the Windows Forms Framework. It displays its own unhandled exception dialog without even consulting the registry keys discussed here. (You can disable this dialog by adding a handler to the `Application.ThreadException` event. If you just rethrow teh exception in this handler, the application will revert to the standard behavior—it will consult the registry and show the appropriate dialogs.)

If an application throws an unhandled classic Win32 exception, a different registry key is used. Windows will launch the program registered under the Debugger value under the `HKEY_LOCAL_MACHINE\SOFTWARE\Microsoft\Windows NT\CurrentVersion\AeDebug` key.

On a system that has had Visual Studio .NET installed, both of these registry keys will point to a program called *VS7JIT.EXE*. and the `DbgJITDebugLaunchSetting` value is set to 2. So the same program will be run immediately when either a .NET or a classic Win32 application throws an unhandled exceptions. This program displays the dialog shown in Figure 3-4. It determines which debuggers to display from a list stored under the `HKEY_LOCAL_MACHINE\SOFTWARE\Microsoft\Machine Debug Manager\JITDebugging` registry key.

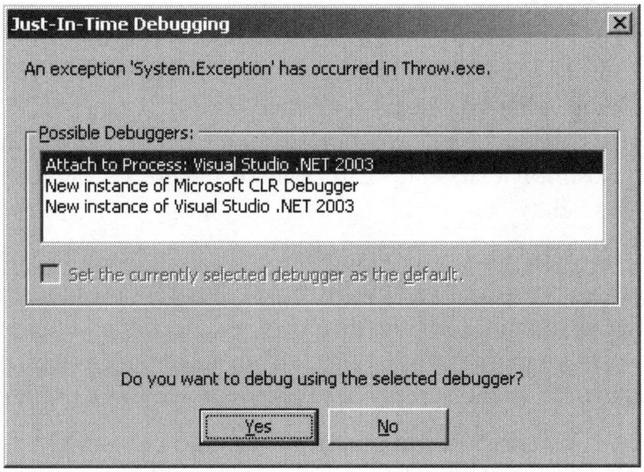

Figure 3-4. Just-in-time debugger selection

This dialog displays a list of suitable debuggers. The first choice it has given us is an instance of Visual Studio .NET that happens to be running. This can be very useful if you already have an appropriate solution loaded. (This is particularly helpful if you launched a program from within VS.NET without attaching the debugger using Debug → Start Without Debugging (Ctrl-F5), only to have the program fail unexpectedly.) It has also given us the option of launching new processes–either a new copy of VS.NET or the Microsoft CLR debugger. (The Microsoft CLR debugger is the free debugger that ships with the .NET Framework SDK, DBGCLR.EXE.)

If you choose to debug using Visual Studio .NET from the Just-in-Time Debugging dialog box shown in Figure 3-4, you will be presented with the program type selection dialog box shown in Figure 3-2, just as if you had attached to the process using the Debug → Process... menu item.

With Visual Studio 2002, you can configure a machine to support remote Just-in-time debugging. You can run the following command on the machine on which you will run the target application:

```
\Program Files\Common Files\Microsoft Shared\VS7Debug\mdm.exe /remotecfg
```

This lets you select which machines will be given the opportunity to debug when a program crashes. You must choose machines that have Visual Studio .NET installed. However, this feature was dropped in Visual Studio 2003 as part of a drive to improve the security of remote debugging. This does not prevent you from debugging remote systems; it simply means that you must attach the debugger to the remote executable before it crashes, rather than relying on JIT debugging.

JIT debugging in Windows Forms applications

.NET Windows Forms applications add an extra complication to JIT debugging. The Windows Forms event-handling loop catches all unhandled exceptions and displays its own error dialog, allowing users to either continue or quit. Neither of these options will start JIT debugging—selecting Continue causes the application to ignore the error, and Quit simply exits. This can be inconvenient for debugging, so it is possible to disable this behavior.

You can enable JIT debugging in a Windows Forms application by adding an entry to the application's configuration file. (If the application is called *Appname.exe*, its configuration file must be in the same directory, and its name must be *Appname.exe.config*.) If you wish to enable JIT debugging for an application that does not currently have a configuration file, simply use the file shown in Example 3-1.

If the application already has a configuration file, you can simply add the `<system.windows.forms jitDebugging="true"/>` element underneath the main `<configuration>` element. The presence of this element will cause Windows Forms applications to start JIT debugging just like any other application when an unhandled error occurs.

If you want to enable JIT debugging for all Windows Forms applications on your development machine, you can modify your *machine.config* file. This file can be found in the *CONFIG* subdirectory of your .NET Framework installation directory, which is typically beneath *%SystemRoot%\Microsoft.NET\Framework*. If you search the standard *machine.config* file for `system.windows.forms,` you will find that it already has a suitable element, which has been commented out. If you uncomment the element and set its `jitDebugging` attribute to true (it is false by default), this will enable JIT debugging for all Windows Forms applications on the whole machine, so you will not need to create or modify individual applications' configuration files.

ASP.NET Debugging

ASP.NET applications are special in that they don't run in their own process. Each application runs in its own AppDomain in the ASP.NET worker process. (With Internet Information Services (IIS) Version 5, the worker process is `aspnet_wp.exe`. On future versions of Windows, this is likely to change.) Fortunately, Visual Studio .NET knows about ASP.NET. If you create a web project, Debug → Start (F5) causes Visual Studio .NET to attach to the ASP.NET worker process, and it simply launches Internet Explorer to show the start page. This means that you do not need to take any special action to attach to an ASP.NET application. However, you will need to make sure that any code generated by the ASP.NET runtime is debuggable.

All *.aspx* pages begin with an `@Page` directive. You can supply a `Debug` attribute for this directive, indicating whether the generated code should be compiled with debugging enabled. This should be set to true to enable debugging of the page:

```
<%@ Page language="C#" Debug="true" %>
```

You can also configure this on an application-wide level. If a particular page does not have the Debug attribute, ASP.NET will use the setting in the *web.config* file. The application debug setting is contained in the <compilation> element, underneath the <system.web> element. The configuration file in Example 3-1 enables debugging for pages that don't explicitly disable it with the Debug attribute.

Example 3-1. Enabling debugging in ASP.NET applications

```
<configuration>
  <system.web>
    <compilation debug="true"/>
  </system.web>
</configuration>
```

These settings apply only to code generated by ASP.NET. Visual Studio .NET web projects usually contain a certain amount of precompiled code in codebehind pages, deployed on the web server as a *.dll* in the application's *bin* directory. To enable debugging of this code, you must make sure that you build the Debug configuration of the project. (By default, new projects will build the Debug configuration.)

 You can debug ASP.NET applications on remote machines, too. However, this will work only if the remote debugging components have been installed on the target machine. (See the "Cross-Machine Debugging" section, later in this chapter.) Your user account will also need to be a member of either the local Administrator group or the local Debugger User group on the target machine.

Client-Side Script Debugging

Although you can debug ASP.NET pages, you will find that if you attempt to debug client-side script code in an *.aspx* file, nothing seems to work. On the face of it, VS. NET appears to support server-side debugging for only *.aspx* files. However, debugging client-side script is entirely possible in VS.NET; it is just a little more involved.

The problem with debugging client-side script is that the web browser does not get to see a server-side file (e.g., the *.aspx* file)—it gets to see the response generated by that file. Since client-side script executes in the web browser, you cannot debug client-side script directly in the *.aspx* file. Instead, you must debug the response that the client browser is working from (i.e., the output of the *.aspx* page, not the *.aspx* page itself).

In order to debug client-side script, you must first enable script debugging in Internet Explorer—it is disabled by default. From Internet Explorer's Tools menu, select Internet Options, and choose the Advanced tab in the dialog that appears. This will display a list of configuration options. Find the Disable Script Debugging checkbox. Make sure that this box is *not* checked. Script debugging will now be enabled.

If you turn on script debugging in this way in the middle of a debug session, it will have no effect until you finish. You will need to stop debugging and start a new session for the change to take effect.

Once IE script debugging is enabled, when you debug an ASP.NET application, VS.NET will be able to show you all of the active HTML files that the browser currently has loaded. This list is shown in the Running Documents tool window, which can be opened with Debug → Windows → Running Documents (Ctrl-Alt-N). Figure 3-5 shows the Running Documents window

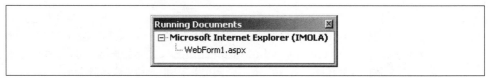

Figure 3-5. The Running Documents window

By default, Visual Studio .NET will show only documents loaded by the instance of Internet Explorer that it launched for this debug session. (If you want to see documents in other instances of IE, you can attach the debugger to those processes.) In Figure 3-5, only one document is shown, but if the web application were using frames, there would be one item for each file in the frameset.

If you double-click on a file in the Running Documents window, VS.NET will display the contents of the page as Internet Explorer sees them. (This is the same text that you would see if you selected View Source in IE itself.) This will be similar to, but not quite the same as, the underlying *.aspx* file—the static content will be the same, but any dynamic items (e.g., runat=server tags or <% ... %> script blocks) will have been replaced with their evaluated content. But you will now be able to use debugging features described in this chapter, such as breakpoints and single-stepping, on all of the client-side script on the page.

Controlling Execution

For the debugger to do its job well, it must make as few changes as possible to the operation of the program, so simply attaching Visual Studio .NET's debugger does not have much immediate effect. In order to examine a program's state and behavior, you must suspend its execution, so you will need to give VS.NET the criteria under which it should freeze the application and show you what is going on.

You can control program execution in three ways with the debugger. Breakpoints enable you to bring the program to a halt on selected lines of code. You can configure the debugger to suspend execution when particular error conditions occur. And once the program has been brought to a halt, you can exercise fine control by single-stepping through the code.

Breakpoints

As you would expect, Visual Studio .NET allows you to set breakpoints—requests to suspend the program when it reaches certain lines of code. You can set a breakpoint by placing the cursor on the line at which you want execution to stop and pressing F9. F9 will toggle the breakpoint—if the line already has a breakpoint set, F9 will remove it. (You can also toggle breakpoints by clicking in the gray column at the left of the editor.) Visual Studio .NET indicates that a breakpoint has been set by placing a red circle to the left of the line, as Figure 3-6 shows. It can also optionally color the line's background—you can configure this with the Options dialog. (Use Tools → Options, and select the Fonts and Colors properties in the Environment category.)

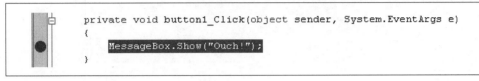

```
private void button1_Click(object sender, System.EventArgs e)
{
    MessageBox.Show("Ouch!");
}
```

Figure 3-6. A breakpoint

Breakpoints have an effect only when the debugger is attached—if you run a program outside of the debugger, it will not stop at a breakpoint. Old-style compiled-in breakpoints that work under any circumstances are still available if you need them. With .NET applications, you simply call the Break method of the System.Diagnostics.Debugger class. In classic C++ applications, you can either compile in an __asm int 3 or call the DebugBreak API. When a debugger is attached, all of these techniques have the same effect as hitting a breakpoint. If a debugger is not attached, the just-in-time debugging process described earlier will begin, allowing you to attach a debugger.

Sometimes, specifying the line at which to stop is not enough—it is not unusual to need to stop at a line that is executed many thousands of times but that you want to debug only under certain circumstances. In this case, you will need to be a little more selective. Instead of using F9 to set a breakpoint, you can use Ctrl-B, which will display the window shown in Figure 3-7.

As you would expect, the dialog indicates the location of the breakpoint. The File tab shown here allows the location to be specified as a particular line in a file. (Breakpoints set using F9 work this way.) The Function tab allows you to set a breakpoint on a function by name. Figure 3-8 shows how to use this to trap all calls to a particular .NET system API. (This technique relies on having symbolic information for the function being trapped. This means that it doesn't work on system APIs in unmanaged applications unless you have installed the debug symbols—to trap such calls without system debug symbols installed, you will need to use the Address tab.)

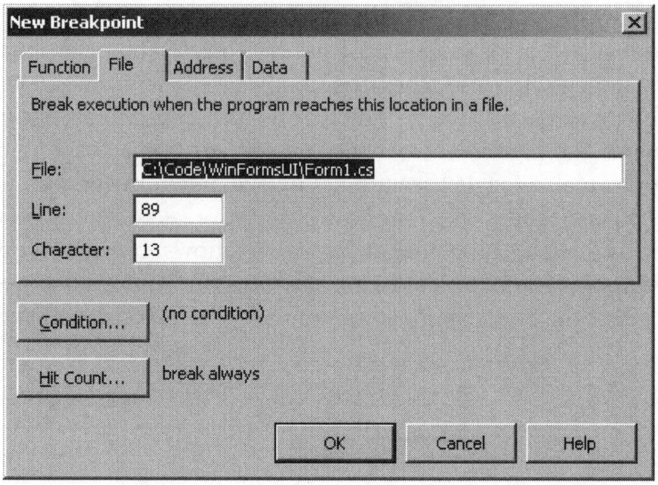

Figure 3-7. Setting a selective breakpoint

 If you use the Function tab to set a breakpoint on a .NET API, Visual Studio .NET will give you two warnings. When you set the break-point, it will indicate that it has not recognized the function name. This is because the function is not defined in your project. The second warning will be at runtime, when you hit the breakpoint: it will tell you that it has no source code for the relevant location.

Both of these warnings are unavoidable, because Microsoft does not supply the source for the .NET Framework Class Libraries. So you cannot use this technique to step through the system libraries, but it can still be useful to halt when a call to particular a system function occurs.

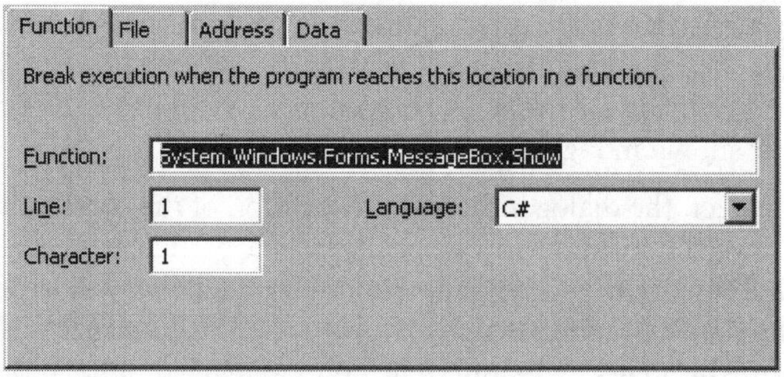

Figure 3-8. Setting a breakpoint by function name

The third tab, Address, allows you to set a breakpoint based on the address of a specific instruction. This is available only with Native Win32 debugging—with managed code (CLR programs), JIT compilation means that methods can be relocated dynamically, which makes address-based breakpoints useless. (The fields on this tab will be grayed out when working with .NET applications.) The fourth tab, Data, lets you specify location-independent breakpoints that fire only when certain data items are accessed. Data breakpoints are also available only with native debugging.

Regardless of which tab you use to specify a breakpoint's location, the bottom half of the dialog will always show the same two buttons: Condition... and Hit Count... These allow you to narrow down the conditions under which the breakpoint will suspend the program.

The Hit Count... button displays the dialog shown in Figure 3-9. The drop-down listbox provides four options. Break Always, the default, disables hit counting. "Break when hit count is equal to" causes the breakpoint to be ignored except when it is hit for the Nth time, with N the number specified in the text box. This can be particularly useful when tracking down memory leaks in C++ applications—see the sidebar. You can also specify "Break when the hit count is greater than or equal to," which is useful in situations in which code operates correctly at first but malfunctions after several executions. Finally, you can specify that the breakpoint should "Break when the hit count is a multiple of" the specified figure, which can be useful if you only want to examine occasional calls to suspect code. The Reset Hit Count button lets you reset Visual Studio .NET's record of the number of times that this breakpoint has been hit so far.

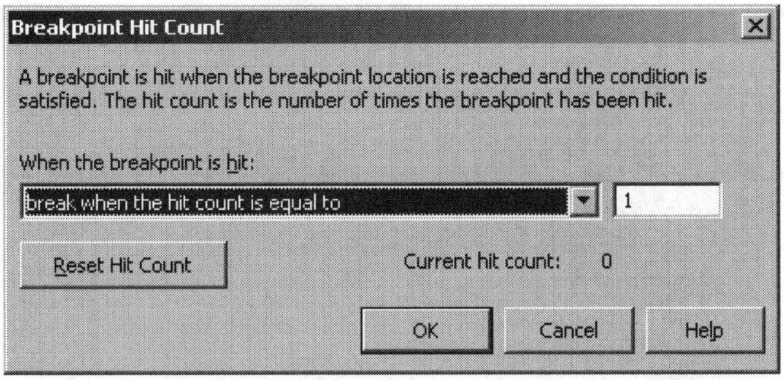

Figure 3-9. Specifying a hit count for a breakpoint

The Condition... button of the Breakpoint Properties dialog in Figure 3-7 provides another way of being selective about when the breakpoint will halt the program. If you click this button, the dialog shown in Figure 3-10 will appear.

Finding Memory Leaks in C++

The C++ runtime library is able to report leaked heap blocks. Simply add the following lines to your project's *stdafx.h* file:

```
#define CRTDBG_MAP_ALLOC
#include <stdlib.h>
#include <crtdbg.h>
```

With this in place, call the _CrtDumpMemoryLeaks function at program exit. (Applications created with the MFC Wizard will do this automatically.) This will scan the heap looking for unfreed blocks, reporting everything it finds to the debugger's Output window. The report includes the allocation number (i.e., the number of times that the heap allocation method had been called when that block was allocated). For example, the following output shows that the fiftieth block of memory to be allocated was 5 bytes long and was never freed:

```
Detected memory leaks!
Dumping objects ->
{50} normal block at 0x00323AE8, 5 bytes long.
 Data: <     > CD CD CD CD CD
Object dump complete.
```

If you can reproduce a memory leak in such a way that the allocation number is the same every time you run the program, it is easy to locate the source of the leak. Just set a breakpoint on the library's memory allocation method (_heap_alloc_dbg, in the *dbgheap.c* file) and set its hit count to be whatever the offending allocation number is (50 in this case). If you choose the "Break when hit count is equal to" option in the Breakpoint Hit Count dialog (as shown in Figure 3-9), the debugger will ignore the first 49 heap allocations but then stop when the offending allocation occurs. You can then simply look at the call stack to find the line of code that allocated the leaked block.

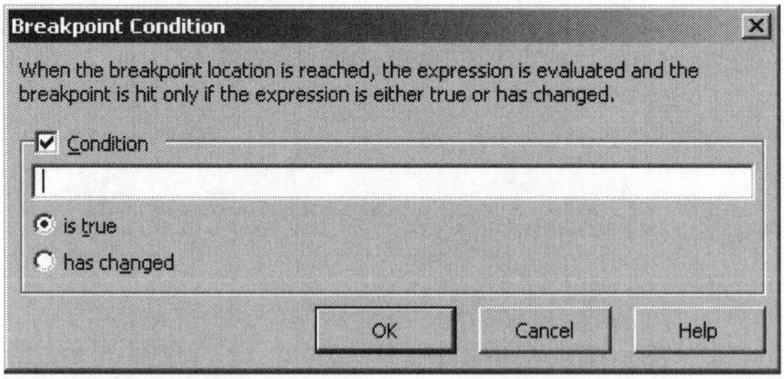

Figure 3-10. Setting a conditional breakpoint

This dialog allows you to specify an expression that will be evaluated when the breakpoint is hit. (It will be evaluated at the scope of the breakpoint, so you may use local variables and method parameters in the expression. You can even call methods in the expression.) You can use the expression in two ways. You can choose to halt execution only if the expression is true. Alternatively, you can halt only if the expression is different from what it was last time the breakpoint was hit.

Choosing to halt when an expression is true can be very useful when particular function may be called extremely frequently but you want to debug only a small subset of the calls. Consider some code in a Windows application that is responsible for repainting the window. Redraw code is often particularly awkward to debug with normal breakpoints because the act of hitting a breakpoint will bring the debugger to the front. This obscures the window of the application being debugged, so when you let the program continue, its redraw code will run again, at which point it will, of course, hit the breakpoint again. While this issue can often be solved by using a hit count to stop in the debugger only every other redraw, the fact that repaint code is often called tens of times a second makes them a frequent candidate for a more selective breakpoint.

For example, suppose you notice that your window's appearance is wrong whenever the window is square, but correct otherwise. (Certain drawing algorithms have an edge case for perfectly square drawing areas that is easy to get wrong, so this is a fairly common scenario.) Conditional breakpoints can make it easy to catch the one case you are interested in and single-step through that. You can just put a breakpoint on the first line of the redraw handler and set an appropriate condition. For example, in a Windows Forms application, you could use this expression: `DisplayRectangle.Width==DisplayRectangle.Height`.

In order to use a conditional breakpoint, the inputs you require for the expression must be in scope. So for an MFC application you would be able to use this trick only if the window width and height had already been retrieved—unlike Windows Forms, MFC does not make these values available directly through class properties. Figure 3-11 shows an example program in which the width and height have been read into local variables, and a suitable conditional breakpoint has been set.

 Conditional breakpoints don't enable you to do anything that couldn't be done by modifying the code being debugged and setting normal breakpoints. Obviously, it is best not to change the target if at all possible, since such modifications may change the behavior. Conditional breakpoints are therefore very useful because they allow you to be selective without touching the code. However, if you find that you cannot set a breakpoint for the exact set of conditions you need (because the relevant information is not in scope), remember that you always have the fallback position of compiling the test you require into the target instead.

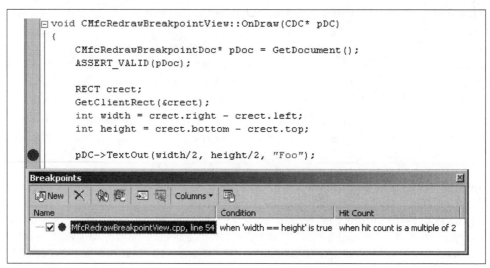

```
void CMfcRedrawBreakpointView::OnDraw(CDC* pDC)
{
    CMfcRedrawBreakpointDoc* pDoc = GetDocument();
    ASSERT_VALID(pDoc);

    RECT crect;
    GetClientRect(&crect);
    int width = crect.right - crect.left;
    int height = crect.bottom - crect.top;

    pDC->TextOut(width/2, height/2, "Foo");
```

Breakpoints			☒
📝 New ✕ 🖐 🗐 🐷 🗐 Columns ▾ 🗐			
Name		Condition	Hit Count
☑ ● MfcRedrawBreakpointView.cpp, line 54		when 'width == height' is true	when hit count is a multiple of 2

Figure 3-11. Conditional redraw breakpoint in an MFC application

Data breakpoints

The New Breakpoint window shown in Figure 3-7 has a fourth tab, Data, which allows you to set a kind of breakpoint that is different from all the others. Data breakpoints are not associated with any particular line of code. With a data breakpoint, you simply specify the name of a variable, and the debugger will halt if that variable changes, regardless of which line of code made the change. This can be very useful for tracking down bugs when a value has changed but you do not know when or why the change occurred.

> Data breakpoints are not supported in .NET programs. They are available only in native code.

Figure 3-12 shows the tab for setting a data breakpoint. The variable name must be a global variable. If it is a pointer variable and points to an array, you can use the Items field to specify the number of array elements that the debugger will monitor. The Context field allows you to specify the lexical scope in which the variable name should be evaluated—this is useful when the expression is otherwise ambiguous. This field takes strings of the form {*[function],[source],[module]*} *location*. The *function* is the name of a method. Since function names are not necessarily globally unique, *source* specifies the source file in which the function was defined. When debugging across multiple modules (e.g., in a program that uses several DLLs), even source file names may not be unique, so you can specify which particular module you mean with *module*. Finally, *location* specifies the exact position—this is specified as a line number.

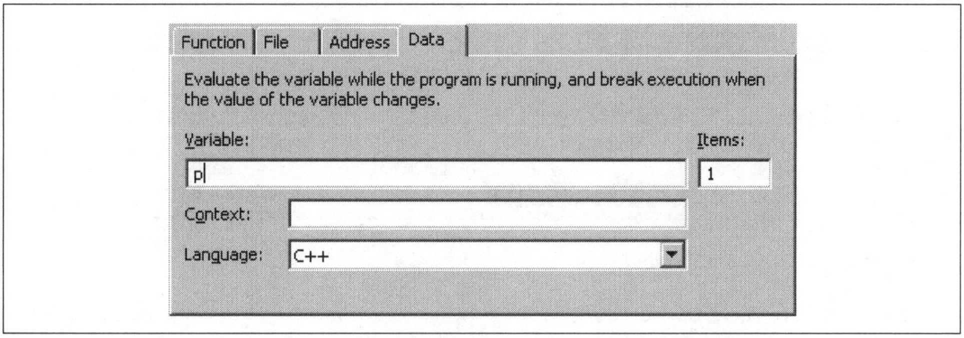

Figure 3-12. A data breakpoint

The various parts of the context string are all optional—you need supply only as many as are required to be unambiguous. For example, to specify that the expression should be evaluated with respect to line 123 of the *Hello.cpp* source file, use the string {,Hello.cpp,} @123. Because no *function* was provided, *location* was relative to the top of the file. However, if you supply a *function*, *location* is not required.

> Using data breakpoints can make your program run very slowly in the debugger, because Visual Studio .NET has to go to great lengths to provide this functionality. If the code you are debugging is very processor intensive, data breakpoints will probably not be the most appropriate tool.

The Breakpoints window

You can review, modify, and remove all of the breakpoints currently in place for your project with the Breakpoints window. You can open the window using Debug → Windows → Breakpoints (Ctrl-Alt-B).

As Figure 3-13 shows, the Breakpoints window lists all of the breakpoints. You can choose which information will be displayed about each breakpoint—the Columns button on the toolbar lets you select any aspect of a breakpoint. By default, the window will show each breakpoint's location and whether it has condition or hit count requirements specified, and the Hit Count column also indicates how many times the breakpoint has been hit so far in the current debugging session. You can modify the breakpoint by selecting it and choosing Properties from the context menu—this will open the Breakpoint Properties window, which is essentially identical to the New Breakpoint window (except that it doesn't let you change a location-based breakpoint to a data breakpoint or vice versa).

The tick box next to the breakpoint indicates that the breakpoint is enabled. If you uncheck this, the breakpoint will be disabled, but not forgotten. (You can also toggle this setting in the editor window by moving the cursor to the relevant line and pressing Ctrl-F9.) This is useful if you want to prevent a breakpoint from operating temporarily

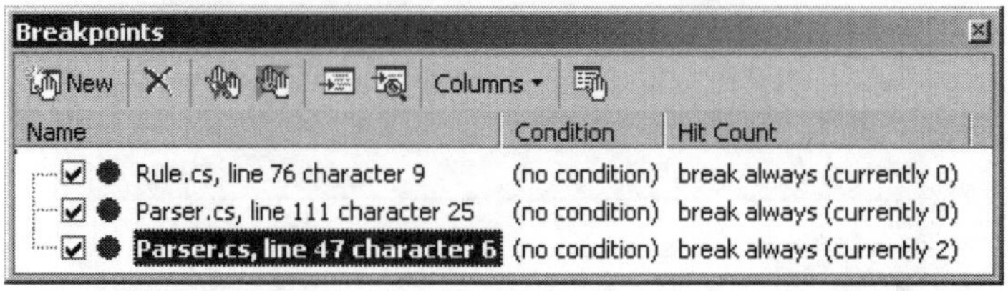

Breakpoints			⊠
🔲New ✕ 🖐 🖐 🖅 🔍 Columns ▾ 🗐			
Name	Condition	Hit Count	
☑ ● Rule.cs, line 76 character 9	(no condition)	break always (currently 0)	
☑ ● Parser.cs, line 111 character 25	(no condition)	break always (currently 0)	
☑ ● **Parser.cs, line 47 character 6**	(no condition)	break always (currently 2)	

Figure 3-13. The Breakpoints window

but don't want to have to recreate the breakpoint again later. (This is particularly help-ful for complex breakpoints such as those with conditions or data breakpoints.) You can also enable and disable breakpoints using the context menu in the source window.

 Visual Studio .NET saves your breakpoint settings when you save the solution, including whether they are enabled or not. These settings are not stored in the *.sln* file itself, but rather in the associated *.suo* file. Note that if you move the *.suo* file to another machine, you may find that some of your breakpoints stop working—the location of source files for components outside of the project may not be the same from one machine to the next. (For example, they could be on a network share that might be mapped to different drives.) If you find that some breakpoints have disappeared after changing machines, open the Breakpoints window and check that none of the breakpoints have file-names that are no longer valid.

The toolbar at the top of the window provides the ability to create and delete break-points, to enable and disable them, to examine the code on which they are set, and to display their properties window. (All of these facilities are also available from the context menu.)

Halting on Errors

Breakpoints are very useful when you know exactly which part of your program you wish to examine, but in practice, debugging sessions often start when an unexpected error occurs. Just-in-time debugging always works this way—when you attach the debugger just-in-time, it will halt the program and attempt to show you where the error occurred. But you do not need to rely on just-in-time attachment for this behavior—programs started from within the debugger can be halted automatically when an unhandled error occurs.

Visual Studio .NET can identify many different sources of errors. There are four gen-eral categories: C++ exceptions, CLR exceptions, CLR runtime checks, and Win32 exceptions. These categories are subdivided into specific exceptions. You can config-ure how VS.NET handles these error types with the Exceptions dialog, which is dis-played using Debug → Exceptions... (Ctrl-Alt-E). This dialog is shown in Figure 3-14.

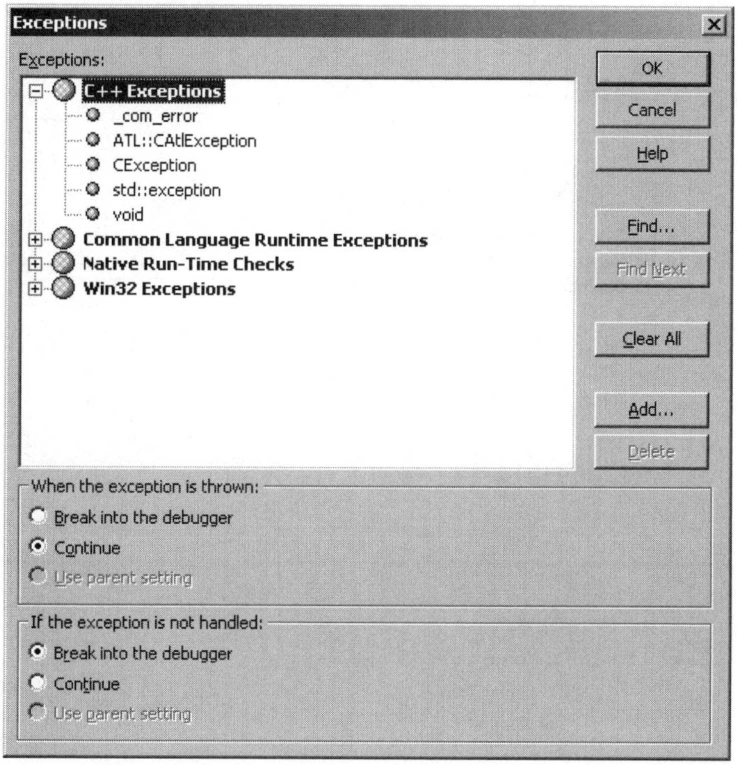

Figure 3-14. Configuring exception handling

For each error type, Visual Studio .NET allows two error-handling behaviors to be specified: unanticipated errors can be treated differently from those the application is able to handle itself. Unhandled exceptions will use the setting in the "If the exception is not handled" group box. Exceptions that the application handles itself will use the setting in the "When the exception is thrown" group box.

The gray circles in Figure 3-14 indicate that the debugger will suspend the code only when an unhandled error occurs. This is the default for all categories. If you change the category's setting, the members of that category will inherit that setting unless they have been explicitly configured to override it. (The default for most category members is Use Parent Setting.) Figure 3-15 shows the effect of changing the C++ Exceptions category settings. The X in a red circle indicates that the error will always cause the debugger to break, regardless of whether the program handles the error. Notice how all of the entries inside the C++ Exceptions category have changed to a red cross—they have all inherited their parents' settings.

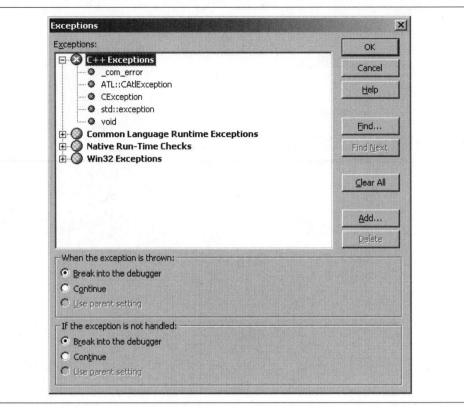

Figure 3-15. Exception setting inheritance

The Exceptions dialog indicates that an entry will inherit its parent's settings by drawing a smaller icon—all of the items in the C++ Exceptions category have small circles by them. If you set an item's behavior explicitly, making it ignore the parent setting, you will see a full-sized icon. Figure 3-16 shows how this looks—Visual Studio .NET's default configuration has two Win32 exceptions that override their category's default, breaking into the debugger regardless of whether the exceptions are handled by the application. These are the Ctrl-C and Ctrl-Break exceptions.

 The Ctrl-C and Ctrl-Break error settings mean that if a program is running with the debugger attached, you can always halt the program and examine it by pressing one of these key combinations. (You must do so when the target program itself has the focus.)

Note that using Ctrl-C to enter the debugger works only for console applications. In Windows applications, Ctrl-C does not have the same meaning and just copies data to the clipboard, so normally only the Ctrl-Break key combination will work.

If Visual Studio .NET has the focus, you can always suspend the program with Debug → Break All (Ctrl-Alt-Break).

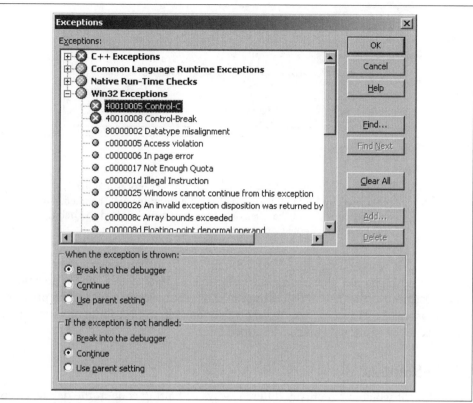

Figure 3-16. Overriding parent behavior

The Exceptions window does not show every possible exception, it simply lists some of the more common ones. If an unlisted exception occurs, it will simply use the category defaults. If this is not what you require, you can use the Add... button to add an entry for the particular exception you wish to configure. Make sure that you select the appropriate category in the tree view before clicking Add.... (For example, don't try to add settings for a .NET exception when the Win32 Exceptions item is selected.)

Unless you are debugging your error-handling code, you will not normally need to change the default settings—they will cause Visual Studio .NET to suspend your code only when there is an unhandled error. This is usually the most helpful behavior. When an unhandled error does occur, you will see the dialog shown in Figure 3-17. This tells you about the error and gives you the option of halting the code in the debugger or continuing with execution (the Break and Continue buttons, respectively).

If you select Continue, the application's normal unhandled error management code will run. This will allow execution to continue instead of halting in the debugger. This can be useful if you have written your own application-level unhandled exception handler and wish to debug it.

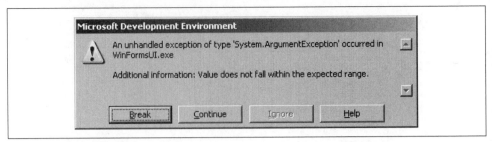

Figure 3-17. An unhandled exception

 The presence of an application-level default exception handler is not considered by VS.NET to mean that all exceptions are "handled." It will run your default handler only after you have allowed the debugger to continue in the face of an unhandled error.

Be aware that when configuring Visual Studio .NET to halt when an error occurs, you have no guarantee that there will be source code available for the location at which execution halts. If VS.NET cannot find the source code, you will be presented with disassembly. However, you will normally be able to find some of your code in the Stack Trace window, which is described later.

Single-Stepping

Regardless of which of the many different ways of halting code in the debugger you choose, you will end up with Visual Studio .NET showing you where the program has been stopped. It indicates the exact line with a yellow arrow in the gray margin at the left of the source code window, and it also highlights the source code in yellow, as Figure 3-18 shows. (The arrow will be drawn over the red circle if the line at which the code stopped has a breakpoint set.)

Figure 3-18. The current line in the debugger

When execution is suspended like this, there are various things you can do. You can examine the value of any program data that is in scope, as described later. You can terminate the program with Debug → Stop Debugging (Shift-F5). You can resume execution with Debug → Continue (F5). Or you may decide that you want to follow the program's execution through in detail, one line at a time, by single-stepping.

The single-stepping shortcut keys are probably the ones that you will use the most, so although you can use Debug → Step Over or Debug → Step Into or their toolbar equivalents, in practice you will normally use their keyboard shortcuts, F10 and F11. Both Step Over (F10) and Step Into (F11) execute a single line of code; the only difference is that, if the line contains a function call, F11 will let you step into the code of the called function, whereas F10 will simply call the function and stop on the following line. (In .NET applications, properties are implemented as functions, so F11 will also step into property accessors.)

If you are currently viewing source code, Step Into (F11) will work only if source code is available for the method you are stepping into. (If no source code is available, it simply steps over the current line.) However, if you change to assembly language debugging, you can step into almost any CALL instruction. You can switch to a disassembly view with Debug → Windows → Disassembly, or Ctrl-Alt-D. (Certain calls into the .NET runtime cannot be stepped into in a .NET debugging session. A native debugging session can step into any CALL instruction.)

You can see assembly language when debugging by selecting Go to Disassembly from the context menu. Alternatively, you can use Debug → Windows → Disassembly (Ctrl-Alt-D). There is currently no way of seeing the Intermediate Language (IL) for a method in the debugger.

In versions of Visual Studio prior to .NET, Step Into suffered from ambiguity in the face of multiple method calls. Consider the following code:

```
printf("Name: %s %s", GetTitle( ), GetName( ));
```

This one line involves three functions: printf, GetTitle, and GetName. Pressing F11 will step into whichever executes first. (The C++ spec doesn't actually dictate the precise order in which the calls will occur in this particular example, beyond requiring printf to be called last. With Microsoft's C++ compiler, it turns out to call GetName first.) When that returns, you can press F11 again to call the second and so on. If you care about only one of the methods, it can be tedious to step through the rest. And although you can always drop down into disassembly mode and locate the call you want, that is hardly an elegant solution.

Fortunately, Visual Studio .NET provides a better solution for unmanaged (non-.NET) Win32 C++ applications. (Other languages don't get this feature, sadly.) If execution is halted at a line with multiple method calls, the context menu will have a Step Into Specific menu item. As Figure 3-19 shows, this item has a submenu with each of the functions shown. If you select an item from this list, the debugger will step into that one.

If the method you select happens not to be the one that will execute first, the others will not be skipped. They will simply be executed silently, just as function calls stepped over with F10 are.

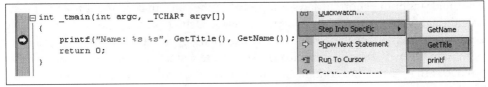

Figure 3-19. Stepping into a specific function

Single-Stepping and IL

Although VS.NET provides no support for examining IL at debug time, it is possible to work around this limitation if you are sufficiently determined. The IL Assembler (*ILASM.EXE*) is able to generate debug information. So if you write all your software in IL, then source-level debugging will consist of single-stepping through IL.

Of course, switching to IL is a high price to pay. However, if you want to carry on writing your code in C# or VB.NET but still see IL in the debugger, there is a way: compile your component as usual and then run it through ILDASM, the IL Disassembler, passing the /out=<filename> switch. This will generate an IL source file. You can then compile this using ILASM, passing in the /debug+ switch in order to generate IL debugging information. You will now be able to single-step through the IL.

There are two problems with this technique. The first is that you have to do this all by hand—VS.NET does not automate this for you. The second problem is that you will no longer be able to single-step through the original source code—VS.NET will consider the IL generated by ILDASM to be the source code! You can mitigate this second problem by passing the /source switch to ILDASM, which will cause it to annotate the IL with the original source code, providing you with a mixed IL/source view, which is a lot better than raw IL. (This works only if the original component was built with debugging information of course.)

Unfortunately, C# and Visual Basic .NET are not blessed with this feature. However, the debugger does provide a feature that can mitigate this shortcoming. Any method that has been marked with the System.Diagnostics.DebuggerStepThrough attribute will not be stepped into when F11 is pressed—it will be executed without single-stepping. This attribute is particularly appropriate for simple property accessors. The accessor in Example 3-2 is so straightforward that it is unlikely to be informative to step into it, so the attribute will make it effectively invisible to Step Into (F11). (The code can still be stepped through if it turns out to be necessary by setting a breakpoint inside the accessor, so there is no harm in using this attribute on such methods.)

Example 3-2. Disabling Step Into for trivial methods

```
private int _index;
private int CurrentIndex
{
```

Example 3-2. Disabling Step Into for trivial methods (continued)

```
[System.Diagnostics.DebuggerStepThrough]
get { return _index; }
}
```

Stepping through multiple lines

Sometimes, you will need to single-step through some code that has regions that are tedious to work through one line at a time. A common example is code with a long, uninteresting loop. It is relatively straightforward to avoid having to single-step through such a section by placing a breakpoint at the end and letting the code run. But there is a slightly quicker way. You can simply move the cursor past the dull section, to the first line at which you would like to resume single-stepping, and press Ctrl-F10. (Alternatively, you can select Run to Cursor from the context menu, which has the same effect; for some reason this option is not available from the main menu.)

There is another common situation in which you will wish to step through several lines in one go. Sometimes when you step into (F11) a method, it will become apparent that the method is not interesting enough to warrant stepping through all of it. You could use Run to Cursor (Ctrl-F10) to move back to the parent method, but it is easier to use Debug → Step Out (Shift-F11). This will allow the code to run until it returns from the current subroutine, and it will then resume single-stepping.

Changing the current point of execution

Occasionally you will want to disrupt the natural flow of execution. You can manually adjust the current execution location of the code by using the context menu's Set Next Statement item. You can only move within the currently executing method, but you can move both forward and backward. (So you can either skip code or rerun code.)

Adjusting the execution location can be powerful technique. It can allow you to go back and watch a piece of code's execution a second time in case you missed some aspect of its behavior. Used in conjunction with the ability to modify the program's variables (see "Displaying Variables and Expressions," later in this chapter) it can also provide a way of experimenting with the code's behavior in situ. However, you should avoid using this feature if possible, because it may have unintended consequences. Compilers do not generate code that is guaranteed to work when you leap from one location to another, so anomalous behavior may occur. Variables may not be initialized correctly, and you may even see more insidious problems like stack corruption. So you should always prefer to restart a program and recompile it if necessary. However, if you are tracking down a problem that is very hard to reproduce, this feature can be extremely useful, because it allows you a degree of latitude for experimentation on the occasions when the behavior you are looking for does manifest itself.

Edit and continue

Edit and continue is a feature that allows code to be edited during a debugging session. The only language that supports this feature in the first release of Visual Studio .NET is C++. This is a little surprising because Visual Basic was the first language to get edit and continue. Unfortunately, certain features of the .NET runtime make it extremely hard to implement edit and continue, so now that Visual Basic is a .NET language, only classic unmanaged Win32 C++ applications get this feature. However, we hope for its return in a future version of Visual Basic .NET.

Edit and continue can be a great time-saver, because it enables you to fix errors without having to stop your debug session, rebuild, and restart. This can be particularly helpful in scenarios in which a bug is tricky to reproduce. If you have spent half a day getting to the point to see the program fail, it can be very useful to try out a fix in situ without having to rebuild and then start again from scratch.

Edit and continue can also sometimes be useful for experimenting with a program's behavior. In combination with the ability to change the next line to be executed and to modify program variables, the ability to change the code makes it very easy to try out several snippets of code in quick succession to see how they behave.

Observing State

The ability to watch the progress of a program's execution line by line is important, but debugging would be much harder if we were not also able to examine the program's state. Visual Studio .NET therefore provides us with a range of tools for examining a process's memory. We can access global variables, the stack (which contains local variables and parameters of the currently executing method and its callers), and raw memory.

Displaying Variables and Expressions

Several windows can be used to display variables and expressions while single-stepping through code in the debugger. They all work in more or less the same way, displaying the name, value, and type of a number of expressions. They are all dockable tool windows. They all keep their value displays up-to-date as you single-step through the code, highlighting any changed values in red. The only difference between these various windows is the exact selection of expressions displayed.

Watch windows

A watch window is a grid into which you can type arbitrary expressions. These will be evaluated whenever code is halted in the debugger and updated as you single-step. All expressions are evaluated with respect to the scope of the current line of code.

Figure 3-20 shows a watch window with two expressions. (New expressions are added by typing into the Name column in the blank line at the bottom of the grid.) The first expression, this, illustrates that the watch window allows objects to be expanded so that the individual fields can be shown. The second expression, ((Button) sender).Text, illustrates that we are not restricted to simple variable names—this is a snippet of C# that performs a cast on a variable and then retrieves a property.

Name	Value	Type
Watch 1		
⊟ this	{WinFormsUI.Form1}	WinFormsUI.Form1
└ ⊞ System.Windows.Forms.Form	{WinFormsUI.Form1}	System.Windows.Forms.Form
└ ⊟ button1	{Text="button1"}	System.Windows.Forms.Button
└ ⊞ System.Windows.Forms.ButtonBase	{System.Windows.Forms.Button}	System.Windows.Forms.ButtonBase
└ ⊞ CreateParams	{System.Windows.Forms.CreateParams}	System.Windows.Forms.CreateParams
└ DialogResult	None	System.Windows.Forms.DialogResult
└ dialogResult	None	System.Windows.Forms.DialogResult
└ components	<undefined value>	System.ComponentModel.Container
((Button)sender).Text	"button1"	string

Figure 3-20. A watch window

Remember that in .NET, properties are really functions, so the implication is that expressions in watch windows are able to cause code to be executed. This is indeed the case, and you can even include method calls inside the expressions that you want to be evaluated. You should exercise caution when doing this—in particular, you don't want the presence of your watch window expression to have side effects that modify the program's operation.

If the ability to execute code as a side effect of evaluating a watch expression makes you nervous, you can disable this facility. Open the Options dialog with Tools → Options..., and select the Debugging folder. If you uncheck the "Allow property evaluation in variable windows" option, this will prevent Visual Studio .NET from calling functions in watch windows. It disallows all function calls, not just those required to evaluate properties, despite what the text seems to imply.

The watch window in Figure 3-20 is labeled Watch 1. You can have up to four watch windows open. These can be opened from the Debug → Windows → Watch menu. Expressions will stay in the windows until you delete them; they persist across debug sessions. If you write an expression that makes sense in only a particular scope, Visual Studio .NET will display an error message in that line of the watch window, but this is easily ignored. It doesn't do anything disruptive like opening an error dialog, so it is common practice to leave useful but context-specific expressions in place and to ignore the errors when debugging in a different context.

Watch windows are not read-only—you can change the values of watched expressions. (The expressions must be writable, of course; you can't meaningfully change the value of an expression that calls a method.) This allows you to modify the values of parameters and local variables, which may be useful for experimenting with the behavior of the code you are debugging. This can be especially useful for checking the behavior of error-handling code when it is difficult to generate the error conditions by normal program execution. (Of course, this is no substitute for good unit testing, but it is a useful extra tool to have available.)

Watch Window Format Specifiers

Watch windows allow you to modify the way in which data is presented. By default, they will show values formatted according to their type—integers will be displayed numerically, strings will be shown as text, and so on. However, Visual Studio .NET supports a variety of format specifiers that allow certain types to be displayed in different ways.

Format specifiers are placed after the expression itself, following a comma. For example, you can ask for a variable foo to be displayed in hexadecimal by typing foo,x into the watch window. The standard numeric specifiers are:

Signed decimal (d or i)
Unsigned decimal (u)
Octal and hexadecimal (o and x)
Standard, scientific, and automatic (shortest) floating point (f, e, and g)

You can also ask Visual Studio .NET to interpret integers as being of one of the following types, in which case the value will be displayed as the appropriate text constant:

HRESULT or Win32 error code (hr)
This will look up both the constant, such as E_OUTOFMEMORY, and a textual description of the error if one is available. Note that if a variable's type is HRESULT, the debugger will normally use this format style automatically, so you need to specify only hr when the debugger does not know the value's type (e.g., when examining a CPU register).

Windows Class flag (wc)
This will look up Windows Class constants such as WC_DEFAULTCHAR.

Windows Message (wm)
This will look up the name of a Windows message such as WM_ACTIVATE.

There are also format specifiers for strings:

Single character (c)
String (s)
Unicode string (su)

Autos, Locals, and This

Watch windows require you to type in the expressions that you want to evaluate. The Autos, Locals, and This windows are essentially watch windows that provide a useful sets of expressions without the need for you to type anything.

The This window (Debug → Windows → This) is fairly self-explanatory. (At least it is for C++ and C# developers; for Visual Basic .NET programmers, the Me window might have been a better name.) It is simply a watch window with a single fixed expression, the this (or Me) reference. The Locals window is also straightforward. It is a watch window that shows all local variables and parameters currently in scope.

Although the This and Locals windows are useful, they can often provide information overload. Complex code may have so many locals and object members that you will continually be scrolling these windows to find the values you care about for the current line of code. The Autos window attempts to alleviate this.

The Autos window guesses which expressions in the current line of code would be useful for you to see. It seems to use a heuristic that includes any variables that are used on this line or its immediate neighbors and any variables explicitly modified by the last line that executed. (Implicit side effects are not shown, since these could be arbitrarily extensive if the previous line made any function calls.)

Figure 3-21 shows a typical selection of variables from the Autos window. Both the count and total variables were modified on the previous line, so it has shown these. (It has colored them red, to draw attention to the fact that they have just changed.) It also shows the expressions that will be used on the line about to be executed.

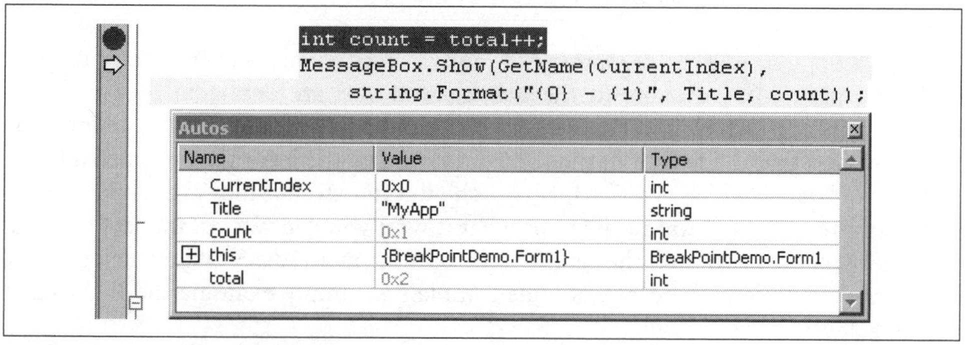

Figure 3-21. The Autos window

The Autos window is extremely useful. It shows all of the expressions you need to see most of the time. This, in conjunction with the fact that you can evaluate any expression visible in a source code window merely by hovering the mouse over it, means that you will rarely need anything else. (Sometimes the Autos heuristic doesn't guess at all the things you need, in which case watch windows are very useful, but most of the time you will need only Autos.)

Registers

The ability to evaluate expressions while debugging is very powerful. Unfortunately, in some situations expressions cannot be used—the debugger requires a certain amount of symbolic information* in order to perform expression evaluation. Sometimes you will find yourself in a situation with no such information available, either because you needed to attach a debugger to a release build or because an error occurred in a third-party or OS component for which source code and symbols are simply unavailable.

This makes life much harder, but it is still possible to debug code in these circumstances. You must drop back to the old-fashioned techniques of assembly-level debugging, but that is better than nothing. To make sense of single-stepping through assembly language, you will need to examine the contents of the CPU's registers. Visual Studio .NET has a window for precisely this purpose, the Registers window. It can be displayed with Debug → Windows → Registers (Ctrl-Alt-G). It simply displays the current values of all of the CPU's registers, as Figure 3-22 shows. Old-time developers will appreciate the retro feel of this window (although probably not as much as they will appreciate not having to use it most of the time).

Figure 3-22. The Registers window

There is a popular reason for wanting to look at register values even when full symbolic information is available to the debugger. If you are debugging some classic unmanaged (non-.NET) Win32 code that has less than thorough error handling, you will often find that the author of the code did not store the return code of an API that you suspect may have failed. The fact that she did not store it in a variable does not, however, prevent you from finding out what it was: you can rely on the fact that the EAX register is used to hold the return value of most methods. So if you suspect that an unchecked error is the cause of your complaints, simply examine the EAX register immediately after the call.

In fact, you don't need to use the Registers window at all to do this. If you are running in native mode (i.e., not .NET), you can simply type EAX into a watch window.

---

* *Symbolic* information is data about named items such as functions, variables, and parameters. Compilers usually discard such information in release builds—executable code deals with raw data and has no need for the symbolic names used to represent the data in source code.

Better than that, you can type EAX,hr. This informs the watch window that the value should be interpreted as an error code. Visual Studio .NET will then look up the error number to see if it is either a well-known COM HRESULT, or a standard system error code, and will display some explanatory text for the error. Another useful trick is that you can type @hr, hr, which will display the value returned by the GetLastError API, along with a text explanation when available. These tricks are not available when debugging .NET applications, but since .NET uses exceptions for most error handling, these kinds of problems tend not to arise so often.

The Call Stack

A program's state consists of more than just the location of the next line to be executed and the values of local and global variables. How it got to its current position is also important. Very often when debugging some code, the most interesting questions are not of the form "what is happening here?" but more along the lines of "how did we get to this state in the first place?" Unfortunately, Visual Studio .NET cannot provide you with a complete history of every step of your program's execution, but it can tell you which method called the current method and which called that and so on all the way back up to the start of the thread. It can even take you to the source code location of every call and show the local variables in scope for each call in the chain.

This information is visible in the Call Stack window. This can be displayed with Debug → Windows → Call Stack (Ctrl-Alt-C). Figure 3-23 shows an example. You can examine the code for any entry on the call stack by double-clicking on it. Visual Studio .NET will take you to the next line that will execute when the code returns to the function in question (i.e., it will highlight the line *after* the call currently in progress). The lines shown in gray are those for which Visual Studio .NET does not have source code information—if you attempt to show the source code by double-clicking on these, you will instead be shown disassembly for that location. The example here is fairly typical for a Windows Forms application—most of the code is inside the Windows Forms Framework, with the application's main method visible at one end and an event handler at the other.

Native Win32 applications don't always display such a complete call stack when symbols are not available. .NET programs run in a managed environment that knows about which methods are called and what types are in use. In Win32, this is not guaranteed, so be prepared for the call stack to be absent, uninformative, or even misleading when it delves into areas outside of your own code—optimized code often doesn't provide all of the information the debugger needs, so Visual Studio .NET is not always able to interpret the entire call stack correctly. (Although be aware that you can download debugging symbols for most Windows system DLLs from Microsoft's web site, which can considerably improve the readability of native call stacks.)

```
Call Stack                                                                    X
  Name                                                                    Langi ▲
➡ BreakPointDemo.exe!BreakPointDemo.Form1.button1_Click(System.Object sender = {Text="button1"}, Sy C#
  system.windows.forms.dll!System.Windows.Forms.Control.OnClick(System.EventArgs e = {System.EventA
  system.windows.forms.dll!System.Windows.Forms.Button.OnClick(System.EventArgs e = {System.EventAr
  system.windows.forms.dll!System.Windows.Forms.Button.OnMouseUp(System.Windows.Forms.MouseEver
  system.windows.forms.dll!System.Windows.Forms.Control.WmMouseUp(System.Windows.Forms.Message
  system.windows.forms.dll!System.Windows.Forms.Control.WndProc(System.Windows.Forms.Message m =
  system.windows.forms.dll!System.Windows.Forms.ButtonBase.WndProc(System.Windows.Forms.Message
  system.windows.forms.dll!System.Windows.Forms.Button.WndProc(System.Windows.Forms.Message m =
  system.windows.forms.dll!ControlNativeWindow.OnMessage(System.Windows.Forms.Message m = {Syste
  system.windows.forms.dll!ControlNativeWindow.WndProc(System.Windows.Forms.Message m = {System.\
  system.windows.forms.dll!System.Windows.Forms.NativeWindow.DebuggableCallback(int hWnd = 0xb507l
  system.windows.forms.dll!System.Windows.Forms.Application.ComponentManager.System.Windows.Form:
  system.windows.forms.dll!ThreadContext.RunMessageLoopInner(int reason = 0xffffffff, System.Windows
  system.windows.forms.dll!ThreadContext.RunMessageLoop(int reason = 0xffffffff, System.Windows.Form
  system.windows.forms.dll!System.Windows.Forms.Application.Run(System.Windows.Forms.Form mainForn
  BreakPointDemo.exe!BreakPointDemo.Form1.Main() Line 118                                    C# ▼
```

Figure 3-23. The Call Stack window

 You can obtain debugging symbols in various ways. They are shipped with the MSDN subscription, but the problem with these is that they will go out-of-date as you apply hot fixes and service packs. Information on how to keep your symbols in sync with your OS updates is available at *http://www.microsoft.com/ddk/debugging/symbols.asp*.

You can also configure VS.NET to automatically download symbols from Microsoft's public symbol server—see the "Symbol Servers" section later in this chapter.

As well as double-clicking on entries in the call stack to go to the listed functions, you can select a line in the call stack and press F9 to set a breakpoint. This will create a breakpoint that is positioned so that it gets hit when execution returns to the selected function.

Memory Windows

Just as you will not always have access to source for the code you wish to debug, you may not always have the symbolic information you require to view state using expressions. And just as Visual Studio .NET can drop back to disassembly when the source code is not present, it can also provide you with access to raw memory when you cannot use expressions.

Memory windows simply provide a hexadecimal dump of the memory at the address of your choice. As with watch windows, you can have up to four memory windows open, which can be displayed using Debug → Windows → Memory.

Figure 3-24 shows a memory window. By default, Visual Studio .NET will display as many bytes as will fit across the window. However, it is often useful to fix the column size to something more regular since this can make it easier to see patterns in the data. So the drop-down list labeled Columns can be used to set an explicit width. It provides a list of various powers of two (2, 4, 8, 16, etc.), which are popular choices, but you can type in any value you like.

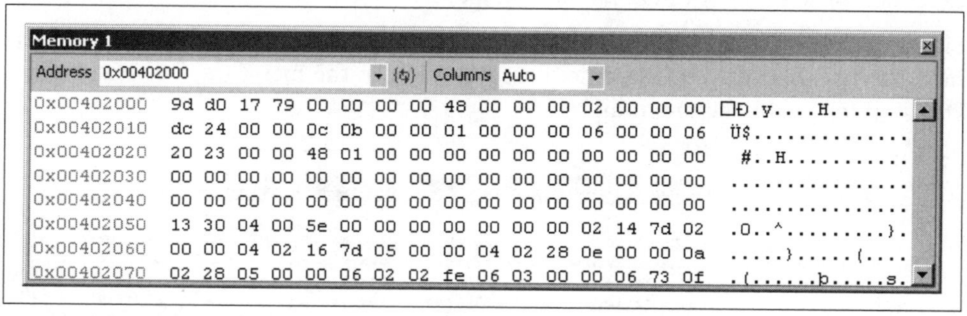

```
Memory 1                                                                    ×
Address  0x00402000                        ▼ {ɸ}  Columns  Auto        ▼
0x00402000    9d d0 17 79 00 00 00 00 48 00 00 00 02 00 00 00   ☐Đ.y....H.......  ▲
0x00402010    dc 24 00 00 0c 0b 00 00 01 00 00 00 06 00 00 06   Ü$..............
0x00402020    20 23 00 00 48 01 00 00 00 00 00 00 00 00 00 00    #..H...........
0x00402030    00 00 00 00 00 00 00 00 00 00 00 00 00 00 00 00   ................
0x00402040    00 00 00 00 00 00 00 00 00 00 00 00 00 00 00 00   ...............
0x00402050    13 30 04 00 5e 00 00 00 00 00 00 00 02 14 7d 02   .0..^.........}.
0x00402060    00 00 04 02 16 7d 05 00 00 04 02 28 0e 00 00 0a   .....}.....(....
0x00402070    02 28 05 00 00 06 02 02 fe 06 03 00 00 06 73 0f   .(......b.....s. ▼
```

Figure 3-24. A memory window

By default, memory will be shown in 1-byte units. However, it is often useful to group the display into larger units. The window's context menu allows you to group numbers into 2-byte or 4-byte integers. (Since Intel's processors are little-endian, this is useful, because it saves you from reversing the order of the bytes in your head.) It also allows you to make the window interpret the data as 32-bit or 64-bit floating point numbers.

Next to the Address field is a tool button with two small arrows. This button is relevant only if you type an expression (instead of a constant) into the Address field. If the button is not pressed (the default), any expression you type into the Address field will be evaluated just once when you type it. (In fact, the expression will be replaced with its value when you press Return.) If the button is clicked, however, the expression you typed in will remain in the Address field and will be reevaluated each time the debugger halts at a breakpoint or each time you step over a line of code. So if you type in the name of a pointer variable, the window will always display whatever memory the pointer points to, even if the pointer changes.

The Output Window

The various windows Visual Studio .NET supplies for observing your program's state are very useful, but they all suffer from two limitations. First, you can use them only when the program is suspended in the debugger—their contents all vanish when the program is running freely. Second, they cannot show you any historical information—they can show you only the current status.

The Output window does not suffer from either of these restrictions. It is visible during normal execution and can even be viewed after the program has terminated. And once items have been shown in the Output window, they remain there until you clear the window explicitly (or start a new debugging session). The price of this is that the Output window is a little less sophisticated than the other windows we have seen so far—it can show only text. But its ability to function without needing to halt execution makes it an invaluable debugging tool.

Figure 3-25 shows the Output window. Visual Studio .NET itself sends certain messages to this window. For example, here you can see the messages it displays when DLLs are loaded by the program.

```
Output                                                                    ☒
Debug                                                                     ▼
  'BreakPointDemo': Loaded 'C:\try\clr\WinForms\BreakPointDemo\bin\Debug\BreakPointDemo.exe', ▲
  'BreakPointDemo.exe': Loaded 'c:\windows\assembly\gac\system.windows.forms\1.0.5000.0__b77a5c
  'BreakPointDemo.exe': Loaded 'c:\windows\assembly\gac\system\1.0.5000.0__b77a5c561934e089\sys
  'BreakPointDemo.exe': Loaded 'c:\windows\assembly\gac\system.drawing\1.0.5000.0__b03f5f7f11d5
  'BreakPointDemo.exe': Loaded 'c:\windows\assembly\gac\system.xml\1.0.5000.0__b77a5c561934e089
  Button1 clicked - count: 0                                              ▼
◄                                                                      ► 
```

Figure 3-25. The Output window

The final line shown in Figure 3-25 is a custom message generated by the author of the program by including the following code at some appropriate point in the code:

```
Debug.WriteLine(string.Format("Button1 clicked - count: {0}", count));
```

This C# code uses the Debug class in the System.Diagnostics namespace. Calls to this API will be compiled into only debug builds. The Trace class allows you to generate output in release builds. So this code will generate debug output in all builds:

```
Trace.WriteLine(string.Format("Button1 clicked - count: {0}", count));
```

 The Trace class in the System.Diagnostics namespace is unrelated to the ASP.NET tracing facilities.

Note that, unlike the Console.WriteLine method, Debug.WriteLine does not support string formatting with variable length argument lists. If you need to place dynamic information in your output, you must use the String class's Format method as shown here.

Classic Win32 applications can send messages to this window too, using the OutputDebugString API. You would normally use this API indirectly through macros such as MFC's TRACE or ATL's ATLTRACE. As with the .NET Debug class, these macros generate output only in debug builds.

The Modules Window

The Modules window allows you to see which modules (DLLs and EXEs) have been loaded in the current debug session. It also allows you to see which of them Visual Studio .NET has found debug symbols for and to control where it looks for symbol files.

You can display the Modules window with Debug → Window → Modules (Ctrl-Alt-U). As Figure 3-26 shows, the window displays a considerable amount of information for each loaded module. It shows the filename, the address at which it has been loaded, the file path, the order in which the modules were loaded in this particular process, the version and timestamp of each module, and the process in which the module is loaded (this is used in multiprocess debugging). It also shows whether debug symbols have been loaded for the DLL.

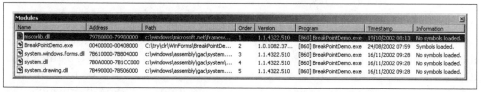

Figure 3-26. The Modules window

If you are debugging code from just one project, you will probably not need to use the Modules window much, but if your program uses multiple components from many projects, this window is extremely useful. It enables you to find out exactly which components got loaded. (For complex build environments, it is not always trivial to work out exactly where a component will be loaded from, so the ability to find out exactly which one is running is important.)

A common problem that occurs in debugging large componentized applications is that Visual Studio .NET might not be able to locate the debug information it requires for all components automatically. Fortunately, the Modules window enables you to tell Visual Studio .NET where the symbols are—if you right-click on a module and select Reload Symbols..., you will be shown a dialog that lets you choose the *.pdb* file that contains the symbols. You can even do this with modules for which Visual Studio .NET has already loaded symbols—this is useful because under certain circumstances, the wrong symbols may get loaded.

Debugging and Project Settings

The Visual Studio .NET debugger relies on having detailed information about your program. To be able to provide source-level debugging, it needs to know how compiled code relates to source code. In order to be able to evaluate expressions, it needs to know about the variables and types in use in your program. And for .NET programs, it needs the CLR's cooperation to be able to display the values of local variables and parameters.

The information required for debugging does not come for free. The symbols and line number information take up space. Making local variables and parameters available to the debugger places extra constraints on the compiler, reducing performance. Furthermore, this information makes it much easier to reverse engineer code. For all of these reasons, you will probably not want to ship debug versions of your programs.

 With .NET, even release builds are relatively easy to reverse-engineer, because all symbol names apart from local variables are left in release builds. One way to mitigate this is to use an obfuscation tool. (VS.NET 2003 ships with such a tool.) Of course, the only thing that can stop the truly determined from reverse-engineering your applications is to not give them the applications in the first place.

When you create a new project, Visual Studio .NET will create at least two different configurations for that project, enabling you to build debug and release versions of the code. Release builds usually have no symbols beyond those required by the target technology. (For native Win32 applications, the only symbols will be those needed for DLL import and export tables. For .NET applications, full type information, but not enough information to perform source-level debugging, will be present.) Release builds are also normally compiled with full optimizations enabled. (And in the case of .NET applications, where most of the compilation process is done by the CLR, the binary will be marked as nondebug, enabling the CLR to perform full optimizations.) Optimizations are disabled in debug builds because they tend to interfere with the debugger's ability to display the program's state.

Debug builds will have the DEBUG symbol defined. Some programs use this to make sure that certain code appears only in debug build. For example, the debug trace output mentioned earlier uses this. Note that in .NET projects a TRACE symbol will also be defined, both in debug and release builds—this controls the use of the Trace class. So, you could add another build configuration that omits all trace output, whether it came from the Debug or the Trace class, by defining neither the DEBUG nor the TRACE symbol.

Figure 3-27 and Figure 3-28 show the parts of the project property pages where optimization and trace settings are controlled. (You can find these by right-clicking on the project in the Solution Explorer and selecting Properties.)

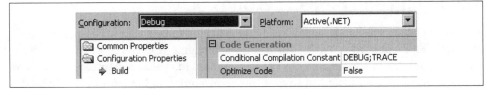

Figure 3-27. Debug project settings

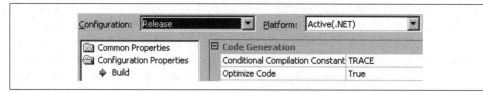

Figure 3-28. Release project settings

Release-Only Bugs

Some bugs occur only in release mode. This is usually because enabling full compiler optimizations can allow bugs, which would remain silent in debug mode, to manifest. Mostly this is due to problems such as reading uninitialized variables. Unfortunately, such faults can be hard to diagnose because, as soon as you try to debug them, they disappear.

Although the .NET runtime checks for and prevents the main kind of bug that causes different behavior in release modes (use of uninitialized variables), there is a class of behavior change specific to .NET applications. When running debug builds, the CLR ensures that variables live for their whole lexical scope. With release builds, it discards variables as soon as they fall out of use. The reason for disabling this optimization in debug mode is that it could prevent you from reading the values of those variables while debugging.

This extended lifetime can sometimes change program behavior. In particular, it can cause objects to be garbage collected later in debug mode than they would be in release mode. In extreme cases, some objects may never be collected in debug mode.

Fortunately, you can attach a debugger to a release build. However, you must be careful how you do so if you want the results to be useful. By default, you will get nothing but assembly language in the debugger when you do this, but it is possible to get a little more information.

Note that, as Figure 3-27 shows, a Debug project will be set to generate unoptimized code. You can change the Debug project's Optimize Code setting to true and still get most of the debugging symbols created. (The generation of debugging information is controlled by a separate compiler flag further down on the same property page under the Outputs category, as Figure 3-29 shows.)

Generate Debugging Information	True

Figure 3-29. Enabling debug symbol generation

If you build with a project configuration that has both debugging information and optimization enabled, you will still be able to use most of the debugger's normal functionality. Certain variables may not be accessible at runtime, and you may even see strange behavior when single-stepping—the compiler sometimes reorders code execution as part of the optimization process. But if this lets you observe a bug in action that does not manifest when optimizations are disabled, then these inconveniences are worthwhile. (Of course, you may still find that the bug occurs only when the debugger is not attached, in which case you must resort to more old-fashioned techniques.)

 With managed (.NET) code, compiling in debug information always affects the way the JIT compiler works. So, even in a release build, turning on debug information for managed code always disables optimizations. So the trick of generating debuggable optimized code works only for unmanaged code.

Choosing Debugging Modes

When using just-in-time debugging to attach to a process, you were presented with a list of different program types to debug, as shown in Figure 3-2. You will not be shown this list if you simply launch your program from within Visual Studio .NET using Debug → Start (F5). Usually this is not a problem, since it will use a debugging session appropriate to your project type. But what if this default is not correct? Perhaps you have written a .NET application but want to enable native debugging because you are using COM interop.

Fortunately, you have the same flexibility when launching a program from within Visual Studio .NET as you do when attaching to an existing one. It is simply that the program type decision is determined by the project's settings rather than by opening a dialog every time you debug. Figure 3-30 shows the relevant section of the project properties dialog for .NET projects.

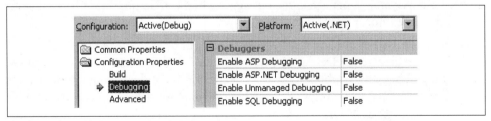

Figure 3-30. Managed project debug settings

The Unmanaged Debugging, SQL Debugging, and ASP Debugging settings are equivalent, respectively, to the Native, T-SQL, and Script settings of the Attach to Process dialog shown in Figure 3-2. The Attach to Process dialog also has a Common Language Runtime option. There is no direct equivalent in Figure 3-30—Visual Studio .NET simply knows that this particular project is for the .NET platform and will always enable CLR debugging. For native Win32 projects, the project settings look a little different, as Figure 3-31 shows.

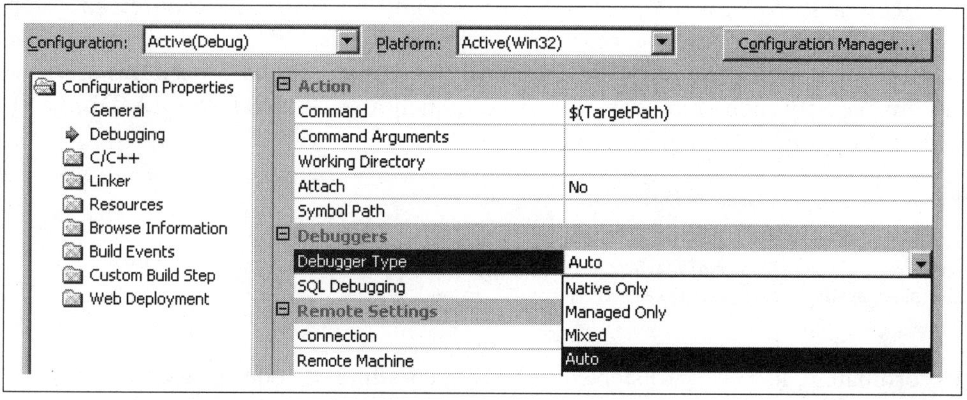

Figure 3-31. Unmanaged project debug settings

For unmanaged projects, you can select whether you want CLR (Managed Only), Native, or both. (Auto will examine the *.exe* file and choose CLR or Native according to its contents.) The SQL Debugging option enables or disables T-SQL debugging. (Remember that native debugging and script debugging are mutually exclusive, so you are not presented with the option of script debugging for a native application.)

Advanced Debugging Techniques

So far we have looked at debugging relatively straightforward solutions. Visual Studio .NET is capable of debugging multiple solutions simultaneously, even when those solutions span multiple threads, processes, languages, technologies, and even multiple machines. While such projects require a little more configuration, it is much easier to debug these scenarios than it was with previous versions of Visual Studio.

Crossing Language and Technology Boundaries

The .NET runtime is often referred to as the CLR—the Common Language Runtime. It is so called because all languages that target the .NET platform share the same runtime environment. One of the benefits of this is unified debugging. If your solutions contain components written in multiple languages, then as long as those components have all been built with debug support enabled, traversing language boundaries works seamlessly. No special configuration is required.

When crossing technology boundaries, however, you will need to make sure that things are set up correctly before you start. So if your system contains a mixture of .NET and native Win32 code, you will need to ensure that your startup project's configuration enables both types of debugging, as described earlier. (Or if you are attaching to an existing process, you must make sure that both the Common Language Runtime and the Native options are checked in the Attach to Process dialog.)

T-SQL is a special case. You can set breakpoints in stored procedures and step through T-SQL code just like other languages. However, T-SQL is different, in that you cannot step directly into it from another language.* Stored procedures are usually invoked through some data access API, such as ADO.NET or OLE DB, using code such as that shown in Example 3-3.

Example 3-3. Calling a stored procedure from C#

```
. . .
cmd.CommandType = CommandType.StoredProcedure;
IDataReader dr = cmd.ExecuteReader( );
. . .
```

Unfortunately, if you try to step into (F11) such a line of code, Visual Studio .NET will ignore you. It is not smart enough to realize that this code is executing a stored procedure on a SQL Server database. To debug the stored procedure, you must therefore set a breakpoint in the T-SQL itself. You can open the stored procedure from the Server Explorer window—just locate the relevant SQL Server database and expand its Stored Procedures node. If you double-click on a stored procedure, Visual Studio .NET will open its source code. (This feature is available only on Enterprise editions of VS.NET.) You can set breakpoints in this code just as with any other code.

Multiple Threads

When Visual Studio .NET suspends a process during debugging, it halts all of the threads. You can look at only one thread's state and call stack at a time, but it is possible to switch to other threads in the process and examine those using the Threads window. You can display the Threads window using Debug → Windows → Threads (Ctrl-Alt-H).

The Threads window, shown in Figure 3-32, shows all of the threads in the target process. It indicates the one currently selected for debugging by highlighting it with a yellow arrow. For each thread, it shows the thread ID, the thread name, the function in which the thread is currently executing, the thread's priority, and whether it is suspended. The function name will often be blank when the code is executing a system call. For example, the worker thread in Figure 3-32 is actually inside the Thread. Sleep method.

---

* We may be able to do this in the future. The upcoming "Yukon" is slated to have much tighter integration of the .NET runtime and SQL Server stored procedures.

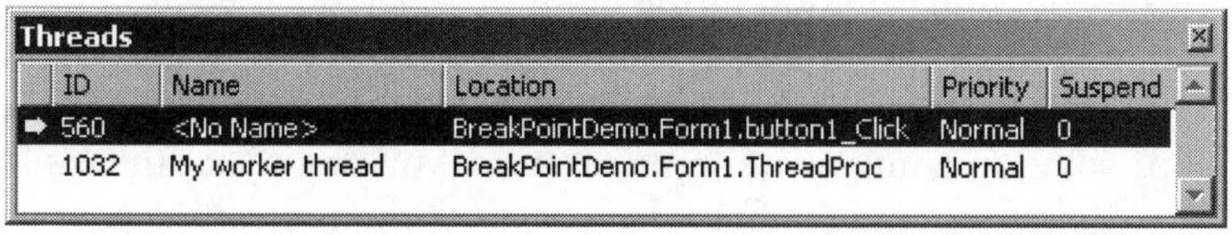

Threads					
ID	Name	Location	Priority	Suspend	
➡ 560	<No Name>	BreakPointDemo.Form1.button1_Click	Normal	0	
1032	My worker thread	BreakPointDemo.Form1.ThreadProc	Normal	0	

Figure 3-32. The Threads window

In .NET applications, you can set a thread's name using the Thread class's Name property. In native Win32 applications, you must use a slightly curious hack—you raise SEH (Structured Exception Handling) exception number 0x406D1388, passing in a pointer to a THREADNAME_INFO structure. The Visual Studio .NET documentation provides sample code for this in the "SetThreadName function" help entry.

Visual Studio .NET allows you to suspend individual threads manually in the debugger. The Threads window's context menu has a Freeze option, which will prevent the selected thread from running when you allow the program's execution to continue. (The context menu for a frozen thread has a corresponding Thaw option, which will allow the thread to continue.)

Freezing threads can occasionally be useful when single-stepping through code. Every time you step through a line of code, all of the other threads in the system will be allowed to run for a short while too. If you have breakpoints set elsewhere in your code, this can be inconvenient—if some thread other than the one that you are single-stepping with hits a breakpoint, Visual Studio .NET will switch to that thread. This can be somewhat disorientating. You can avoid this by temporarily freezing all of the threads other than the one you wish to examine.

Multiple Processes

Visual Studio .NET can attach to any number of processes in a single debugging session. The simplest way to exploit this is to use the Processes window (Debug → Processes...) described earlier (see Figure 3-1). This dialog can be opened even when a debugging session is already in progress, and you can simply add more processes to the list. Also, if you are using a technology that supports cross-process method calls such as COM or .NET Remoting, you will then be able to step into (F11) code across process boundaries.

For some projects (especially those involving remoting), you may need to launch a particular set of processes and then attach to them every time you debug. It can be tedious to use the Processes dialog for this. Fortunately, a Visual Studio .NET solution can be configured to launch several processes and attach the debugger to all of them whenever you use Debug → Start (F5).

If you right-click on your solution in the Solution Explorer (be sure to click on the solution itself, not one of its projects), you will see a Set Startup Projects... item. This displays the Startup project page in the solution's property pages, as Figure 3-33 shows. If your solution contains multiple projects, you can select the Multiple Startup Projects radio button and configure any or all of the projects in your solution to be run when debugging starts. As the drop-down list shows, you can also choose to start a project without attaching the debugger. You can control the start order too—projects will be started in the order in which they appear, and you can change this with the Move Up and Move Down buttons.

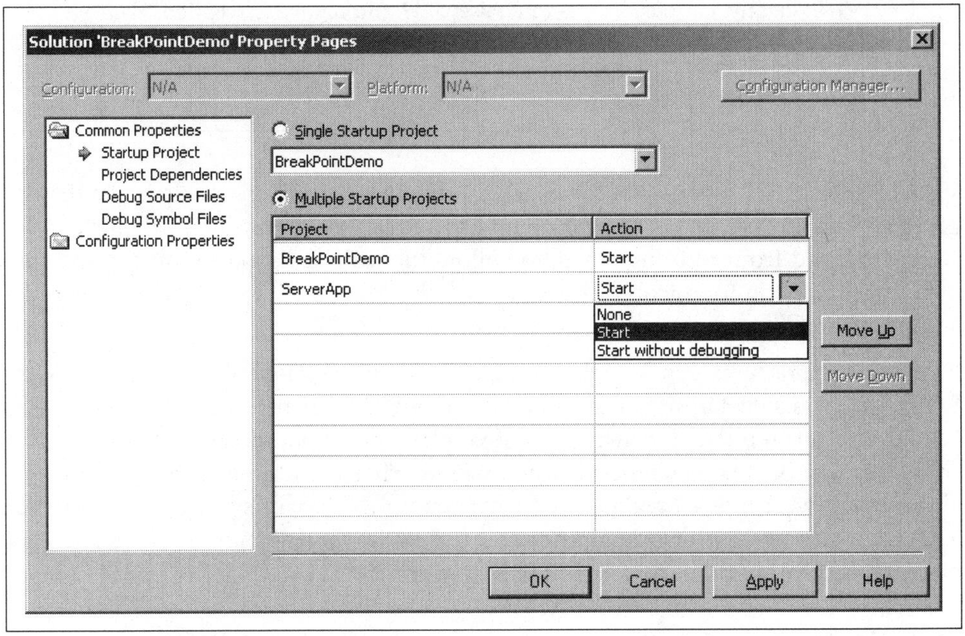

Figure 3-33. The Solution startup projects page

Cross-Machine Debugging

Debugging processes on multiple machines in Visual Studio .NET is almost as easy as debugging multiple processes on a single machine. The only restrictions are that the remote machine must have the appropriate remote debugging support installed, you must have the appropriate DCOM and security settings on the remote machine, and you cannot launch remote processes automatically when you start debugging.

If the target machine has Visual Studio .NET installed, you do not need to install any extra software. But if it does not have Visual Studio .NET installed, you can instead install the Remote Debugging Components. (These components can be installed from the Visual Studio .NET installation disks.) The Remote Debugging Components install just enough functionality to allow code to be debugged remotely.

Remote debugging relies on DCOM, so you may need to adjust the DCOM settings on the target machine before remote debugging will work. You can use the *dcomcnfg* utility to grant developers permission to use DCOM. In Windows XP, you do this by expanding the Component Services node in *dcomcnfg*, locating the computer you wish to configure, and selecting properties—this will display the DCOM properties window for your computer. Under Windows 2000, this window will appear as soon as you run *dcomcnfg*. From this dialog, select the Default COM Security tab and click on the Edit Default... button in the Access Permissions section. Make sure that any developers who require access are listed here. Also, make sure that the SYSTEM account is listed.

Finally, the developers will need to be a member of either the Debugger User group or the local Administrator group on the target machine.

Once the remote machine has the appropriate software installed and the security and DCOM settings are configured correctly, you can attach the VS.NET debugger to processes on that remote machine. Simply type the machine's name into the Name field of the Processes dialog, or select the machine from the "..." button. The dialog will show a list of processes running on the remote machine, and from there on, everything works in much the same way as it does for local debugging.

T-SQL debugging

VS.NET is able to debug SQL Server-stored procedures, but to use this feature, you will need to make sure that your systems are configured appropriately. If you are running SQL Server locally (i.e., on the same machine as you are running VS.NET), you will usually find that it just works out of the box but in distributed scenarios a little more work may be required.

The VS.NET remote debugging components must be installed on the server machine as described earlier. You will also need to make sure that security and DCOM are configured appropriately, just as you would for normal remote debugging. (If you make any changes to the DCOM settings, you must restart SQL Server for the changes to take effect.)

You must also make sure you have the appropriate SQL security configuration. The only requirement here is that the developer is able to call the sp_sdidebug stored procedure. Use SQL Server Enterprise Manager to grant the developer access to this procedure. (The related *mssdi98.dll* component must also be installed in SQL Server's *bin* directory in order for this stored procedure to work.)

Alternative Debugging Protocols

The remote debugging features of Visual Studio .NET use DCOM to communicate with the target machine. Unfortunately, in certain network configurations, it may be awkward or even impossible to use DCOM. Also, DCOM debugging is not supported when the target machine is running Windows 9x, Windows ME, or the Home Edition of Windows XP. VS.NET therefore supports two other protocols, although with some loss of functionality; they are named pipes and TCP/IP. (VS.NET 2002 does not support named pipes.)

Named pipes and TCP/IP are less secure than DCOM. (The documentation is not precise about what this means—it merely says that pipes are less secure than DCOM and TCP/IP is less secure than pipes.) These protocols also support only native debugging—to debug managed code, T-SQL, or script, you must use the default DCOM protocol. So you should resort to named pipes or TCP/IP only if you have no other choice.

To use named pipes or TCP/IP, you must run the Remote Debug Monitor on the target machine. This is installed as part of the remote debugging setup described earlier, but it is not a service; it is a console application called *msvcmon.exe* and must be started manually—it is not left running by default due to the lower security offered by these transports. It can be found under Visual Studio .NET's Tools menu in the Start menu as the Visual C++ Remote Debugger item. (Or you can run the same program from the command line, although unlike Visual C++ 6, Visual Studio .NET does not install the program on the path, so you must find it first. It is usually in the *Common7\Packages\Debugger* subdirectory of the VS.NET installation.)

 By default, *msvcmon.exe* accepts only named pipe connections. You must run it from the command line with the -tcpip option.

Once the Remote Debug Monitor is running on the target, you can select one of the alternate protocols in the debugger. You attach the debugger using the Process dialog (see Figure 3-1) as usual, but you can select either Pipe or TCP/IP from the Transport drop-down list at the top of the dialog. You must then specify the name of the machine to which you wish to connect as usual, and debugging will proceed as normal (except that only native debugging will work).

Symbol Servers

The Windows Platform SDK ships with a set of tools designed to allow debugging symbols to be distributed from a central server. VS.NET is able to make use of these tools when debugging applications. This can be very useful if you are working on a large project. It enables you to ensure that you are always debugging with up-to-date symbols, without having to ship complete copies of all the debug symbols with each distribution of binaries.

There are two parts to the symbol server technology: the symbol server store manager (*symstore.exe*) and a client DLL (*symsrv.dll*). *symstore.exe* is responsible only for maintaining the contents of the store. It does not serve up the files themselves—this is done with either HTTP, HTTPS, or normal Windows file shares. (So symbol stores can live on either web servers or file servers.) VS.NET 2003 ships with *symsrv.dll*, so you will not need to install the debugging tools simply in order to access a symbol store. However, if you want to create or maintain a symbol store, you will need to install the Platform SDK as well as Visual Studio .NET.[*]

Using a symbol store

You can instruct Visual Studio .NET to use a symbol server by modifying your solution's debugging properties. Right-click on the solution in the Solution Explorer and select Properties, then in the Solution Property Pages, select the Debug Symbol Files item under Common Properties. Add a new path to the list on the right. This path should be of following form:

```
symsrv*symsrv.dll*LOCALCACHE*STOREPATH
```

The first part, symsrv*, indicates to VS.NET that this is not a simple file path, but rather an instruction to use a symbol server DLL. The next part tells VS.NET the name of the client DLL to use—*symsrv.dll* in this case. (The architecture is designed to allow anyone to write his own symbol clients and servers. *symsrv.dll* is the client supplied by Microsoft.)

LOCALCACHE should be the path of a local directory, which will be used as a download cache for symbol files. In order to avoid loading symbol files from the symbol server every time the debugger starts, *symsrv.dll* will copy them into this local directory. The contents of this cache can always be reconstructed from the main server, so if you need to free up some disk space, you can delete the contents of this directory whenever you like. (This will, of course, slow things down a little next time you start debugging but will have the benefit of clearing out any files that you have long since stopped using.)

 Symbol stores can store symbol files for many different versions of each binary. So local caches tend to fill up with out-of-date symbols over time. We therefore recommend that you delete the cache from time to time—old symbol files are not deleted automatically.

STOREPATH should be set to the path of the symbol store. This can be a UNC share name or a URL. (Only HTTP and HTTPS URLs are supported.) Consider this example:

```
symsrv*symsrv.dll*c:\websymbols*http://msdl.microsoft.com/download/symbols
```

This instructs VS.NET to download symbols from Microsoft's symbol server. (Windows debug symbols can be downloaded from here.) It tells it to cache the

---

[*] If you are running VS.NET 2002, not even the client component is installed by default, so you must install the debugging tools and then make sure that *symsrv.dll* is available to VS.NET—you can do this by copying it from the debugging tools directory into the *Common7\IDE* directory inside your VS.NET installation.

downloaded symbol files in a local directory called *c:\websymbols*. This example can be rather useful as it means that symbols for your system DLLs will always be kept up-to-date. However, be aware that this can slow down the debugger quite considerably at startup, especially if you have a slow Internet connection.

Visual Studio .NET 2003 supports an abbreviated form of symbol store path:

```
srv*c:\cache*http://msdl.microsoft.com/download/symbols
```

The srv* prefix tells it to use the default client DLL, *symsrv.dll*. The cache and store location are specified in exactly the same way as before.

> VS.NET 2002 would download symbol files only from a symbol store path for unmanaged code. If you are using VS.NET 2002, you can still place debug files for managed (.NET) code in symbol stores, but you must place the store path in the _NT_SYMBOL_PATH environment variable rather than configuring it in the solution properties. VS.NET 2003 does not use this environment variable.

Creating and maintaining a symbol store

You will, of course, need a symbol store from which to download symbols. The earlier example uses Microsoft's public store, but if you want to use this feature on your own projects, you will need to create a symbol store yourself. All you need is a directory that is accessible either as a file share or via HTTP. You will use the *symstore.exe* command-line utility to maintain the contents of the directory.

The first parameter to *symstore.exe* should be add when you are adding files. This can optionally be followed by switches: /r indicates that a directory and its files should be copied recursively. /p specifies that the file will not actually be placed in the store but that the store will merely contain a pointer to the file (i.e., the location of the file). If you specify /p, *symstore.exe* will usually complain if you attempt to add files with a local path instead of a network path—usually you wouldn't want to do that, since symbol stores are meant to be accessed remotely and local paths will not be meaningful, but the /l switch suppresses this error.

> The /l switch can be useful if you want to create a local symbol store on your machine. You may want to do this if you have many projects, all of which use the same set of shared components—it enables you to put the shared components' debug files in just one place. With local symbol stores, you can also omit the LOCALCACHE part of the symbol store path—since the store is local, VS.NET has no need to download copies and can just use the files in the store directly.

Next, follow the mandatory switches. /f *PATH* indicates the file or directory that is to be added. /s *STOREPATH* indicates the path of the symbol store directory itself. /t *PRODUCT* and /v *VERSION* specify the product name and version of the debug information. These should match the corresponding items in the version resource of the binary. (*symstore.exe* has further options, supporting the generation of index files that can later be used to load symbols into the store automatically. For more information on this, and the internal workings of *symstore.exe*, consult the Platform SDK documentation.)

Conclusion

Visual Studio .NET provides an exceptionally powerful debugging environment. It can debug normal executable applications, ASP.NET applications, client-side script, and T-SQL stored procedures. Furthermore, it can manage all of these from within a single debugging session, even when these components are running on different machines. For all of these different technologies, it provides extensive facilities for controlling the flow of execution and monitoring the state of your programs.

Now that we have looked in detail at how to manage, build, and debug solutions in VS.NET, it is time to look in more detail at some specific project types, so in the next chapter we will be examining web projects.

CHAPTER 4
Web Projects

Microsoft wanted its first truly integrated development environment to be usable for all layers of your application; they did a pretty good job at making that happen. Class libraries, Windows applications, database code, web applications, and web services can all be developed and debugged in VS.NET, even though these various components may be distributed across multiple machines. Web applications and web services get a certain amount of special handling—VS.NET can communicate with local or remote web servers on your behalf in order to create and debug the web-based parts of your distributed systems. Also, certain aspects of the development process are different for web projects than for other project types, so this chapter will outline the basic operation of VS.NET when dealing with web projects.

Web Project Templates

When you create a new project, the project template you choose determines whether your project is web-based. A web-based project is one that is accessed or managed via a web protocol, such as HTTP, HTTPS, or FTP. The list of web project templates is listed in Table 4-1.

Table 4-1. Web-based projects

Project template	Managed	Description	Output
ASP.NET Web Application (C#/VB/J#)	Yes	ASP.NET Web Forms Application	Managed DLL and content files
ASP.NET Web Service (C#/VB/J#/MC++)	Yes	ASP.NET Web Service	Managed DLL and content files
ASP.NET Mobile Web Application	Yes	ASP.NET Web Forms Applications for mobile devices	Managed DLL and content files
Empty Web Project (C#/VB/J#)	Yes	An empty project to which to add source and content files	Managed DLL and content files
ATL Server (VC++)	No	ATL-based web application	Unmanaged DLL and content files
ATL Server Web Service (VC++)	No	ATL-based web service	Unmanaged DLL and content files

Although web projects look like normal projects when viewed in the IDE, they behave quite differently behind the scenes. Any content files (web pages, graphics, etc.) must reside on a web server; the same is true for the build output (a managed or unmanaged DLL).

VS.NET has two completely different strategies for ensuring that all of the necessary files are in the right place. One is used by C#, VB.NET, and J# projects, and the other is used by Visual C++ projects. We will talk about each separately, in the "Managed Web Projects" and "Visual C++ Projects" sections later in this chapter. Before we do that, we need to talk about IIS web applications, since both types of projects depend on the separation provided by web applications to function properly.

IIS Virtual Directories and Web Applications

In IIS, every directory is considered to be either a nonvirtual directory or a virtual directory. Nonvirtual directories are stored under the web server's root directory. A virtual directory can be anywhere on the server's filesystem, but the URL that is used to access that content makes it appear to the end user that it is physically below the root directory (hence the term virtual).

For example, suppose that the web server root is in the default location, *c:\inetpub\ wwwroot*. If that directory were to contain a file called *default.htm*, a web browser would use the address *http://server/default.htm* to access that resource. If there were a directory at *c:\inetpub\wwwroot\dir1* containing a file *foo.htm*, then the URL would be *http://server/dir1/foo.htm*. *dir1* would be a nonvirtual directory within the web server's root directory. The structure of nonvirtual directories is presented directly through the structure of the URLs used to access their contents.

IIS does not force us to have such a strict mapping between URLs and the structure of our filesystem. Virtual directories allow us more flexibility. For example, we could use the IIS administration tool (located in the Administrative Tools section of the Control Panel) to map the *e:\website* directory as a virtual directory called *dir2*. (A virtual directory can have a different name than the actual directory on which it is based.) If *e:\website* contains a *page.htm* file, a web browser could access this with the URL *http://server/dir2/page.htm*. Because we set up a virtual directory called *dir2*, IIS will map the request for */dir2/page.htm* to the *e:\website\page.htm*.

A web application is a directory tree with its own application settings. These application settings include security configuration, error handling, and file extension mappings. By default, a directory (virtual or not) will belong to its parent directory's application. However, any directory can be set as having its own application, at which point it gets its own settings. (Of course, these settings will propagate to any subdirectories that do not have their own application.)

You make a directory the root of a web application using the IIS administration utility. Open the directory's Properties page by right-clicking on the directory in the tree and selecting Properties from the context menu. If the directory is not a web application directory (i.e., if it picks up its application settings from its parent), you will be able to turn it into a web application by clicking on the Create button in the Application Settings section of the Directory tab, which is shown in Figure 4-1. (If the directory is already a web application, in place of a Create button, you will see a Remove button, enabling you to remove the web application—this will cause the directory to revert to using its parent's settings.)

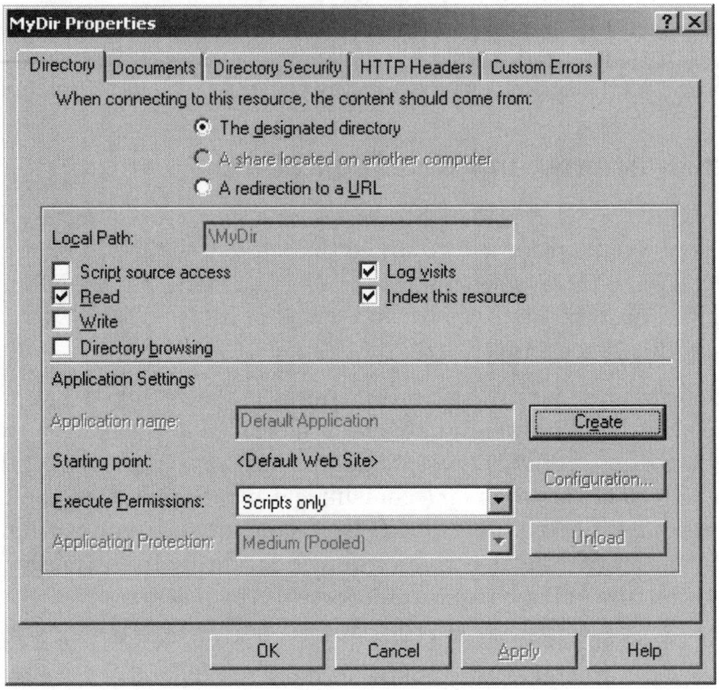

Figure 4-1. A directory's Properties page in IIS

Windows XP lets you add new virtual directories using Windows Explorer. The Properties page for a directory will have a Web Sharing tab. (Certain directories do not support web sharing, so the Web Sharing tab will not always be present.) If you share a directory in this way, Windows Explorer will create both a new virtual directory and a new web application for that directory.

A web server will always have at least one web application—even if you do not create any web applications of your own, there is an application for the web server's home directory. You can configure this from the Properties page for the web site itself. The tab has a different name in this case—it is labeled Home Directory instead of just Directory, but it otherwise works in the same way.

Once you create an application by clicking the Create button, all of the code in that application and all of the directories below it (at least those that are not applications themselves) now share application-wide settings. In an ASP application, Session and Application state are scoped by the web application. Process isolation settings are also configured on a per-application basis. In ASP.NET, the Session and Application state are partitioned in a similar way, but the process isolation settings are ignored in favor of an ASP.NET worker process.

Although ASP.NET ignores the IIS isolation settings, it gives each web application its own AppDomain, which serves a similar purpose. Web applications also determine the scope for configuration settings in the application's *web.config*.

Web applications and web projects

Whenever you create a new web project, VS.NET creates a new web application (unless an appropriate one already exists). This means there is a one-to-one mapping between VS.NET web projects and IIS web applications. For a .NET web project, VS.NET will also create a *bin* directory underneath the web application directory. The *bin* directory is where VS.NET places the project's build output. (ASP.NET automatically loads any assemblies in the *bin* directory into the web application's AppDomain.)

Managed Web Projects

Visual Studio .NET allows managed (.NET) web projects to be written in C#, VB. NET, or J#. Each of these languages has four web project templates: ASP.NET Web Application, ASP.NET Web Service, ASP.NET Mobile Web Application, and Empty Web Project. (Mobile Web Applications are not available in VS.NET 2002.)

Visual C++ has only one .NET web project type: ASP.NET Web Service. However, the way it works within VS.NET is more like the other unmanaged Visual C++ web projects than the C#, VB.NET, or J# managed projects. We will therefore describe that project type in the later section, "Visual C++ Projects."

The ASP.NET Web Application template is used for building web applications that will be accessed from a normal web browser. The ASP.NET Web Service template is used to build web services—programs that present a programming interface instead of a user interface, but which are still accessed using HTTP. The ASP.NET Mobile Web Application template is designed for building web applications that will be accessed from a web browser on a mobile device such as a PDA or mobile phone. The Empty Web Project template can be used to build any kind of web application.

.NET Framework Versions

Visual Studio .NET 2003 shipped with Version 1.1 of the .NET Framework. This was the second release of the .NET Framework, and it saw the introduction of so-called *side-by-side* support.

Side-by-side support simply means that multiple versions of a software product may be installed simultaneously on a single machine. The idea is that if you have applications that have been developed on and regression tested against Version 1.0 of the .NET Framework, you can carry on running those applications against that version even though you may have newer applications on the same machine using Version 1.1 or later.

Normal executable files indicate which version of the framework they require using settings in their file headers. However, for web applications, this is not good enough— the ASP.NET Framework will be up and running long before any executable files get loaded, so we must use a different technique to indicate which version of the framework we require.

The .NET Framework version is chosen on a per-web application level. By default, a newly created web application will use the latest version of the framework on the machine, but it is easy to downgrade to an earlier version—each version of the framework ships with a tool called *aspnet_regiis.exe* that can do this.

It is vitally important that you run the right copy of this tool—if you have multiple versions of the .NET Framework, you will have multiple copies. The tool is typically found here:

> *\Windows\Microsoft.NET\Framework\v1.0.3705*

(The final directory indicates the version number—this is the normal location for Version 1.0.) Having located the correct version of the tool, simply run it thus:

```
aspnet_regiis -s W3SVC/1/ROOT/WebApp
```

where *WebApp* is the name of the web application that requires the old version of the framework.

The *aspnet_regiis* utility can also be used to set up the IIS default application configuration. This is useful when you have installed IIS after installing the .NET Framework—if IIS is not present when the framework is installed, it obviously cannot be configured. Running *aspnet_regiis* with the -i switch will perform this configuration.

These four template types are very similar to one another—they manage and build their files in much the same way. The only differences between them are the default set of files that are added to the project initially. For the ASP.NET Web Application project, the main file added to the project is an ASP.NET Web Form named *WebForm1.aspx*, while for a Mobile Web Application, the main form is called *MobileWebForm1.aspx*. (Mobile Web Applications also have an additional reference to System.Web.Mobile.) For ASP.NET Web Service projects, the main file is

Service1.asmx, which acts as the main web service entry point. An Empty Web Project contains no files at all to start with.

VS.NET treats all of these project types in exactly the same way once they have been created. So for the rest of this section, we will not distinguish between the different types of managed web projects.

Creating a New Web Project

You create new managed web projects using the New Project dialog (Ctrl-Shift-N) as usual. When you have selected a managed web project type, you must enter a URL into the Location text box, as shown in Figure 4-2.

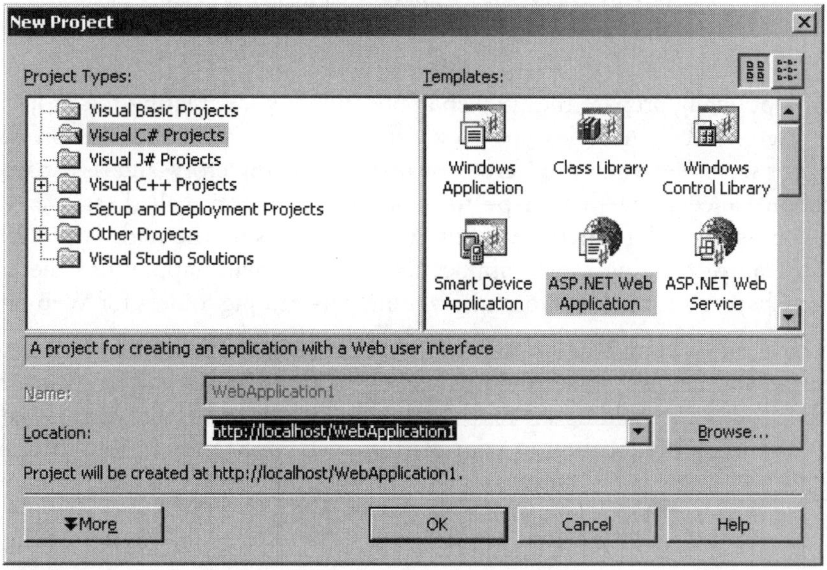

Figure 4-2. The New Project dialog for a web application

When you click OK, VS.NET immediately communicates with IIS to see if a web application with the specified name exists. If not, VS.NET will create a new application that takes its name from the last part of the location name (i.e., the string typed in after the last forward slash). For example, if the string *http://localhost/app1* is entered into the Location text box, VS.NET will create a new web application called *app1*. It will not create a virtual directory however—when VS.NET creates a new application in this way, it just adds a nonvirtual directory underneath the web server's home directory. So if the home directory were the default *c:\inetpub\ wwwroot*, VS.NET would create the new directory at *c:\inetpub\wwwroot\app1*.

The URL of the web project is stored in the VS.NET solution file. If you choose to create a web project on your local web server by using a URL of the form *http://localhost/project*, this may cause problems if you copy the solution to another developer's machine—VS.NET will look for the corresponding web application on the local web server. You will therefore need to make a local copy of the web application. (If you put your development machine name in the URL instead, you won't encounter this problem, but this will, of course, mean that the other developer will now be using your machine's local web server to do her development, which is probably not a great idea.)

Fortunately, source control offers a better solution to this problem. If your projects are in a source control database, VS.NET will be able to create a new copy of a web project when you check it out. If the web project's URL refers to *localhost*, VS.NET will offer to build a new web application on your local server to contain the copy.

You can optionally prepare the IIS web application before creating the project. This can be useful since it enables you to control the location of the files on the web server. For example, you could create a new virtual directory and associated web application called *app2* that maps to a physical directory called, say, *e:\MyApp*. When you use VS.NET to create a new web project using the path *http://localhost/app2*, instead of creating a new application, VS.NET will happily use the existing one. See Chapter 1 for more information about pre-creating folders for Web projects.

If you have an existing web application, you can create a VS.NET project for the application and its files, rather than having to build a new application from scratch. You can do this by building an Empty Web project (based upon your language of choice) and using the location of your existing web application in the Location box of the New Project dialog. Once you have created the project, it will, of course, be empty as far as VS.NET is concerned, so the next step will be to add the files in the web application to the VS.NET project. To do this, click on the Show All Files button in the Solution Explorer window (see Figure 4-3) to show all the files that already exist in the application, and then add the files you are interested in working with by right-clicking on them and selecting the Include in Project option.

If you have a web application in which you want to create a project, but you don't recall the exact name, you can use the Browse button from the New Project dialog. This shows the Project Location dialog box, which allows you to browse for projects.

The Project Location dialog is normally used for browsing through the filesystem. However, it can also browse web servers. There is a Tools menu in the upper-right-hand corner of this dialog, and it provides an Open from Web Server... option. This brings up the Connect to Web Server dialog, into which you can type the URL of the web server where you want to create the new project. If you supply a URL that contains only the server name (e.g., *http://localhost/*), VS.NET will show you a list of all the directories on the server, as Figure 4-4 shows. The dialog indicates a directory that is already a web application by embedding a small globe icon in its folder icon.

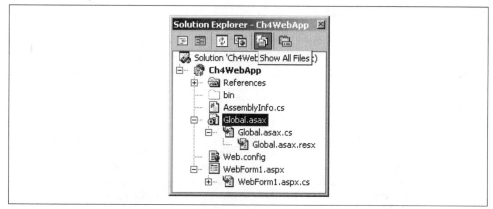

Figure 4-3. The Solution Explorer's Show All Files button

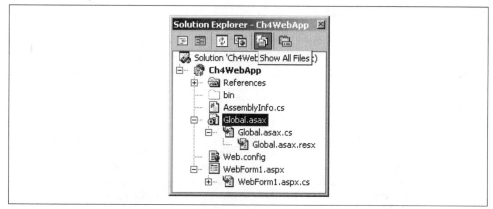

Figure 4-4. Project Location dialog showing a web server's directories

You can pick the directory in which you would like to create the new project. VS.NET will then use that directory for creating all the files based upon the project type you selected. If you select a directory that does not have its own web application, VS.NET will create a new application for that directory.

Storage of Project Files

When you create a managed web project, the project files are not kept on your local hard disk, as they are for other VS.NET project types. Only the solution files (*.sln* and *.suo*) are kept in a local folder. All the other files (including the *.xxproj* file) are kept on the web server.

 The prospect of having all of your source and project files on a web server may sound slightly unnerving. Fortunately, ASP.NET takes steps to prevent end users from accessing the project files (and other source files)—all the project file extensions are mapped to the System. Web.HttpForbiddenHandler in the *machine.config* file. If a user tries to get one of these files with a browser, the server will return an HTTP 403 forbidden error code.

Although the master copies of a web project's files all live on the web server, VS.NET keeps a local copy of all the web project files in a special folder called the web project cache—it needs local copies in order to be able to edit and compile files. The default folder for the project cache is a folder called *VsWebCache* under your user account's Document and Settings folder. You can change the location of this folder using the Tools → Options dialog. Select the Projects folder in the lefthand pane of the Options dialog, and then choose the Web Settings subitem. The cache directory can then be set in the Offline Projects section on the righthand side. (This is a per-user setting—there is no way to configure the cache directory on a per-project basis.)

Codebehind

In ASP.NET, we are discouraged from having all of our source code inside of *.aspx* files, intermingled with HTML code. Instead, the *.aspx* file should contain only user interface elements, while any dynamic server-side behavior should be in a separate source file associated with the *.aspx* page. This separate source file is known as the *codebehind* file—it contains the server-side code behind the HTML frontend. (This same concept is also applied to other ASP.NET-related files, such as the *global.asax* and any *.asmx* or *.ascx* files.) Use of codebehind is not mandatory—you are free to create a spaghetti-like tangle on a single page if you prefer—but it is almost always better to separate user interface from implementation.

To use codebehind, you must put a special attribute into the @Page directive in your *.aspx* file (or the analogous directive for other file types). The attribute is Inherits, which specifies the name of a type. ASP.NET will use this type as the base class for the class that it builds dynamically based upon the HTML and code contained in the *.aspx* file.

This named type obviously needs to be available to ASP.NET at runtime—it can build a class derived from a type only if it has access to that type. One way of doing this is to use the Src attribute. The Src attribute names a source file, and whenever either the *.aspx* file or the file referenced in the Src attribute is modified, ASP.NET will recompile both files. The intended usage model is that the source file contains the source for the page's base class.

However, although VS.NET uses codebehind, it does not use the Src attribute. Instead, it compiles the source file that contains the base class for the *.aspx* page into the main assembly for the web application. VS.NET will copy this assembly into the web application's *bin* subdirectory, and ASP.NET automatically loads any assemblies in that directory into the web application's AppDomain. This means that when ASP.NET compiles the *.aspx* page, it will already have loaded the application's main assembly and will therefore already have access to the base class. So VS.NET has no need to use the Src attribute—it needs to use only the Inherits attribute.

 The fact that VS.NET builds the codebehind class into the main assembly instead of using the Src attribute means that you always need to build your project in order to push changes to the web server. When using the Src attribute, it is sufficient just to save the file and let ASP.NET do the compilation. (One advantage of not using the Src attribute is that VS.NET is able to provide IntelliSense for classes that are built into the main assembly but cannot do so for classes compiled by ASP.NET. It also means that the page will be served up slightly faster the very first time it is used, as ASP.NET will not need to compile the codebehind page.)

Although it does not use the Src attribute, VS.NET does place an attribute in the @Page directive that refers to the source file: the Codebehind attribute. ASP.NET ignores this attribute—it is present only for VS.NET's benefit. It tells VS.NET which source file is associated with a particular content file.

By default, VS.NET hides the codebehind files in the Solution Explorer. However, if you want to see them, you can click on the Show All Files button. This will cause the Solution Explorer to show you all the source files associated with particular content files—codebehind files appear as children of their corresponding content files in the tree. (You do not need to do this merely to edit the codebehind file. If you right-click on an *.aspx* file in the Solution Explorer and select View Code, VS.NET will open the codebehind file instead of the *.aspx* file.)

Source files do not have to be codebehind files in a web project—you can also add raw source files as you would with any other kind of project. These files get built into the main application assembly as usual.

Opening an Existing Web Project

If someone else has created a project for an existing web application, you may need to open it in order to work on the files in the project. To do this, you select File → Open → Project from Web. This brings up the Connect to Web Server dialog in which you can type the URL of the web server from which you want to open up the project. This dialog presents a view of the web applications on the web server like the one shown in Figure 4-4. Once you open the correct web application folder, you should find the project file (with a *.csproj*, *.vbproj*, or *.vjsproj* file extension) on the server. When you open it, VS.NET will create a local solution file for you (unless you are adding this to an existing solution).

 If you are using a source control database that is integrated with VS. NET, such as Visual Source Safe, you will not normally need to locate an existing web project manually like this. When you open an existing solution that contains a web project from a source control database, VS.NET will automatically connect to the web server for you—the solution file contains enough information for VS.NET to locate the web server.

Building and Debugging

You build a managed web project in the same way as all other projects, using Build → Build Solution (Ctrl-Shift-B). However, VS.NET performs some extra work when building a web project. As usual, VS.NET takes all of the source files in your project and builds them into a single assembly. (Since the compilers cannot work directly from a web server, this compilation takes place in the folder in the local web cache that corresponds to this project.) Once compilation is complete, VS.NET copies the results to the actual web application.

To get debugging to work, you need to make sure that you are building a debug configuration (which causes VS.NET to create a *.pdb* file for your assembly). The configuration can be selected from the Solution Configuration drop-down list in the Standard toolbar or you can use the Build → Configuration Manager... menu option. (The Debug solution will be selected by default for a newly created web project, so you will normally need to select only the Debug configuration if you have previously selected a different configuration.) You will also need to tell ASP.NET that you want to debug your application. The simplest way to do this is to make sure that the *web. config* in your application has the debug attribute on the `compilation` element set to true. Example 4-1 shows a suitable minimal configuration file. (Note that the default *web.config* generated by VS.NET for a new web project will already contain a `compilation` element with `debug` set to `true`, so again, you will not need to take any special action on a newly created .NET web application.)

Example 4-1. Minimal web.config compilation element

```
<?xml version="1.0" encoding="utf-8" ?>
<configuration>
  <system.web>
    <compilation debug="true" />

    ...other configuration stuff here...
  </system.web>
</configuration>
```

Setting this attribute will tell the ASP.NET compilation system to generate debugging information for dynamically compiled files (e.g., *.aspx*, *.asmx*). This enables source-level debugging of such files in VS.NET.

Once the debug symbols are in place, you can debug this project like any other. See Chapter 3 for detailed information about debugging.

Debugging with team projects

Note that when you debug a web application, the application effectively becomes unusable for anyone else—whenever you suspend execution in the debugger, the application will not be able to respond to requests until you allow it to continue.

IIS 6 can mitigate this with application pools, but usually the simplest solution is for developers to have their own copies of the application on their machines' local web servers.

FrontPage Versus File Share

One of the choices you need to make when working with a web project is whether to use File Sharing or FrontPage Server Extensions to access your project files on the web server. By default, VS.NET will use File Sharing.

When using File Sharing, VS.NET copies your files to the web server using normal Windows File Sharing. If your project points to a remote web server, you will need to have a share open on the server (VS.NET looks for a wwwroot$ share by default). For this to work, the web server will have to be able to recognize your Windows login credentials. This will usually mean that the web server must be in the same Windows domain as you. (Or if you are not using domain authentication, the web server will need to have an account with the same name and credentials that you use.)

If the machine you are trying to connect to does not have a share named wwwroot$, you will get the dialog box shown in Figure 4-5. With this dialog, you can either fill in the correct share name or switch the project to use FrontPage Server Extensions (FPSE). Microsoft advises that if you are using File Sharing, you should use the wwwroot$ share name, so although it is possible to use this dialog to select something else, VS.NET can sometimes get confused by this. So you should really use this dialog only to select between File Sharing and FPSE.

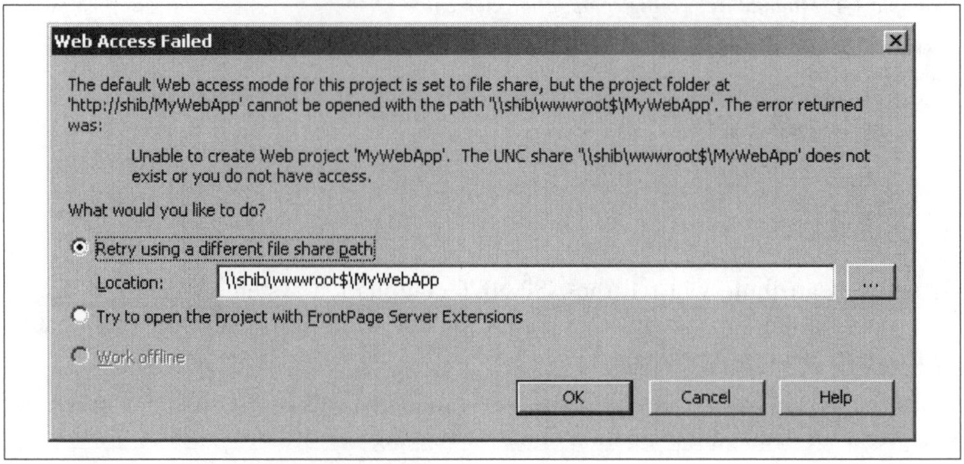

Web Access Failed

The default Web access mode for this project is set to file share, but the project folder at 'http://shib/MyWebApp' cannot be opened with the path '\\shib\wwwroot$\MyWebApp'. The error returned was:

> Unable to create Web project 'MyWebApp'. The UNC share '\\shib\wwwroot$\MyWebApp' does not exist or you do not have access.

What would you like to do?

☉ Retry using a different file share path

Location: [\\shib\wwwroot$\MyWebApp] [...]

○ Try to open the project with FrontPage Server Extensions

○ Work offline

[OK] [Cancel] [Help]

Figure 4-5. Web Access Failed dialog

If you switch from File Sharing to FPSE, then instead of using SMB to connect to the files on the web server, VS.NET will use its FPSE libraries to communicate with the web server via the FPSE HTTP protocol.

The main advantage of FPSE over File Sharing is that FPSE can work better when the web server that hosts your web application is not on your local network. When the web server is on your local network, this is not likely to be an issue—you will typically have a large amount of bandwidth, which will make using SMB fast, and the web server will likely be in the same Windows domain as you, so security will not be an issue. If your server is remote, however, FPSE may be a better bet since it uses HTTP. This is less likely to be tripped up by firewalls or other security configuration issues and is also generally faster than Windows File Sharing over longer distances. However, VS.NET prefers the use of File Sharing, so you should use that if possible.

> Use of FrontPage Server Extensions can complicate the use of source control—VS.NET's integrated source control works only for File Sharing. You can use source control with FPSE, but you must perform the source control operations on the machine that hosts the web server rather than using VS.NET.

Visual C++ Projects

VC++ web projects act more like nonweb VS.NET projects than like the managed web projects described earlier. All of the solution, project, and source files are kept on the local hard disk and not the web server. When you build a VC++ web project, all of the usual build and debug build directories are used, and not the local web cache folder. The only real difference between a nonweb project and a VC++ web project is that a VC++ web project has a final build step that copies the appropriate DLLs and content files to the web server.

Creating a New VC++ Web Project

Creating a new unmanaged web project is similar to creating a nonweb project. Unlike with managed web projects, you do not specify a remote web server in the New Project dialog—you just specify a folder on the local filesystem as usual. When you build an unmanaged web project, VS.NET communicates with IIS via DCOM (Distributed Component Object Model) and creates the appropriate web application for your project. (By default, it will use the project name, but you can change this in the Project Property Pages dialog—in the Web Deployment settings, the General section contains a Virtual Directory Name property that you can use to control where VS.NET will send the build output.)

The two basic types of VC++ web projects are ATL Server and ASP.NET Web Service (or Managed C++ Web Service as it was called in VS.NET 2002). Although they create different kinds of output, these projects interact with the web server in the same way.

ATL Server

> An ATL Server project creates a new web application whose main executable is an ISAPI (Internet Server Application Programming Interface) extension DLL. This ISAPI extension responds dynamically to HTTP requests. There are two ATL Server project templates. ATL Server Project creates an ISAPI DLL that uses *.srf* files to create dynamic HTML UIs. ATL Server Web Service creates an ISAPI DLL that exposes a web service via SOAP (Simple Object Access Protocol). See *ATL Internals*, Second Edition (Addison-Wesley) for a more detailed discussion of ATL Server.

ASP.NET Web Service

> An ASP.NET Web Service in Managed C++ is similar to ASP.NET Web Services in other managed languages. The ASP.NET Web Service template creates a project that provides a SOAP-based web service. The project builds a .NET assembly. It puts this assembly in the *bin* directory of a web application and then links a type in that assembly to an *.asmx* file (via the *.asmx* file's WebService directive).

Files

VC++ web projects manage files in the typical VS.NET manner, keeping all of the source files in the project directory. Content files are copied to the web server automatically as part of the build process. (You can tell VS.NET which files are content by selecting the files in the Solution Explorer and setting their Content property to true.)

.asmx Files

The documentation for .asmx files is scant. Their purpose is to map the URL for a web service onto the class that implements the service. The easiest way to see how they work is to look inside one, although that is easier said than done—VS.NET tries to stop you from editing their contents by always showing you the codebehind file instead of the .asmx file itself. (You can force it to open the .asmx file by right-clicking on the file in the Solution Explorer, selecting Open With, and choosing Source Code (Text) Editor.)

Most .asmx files contain just one line, a @WebService directive. This contains a Class attribute, which tells ASP.NET the name of the class that will handle web service requests directed to this endpoint. VS.NET places the class in a codebehind file (and it adds a Codebehind attribute to the directive so that it can find the relevant source file). ASP.NET also allows the source for the class to be placed inside the .asmx file itself, after the directive. (You can supply a Language attribute to tell ASP.NET which compiler it should use.) However, VS.NET doesn't make use of that—it always places the class definition in a codebehind file.

Here is a typical .asmx file generated by VS.NET:

```
<%@ WebService Language="c#" Codebehind="Svc1.asmx.cs"
    Class="WebSvc.Svc1" %>
```

It indicates that all web service requests directed to this file's URL will be handled by a class called WebSvc.Svc1, and the Codebehind hint tells VS.NET that this class is implemented in a file called Svc1.asmx.cs.

Building and Debugging

When a project is built, the files necessary for the web application are copied to the corresponding directory on the web server. If you need to deploy a VC++ project to another server, you will have to move the appropriate files by hand (as well as set up an appropriate IIS application).

When building an unmanaged project for debugging, all you need to do is make sure that you are building a Debug configuration. Otherwise, debugging is the same as any other project. See Chapter 3 for more detailed information about debugging.

Conclusion

VS.NET provides two kinds of web projects—C#/VB.NET/J# web projects and VC++ web projects. C#/VB.NET/J# projects keep all the project files on the web server, using a local cache directory when local copies are required. VC++ web projects (whether managed or unmanaged) keep project files on the local machine and copy all necessary files to the web server as part of the build process. Both types have a one-to-one mapping between projects and IIS web applications.

CHAPTER 5

Databases

Many applications rely on database management systems, such as SQL Server or Oracle, to provide robust, high-performance storage and retrieval of information. Visual Studio .NET provides tools that enable you to design, maintain, and use databases and that help you manage changes as your application evolves.

Visual tools help you design database objects such as tables, queries, and relationships. Visual Studio .NET is able to observe the changes you make with these tools and save them in a Database project. This allows any changes you make to a development server to be applied at a later date to other servers (e.g., staging servers and production servers). Code generation facilities are also available in certain project types that automate the retrieval and storage of data. For example, .NET projects allow data adapters and type-safe datasets to be created from database schemas. You can also use all of the visual database tools without needing a project at all—they can all be accessed through the Server Explorer.

 The various editions of Visual Studio .NET offer different levels of support for database work. Table 5-1 shows what level of support each of the editions offers for the various database types.

Table 5-1. Database support in Visual Studio .NET editions

Feature	Enterprise Architect/ Developer	Professional	Standard
Browse MSDE or Access	X	X	X
Browse any OLE DB data source	X	X	
Design MSDE databases	X	X	
Design any OLE DB data source	X		

Server Explorer

The Server Explorer is a tool window that allows you to examine various server resources, including databases. Figure 5-1 shows a typical example. You can display the Server Explorer with View → Server Explorer (Ctrl-Alt-S). You can examine databases in two ways with the Server Explorer. One is to expand the tree's Servers node and look in the relevant server's SQL Servers node. (If the server you require is not listed, you can add it to the list with the Servers node context menu's Add Server... item.) Figure 5-1 shows several SQL Server databases running on a machine called *IMOLA*.

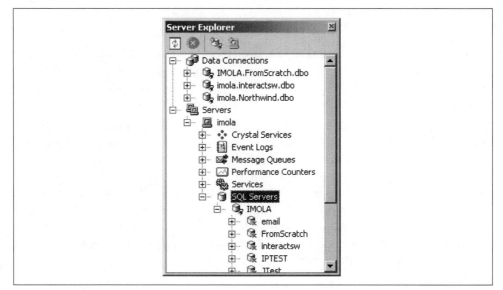

Figure 5-1. Server Explorer

If you will be using the database frequently and want to avoid having to drill so far into a tree view or if the database you require is not a SQL Server database, you can use the second technique—add an item to the Data Connections list in the Server Explorer. The Data Connections item's context menu has an Add Connection... entry, which opens the Data Link Properties window shown in Figure 5-2. By default, you will be shown a dialog for setting SQL Server connection details. However, if you select the Provider tab, you will be able to select any OLE DB provider installed on your system. (Remember, the Standard Edition of Visual Studio .NET can use only MSDE and Access, so you will be able to select arbitrary OLE DB providers only if you have the Professional Edition or better.) If you change the provider, a dialog specific to that provider will be shown in the Connection tab.

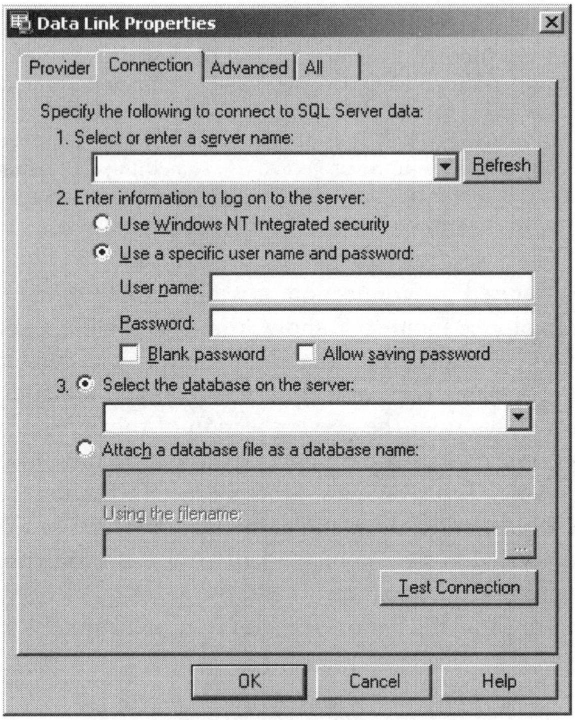

Figure 5-2. Configuring a connection

The credentials you supply when you create a database connection will have an impact on which of the visual database tools you can use. If you do not have permission to create or edit tables, for example, the table designer will not be able to save your designs to the database.

Note that unless you use integrated security when connecting to a database, Visual Studio .NET will need to know your credentials. You can store these in the data connection by checking the Allow Saving Password checkbox shown in Figure 5-2. But then anyone with access to your files will be able to read these, so be wary of creating a connection with a privileged account. If you leave this unchecked, you will be prompted for the password when you connect. (Although this dialog also provides a Blank Password option for accounts that have no password you are strongly advised to avoid this—using accounts without passwords is extremely bad practice because of its inherent insecurity.) If you can, you should use integrated security—Visual Studio .NET doesn't then need to store or prompt for the username and password.

Connection credentials are stored by the designer and are independent from runtime credentials. Using the visual techniques described later for adding database support to your projects means those projects will initially use the same credentials. (Or if you use integrated security, so will your project, to start with.) Changing the connection properties in the project to use something else is easy, so there is no need to worry that your choice of credentials when you browse may have an irrevocable effect on your application.

Once you have configured the connection, it will be added to the Data Connections list in the Server Explorer. Figure 5-1 shows three such connections. You can view various objects in the database by expanding the relevant connection in the Data Connections list. (The same objects will be shown if you expand a database in the SQL Server database list under the Servers section of the Server Explorer instead of creating a connection.) As Figure 5-3 shows, you will be presented with tree nodes for Database Diagrams, Tables, Views, Stored Procedures, and Functions. Each of these can then be expanded to show the individual objects. For example Figure 5-3, shows the Stored Procedures node expanded. And each individual object can be expanded to show further information—here, the SalesByCategory stored procedure has been expanded to show the parameters and returned columns.

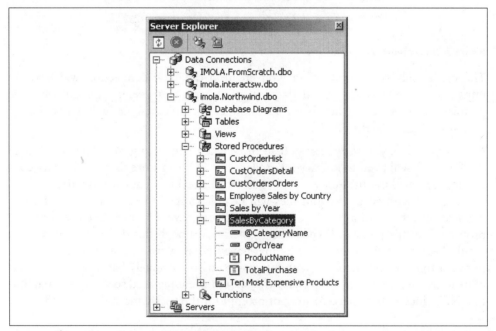

Figure 5-3. Database objects in the Server Explorer

The items that will be visible when you expand an object are different for each type of object. Expanding a database diagram will show a list of the tables present on the diagram, and these can be further expanded to show their columns. For Tables and Views, you will see a list of columns and triggers. For Stored Procedures and Functions, the parameters and return columns are shown.

 VS.NET cannot always determine the correct column information for complex stored procedures, so you should be wary of trusting this for anything other than simple stored procedures.

If you double-click on a table or a view, Visual Studio .NET will display a table showing its contents. This view is the equivalent of a SQL SELECT * statement with no WHERE clause, and it can be useful for examining small tables in development systems. If you need to perform a more selective ad hoc query, you can display either the SQL pane or the Grid pane and specify a filter or WHERE clause. These can be accessed from the View → Panes menu or the Query toolbar, both of which are usually displayed only when the results of a database query are shown. The SQL and Grid panes are described later in the "Query and View Designer" section. (Alternatively, you can create a query in a Database project—see the section entitled "Query Files" later in this chapter.)

Figure 5-4 shows how the contents of a table or view are typically displayed. The entries are usually editable, although certain types of database view will defeat this— you cannot edit entries in a view that uses the DISTINCT keyword for example. But for views in which it is practicable for Visual Studio .NET to apply updates to the database, editing will be permitted.

	ProductID	ProductName	SupplierID	CategoryID	QuantityPerUnit	UnitPrice	UnitsInStock	UnitsOnOrder	ReorderLevel	Discontinued	CategoryName
▶	1	Chai	1	1	10 boxes x 20 bag:	18	39	0	10	0	Beverages
	2	Chang	1	1	24 - 12 oz bottles	19	17	40	25	0	Beverages
	3	Aniseed Syrup	1	2	12 - 550 ml bottles	10	13	70	25	0	Condiments
	4	Chef Anton's Caju	2	2	48 - 6 oz jars	22	53	0	0	0	Condiments
	6	Grandma's Boysen	3	2	12 - 8 oz jars	25	120	0	25	0	Condiments
	7	Uncle Bob's Organ	3	7	12 - 1 lb pkgs.	30	15	0	10	0	Produce
	8	Northwoods Crant	3	2	12 - 12 oz jars	40	6	0	0	0	Condiments
	10	Ikura	4	8	12 - 200 ml jars	31	31	0	0	0	Seafood
	11	Queso Cabrales	5	4	1 kg pkg.	21	22	30	30	0	Dairy Products
	12	Queso Manchego	5	4	10 - 500 g pkgs.	38	86	0	0	0	Dairy Products
	13	Konbu	6	8	2 kg box	6	24	0	5	0	Seafood
	14	Tofu	6	7	40 - 100 g pkgs.	23.25	35	0	0	0	Produce
	15	Genen Shouyu	6	2	24 - 250 ml bottles	15.5	39	0	5	0	Condiments

dbo.Alphabetic...ola.Northwind)

Figure 5-4. Showing a view

You can also run functions and stored procedures from the Server Explorer, although you must do so by right-clicking and selecting Run from the context menu. (Double-clicking will simply open the definition of the stored procedure or function for editing.) If any parameters are required, Visual Studio .NET will present you with a dialog to supply those parameters, as Figure 5-5 shows. However, the results will not be shown in the grid style used by tables and views. Stored procedure results are displayed in the Output window.

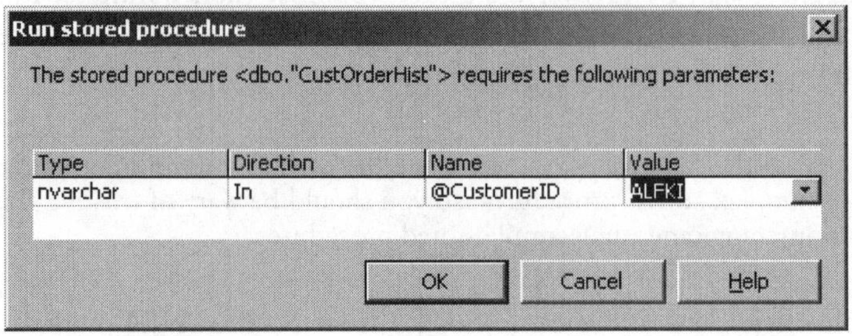

Figure 5-5. Passing parameters to a stored procedure

Double-clicking on any type of node other than a table or view opens a designer window—double-clicking on a database diagram brings up the diagram designer, and for stored procedures or functions, you will be presented with a SQL editor. You can design tables and views too—their context menus have Design Table and Design View entries. These designer windows are all described in the following sections. (Remember, you will be able to save any changes you make with these designers only if your connection to the database has the appropriate permissions.)

Database Diagram Designer

The database diagram designer window allows a considerable amount of information about a database's structure to be presented in one place. A single diagram can show many tables and the relationships among them. It also allows all of the items it displays to be edited. You can open the diagram designer with the Server Explorer, by expanding a database's Database Diagrams node and double-clicking on any existing diagrams. Adding a new diagram using the context menu will also show the diagram designer.

Figure 5-6 shows a diagram representing certain tables from the Northwind sample database. It shows all of the column names in each of the tables present on the diagram and indicates which columns form the primary key by annotating them with a key graphic. The relations have all been shown, with the direction indicated—the key indicates the table containing the primary key, and the infinity sign (∞) indicates the table containing the foreign key. (The the infinity sign indicates that the primary key may be related to any number of rows in the related table. A one-to-one relationship with the relation between the primary keys of both tables will show a key at both ends.)

You can add new relations by dragging from a column in one table to a column in another table. This will cause the Create Relationship dialog to be displayed. The Create Relationship dialog is almost identical to the Relationships tab of the property pages, described later.

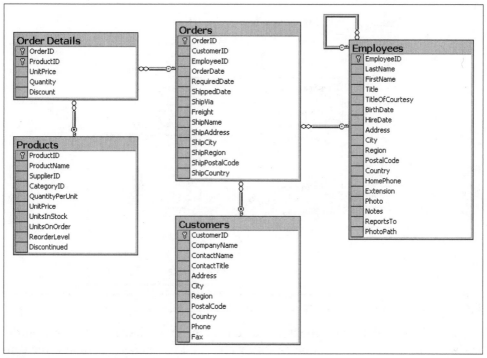

Figure 5-6. Database diagram

At the bottom-right corner of the diagram window is an icon with crossed arrows, as Figure 5-7 shows. If you click and hold down the left mouse button on this icon, a "map" of the entire diagram will be displayed, as Figure 5-8 shows.

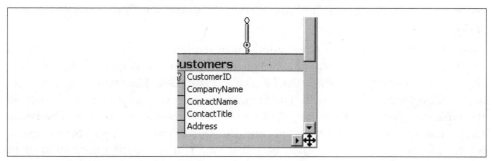

Figure 5-7. Database diagram navigation

A dotted rectangular outline will be displayed on the map to represent the part of the diagram that is currently visible in the window. You can move this rectangle around while the mouse button is depressed in order to choose the part of the diagram you would like to look at. When you release the mouse button, the diagram window will display the chosen portion of the overall database diagram.

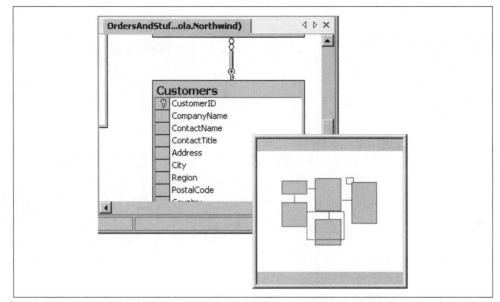

Figure 5-8. Database navigation map

Figure 5-9 shows the two context menus for the diagram designer. The one on the left is shown if you right-click on an empty area, and the one on the right is the context menu for a table. You can use these to create, modify, and delete tables through the diagram editor. You can add and remove columns and choose which columns form the primary key. If you want to include all of the tables related to a particular table, you can select the Add Related Tables item. The Relationships..., Indexes/Keys..., Check Constraints..., and Property Pages menu items all show the database properties pages dialog, which is described in the upcoming "Table Property Pages" section.

Figure 5-10 shows the Table View submenu of the table context menu. This allows you to select the way in which the table is presented in the diagram. The default is the Column Names view, which can be seen in Figure 5-6. The remaining view types are all illustrated in Figure 5-11. The Standard view is the same one that is used in the table designer. The Keys view shows only columns that act as keys. The Name Only view shows no columns at all, and the Custom view allows you to choose which information is shown about each column. You select the information to be shown by choosing Modify Custom... from the context menu.

Because the diagram view shows information about multiple tables, its functionality overlaps with other designer views. (In fact, all of the modifications to the database's structure that the diagram designer allows can also be achieved through other means, either with other designers' views or with property pages—the diagram view is provided merely for convenience.) So if you change two tables in a diagram and then save your changes back to the database, Visual Studio .NET will inform you that it needs to save the two tables you modified as well as the diagram.

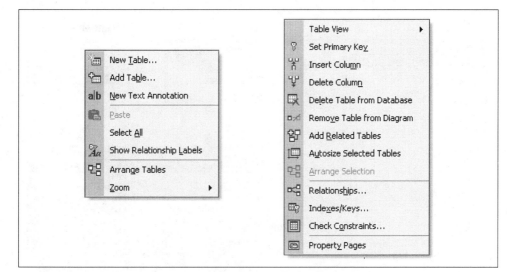

Figure 5-9. Diagram designer context menus

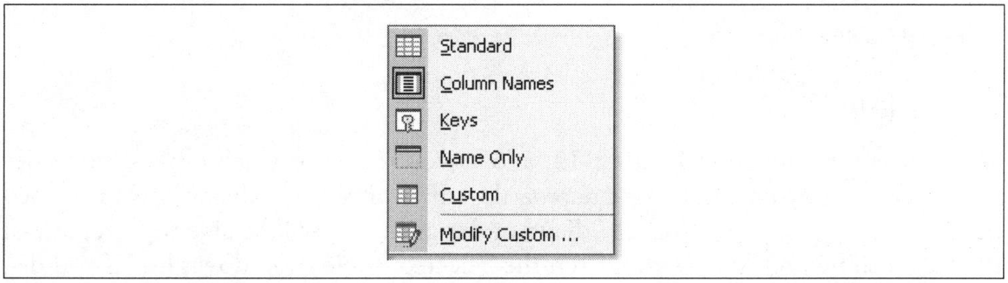

Figure 5-10. Table View menu

Table Property Pages

Certain objects in the database's schema do not have their own designer views. For example, Visual Studio .NET cannot show you an index or a constraint in an editor window. And even though keys and relationships can be displayed in the diagram designer, you cannot see all of their properties in this view. To enable you to set the properties of such database objects, VS.NET provides the database Property Pages dialog.

Property Pages can be displayed by selecting the Property Pages item from a table's context menu, in either the diagram designer or the table designer (but not directly from the Server Explorer). This dialog is divided into either four or five tabs: Tables, Columns (only if opened in the diagram designer), Relationships, Indexes/Keys, and Check Constraints.

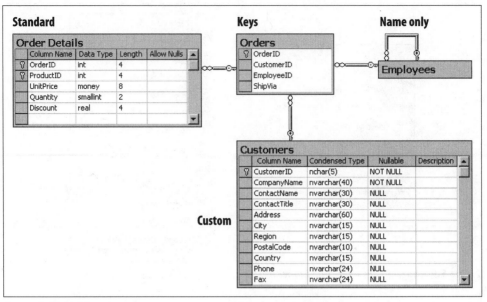

Figure 5-11. Table views

Tables Tab

The Tables tab, shown in Figure 5-12, allows you to select which table's properties will be affected by changes you make on the other tabs in the dialog. If you opened the Property Pages dialog from the diagram designer, you will be able to select any of the tables shown on the diagram from the Selected Table drop-down list. If you displayed the dialog from a table designer view, this list will contain only the table you were designing.

You can also edit certain table properties with this page. The table name and description may be changed. You can also choose the identity column (or ROWGUID column if you are using globally unique identities). You may change the table owner to any SQL Server user or role with the Owner list. If any user file groups are defined for the database, you may choose the file groups that this table will use for its contents and any text or ntext columns.

Columns Tab

Figure 5-13 shows the Columns tab. This tab is present only if the property pages are shown in the diagram editor. This is not shown when you open the property pages from the table designer view because this tab presents information shown in the main table designer window. See the later "Table Designer" section for details on how to edit column properties.

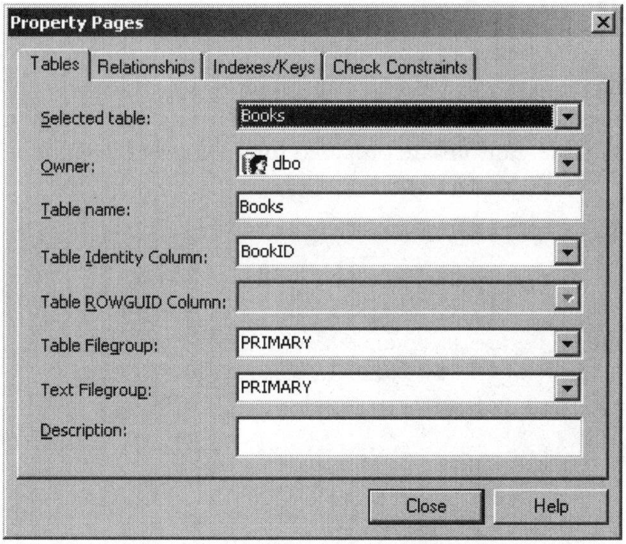

Figure 5-12. Tables tab

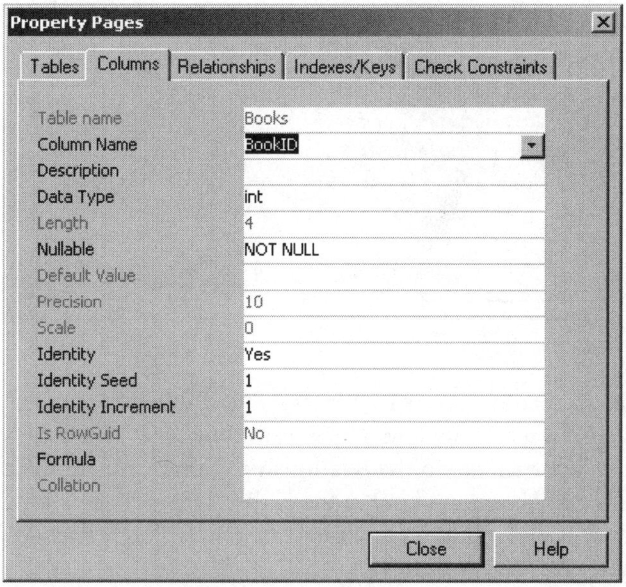

Figure 5-13. Columns tab

Relationships Tab

Figure 5-14 shows the Relationships tab. It allows relationships involving the selected table to be modified. The Selected Relationship drop-down list will allow any relationship involving this table to be selected, whether it is in the role of the primary key table or the foreign key table. Buttons are provided for adding and deleting relationships.

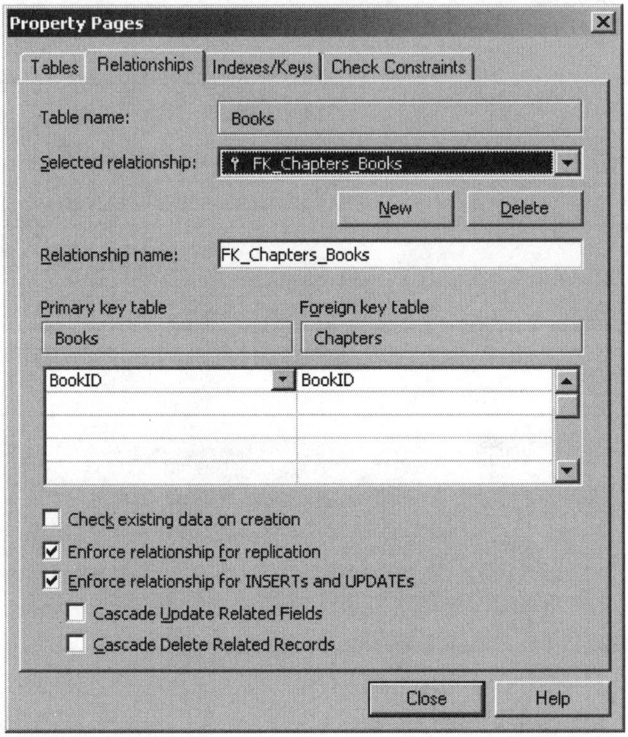

Figure 5-14. Relationships tab

When you create a relationship, the Primary Key Table and Foreign Key Table settings will change from read-only labels into drop-down lists, enabling you to select the two tables that will participate in the relationship. You can then select which primary keys are related to which foreign keys in the listbox. Figure 5-14 shows that the Books table's primary key BookID is related to the Chapters table's foreign key BookID.

 When you create a new relationship, Visual Studio .NET makes sure that one of the two tables involved is the one currently being edited by the Property Pages. (The table is shown in the Table Name field at the top of the page.) If you set one of the two key tables to be something other than the selected table, the other key table will be forced to be the selected table. If you want to add a relationship for some other pair of tables, you must first select one of them in the Tables tab.

When you create a new relationship, the dialog will choose a default name based on the two tables involved in the relationship, such as FK_PrimaryTable_ForeignTable. You can change this name with the Relationship Name field.

You can configure the referential integrity rules for the relationship with the check-boxes toward the bottom of the dialog. When adding a new relationship, the "Check existing data on creation" checkbox allows you to verify that all the data already in the database conforms. You would not normally want to disable checks for replication, INSERTs, or UPDATEs, so these will be enabled by default. However, cascading operations (for example, when deleting a row in the primary key table causes all related rows in the foreign key table to be deleted) are disabled by default.

Indexes/Keys Tab

The Indexes/Keys tab is shown in Figure 5-15. This allows you to view and edit keys and indexes for the selected table. If you assigned a primary key for your table, it will appear in here by default. Nothing else will typically be indexed by default, so you should add any indexes that you require with this dialog.

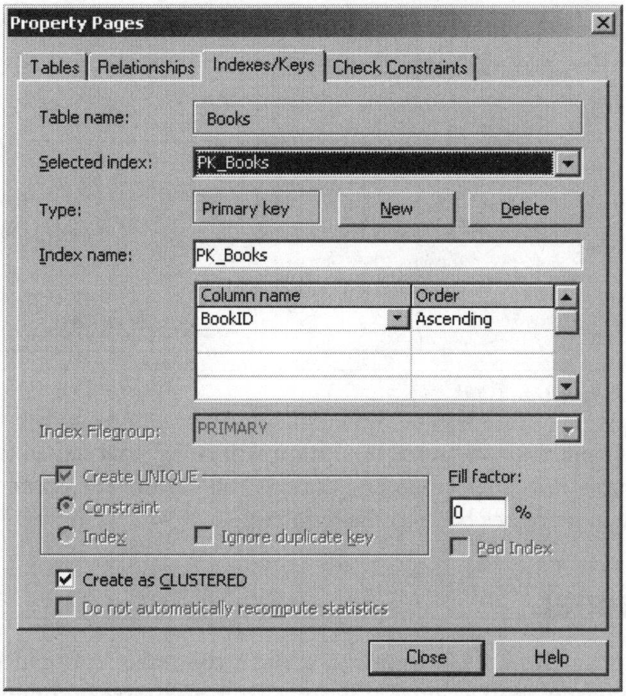

Figure 5-15. Indexes/Keys tab

An index may contain as many columns as you like. You may create as many individual indexes as you require. Note however that only one index can be CLUSTERED for any single table. (By default, the primary key index will be CLUSTERED. If your primary key is a GUID, you will want to turn this off—CLUSTERED indexes do not perform well with GUID primary keys.)

Check Constraints Tab

The Check Constraints tab, shown in Figure 5-16, allows you to add constraints on the selected table that the database will enforce when data is added or modified. (You do not need to add foreign key constraints here—those are dealt with in the Relationships tab.)

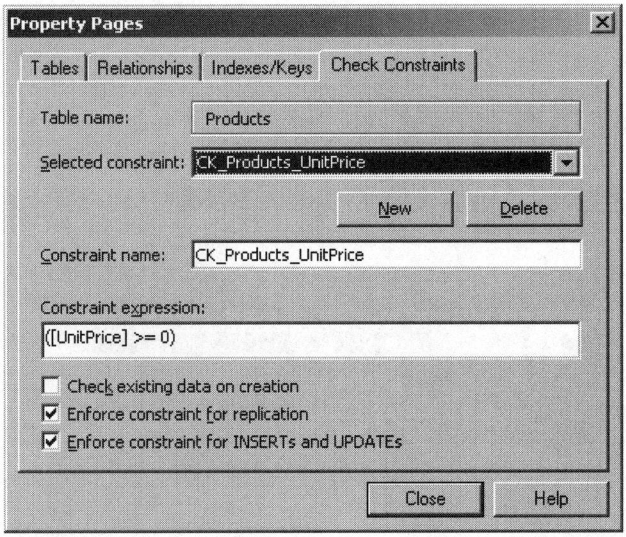

Figure 5-16. Check Constraints tab

The "Check existing data on creation" option will check that any data already in the database conforms to the specified constraint. This check will occur when you save the table to which it applies back to the database.

Table Designer

The table designer allows you to edit a table's columns. You can open the table designer by choosing the Design Table item from the table's context menu in the Server Explorer. Figure 5-17 shows the table designer for the Customers table in the sample Northwind database.

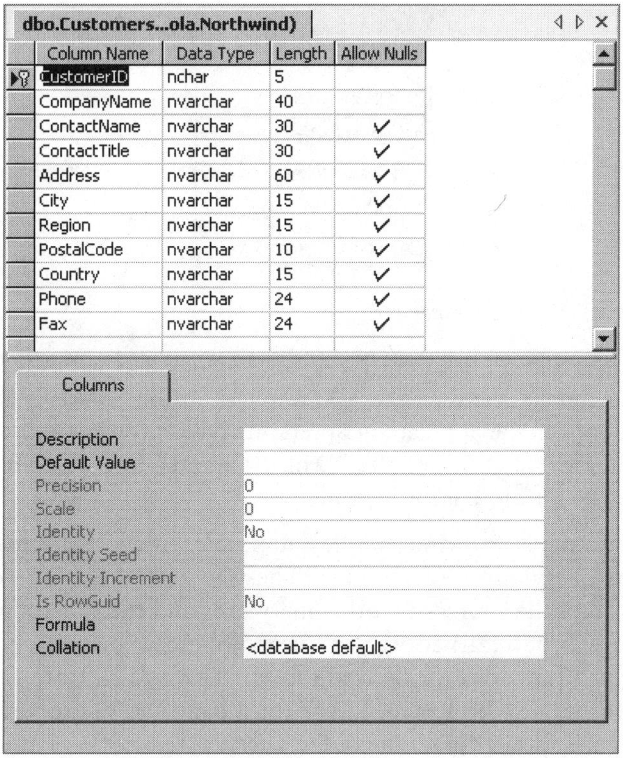

Figure 5-17. Table designer

The top half of the window shows all of the columns defined for the table, allowing their name, type, and length to be set, as well as choosing whether they accept null values. Further column properties for the selected column can be edited in the Columns tab in the bottom half of the view.

If you right-click on any of the rows in the table designer, the context menu, shown in Figure 5-18, will appear. It allows columns to be chosen as part of the primary key. (Primary key columns are indicated with a small key icon in the main view, as Figure 5-17 shows on the CustomerID column.) The context menu allows columns to be added or deleted. You can also add a new column to the end of the list by typing into the first blank row. The menu also provides access to the various pages of the Property Pages dialog.

Query and View Designer

The query and view designer provides a user interface for building SQL statements. You can open the query and view designer from several places. It is used to design views in the database, and you can open the designer on a view by double-clicking

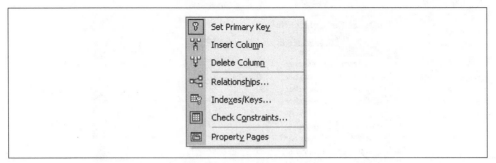

Figure 5-18. Table column context menu

on that view in the Server Explorer. (New views are created with the New View item in the context menu for the database's Views item in the Server Explorer.) It is also used in the Query Builder for data adapters in .NET projects and to build ad hoc queries in Database projects. See the "Data Adapters" and "Query Files" sections later in this chapter for more information.

Figure 5-19 shows the Northwind sample database's Order Details extended view, as presented in the query and view designer. The view is divided into four panes. The diagram pane shows the sources that the query uses and their relations and indicates which columns will be returned by the query. (Sources for a query can be tables, views, table-valued functions, or derived tables.) The grid beneath this allows filtering and sorting criteria to be specified. The third pane shows the SQL for the query, and the fourth pane shows the results of the query.

If you include multiple tables in a query, the query designer will generate a SELECT statement that performs a JOIN on the tables. It will not generate a batch query that returns multiple tables.

Diagram Pane

The query and view designer's diagram pane is very similar to the database diagram designer—it can show many tables, along with their columns and relationships. However, while the database diagram designer allows you to edit tables, the query and view diagram pane does not. It simply allows you to choose which table sources and columns will be included in a query and to control the way in which tables are joined.

The diagram pane shows a checkbox next to each column. For each one you check, the query will include that column in the query. If you want to retrieve all of the columns, simply check the All Columns box at the top of the table.

You are given the chance to decide which tables will appear in the diagram when you create a new view or query. You will be shown the Add Table dialog, as in Figure 5-20. This allows you to add views and table-valued functions as well as tables

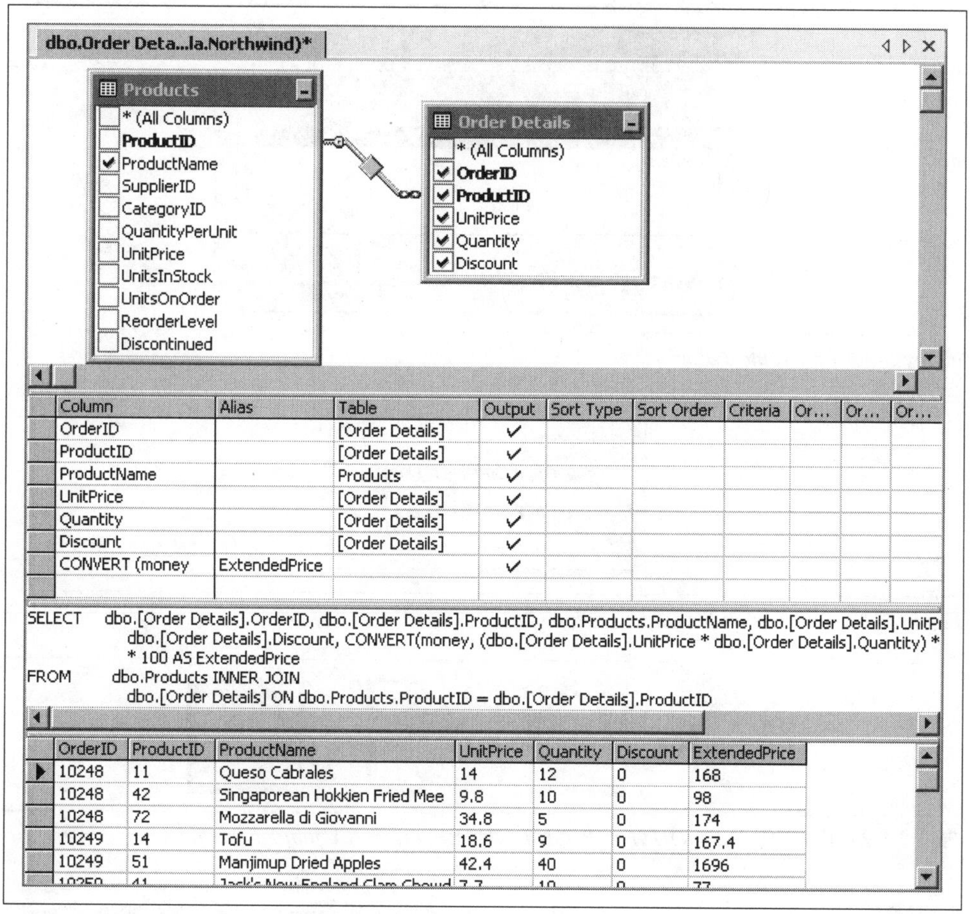

Figure 5-19. Query and view designer

to the diagram. You can always reopen the Add Table dialog to add more tables to the diagram at any time by selecting the Add Table... item from the pane's context menu or from the database view toolbar.

The diagram pane detects relations between tables and shows them with connectors such as the one between the Products and Order Details tables in Figure 5-19. The context menu for these connectors, shown in Figure 5-21, allows you to configure the type of JOIN that will be generated.

By default, an INNER JOIN will be created. Choosing one of the two Select All Rows menu items will turn this into either a RIGHT OUTER JOIN or a LEFT OUTER JOIN. Selecting both will perform a FULL OUTER JOIN. (If you add two tables that are unrelated to each other, a CROSS JOIN will be generated.) Each of the JOIN types is represented with a different graphic on the connector, as Figure 5-22 shows.

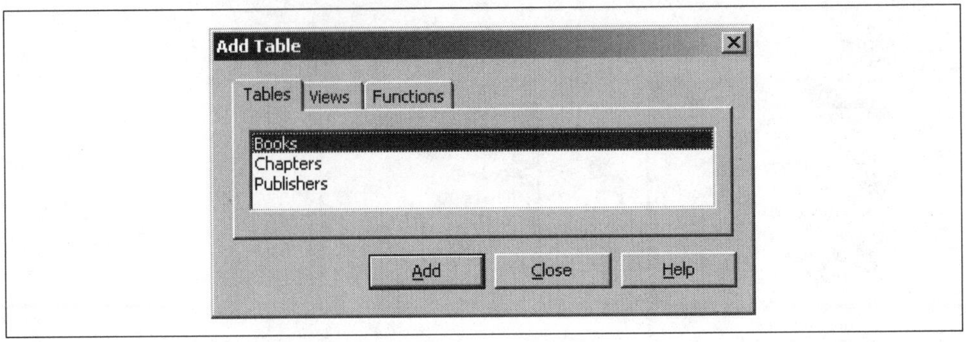

Figure 5-20. Add Table dialog

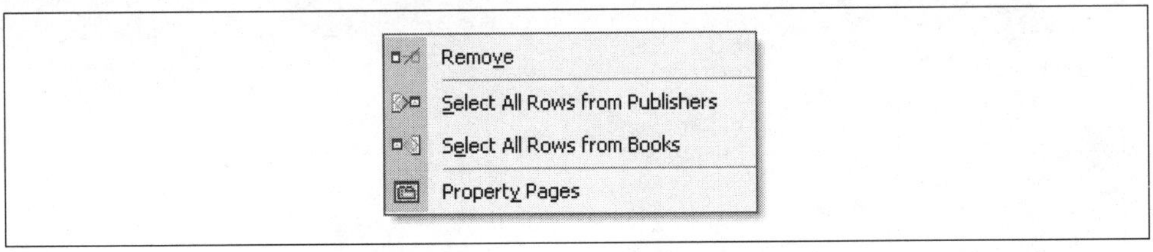

Figure 5-21. Query relations context menu

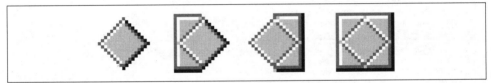

Figure 5-22. INNER, LEFT OUTER, RIGHT OUTER and FULL joins

 If you are using an Oracle database, Oracle's nonstandard `OUTER JOIN` syntax is supported correctly.

If you select Property Pages from the context menu for either a relation or a table, Visual Studio .NET does not show the normal database property pages described earlier. Instead, it shows property pages unique to the query and view designer. The table property page contains only one interesting field. It allows an alias to be assigned for the table, so if the table must be referred to elsewhere in the query, it can be referred to by its alias. If your tables have long names, this can make the generated SQL slightly easier to read.

The property page for a relation is a little more interesting and is shown in Figure 5-23. As well as showing the `JOIN` type information (the two checkboxes correspond to the All Rows from... items on the context menu), it also allows the `JOIN` condition type to be specified. By default, the `ON` part of the `JOIN` will use = as the condition. But you can change this to be any of <, >, <=, >=, or <> (not equal).

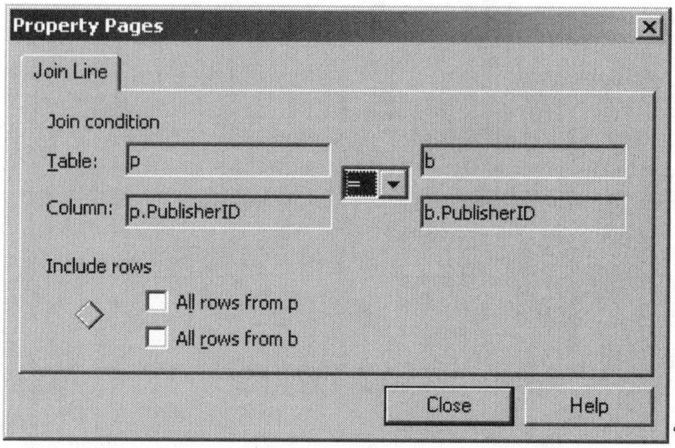

Figure 5-23. Join property page

If you are editing a database view and select the Property Pages item from the background of the diagram pane (i.e., with no particular object selected), you will be shown the view property page, illustrated in Figure 5-24. This allows you to control certain aspects of the view that are not handled by the main panes in the designer. You can elect to show all columns from all tables (the Output All Columns checkbox is equivalent to checking the All Columns item on all of the tables). You may add DISTINCT or TOP specifiers to the generated SQL.

The Encrypt View option stores the view's underlying SQL in such a way that it cannot later be examined. (If you choose this option, you will not be able to edit the view in the designer later on—if you need to change it, you will have to recreate it from scratch.)

The Bind to Schema option will prevent any database schema modifications that would cause the view to break. (For example, if the view uses a particular column from a table, any attempt to remove that column from the table will be rejected by the database.)

The Update Using View Rules checkbox ensures that any updates performed on the view by MDAC (Microsoft Data Access Components) will be applied to the view. (Under some circumstances, MDAC may translate an update request on a view into an update request on the underlying table.) The Check Option checkbox ensures that if data in a view is changed interactively in Visual Studio .NET, the changes conform to any WHERE clause specified in the view.

Grid Pane

The grid pane is the second pane in the query and view designer. It is beneath the diagram pane in Figure 5-19. The grid pane allows you to control detailed column-specific aspects of the query.

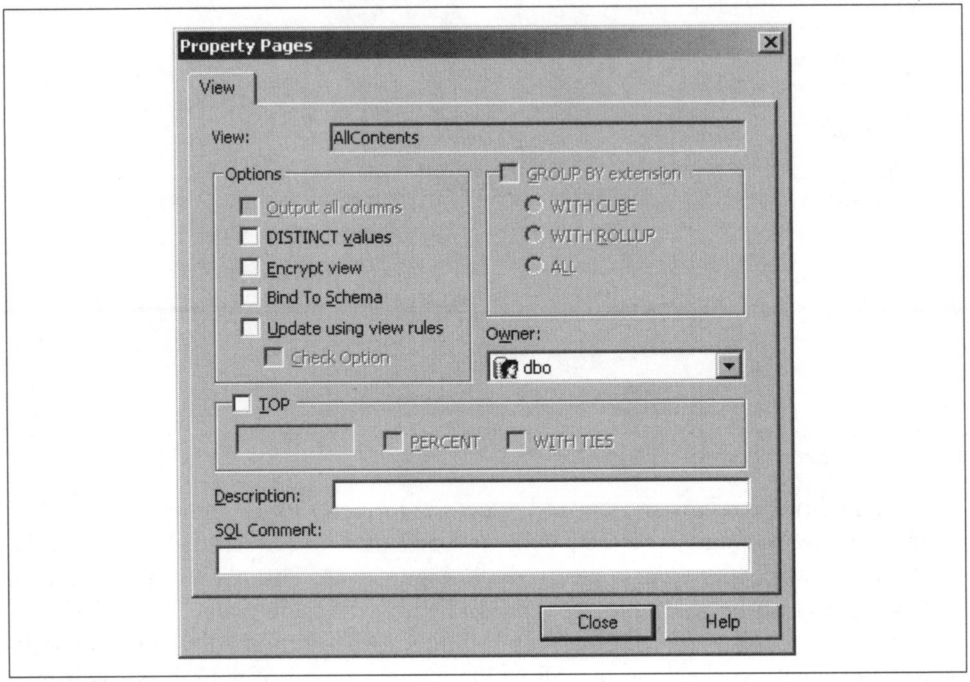

Figure 5-24. View properties

In a multitable query two columns from different tables may have the same name. For example, in a database describing the contents of books, you might expect to find a Title column in both the Books and the Chapters tables. In a query that joins two tables, it is helpful to rename these columns to remove the ambiguity. Figure 5-25 shows grid pane settings that rename two Title columns to the unambiguous BookTitle and ChapterTitle columns and change the Name column of the Publishers table to Publisher.

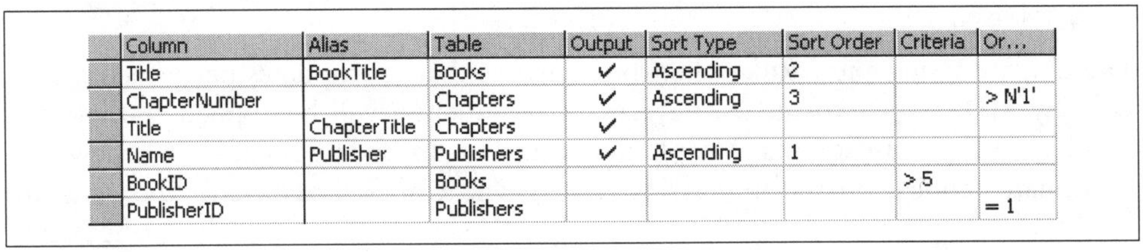

Column	Alias	Table	Output	Sort Type	Sort Order	Criteria	Or...
Title	BookTitle	Books	✔	Ascending	2		
ChapterNumber		Chapters	✔	Ascending	3		> N'1'
Title	ChapterTitle	Chapters	✔				
Name	Publisher	Publishers	✔	Ascending	1		
BookID		Books				> 5	
PublisherID		Publishers					= 1

Figure 5-25. Grid pane

The grid pane has two columns to control the order in which the database will return the rows. These are also shown in Figure 5-25. Each column can participate in controlling the order of the output. To enable this, set the Sort Type column to be either ascending or descending. The Sort Order column defines the order in which the columns will be used to perform the sort. So the example in Figure 5-25 will add the ORDER BY clause shown in Example 5-1.

Example 5-1. Generated ORDER BY clause

```
ORDER BY dbo.Publishers.Name, dbo.Books.Title,
    dbo.Chapters.ChapterNumber
```

You can also use the grid pane to make the query selective. The columns labeled Criteria and Or... allow a WHERE clause to be added to the SELECT statement. Each column (whether it is the criteria column or one of the Or... columns) can contain entries for one or more rows. If a column contains entries for more than one row, these conditions are combined with each other using the AND operator. If you use more than one column, the results of each column's tests will be combined with the OR operator. This means that any given row in the database will be returned if it meets *all* of the criteria in one or more of the columns. For example, the grid shown in Figure 5-25 is using two criteria columns. The corresponding WHERE clause is shown in Example 5-2.

Example 5-2. Generated WHERE clause

```
WHERE (dbo.Books.BookID > 5) OR
    (dbo.Publishers.PublisherID = 1) AND
        (dbo.Chapters.ChapterNumber > N'1')
```

You may sometimes add columns to a query only to specify criteria for them—you might not want them to appear in the output. In this case, you can uncheck these rows in the Output column. In Figure 5-25, the BookID and PublisherID columns are specified only in order to specify search criteria. The Output column is therefore unchecked for them.

You can change the order of the lines in the grid pane, although that is slightly fiddly. You must first select the row representing the column whose position you wish to change. Once the row is selected, you can drag it into the position you require. If you try to drag it without first selecting it, the pane simply enters a mode in which you can select a range of lines by dragging. You have to select a row and release the mouse button before clicking again to start the drag.

SQL Pane

The third pane in the query and view designer shows the SQL statement corresponding to the current settings in the designer. This is useful because it allows you to see exactly the effect of changes in the other designer panes. You can also modify the query directly by editing the text in this pane—for example, you can change the order in which the columns will be returned.

In addition to populating the SQL pane from the settings in the other panes, the query and view designer is able to perform the reverse transformation: when you type SQL directly into the SQL pane, Visual Studio .NET will attempt to interpret it and populate the other panes. (It also goes through this process when you edit a view—the database just stores the SELECT statement for a view, so Visual Studio .NET must reconstruct the remaining panes.) There are limits to what it can read—if you specify a WHERE clause sufficiently complex that it could not have been constructed by filling in fields in the grid pane, the conversion will not be performed, and the diagram and grid panes will not be populated. But for straightforward queries, it will successfully populate the diagram and grid panes.

If you type in invalid SQL, Visual Studio .NET will reject the change. You can check the SQL for validity with Query → Verify SQL Syntax.

Results Pane

The final pane is the results pane, shown at the bottom of Figure 5-19. This is where Visual Studio .NET will show the results of the query or view as currently configured. This pane will initially be blank. To populate it, you must run the query using Query → Run (Ctrl-R).

The values in this panel can normally be modified. Any changes you make will be written back to the database. (Certain types of queries will prevent this—e.g., any query that specifies DISTINCT. It will show the row contents in gray rather than black to indicate that the values are read-only.)

SQL Editor

If you edit a stored procedure, a function, or any SQL script file, Visual Studio .NET will show the SQL editor. This is just the normal Visual Studio .NET text editor window, but in a SQL mode. It supports syntax coloring for various dialects of SQL. (PL/SQL, T-SQL, T-SQL7, and T-SQL8 are all supported.) It also allows stored procedures to be executed and debugged. Unfortunately, IntelliSense is not supported in SQL mode.

If you double-click on a stored procedure or function, the SQL editor window will appear with an ALTER PROCEDURE or ALTER FUNCTION statement containing the SQL source code. (This is to make it easy to modify functions. Note that this use of ALTER is peculiar to SQL Server—some databases use the REPLACE keyword instead.) The editor will also allow you to set breakpoints. You can then execute the statement with Database → Run Stored Procedure (Ctrl-E), and the procedure will run until it hits the breakpoint, at which point you can single-step through the code. You can also start single-stepping straightaway with Database → Step Into Stored Procedure (Alt-F5).

Debugging of stored procedures is supported only for SQL Server. There are also some installation prerequisites—see Chapter 3 for more information on setting up SQL Server debugging.

You can use the query and view designer to add a SQL statement into a SQL editor window. Simply select Insert SQL from the SQL editor's context menu and the query designer will appear. When you save the query, it will insert the generated SQL into the editor. (If you are using this to edit a stored procedure, saving the query will modify only the contents of the SQL editor window. It will not save it back into the database until you save the stored procedure itself.) You can also use the query and view designer to edit existing SELECT, UPDATE, INSERT, and DELETE statements—if you bring up the context menu in the editor on a statement and select Design SQL Block, the query and view designer will be opened, and the diagram and grid will be generated from the SQL.

Database Projects

There is a fundamental difference between working with databases and working with other software development artifacts in Visual Studio .NET. With programs and components, source code is of central importance. Although we must create DLL or EXE files in order for our programs to run, these are usually never checked into revision control systems—they are essentially disposable because they can always be re-created from the source code.

With databases, on the other hand, the model is different. The closest thing we might have to source code is some SQL script that creates a database with a particular schema. However, these are not really at the center of the development model—the database is typically the authoritative source of information. SQL creation scripts are often generated from the contents of the database, so they cannot necessarily be described accurately as containing "source" code. You can use a Database project to hold scripts that contain the master definition for the current database schema, but these scripts would not be run as part of the normal build process—you don't want to re-create your database from scratch every time you build your project.

The role of a Visual Studio .NET Database project is therefore somewhat different from that of most projects—it does not contain the authoritative information required to build the target. In fact, Database projects don't build any kind out output at all—they just act as a container for scripts. Moreover, you do not even need a project in order to use the visual database design tools—when you save any changes you have made in these designers, Visual Studio .NET always writes changes out to the database itself, so there is no need for a project file or source files.

Database projects are useful when you employ the common development practice of having separate database servers for development and production. (And there may also be separate staging and test servers.) Visual Studio .NET can create script files that capture any changes made to a development server. These scripts can then be applied to other servers later on in the development process to apply the same modifications that you applied to the development server.

Creating a Database Project

Database projects are created just like any other projects, using the New Project dialog. (Open this with File → New → Project (Ctrl-Shift-N).) The Database Projects category can be found underneath the Other Projects category. The Database Projects category contains only one kind of project: Database Project.

When you create a new Database project, Visual Studio will ask you to choose a database connection for the project, presenting the dialog shown in Figure 5-26. This lets you select the database for which you will be creating scripts. When you select a connection, this creates a new database reference in the project.

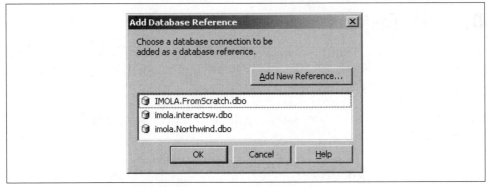

Figure 5-26. Add Database Reference dialog

Connections and References

The list of named database connections displayed in the Server Explorer provides a convenient way of looking at particular data sources—they save you having to navigate through the tree control the long way round. (They also allow non-SQL Server data sources to be used.) However, these connections are stored on a per-user basis, so although they are convenient for interactive use, they are not much use for representing connections in Database projects—project files may be opened by other users who do not have the same connections configured on their system. Visual Studio .NET Database projects therefore have a slightly different mechanism of their own called *database references*.

Database projects usually contain at least one database reference. (You can see one at the bottom of Figure 5-30.) A database reference is very similar to a database connection, except that all of the information is stored in the database project file instead of in the user's Visual Studio .NET settings. This means that anyone who opens the project file will be able to connect to the database even if he didn't have the relevant connection in his local configuration. (This is a good reason to use integrated security with database connections. If you use explicit credentials, they can get stored in the project as part of the connection information, visible to anyone with access to the project file. You might not want database credentials stored in the clear like this. You can prevent passwords from being stored—the Data Link Properties dialog shown in Figure 5-2 has a checkbox labeled Allow Saving Password. If you remember to make sure this is unchecked, the password will not be stored in the settings, and users will be prompted to type credentials in when they try to use the connection. However, if you use integrated security, anyone who opens the project will simply connect with his own credentials automatically.)

When you open a Database project with database references in it, Visual Studio .NET checks to see if the references match any of your database connections. If the project contains a database reference that is different from all of the connections listed in your Server Explorer, it will automatically add a new connection with the same settings as the reference.

When you create a new database project, Visual Studio .NET will ask you which database you wish to connect to. If your system already has an appropriate database connection configured, you can use that. A reference will then be created in your project that has the same settings as the chosen connection. Otherwise, choose the Add New Reference... button to connect to some other data source. This will open the Data Link Properties dialog, allowing you to configure the connection. This is the same window that is used to add data connections to the Server Explorer, as shown in Figure 5-2. This will add a new connection to your Server Explorer and a new database reference to your project, both with the same settings.

Scripts and Databases

Two kinds of scripts—*create scripts* and *change scripts*—can be stored in a Database project. Create scripts contain all of the information required to create a new database from scratch, copying everything except the table contents. Change scripts contain just modifications—they assume that the target database will have the same schema that the development database did before the change was made.

The scripts generated by Visual Studio .NET 2002 and 2003 are designed to be applied to SQL Server databases. Although the visual database design tools work with other databases, database projects and the scripts they contain support only SQL Server.

Create scripts

Create scripts are not normally used on production servers. The only time you would use a create script on a production server would be the very first time the system goes live. Once a system is up and running, you will never want to recreate the database from scratch, because all of the data would be lost.

By default, create scripts check for the existence of items they are about to create and will DROP any existing items they find. You should therefore *never* run a create script on a live server. (It is possible to instruct Visual Studio .NET to omit the DROP statements, but it will still not be productive to run such a script against a live server.)

Create scripts are most likely to be useful in staging and test environments—these systems don't have any real live data. The ability to create a new, empty database instance with exactly the right schema, views, and stored procedures can be very useful in these environments. You can add a create script to a Database project by using the Server Explorer—the context menu will have a Generate Create Script... item on the appropriate nodes. You can either generate scripts for individual objects, such as tables and stored procedures, or Visual Studio .NET can make a set of create scripts for the entire database.

You must install the SQL Server Client Tools in order for the Generate Create Script... option to work.

When you ask Visual Studio .NET to generate a create script, you will see the dialog shown in Figure 5-27. This allows you to control exactly which database items the script will create. The available database objects are shown in the list on the left of the dialog. Figure 5-27 shows the dialog as it appears for the *pubs* sample database when generating a create script for the entire database.

If you open this dialog from the context menu of a specific database item instead of for the entire database, only the selected item will be available, and the checkboxes will all be disabled. However, you can click the Show All button to bring all the other objects back into the list.

By default, no objects will be added to the script—the list on the right shows the items that will be added, and it is initially empty. You can use the Add >> button to add individual items to the list. However, you may find it less work to use the checkboxes toward the top of the dialog. These let you include entire categories of database objects in your create script. The Script All Objects checkbox will cause every database object to be represented, but you can also select just certain categories, such as tables or stored procedures.

The Formatting tab of the Generate Create Scripts dialog, shown in Figure 5-28, allows you to control certain aspects of the SQL script that Visual Studio .NET will generate. You can disable the creation of DROP statements here, which makes the scripts potentially less destructive.

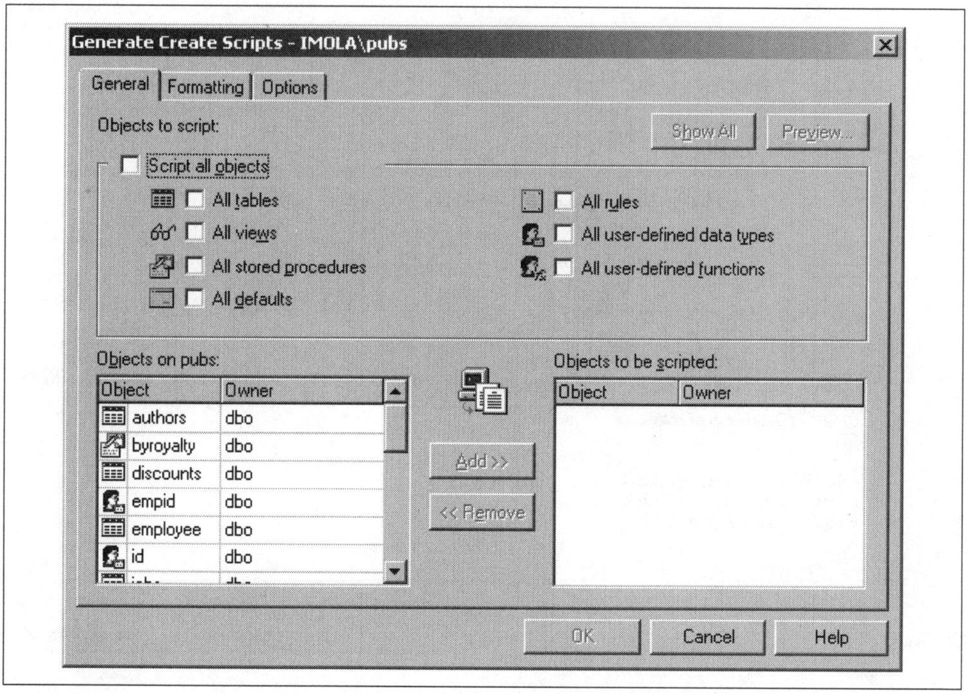

Figure 5-27. Generating a create script

The "Generate scripts for all dependent objects" checkbox will cause Visual Studio .NET to determine which other database objects your selected objects depend upon and generate scripts to create those too. For example, if you generate a create script for a view, selecting this checkbox will generate create scripts for all of the tables the view uses.

The remaining checkboxes allow you to control whether comments describing the file's purpose will be added to the start of the scripts, whether SQL Server 2000 extended properties will be copied across, and whether the script will be limited to using only SQL Server 7 features.

Further options can be set with the Options tab shown in Figure 5-29. Despite being under the Security Scripting Options category, the first option simply determines whether a CREATE DATABASE statement will be created, along with some associated configuration options. The next three determine whether user role, login, and permission settings will be transferred.

The settings under the Table Scripting Options category control how much information will be stored in the script for each table. By default, all indexes, triggers, and keys will be created by the generated script.

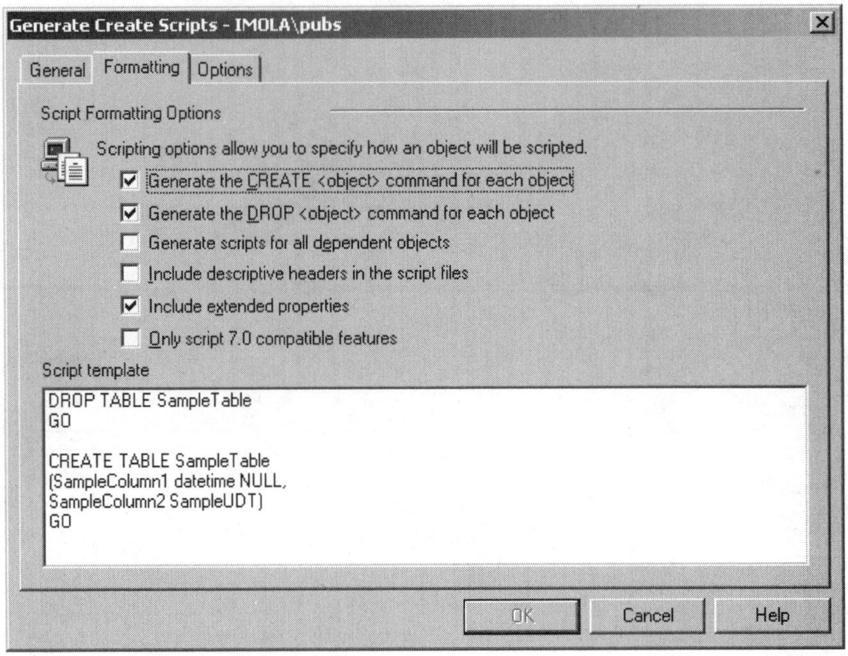

Figure 5-28. Create script code generation options

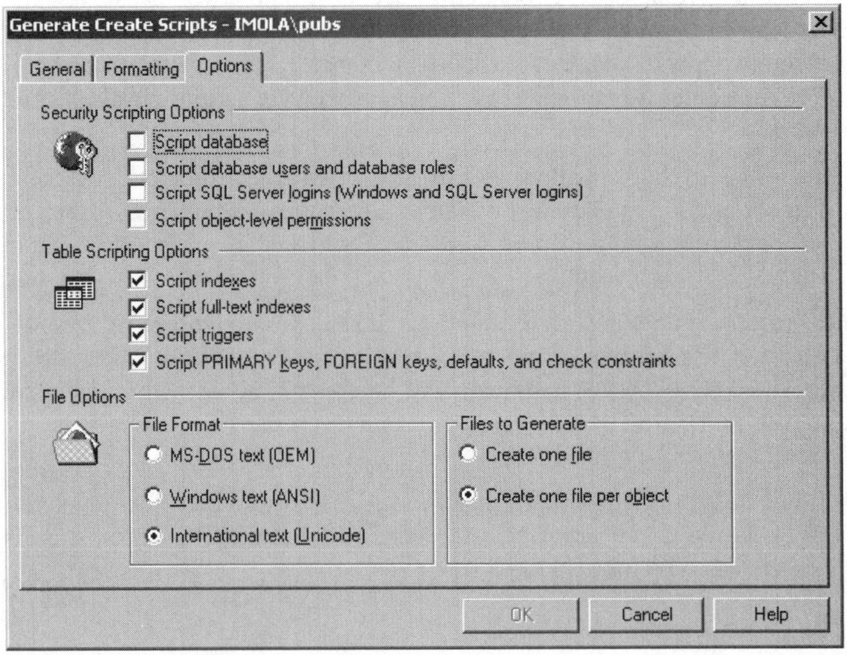

Figure 5-29. Create script options

The File Options category allows you to choose the text encoding of the script files, the default being Unicode. It also allows you to choose between generating a single script file that creates everything and splitting the scripts up so that each object has its own script. Figure 5-30 shows a Database project for a simple database for which the "Create one file per object" option was selected. (This is the default option.) This particular database was fairly small—it contained two tables, ContentText and Transforms, and two stored procedures, GetNewTransformAndContent and GetNewTransformAndNewContent.

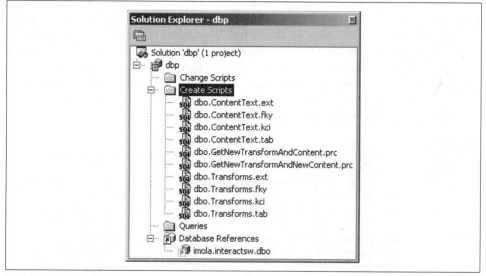

Figure 5-30. Create scripts in a Database project

Create scripts for stored procedures are fairly straightforward—each procedure is represented by a single file with a *.prc* extension, containing a SQL CREATE PROCEDURE statement. Tables are a little more complex however. A table's SQL CREATE TABLE statement is stored in the *.tab* file. Indexing settings are stored in the *.kci* file. The *.fky* files add foreign key constraints, and the *.ext* files contain any extended properties, such as column description strings.

The script files are just series of SQL statements. If you double-click one, it will open in a Visual Studio .NET editor window. You can execute the scripts using the Run or Run On... items from the script's context menu in the Solution Explorer. (Run On... lets you choose which database connection to use.) Remember that, by default, a create script will drop any existing tables before creating new ones, so don't do this on a database if you care about its current contents. If you elected to generate a create script for each object, you will need to be careful about the order in which you execute these files—you must create the tables first, since the keys, indexes, extended properties, and stored procedures all refer back to tables. If you generated a single create script for the whole database, it will create items in the correct order automatically.

Create scripts are useful for building a new database with the required schema from scratch, but they are of no use for modifying an existing database. As projects evolve, schema changes must be applied to the database nondestructively. For certain kinds of changes, it will be possible to use a create script—adding a new table for example. But for any change that modifies an existing object in the schema, you will need to use a change script instead.

Change scripts

Every time you modify a database using the visual database design tools described earlier in this chapter, Visual Studio .NET is able to generate a script containing the changes you made. The intended use of this feature is for you to start from a position in which your development server and production server both have the same schema. You will then make changes to the development server, saving those changes in change scripts. When you are ready to apply the changes to the production server, you can simply run the change scripts on that server. It will then have the same changes applied that you made to the development server.

 Visual Studio .NET will offer to create change scripts only if you have a Database project open. If you don't have a Database project open, you will not be prevented from making changes to the database, but no script file will be generated. (This is often the most convenient way to prototype a design—having Visual Studio .NET generate a change script for every little modification you make can be obtrusive in early experimental stages of development.) Because databases do not normally provide any way of retrieving a change log, you will not be able to recover this information later on, so be sure that you have a Database project open if you need change scripts. Alternatively, you can ask VS.NET to create a change script for you—if you are editing the table, the Diagram → Generate Change Script... item will create a change script even if you don't have a Database project open.

If you have a Database project open, you will be offered the chance to create a change script each time you save your changes to the database. For example, after adding a new column to a table and creating a relationship between that column and one in another table, selecting File → Save causes the dialog shown in Figure 5-31 to appear.

This dialog allows a change script to be created and shows the SQL that will be generated. This one contains an ALTER TABLE statement to add the new column. If you click on the Yes button, a normal Save File dialog will appear asking where you want to save the file. (By default, it will suggest the project's Change Scripts folder.)

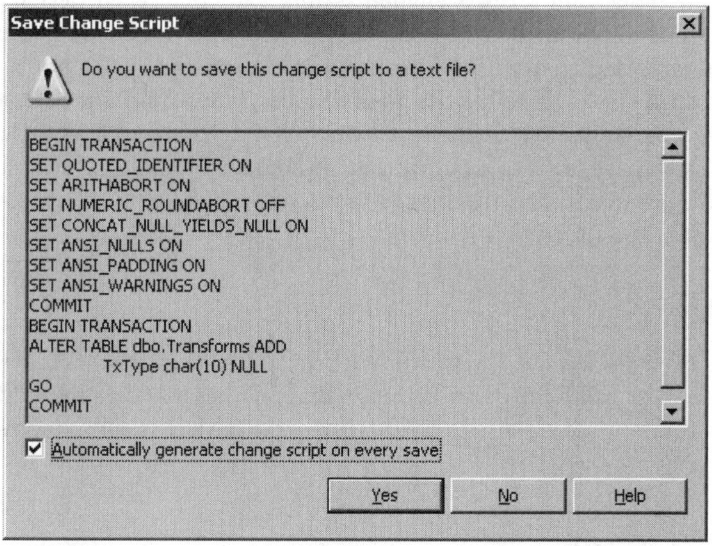

Save Change Script

Do you want to save this change script to a text file?

```
BEGIN TRANSACTION
SET QUOTED_IDENTIFIER ON
SET ARITHABORT ON
SET NUMERIC_ROUNDABORT OFF
SET CONCAT_NULL_YIELDS_NULL ON
SET ANSI_NULLS ON
SET ANSI_PADDING ON
SET ANSI_WARNINGS ON
COMMIT
BEGIN TRANSACTION
ALTER TABLE dbo.Transforms ADD
        TxType char(10) NULL
GO
COMMIT
```

☑ Automatically generate change script on every save

[Yes]   [No]   [Help]

Figure 5-31. Saving a change script

The default name for the change script will usually be the name of the item being changed. So, in this example, Visual Studio .NET suggested *Books.sql*. If you make a series of changes to the same table, you will need to store each set of changes in a separate script file. (A series of changes cannot be merged automatically into a single file.) Fortunately, if you use the same filename every time you save a change, Visual Studio .NET will add a number to the end of the file in order not to overwrite previous changes. So, if you save four changes with the name *Books.sql*, they will be saved into *Books.sql, Books1.sql, Books2.sql*, and *Books3.sql*. (It does not indicate that it is going to do this in the Save dialog—it always shows the name without the number.)

As with create scripts, change scripts just contain SQL statements. And again, you can execute them with the Run or Run On... items from their context menus in the Solution Explorer.

If you attempt to modify a database item that you do not have permission to change, you will not be allowed to save your change into the database. However, Visual Studio .NET will still be able to save these changes into a change script, even if you are not allowed to modify the database itself. You could use this feature to design the changes you want using the visual database design tools, generate a change script, and then submit that script to a DBA.

Unfortunately, you cannot open change scripts with the visual design tools—you will only be able to edit their text. For example, suppose you used the table designer to modify a table and then saved your changes to a change script but not the database. If you then closed the table designer window, you would not be able to reopen the table designer to show your modified view. When you open a table designer window, it will always show what is currently in the database and unfortunately cannot incorporate any work in progress stored in a script file. When you open a script file, you always get the SQL editor view.

Query Files

If you have a Database project, you can write a standalone query that is saved as a *.dtq* file. You edit these using the query and view designer described earlier in this chapter. This allows you to write a query in the designer and execute it without having to store it in the database.

Multiuser Issues

Databases are designed to support multiple users. This presents a potential problem for development teams when multiple developers may be making changes to the database. When you open a database object such as a table in a designer window, Visual Studio .NET does not lock it for exclusive access. Two users may therefore have the same object open for editing simultaneously. This will lead to a problem when the second user tries to save any changes.

Visual Studio .NET deals with this scenario by refusing to save the second user's changes. If it detects that the database object has been modified since editing began, it will not make any changes. The second user will therefore be obliged to reapply the changes. You should therefore save early and save often.

Databases and .NET Projects

Visual Studio .NET has special support for using databases in .NET projects. It can generate data adapters and type-safe datasets from database server metadata.

Data Adapters

A data adapter is an object that is able to retrieve data from and push updates back to a database. You can generate a data adapter by dragging a table, view, or stored procedure in the Server Explorer onto any design surface in a Visual Studio .NET project. A design surface is any design view that allows components to be dropped onto it. Windows Forms, Web Forms, and Web Services are all examples of design surfaces.

When you drag either a table or a view onto a design surface, Visual Studio .NET will add two items to its component tray: a database connection and a data adapter.

If the data source is a SQL Server, these will be of type `SqlConnection` and `SqlDataAdapter`, otherwise they will be `OledbConnection` and `OledbDataAdapter`.

Adapters contain four SQL statements: a `SELECT` for retrieving data, an `UPDATE` for changing data, an `INSERT` for adding data, and a `DELETE` for removing data. You can examine the command strings for these by selecting the data adapter in the component tray, expanding the relevant property in the Properties window. (The properties are called `SelectCommand`, `UpdateCommand`, `InsertCommand`, and `DeleteCommand`). Figure 5-32 shows the `CommandText` for the `SelectCommand` of a typical data adapter.

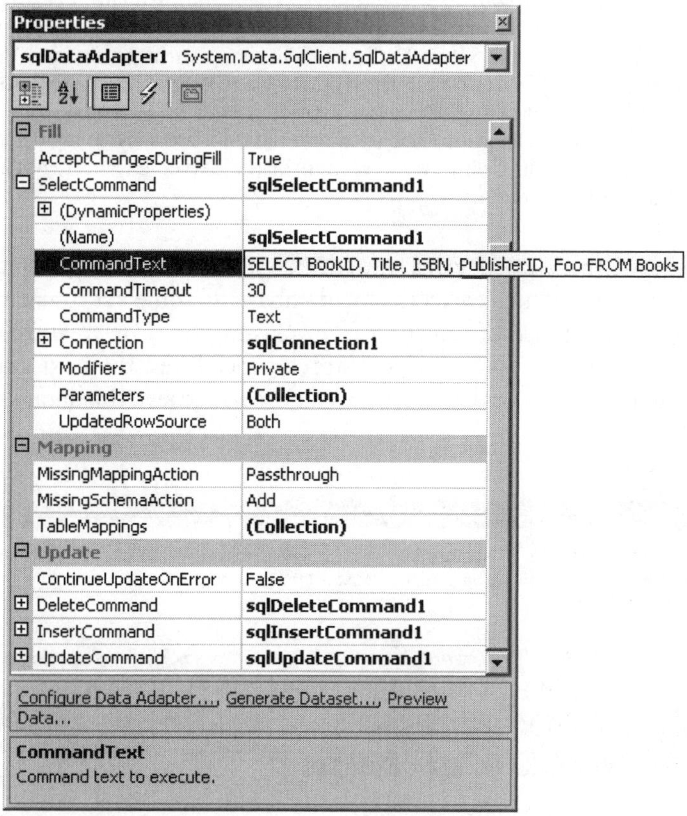

Figure 5-32. Data adapter properties

By default, a data adapter's SQL commands will use all of the columns in a table or view. However, you can change this by clicking on the Configure Data Adapter... verb in the adapter's properties (as shown at the bottom of Figure 5-32) or in its context menu. This displays the Data Adapter Configuration Wizard, which allows you to modify various aspects of the adapter. First, it will ask you which connection to use, which will default to the connection you used to create the adapter in the first place.

This wizard insists on having an appropriate data connection in your Server Explorer. You may not have such a connection—it depends on from where in the Server Explorer you dragged the table or view. If you originally dragged it from a server listed under the Data Connections item, then the wizard will show the connection from which it came. However, if you dragged it from under the Servers section (having expanded a machine node and found the database from its SQL Servers section), then you will encounter a problem. Although a connection object will have been added to your project when you first created the data adapter, there will not be a corresponding data connection in your Server Explorer. This is unfortunate, because the Data Adapter Configuration Wizard insists on having an appropriate connection in the Server Explorer. (This is rather inconsistent—Visual Studio .NET is quite capable of creating a new adapter without such a connection; it just refuses to let you edit it later.) If you plan to use this wizard, it is therefore best to create data adapters by dragging items from the Data Connections section of the Server Explorer, not from the Servers section.

The next page of the wizard gives you the choice of using SQL statements (the default) or stored procedures to access the database. If you elect to use stored procedures, you have the choice of selecting from existing ones or creating new ones. If you choose to use SQL or to create new stored procedures, the next page will show the SELECT statement that the data adapter will use to retrieve the data, as Figure 5-33 shows.

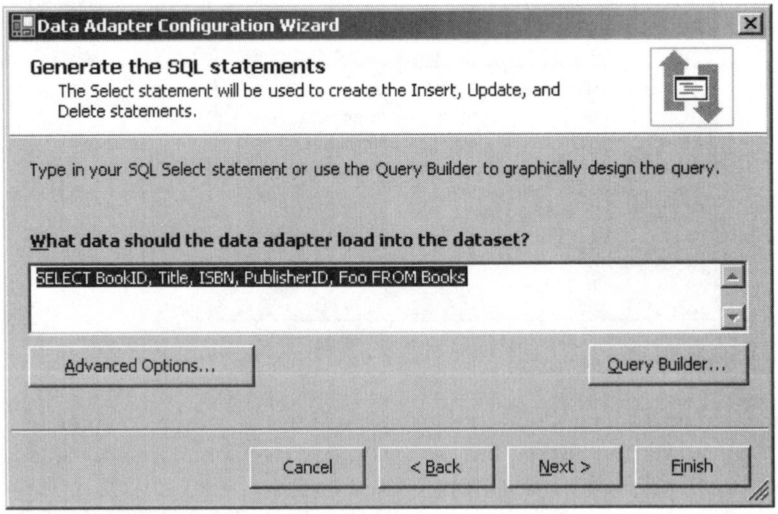

Figure 5-33. Specifying SQL for a data adapter

You can supply your own SQL in this dialog. Alternatively, you can click the Query Builder... button. This will show a dialog containing a query and view designer (as described earlier). You can edit the diagram and grid panes just as you would for any other query, and the SQL pane will show you what SQL will be generated.

Whether you use the default SQL, enter your own SQL, or use the query builder to construct a SELECT statement, by default, Visual Studio .NET will build matching INSERT, UPDATE, and DELETE statements. You can disable this or modify the way they are generated by clicking on the Advanced Options... button. This displays the Advanced SQL Generation Options dialog, which is shown in Figure 5-34.

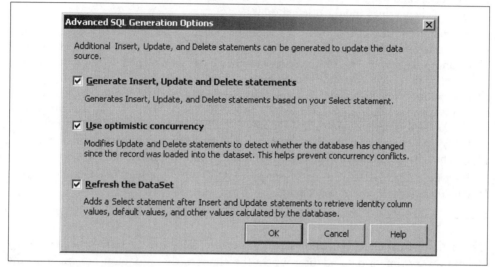

Figure 5-34. SQL generation options

You can disable the generation of INSERT, UPDATE, and DELETE statements by clearing the first checkbox. If you leave it checked, you can choose whether to use the optimistic concurrency option (see sidebar). If you have your own method of dealing with multiple users trying to update the same rows, such as a pessimistic locking strategy or an automatic merging policy, you would typically disable this default behavior.

 If you write your own SQL instead of using the query builder, and you enable automatic generation of INSERT, UPDATE, and DELETE statements, be aware that overly complex SQL will defeat this automatic generation. If Visual Studio .NET is unable to understand your SELECT statement, the wizard will fail. In this case, you should simply abandon the wizard and write all four SQL statements yourself.

Datasets, Adapters, and Optimistic Concurrency

Data adapters are designed to be used in conjunction with a dataset. Typically, some rows are read into a dataset using a data adapter's SELECT statement. (This is done with the adapter's Fill method.) These rows may then be modified by user input. (For example, input fields in a Windows Forms application might modify the dataset using data binding.)

At some point, the program may attempt to push changes back to the database, using the data adapter's Update method. The adapter will obtain a list of changed rows from the dataset and will also retrieve the original values for these rows. (The dataset stores both the new values and the original values.)

By default, the data adapter will use the original values as parameters to the generated UPDATE and DELETE statements—these include a WHERE clause allowing all of the current column values to be checked, making sure they have not changed. If a row has been modified in the database in between being read into the dataset and the modified version being written back out (i.e., some other database client has changed the row since it was read into the dataset), the UPDATE or DELETE will do nothing. The data adapter checks the row update count and will notify the program of any rows that were not correctly updated because they have changed. The program should then notify the user that her changes could not be applied and provide some kind of remedial action.

Pragmatic ADO.NET (Addison-Wesley) and *ADO.NET in a Nutshell* (O'Reilly) discuss these techniques in more detail.

The dialog's final checkbox allows you to disable the standard refresh behavior—by default, every time a data adapter writes the changes that a dataset has made to the database, it will run a SELECT statement to retrieve any autogenerated values for the row. This is useful for tables that have an identity column generated by the database. Autoincrement identity columns can pose a problem for a disconnected data model such as that used by the dataset if you allow end users to add new rows, because a new row's primary key won't be known until the new rows are applied to the underlying database. This can be particularly tricky if your dataset contains multiple related tables and you want to create multiple related rows—in order for the relationship between two newly created rows to be established, the foreign key in one row must match the primary key in the other row. The problem is that, if the primary key is to be autogenerated by the database, the client software cannot know what its value will be until after it executes an INSERT. While this could be solved by adding the two rows in two separate steps, there is an alternative solution. The dataset can be configured to allocate numbers in a range that will be different from what the database will use. (Using a seed and increment of -1 is the usual trick for ensuring this.) When the data adapter performs the updates, it will then retrieve the real identity allocated for the primary key and will then apply that change to the dataset. Since the dataset supports cascading updates, this will change the foreign key in the other table so that, when that row is written out, it will be correctly associated with the newly added row in the other table. (Of course, this still requires two round-trips to the database, but it means that most of the details are dealt with for you.)

 If you run through the Configure Data Adapter Wizard a second time, it forgets any settings you may have made in the Advanced SQL Generation Options dialog the previous time round. For example, if you disabled generation of INSERT, UPDATE, and DELETE operations, they will be reenabled when you run the wizard again. So if you don't want the defaults, you have to remember to click the Advanced Options... button every time.

If you elected to use existing stored procedures instead of building new SQL statements or new stored procedures, you will be shown a different dialog from the one in Figure 5-33. Instead, you will see the one in Figure 5-35.

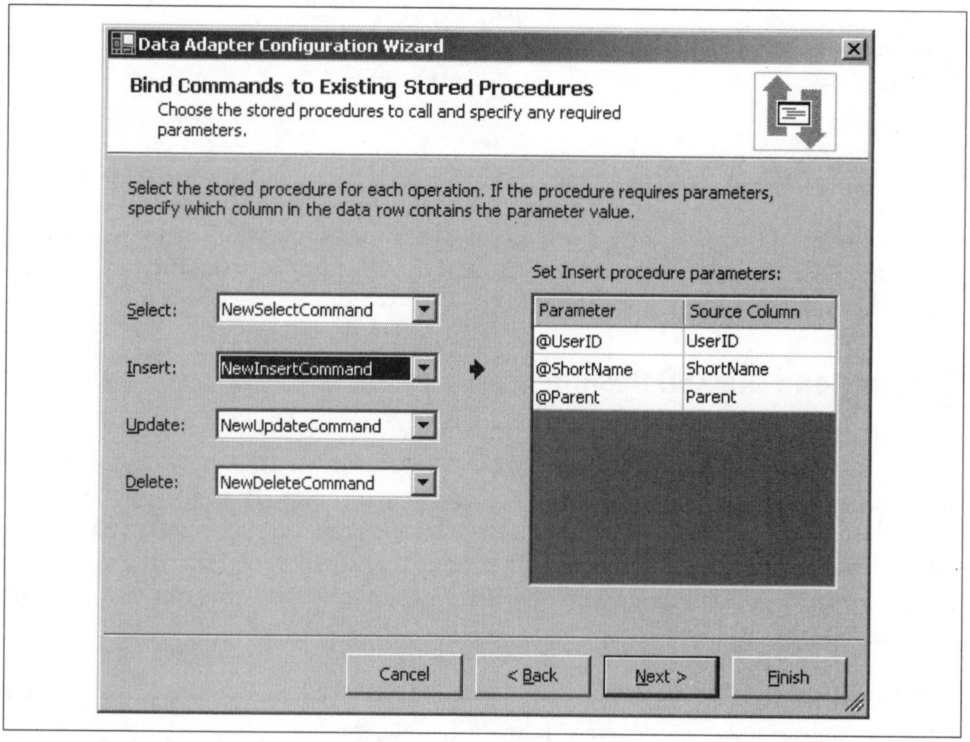

Figure 5-35. Choosing stored procedures for a dataset

The stored procedures can be selected from the drop-down listboxes. Stored procedures typically take parameters. For example, you will need to pass at least one parameter to the DELETE procedure to identify the row to be removed. The UPDATE operation will also require parameters for the values being changed as well as for row identification. Likewise, the INSERT operation will need the column values for the row to be created (although it doesn't need a row identifier). The appropriate values for all of these values will typically be columns in the dataset. Visual Studio .NET can populate such parameters for you—if the INSERT, UPDATE, or DELETE procedures require one or more parameters and those parameters correspond to columns returned by the SELECT procedure, you can set up the association in the table on the right of the dialog.

The code for the stored procedure that performs the INSERT is shown in Example 5-3. This procedure is also selected in Figure 5-35. As you can see, the dialog shows the parameters that the procedure requires as well as which columns in the dataset will be passed for each of those parameters.

Example 5-3. INSERT stored procedure

```
CREATE PROCEDURE dbo.NewInsertCommand
(
@UserID nvarchar(50),
@ShortName nvarchar(100),
@Parent int
)
AS
SET NOCOUNT OFF;
INSERT INTO Mailboxes(UserID, ShortName, Parent) VALUES (@UserID, @ShortName, @Parent);
```

The final page of the wizard simply tells you that it has successfully generated all the necessary SQL. You simply need to click the Finish button to write the settings into the data adapter.

Datasets and the XSD Designer

You can use a data adapter with a generic dataset. However, Visual Studio .NET is able to generate type-safe datasets—these are classes derived from the standard DataSet class that add properties specific to particular tables. They also define classes derived from DataTable for each table in the dataset, providing strongly typed properties for each column in the table. This means that instead of retrieving data with generic properties using code such as that in Example 5-4, you can use strongly typed access like Example 5-5 shows.

Example 5-4. Generic dataset access

```
int eID = int.Parse(ds.Tables["Orders"].Rows[0]["EmployeeID"]);
```

Example 5-5. Strongly typed dataset access

```
int eID = ds.Orders[0].EmployeeID;
```

As well as being simpler, the code in Example 5-5 offers the added advantage of detecting certain programming errors at compile time. If you get the name of a table or column wrong, the compiler will complain. With Example 5-4, you would not discover such an error until runtime. Furthermore, with strongly typed datasets, the table and column names will be available through IntelliSense in the code editor. (Of course, strongly typed datasets are less likely to be of use when you need to be able to adapt to a variety of different schemas, such as automated reporting software.)

You can generate a strongly typed dataset by selecting Generate Dataset... from a data adapter's context menu or Properties window. This will show the Generate Dataset dialog, Figure 5-36. This lets you choose between modifying an existing strongly typed dataset (with the Existing radio button) or creating a new one. In either case, you can choose which tables will be represented in the dataset from the list in the middle of the dialog. There will be one table shown for each data adapter that you have created. The "Add this dataset to the designer" option will add a new item to your component tray using the newly created dataset type.

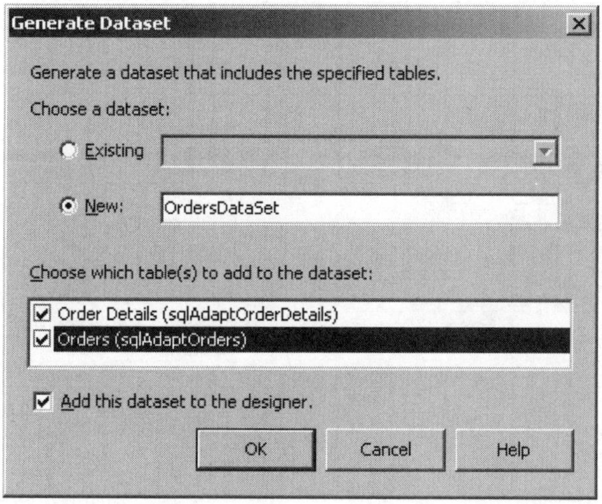

```
Generate Dataset                                    [X]

Generate a dataset that includes the specified tables.

Choose a dataset:

  ○ Existing  [                              ▼]

  ● New:      [OrdersDataSet                  ]

Choose which table(s) to add to the dataset:

  ☑ Order Details (sqlAdaptOrderDetails)
  ☑ Orders (sqlAdaptOrders)

  ☑ Add this dataset to the designer.

          [   OK   ]  [ Cancel ]  [  Help  ]
```

Figure 5-36. Generating a strongly typed dataset

When you click on OK, two new files will be added to your project. (Or two existing ones will be modified if you chose to change a dataset you created earlier.) Figure 5-37 shows a typical pair of files—*OrdersDataSet.xsd* and *OrdersDataSet.cs*.

> By default, the Solution Explorer will hide the *.cs* file and show only the *.xsd*. You must select the Show All Files button to see both. Visual Studio .NET hides the *.cs* file because it will be regenerated every time you modify the *.xsd* file.

Figure 5-37. A strongly typed dataset in the Solution Explorer

The *.xsd* file is an XML Schema Definition. It contains type definitions for the tables in the dataset. The *.cs* file contains the generated strongly typed dataset class. You can edit the *.xsd* file either as raw XML or using Visual Studio .NET's XML Schema editor. Figure 5-38 shows the editor. You can switch between schema and XML mode using the buttons at the bottom of the view.

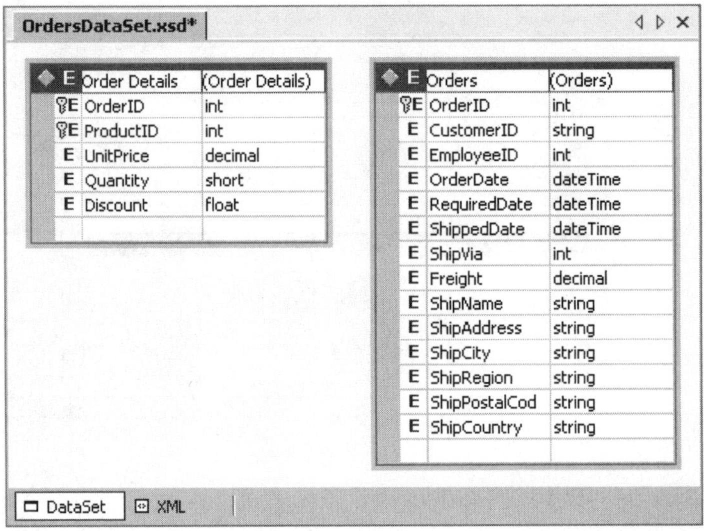

Figure 5-38. An XML Schema Definition

This particular schema shows the Order Details and Orders tables from the Northwind sample database. These two tables are related on their OrderID columns. Unfortunately, the dataset generator does not detect this. (It retrieves the type information from the data adapters, not from the database, and the adapters do not preserve relational information.) You must add relations by hand if you need the dataset to be aware of them. To do this, bring up the context menu on the primary key for which you wish to add a relation (for example, the OrderID column in the Orders table). From the menu's Add submenu, select the New Relation... item. This will show the Edit Relation dialog, Figure 5-39.

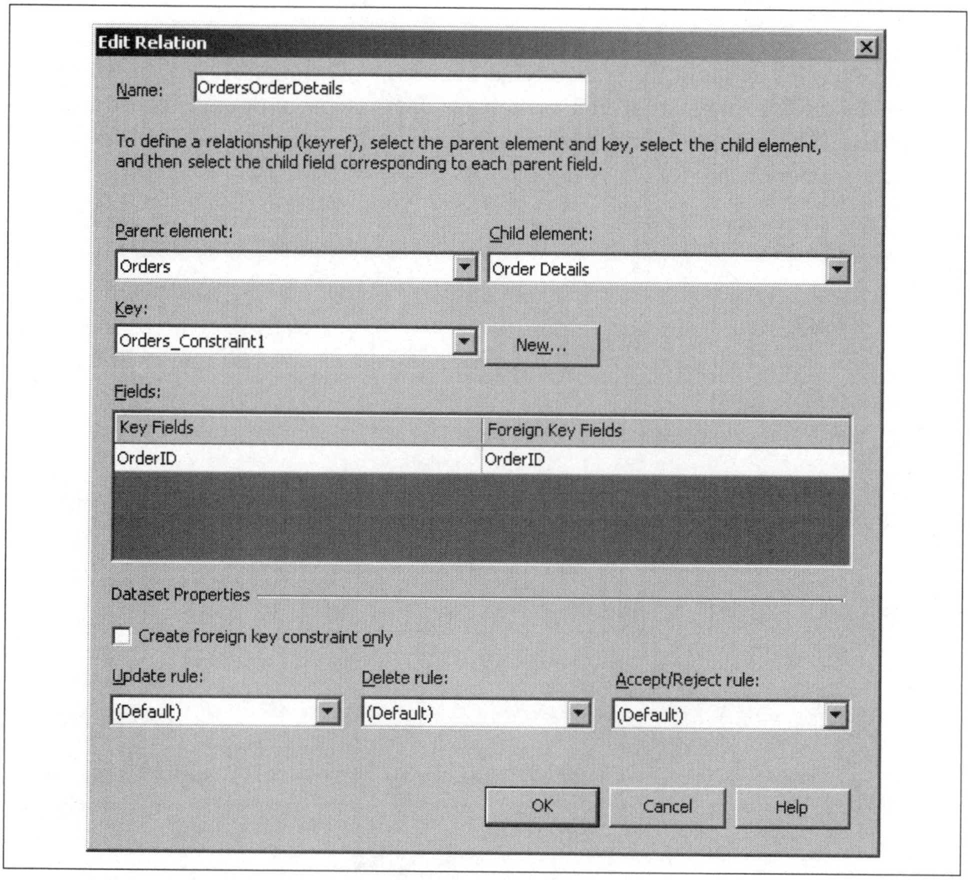

Edit Relation   [x]

Name: OrdersOrderDetails

To define a relationship (keyref), select the parent element and key, select the child element, and then select the child field corresponding to each parent field.

Parent element:

Orders   [▼]

Child element:

Order Details   [▼]

Key:

Orders_Constraint1   [▼]   New...

Fields:

Key Fields	Foreign Key Fields
OrderID	OrderID

Dataset Properties

[ ] Create foreign key constraint only

Update rule:

(Default)   [▼]

Delete rule:

(Default)   [▼]

Accept/Reject rule:

(Default)   [▼]

OK   Cancel   Help

Figure 5-39. Editing a relation in an XML Schema

You can add new table definitions to an existing schema by dragging them from the Server Explorer onto the schema designer. This also works for views and stored procedures.

You should set the parent element to be the table containing the primary key, and the child element to be the table containing the foreign key. (The dialog talks of elements instead of tables because it has an XML-centric view of the world.) Having selected the tables for which you wish to add a relation you must select the related keys in the Fields list. When you click OK, the schema view will now show a connector between the two tables, representing the relation. You will now be able to use this dataset in data binding scenarios that exploit relational datasets, such as master/details views.

Conclusion

Visual Studio .NET provides sophisticated visual tools for working with databases. You can examine and edit the structure and contents of databases. Database projects are able to track changes that you make to a database schema and record these in script files. .NET projects also get extensive support for automatic generation of queries and wrapper classes for accessing databases.

CHAPTER 6

Setup and Deployment

Once you have created and perfected your application, you will no doubt be keen to get it into the hands of your users. Unfortunately, putting a program onto a computer in such a way that it will run successfully can be a nontrivial process. There may be many files to copy, potentially to several different locations. Even if your application consists of just one file, you will need to check that suitable versions of the libraries it requires have been installed, and you may want to provide the option to add an entry to the Start menu or the Desktop. In addition to file copies, system configuration changes may be required.

Visual Studio .NET's Setup projects make light work of the installation process. Setup projects create installers that can copy all of your application's files onto the target computer, making sure that the right libraries are available. They can perform any necessary configuration, such as adding registry entries or creating virtual directories on IIS. They also provide an installation user interface that can collect configuration information from the user if required. It integrates with Windows' Add/Remove Programs feature, providing automatic support for uninstallation.

Windows Installer

Visual Studio .NET relies on Windows Installer for the underlying installation technology—a Setup project simply produces a Windows Installer file. Windows Installer provides a standard way of dealing with the installation issues that most applications encounter, such as dependency management, uninstallation, and system configuration. Windows Installer has been built into Windows since Windows 2000 and Windows Me, but it can also be retrofitted to older versions of the OS back as far as Windows NT 4.0 and Windows 95.

When you build a Setup project, Visual Studio .NET creates an installer file containing all of the components required for the application to run, and any installation details such as registry settings. When this file is run, a standard Windows Installer user interface such as the one shown in Figure 6-1 will appear.

Figure 6-1. A typical Windows Installer

You do not usually need to write any code for a Setup project. Windows Installer uses a declarative approach—it examines the contents of the installer file and works out what steps are required to complete the installation. For example, Windows Installer detects whether any of the required components have already been installed (which would often be the case for any libraries that your application depends on) and makes sure it copies only the files it needs to. Windows Installer deals with issues such as component version conflict resolution for you. You may, of course, add bits of code (called custom actions) when the built-in installer facilities do not meet all of your requirements, but for many projects, you will be able to create an installer without writing any code at all.

As well as providing a basic user interface and installing files, a Windows Installer file can configure the registry, create and configure IIS applications, and register new file types with the system. You can always write installation code if you have special nonstandard installation steps to perform, but for many applications, you will never need to do this.

> Visual Studio .NET Setup projects provide a level of abstraction above the Windows Installer technology. This is useful because it simplifies the creation of installers quite considerably. However, it does mean that there are certain restrictions on how what can be achieved. (For example, your installer's user interface can use only the templates supplied by Visual Studio .NET—you cannot design your own.) If you have to build a particularly complex installer, you may need to consider using either the Windows Installer SDK or third-party installer builders, such as InstallShield or Wise.

There are two kinds of Windows Installer files. The type you choose to create will depend on whether you have written an application or a component that will be used in another application. Applications are represented with *.msi* files, or as they are sometimes somewhat confusingly called, *Windows installers*. Components are represented with *.msm* files, also known as *merge modules*.

Merge Modules

Merge modules represent a body of code likely to be used by more than one application. They are the reusable black boxes of the installer world. Merge modules are never installed in isolation—they are installed as a result of being contained inside the *.msi* file of an application that needs the component.

If you have created a shared component such as an ActiveX control, a Windows Forms Control, or a .NET class library, this would be an ideal candidate for a merge module. Such components are made to be reused and would usually be installed only as a result of installing an application that uses them. You should create a merge module for any such component. This will make it simple for whomever writes the installer for an application that uses your code to ensure that your component is installed correctly—he will just include the merge module in his installer.

 Merge modules vary in size and complexity. Some contain just a single DLL. For example, Microsoft provides a merge module for GDI+, which installs only the single redistributable *GDIPLUS.DLL* file. Others can contain tens or hundreds of files—for example, *dotnetfxredist_x86_enu.msm* contains more than 200 files.

The main purpose that merge modules serve is to make sure that shared components are installed correctly. Without merge modules, application *.msi* files could just contain all of the files that make up the components they are using. (For example, an application might copy *GDIPLUS.DLL* directly into the Windows system directory as part of its installation procedure.) However, if the components in question have installation requirements of their own, such as registry configuration or custom installation steps, it becomes harder for an application installer to install the component correctly. But since a merge module can contain its own complete set of installation requirements, an application *.msi* can simply contain a copy of the merge module and rest assured that Windows Installer will perform all of the necessary steps.

Also, because all merge modules have unique identifiers, Windows Installer is able to recognize when an application depends on a component that has already been installed. This allows it to avoid trying to install components that are already present. Furthermore, it allows Windows to maintain an accurate list of which components are being used by which applications. This prevents the uninstallation of an application from removing shared components that are still in use. It also makes it possible for an application to be repaired—if a file required by a program has been deleted (e.g., the user inadvertently removed a directory), Windows Installer can detect that the necessary files are missing and put them back.

This technology also makes it much easier for component developers to make sure that consistent sets of files are installed. Without merge modules, an application could easily ship a subset of the files that constitute a component. And this could easily result in a machine having a mixture of files from multiple different versions of the component, which would be likely to cause problems. But if components are always installed as merge modules, this cannot happen, since the suite will always be installed as a single unit.

 Windows XP introduced the capability of having multiple versions of a shared component installed simultaneously. This is known as *side-by-side* installation. For this to work, it is particularly important for the OS to know which DLLs belong to which versions and which applications are using which versions. The use of merge modules makes it easier for Windows to detect this.

So if you are using a shared component, always include its corresponding merge module in your Setup project. If you are writing a shared component, you should create a merge module for that component. You choose between creating an application installer (*.msi*) and a merge module (*.msm*) by selecting the appropriate Setup project type.

Setup Project Types

A Setup project should be in the same Visual Studio .NET solution as the project whose output it will be installing. New Setup projects are added to a solution in the same way as any other project. (Either use File → Add Project → New Project... or use the solution item's context menu in the Solution Explorer, choosing Add → New Project....) There are several different project types in the Add New Project dialog's Setup and Deployment Projects category, as Figure 6-2 shows.

 When you add a new Setup project, the project will not be added to any of your configurations by default. This is because Setup projects take a while to build—since the output of a Setup project is usually needed only toward the end of the development cycle, it would be a waste of time to wait for an *.msi* file to be built every time.

You can get Visual Studio .NET to build your project either by adding it to one of your configurations or by selecting Build from the project's context menu in the Solution Explorer.

All Setup projects work in much the same way. The main differences are related to the way in which the component will actually be deployed. The role of each project type is shown in Table 6-1.

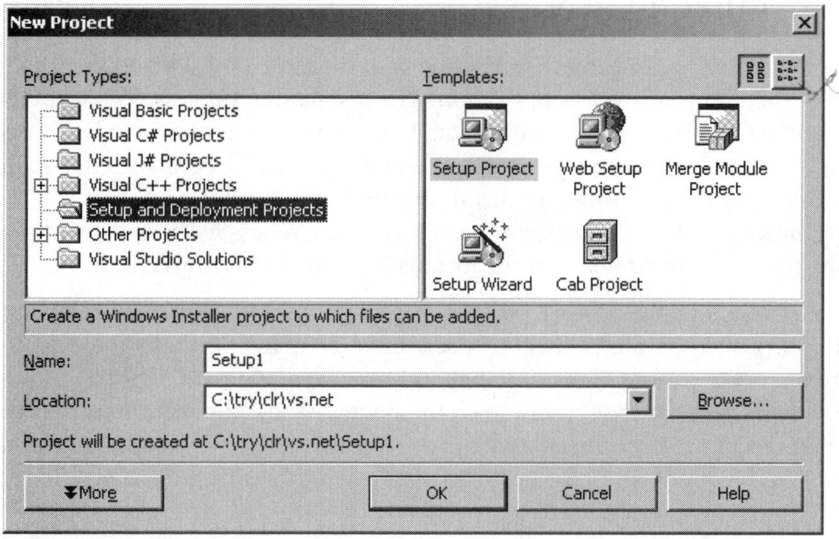

Figure 6-2. Setup project types

Table 6-1. Setup project roles

Project type	When to use
Setup Project	For applications that will be installed on the end user's computer.
Web Setup Project	For applications that will be installed on or deployed through a web server.
Merge Module Project	For components that will be used by other applications. (Merge modules can be imported into either normal applications or web applications.)
Cab Project	For legacy component installation through a web browser. (Typically used for ActiveX controls.)
Setup Wizard	To create one of the four other project types, according to the selection made in the wizard.

Although it is usually fairly obvious which kind of Setup project you require, there is one exception. If you were writing a .NET Windows Forms application, you would expect to create a normal Setup project, since the application runs on the end user's computer. And usually you would be right. However, .NET allows such applications to be deployed via a web server. In this case, although the code ultimately ends up running on end users' machines, the installation step is done on the web server. So if you plan to deploy your Windows Forms applications via a web server, you need a Web Setup project.

Cab projects are provided only for support of legacy scenarios. Cab files do not use Windows Installer, so there is a great deal less flexibility about how the target machine will be configured. You should use one of the other project types unless backward compatibility requirements force you to use a Cab file. Cab projects are discussed in more detail toward the end of the chapter.

The Installation Process

When building a Setup project, it is important to know how Windows Installer will operate when it installs your application. The installation process goes through three phases. First, any required information is collected from the user—this includes details such as the directory in which the application will be installed. Second, the necessary steps are performed to install the application, which includes file copying, adding registry entries, and performing any other necessary system configuration. Finally, the user is informed that the installation process is complete.

This relatively straightforward process is complicated by two requirements. First, applications must be uninstallable—users must be able to go into the Add/Remove Programs section of the Control Panel and remove a program. The Windows Logo requirements demand that all of the components that an application installs must be removed. Second, if the installation process fails halfway through, the installer is required to back out any changes it made, leaving the machine in the state it was before the installation was started.

Fortunately, Windows Installer handles uninstallation and rollback for all standard installation operations. If you add custom installation code, you must provide support for backing out changes, but for normal installation steps such as file copying, component registration, and registry editing, everything is done for you.

Views

Visual Studio .NET presents all the Microsoft Installer Setup project types (i.e., Setup projects other than Cab projects) in the same way: it provides several views onto the project, letting you explore and configure the various aspects of your installation. You can open any of these views by selecting the appropriate item from the project context menu's View submenu, shown in Figure 6-3. These can also be selected from the main menu's View → Editor submenu. (This submenu will be present on the View menu only if you select an item from a Setup project in the Solution Explorer.) Visual Studio .NET will also display buttons corresponding to each of these menu items at the top of the Solution Explorer when you select a Setup project.

The File System view lets you choose which files are to be installed as part of your application. The Registry view allows registry keys and values to be created on installation. You can register file extensions and MIME types for your application with the File Types view. The User Interface view allows you to select and customize the dialogs that will be shown during your application's installation. If you need to perform any operations not supported by Windows Installer, you can supply code for these under Custom Actions. Finally, the Launch Conditions view lets you specify prerequisites for the system. (For example, you might make your application refuse to install on certain OS versions.)

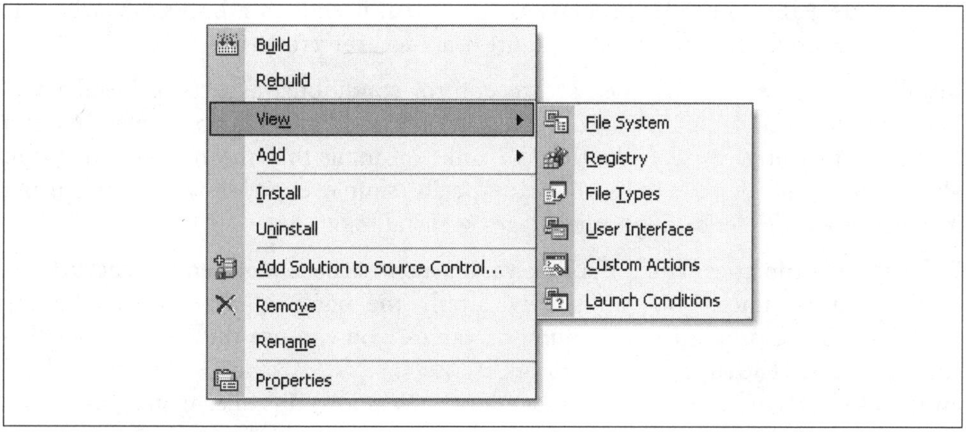

Figure 6-3. Setup project views

Not all views are available on all project types. The User Interface view is not present on Merge Module projects. Cab projects present no views at all.

Project Properties and Conditions

It is often necessary for one stage of the installation process to pass information to a later stage. For example, the data collected from the user prior to installation usually needs to be available to the installation phase. To enable information to be exchanged, Windows Installer allows properties to be created and read. Some of these properties, such as Manufacturer and ProductName are set in the Properties window for the project. Others are determined at installation time—if you add a page to the installation user interface, all user input will be stored in named properties. For example, the Checkbox (A) page stores the user's selections in properties called CHECKBOXA1, CHECKBOXA2, CHECKBOXA3 and CHECKBOXA4.

There is potential for ambiguity when talking about "properties." These properties made available by Windows Installer at install-time are distinct from the properties displayed in Visual Studio .NET's Properties windows.

To avoid ambiguity, the install-time properties will henceforth be referred to as *installer properties*.

These installer properties can be used in most places where a text string is required. If you enclose the installer property name in square brackets within a string, the value will be substituted at runtime. For example, the default installation location in a Windows application Setup project is [ProgramFilesFolder][Manufacturer]\ [ProductName]. This will be expanded at runtime to the real path. (When the

`ProgramFilesFolder` installer property is expanded, it ends in a backslash, which is why there is no slash between that and the `Manufacturer` property.)

Installer properties can also be used to control conditional aspects of installation. Most of the installable items (files, registry keys, custom actions, etc.) have a `Condition` property. By default, this is blank, meaning that the relevant item will always be installed. However, you can specify simple expressions in here, using installer properties set during earlier stages of installation.

For installer properties with a Boolean value, such as those representing checkboxes in the user interface, you can simply supply the name of the property as the `Condition`. If the properties have numeric values, you can use the normal comparison operators. (The supported operators are >, >=, <, <=, ==, and !=.) For example, if an item's `Condition` was set to `VersionNT>=501`, Windows Installer would install the item only on Windows XP or later versions of Windows. You can also compare string values with these operators.

User Interface View

Setup projects automatically provide a user interface for your installation. It follows the normal Windows Installer style in which a dialog presents a series of pages that guide the user through the installation process. The User Interface view lets you edit this user interface.

 Merge Module projects do not provide the User Interface view. This is because merge modules are designed to be merged into application installer files, and it is up to the application to decide what user interface to present.

For simple applications, you will not need to edit the user interface at all. Whether you use the Setup Wizard or simply create a blank Setup project, Visual Studio .NET will add a basic user interface for you. The default user interface just provides an introduction screen, asks where to install the application, and then gets on with it. It uses installer properties to put the name of your application where it is required and otherwise uses generic text so you will not even need to modify any of the default strings. However, if the standard boilerplate is not to your liking or if you want to collect information from the user during the installation process, you will need to modify the user interface.

As Figure 6-4 shows, the User Interface view consists of a pair of trees. The Install tree represents the sequence of pages that will be displayed when installing the application. The Administrative Install tree shows the sequence that will be used if an administrator installs the application onto a network share (see sidebar).

The installation UI is divided into three phases—Start, Progress, and End. These map directly onto the installation phases discussed earlier. Each item within a phase

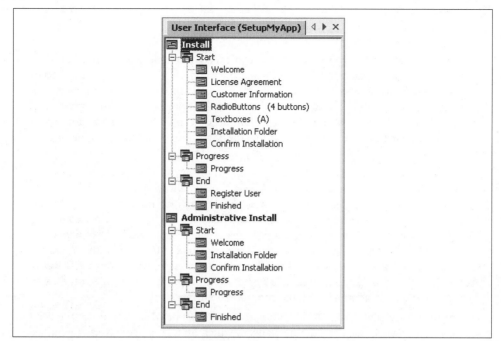

Figure 6-4. User Interface view

represents a single page in the user interface. You cannot add or delete phases—you can only add or remove pages from them.

The Start phase contains pages that will be displayed before anything is done to the target computer. This phase is used for presenting information to and gathering data from the user. The default settings display three pages in this phase. The first page, Welcome, is usually used to provide a short description of what will be installed, along with a copyright warning. The second page, Installation Folder, asks the user which folder the program files should be copied into. The third page, Confirm Installation, informs the user that installation is about to begin and offers one last chance to cancel the installation.

The Progress phase contains just one page, Progress. This will be displayed while the various installation steps such as file copying and registry configuration are performed. It shows a progress bar indicating roughly how far through the process the installer is. This gives users something marginally more interesting than a blank window to watch and provides an approximate idea of how much longer the installation is likely to take. You should not attempt to add any extra user interface pages to the Progress phase—it should contain just the Progress page. (The installer has no way of using more than one page in the Progress phase—it displays the Progress page when installation is in progress, and automatically moves on to the end phase once installation is complete.)

Administrative Installation

Windows Installer allows applications to be installed onto a network share. This does not install the application in such a way that it can be run directly—it simply means that users with access to this share can then install the application on their own machines. This is mainly useful for large and complex applications that have optional features—if the user does not elect to install an option at first, the feature can be installed on demand from the shared installation, without prompting for the original installation media.

Administrative installation makes the most sense for applications that use the Windows Installer "install on demand" technology. This allows partial installations of applications without having to sacrifice functionality. For example, most components of Microsoft Office can be configured to be installed the first time they are used instead of being installed up front. If you attempt to use a feature that you had not previously used, (e.g., you might be using the clip art browser for the first time), the Windows Installer will be invoked dynamically. If you installed the program from a CD-ROM, you will be prompted for the original disks, but if the program was installed off the network, it will download and install the component automatically.

Unfortunately, Visual Studio .NET Setup projects do not provide support for the Windows Installer install-on-demand mechanism, which limits the usefulness of administrative installs. They are supported, but they provide no advantages over simply making the *.msi* file available on a network share. Administrative installs are usually useful only for more complex installers that support install on demand. Such installers cannot be built with a Visual Studio .NET Setup project—they can only be created using the Windows Installer SDK or third-party tools such as InstallShield or Wise.

An administrative install is invoked by running Windows Installer from the command line, using `msiexec /a App.msi`.

You will not normally need to change the administrative installation user interface, because all that is required is the installation location. All other information will be collected as individual users install the application.

The End phase contains pages that will be shown after the installation is complete. By default, this contains just the Finished page, which informs the user that installation has completed successfully. If your application has an online registration system, you might add an extra page here to support it.

UI Pages

Each page in the installation process is represented in the User Interface view by a node under one of the three phases. Visual Studio .NET does not let you view the pages as they will appear—all editing is done through the Properties window for each page. If you wish to see how the pages will appear, you must build the Setup project and run the *.msi* file itself.

If you select Add Dialog from the context menu of either of the Start nodes in the User Interface view, the Add Dialog dialog, shown in Figure 6-5, will be displayed. You can add dialogs only from the list offered—you cannot design your own pages. (Visual Studio .NET does not provide a tool for creating the appropriate resources, it just supplies a number of prebuilt dialogs. If you want to design your own, you will need to use a more advanced tool such as the Windows Installer SDK, Wise, or InstallShield.)

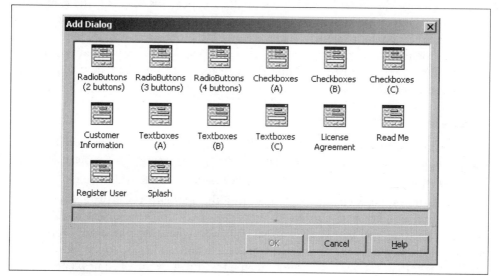

Figure 6-5. Adding a dialog

Most of these dialogs are concerned with getting user input—RadioButtons and Checkboxes pages allow choices to be made, while the Customer Information and Textboxes pages allow strings to be entered. The Register User page allows you to support installation-time registration. There are also special pages for displaying a splash screen, a license agreement, and a Read Me file.

 You can add any particular kind of dialog to a project only once. (The Add Dialog dialog will not offer you pages of a type you are already using.) So you cannot have, for example, two pages with four radio buttons. This is why there are three versions of the text box and checkbox pages—you can have up to three of each by using the (A), (B), and (C) forms.

The text shown on each of the pages is edited through the Properties window. There is only one property common to all page types, and that is the BannerBitmap. You may use this to replace the default bitmap that appears at the top right of the dialog during installation. If you change this on one dialog, Microsoft recommends that you change it on all dialogs, in order for the same picture to be displayed throughout installation.

The banner bitmap should be 500 pixels wide and 70 pixels high. You may make it narrower if you want only a small picture, but if you make it less high, it will be scaled to fit, degrading the quality of the image. Be aware that up to the first 420 pixels may be covered by the banner text, so if you use this region, make sure it is designed to look right when text is drawn over it.

You can change the order in which the dialogs appear by dragging them into the required position in the view. You can also move them up or down one position at a time using their context menus. Visual Studio .NET does not provide direct visual editing of the pages—if you want to see what they will look like, you have to run the installer. Pages are edited by selecting them in the User Interface view and editing their properties in the Properties panel.

Welcome page

This page introduces the user to the installation process for an application by showing a welcome message along with a short copyright warning. This either should be the first page shown or should follow the Splash page where present.

Figure 6-1 shows the Welcome page, featuring the standard boilerplate. If you want to change this text, you can use the page's two properties, WelcomeText and CopyrightWarning. You can change these strings to whatever text is appropriate for your application within the limits of the space available. The copyright warning cannot be longer than six lines, and the welcome text must fit into 11 lines. (Visual Studio .NET will not prevent you from entering too much text, it will simply be truncated at runtime to fit the space available.)

The default WelcomeText uses the ProductName installer property to insert the name of your product into the text. This installer property can be set by selecting the Setup project in the Solution Explorer and modifying its ProductName property in the Properties window. By default, it will be whatever name you gave the Setup project.

You cannot change the banner text at all—it will always say "Welcome to the [ProductName] Setup Wizard."

Installation Folder page

This page allows the user to choose the folder in which the application's files will be installed. (This is used only with normal Windows applications. Web applications use the Installation Address page instead.)

This page only has one property: BannerBitmap. The content and text are fixed, except in that the name of your application will be substituted in a couple of places, as Figure 6-6 shows.

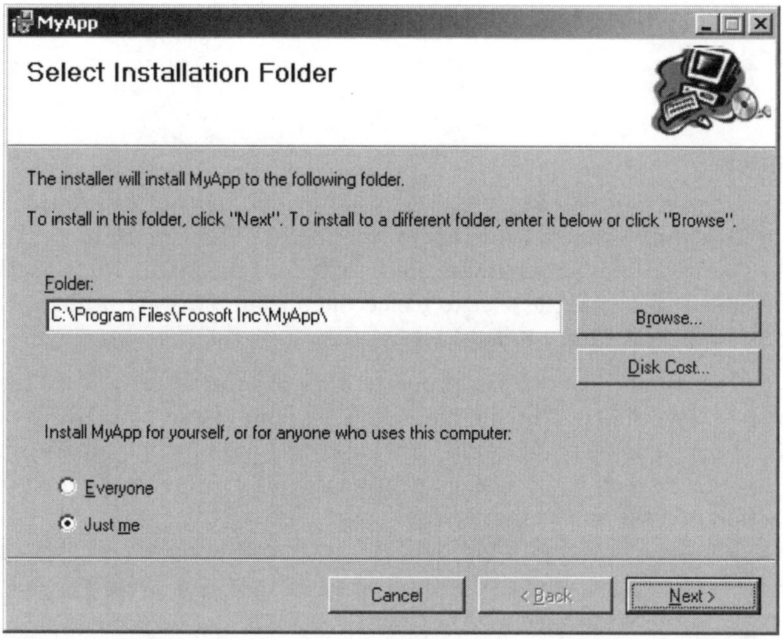

Figure 6-6. The Installation Folder page

If the installing user is an administrator, Windows Installer will allow the application to be installed for either all users or just the installing user. This allows Start menu shortcuts to be placed in the All Users folder, making the application accessible to all users on the machine. When users who are not in the Administrators group install the application, the bottom part of this page will simply be blank.

Installation Address page

This page should be present in any web application installer. (Normal applications use the Installation Folder page instead.) It allows a virtual directory and port number to be chosen for the application.

As with the Installation Folder page, the Installation Address page has only one property: BannerBitmap. The rest of the page's form and content are nonnegotiable.

Confirm Installation page

This page informs the user that the installation is about to proceed and provides a last opportunity to cancel. This page supports only the BannerBitmap property. The banner text will always be "Confirm Installation." The body text will always be:

> The installer is ready to install [ProductName] on your computer.
>
> Click "Next" to start the installation.

This should always be the final item in the Start phase.

Progress page

The Progress page will be displayed while the various steps of installation are performed. It displays a progress bar to give a rough idea of how much longer the install will take. The Back and Next buttons are disabled on this page. The Cancel button remains enabled, allowing the user to cancel the install partway through. Cancellation causes any changes to be rolled back.

As well as the usual `BannerBitmap` property, this page provides a `ShowProgressBar` property. If you set this to false, the progress bar will not be shown. This is occasionally useful, because some applications provide erratic or unhelpful progress bar feedback. (This can happen if the install spends most of its time performing one slow custom action or if the application is very small.)

 This page must always be present as the only page in the Progress phase. Visual Studio .NET will complain if you try to add other pages, since the installer is able to show only one page during this phase.

Once the installation has completed, the installer will move on to the first window in the End phase.

Finished page

This page tells the user that the installation is complete. It should be the last page in the End phase. (By default, it is the only page in the End phase.)

This page has no properties. Its banner is always "Installation Complete," and its body text always indicates that the installation was successful. The Cancel and Next buttons will be grayed out, leaving just a Close button.

RadioButtons pages

There are three RadioButtons pages, allowing you to present a selection of two, three, or four mutually exclusive options. Remember that each different page type can be used only once in any given installer. So, although you can have an installer with both a RadioButtons (2 buttons) and a RadioButtons (4 buttons) page, you cannot have two pages with four buttons. (Again, you will need to use a more powerful tool to build your installer if you absolutely must have more than one page with the same number of radio buttons.)

The various RadioButtons pages all work in the same way. As Figure 6-7 shows, you can set the text that appears in the banner and at the top of the main dialog area. This is done with the `BannerText` and `BodyText` properties. There are also properties for setting the button text: `ButtonNLabel`, where *N* is a number from 1 to 4. You should keep this text to one line—although it can wrap to two lines, the button control isn't quite large enough, and any characters that descend below the text baseline (such as a lowercase *g* or *y*) will have their descenders truncated.

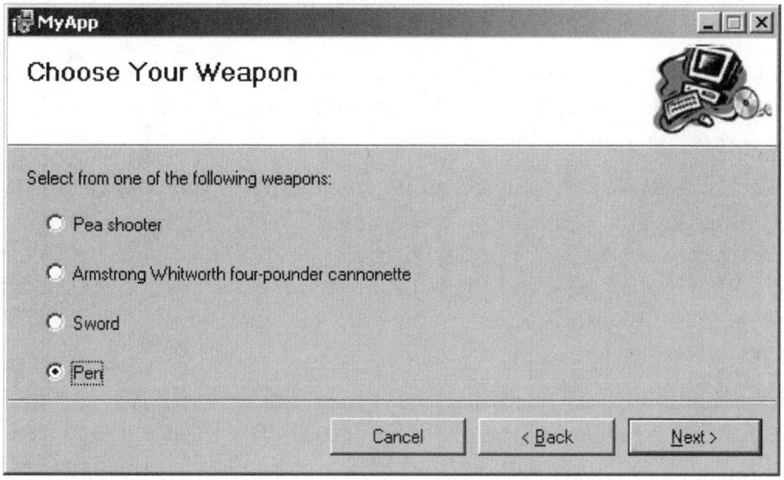

![MyApp dialog titled "Choose Your Weapon" with label "Select from one of the following weapons:" and radio buttons: Pea shooter, Armstrong Whitworth four-pounder cannonette, Sword, and Pen (selected). Buttons at bottom: Cancel, < Back, Next >]

Figure 6-7. A RadioButtons page

The results of the selection will be available to later installation stages and can be used to control conditional installation or passed as parameters to custom actions. The default name of the installer property that stores the user's selection is `BUTTON2`, `BUTTON3`, or `BUTTON4`, depending on whether you are using the two-button, three-button, or four-button dialog. You can change this name by setting the page's `ButtonProperty` property.

The value of this installer property is determined by the radio button the user selects. By default, it will be 1, 2, 3, or 4, but you can change the value that each button will assign if you want. Simply set the `ButtonNValue` properties (where *N* is a number from 1 to 4).

> As with all input pages, you should make sure that any RadioButtons pages appear before either the Confirm Installation or the Installation Folder pages. Unhelpfully, Visual Studio .NET always adds new dialogs to the end of the phase. Since this breaks VS.NET's own rules about the order in which dialogs must appear, you will need to move each dialog after you create it.

Checkboxes pages

Checkboxes pages are similar to RadioButtons pages in that they allow the user to select from a list of options. The most obvious difference is that radio buttons are mutually exclusive while checkboxes can be selected in any combination. However, the

Checkboxes dialogs work slightly differently from the RadioButtons ones. There are still three (named (A), (B), and (C)), but all three are identical.

The only reason there are three different Checkboxes dialogs is to allow an installer to have up to three pages with checkboxes. Each page can have up to four checkboxes. (And unlike the RadioButtons dialogs, all three pages can have the same number of buttons.)

The usual, BannerText and BodyText properties are supported. There are also four CheckboxNVisible properties that determine which checkboxes are visible. The text labels are controlled with the CheckboxNLabel properties.

Because each checkbox can be checked independently of the rest, each sets its own installer property. You can choose the name of each installer property with the CheckboxNProperty properties. By default, it will be CHECKBOXXN, where X is the name of the Checkboxes dialog—either A, B, or C—and N is the number of the checkbox. These properties are all Boolean. You can set their initial settings with the CheckboxNValue properties.

As with the RadioButtons pages (and all other input pages), Visual Studio .NET places new pages at the end of the phase by default. You must move them to an earlier position, since you are not allowed to have pages following the Confirm Installation dialog.

Textboxes pages

Textboxes pages let the user type in arbitrary strings. There are three Textboxes pages, named (A), (B), and (C), and as with the Checkboxes, all three are identical. The reason there are three is to allow an installer to have more than one page with text boxes.

A Textboxes dialog has the usual BannerText and BodyText properties as in Figure 6-8, and it can have up to four text boxes. The presence or absence of each text box is determined by the EditNVisible properties (where N is between 1 and 4). Text box labels are set with the EditNLabel properties.

The values the user types in each text box are made available to later stages of the installation process through installer properties. By default, these properties are named EDITXN, where X is the name of the Textboxes dialog—either A, B, or C—and N is the number of the text box. You can change these variable names with the EditNProperty properties. You can set default values for the fields with the EditNValue properties.

Customer Information page

The Customer Information page allows certain information about the customer to be collected. This page will always ask the user's name. Optionally, it can also ask for the name of the user's organization and even for a serial number to be entered.

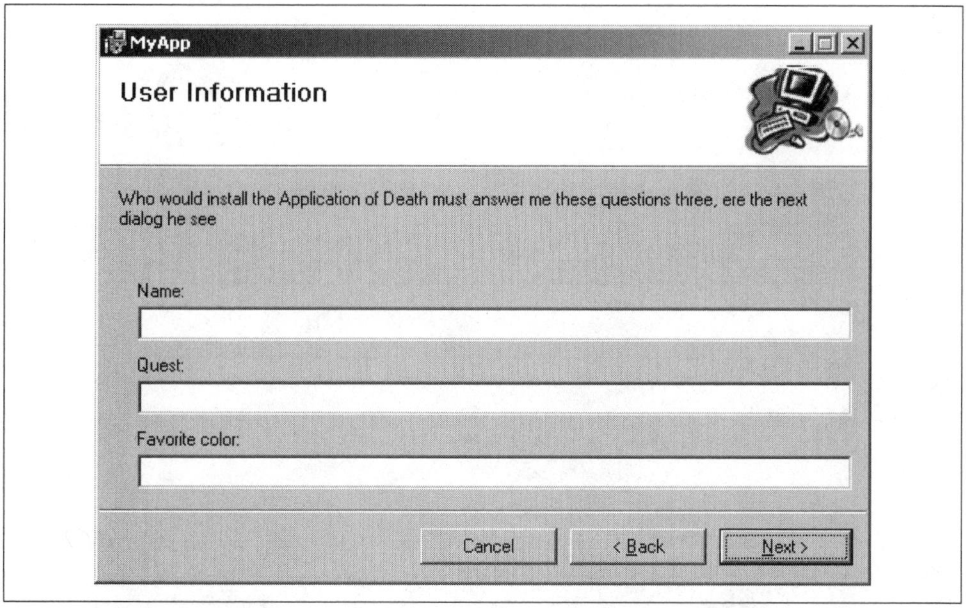

Figure 6-8. A Textboxes page

Figure 6-9 shows the page with all three fields present. The optional fields are enabled by setting the ShowOrganization and ShowSerialNumber properties to true. If you ask for a serial number, you must tell Windows Installer what the format of the number should be by setting the SerialNumberTemplate property.

A serial number template defines the pattern of characters required to make a valid serial number. The template will be used to arrange the text boxes on the dialog and to enforce a valid-looking serial number to be entered. The template includes special characters from Table 6-2. Any other characters will simply be copied verbatim into the dialog between any text boxes. (This is how text and hyphens have been displayed between the boxes in Figure 6-9.)

Table 6-2. Serial number template special characters

Character	Use
<	Delimits the start of the template—characters to the left of this will be ignored.
>	Delimits the end of the template—characters to the right of this will be ignored.
#	Requires a digit.
%	Requires a digit. It will be tested with the Windows Installer validation algorithm (see later).
?	Allows any alphanumeric character.
^	Requires a digit or an uppercase character.

The template used for Figure 6-9 is:

```
<###-%%%%%% - FOO - %%%>
```

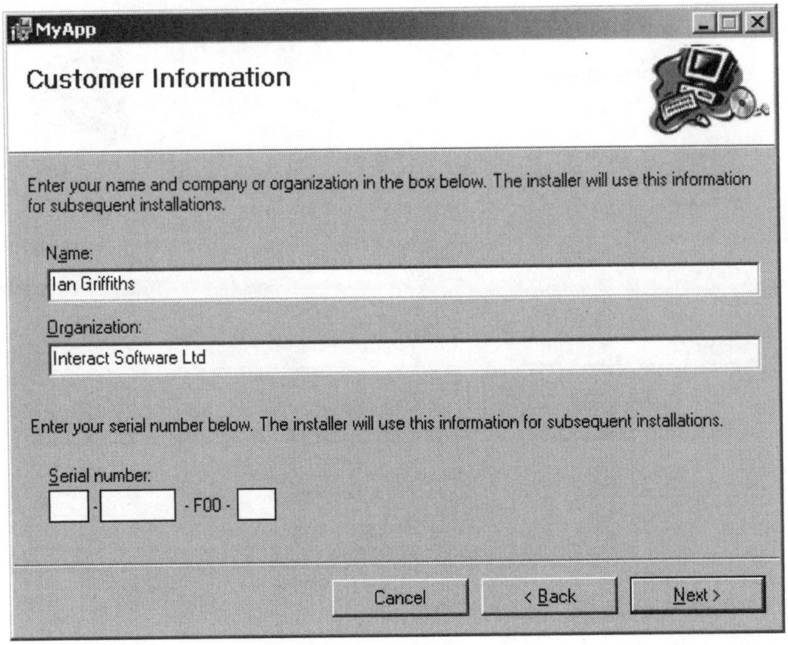

Figure 6-9. Customer Information page

The ranges of special characters (three digits, seven checked digits, three checked digits) have been displayed as three text boxes. The remaining characters have simply been shown between the text boxes. Interspersing short, easily recognized fixed sequences of characters can be useful for long serial numbers—displaying the fixed sequences in the dialog can help users not lose their place as they copy the serial number.

The digits marked with a % in the serial number template get special treatment—as Table 6-2 says, they will be checked with the Windows Installer validation algorithm. This is the venerable old algorithm that has been used for many years in some of Microsoft's own products. It works by adding up all of the checked digits and then dividing the result by seven. If the remainder is zero, the number is valid; otherwise it is not. This is not an antifraud technique—not only is the algorithm extremely well known, even someone who doesn't know the algorithm will not have to guess many different serial numbers until one is accepted. The purpose of this validation is simply to reduce the chances of a transcription error when the user types in the serial number.

The data entered in this dialog is stored in Windows Installer's database in the registry. All three properties can be retrieved by calling the MsiGetProductInfo API, and asking for the ProductID, RegOwner, and RegCompany properties.

The Visual Studio .NET documentation does not mention any way of retrieving this information through installer properties. If you are happy to use undocumented features, you may be interested to know that with projects built using the version of Visual Studio .NET that was shipping when this was written, the [ProductId], [USERNAME], and [COMPANYNAME] installer properties contain the data from this form.

License Agreement page

If you want users to agree to the terms of a license before letting them install your product, you can add a License Agreement page (see Figure 6-10) to the installer. This page simply displays any Rich Text Format (RTF) file, along with a pair of radio buttons allowing the user to indicate whether the terms are acceptable. Users will not be allowed to proceed unless they agree to the terms—the Next button is enabled only when the I Agree button is clicked.

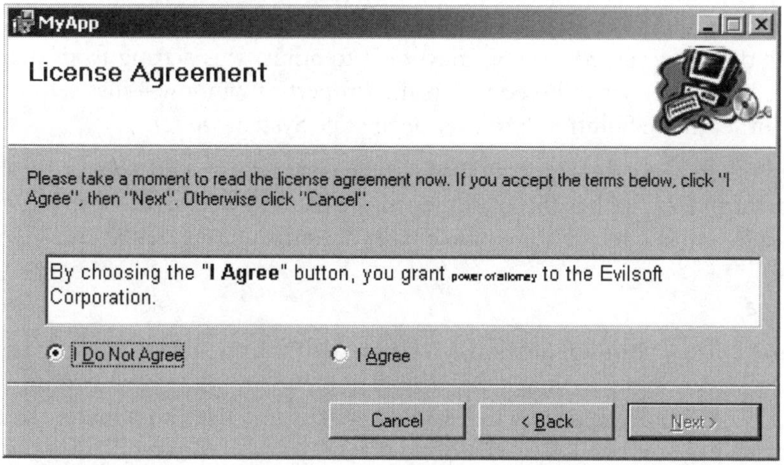

Figure 6-10. License Agreement page

The RTF file must be in the Setup project's File System view. It is chosen with the LicenseFile property. Editing this property brings up a browser that allows files that have been added to the File System view to be selected, as shown in Figure 6-11.

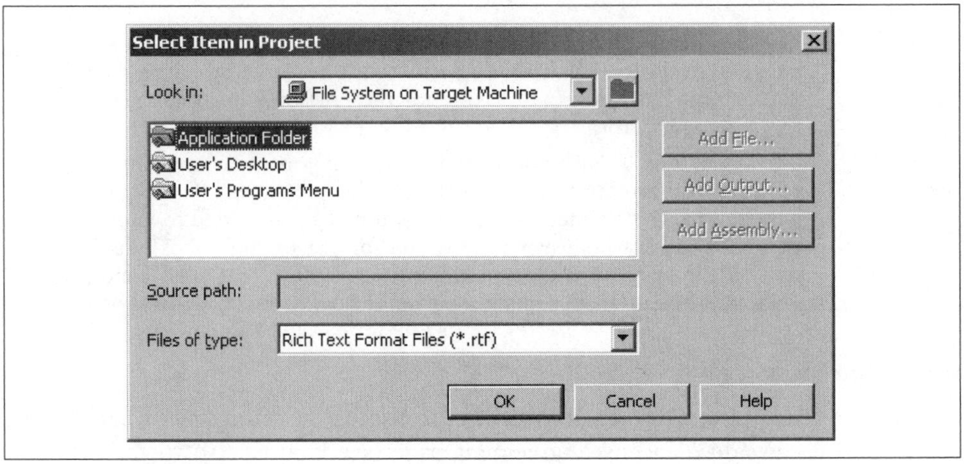

Figure 6-11. Choosing a license agreement file

If you have not already added a license file with the File System view, you can do it from within this browser. Be aware though that the Exclude property of files added this way will be set to false. This means that, although the license file will be built into the MSI, enabling it to be shown during installation, it will not be copied onto the user's computer. Depending on how you feel about not giving the user a copy of the terms they just agreed to, you may wish to adjust this setting from the default. (The Exclude property can be edited in the Properties window—just select the relevant file either in the Solution Explorer or the File System view.)

The only other property supported by the License Agreement page is Sunken. This simply determines whether the RTF file will be displayed in an area with a 3D-effect sunken edge or in a control drawn flush with the surrounding dialog.

Splash page

When users install your application, you may wish for the first thing they see to be a piece of visual design, to make the installer blend in with your product's visual branding. The Welcome page's inflexibility makes this hard to achieve, so you can add a Splash page that will display a bitmap at the start of the installation process.

Your bitmap will fill the parts usually occupied by the banner and body. Accordingly, this is the only page not to have the BannerBitmap property; you specify the splash bitmap with the SplashBitmap property. You should ensure that the bitmap is the correct size. The appropriate dimensions are 480 pixels wide and 320 pixels high. If your image is a different size, Windows Installer will stretch it to fill the available space, which may distort the image.

This page also supports the Sunken property, letting you control whether a 3D-effect edge will be drawn around your bitmap.

Read Me page

Many applications provide a file that contains useful information a user might need to know before running an application. Such files have traditionally been called ReadMe. With Windows Installer, you can provide such information within the installer user interface by adding a Read Me page.

 Read Me pages are usually placed in the End phase of the installer user interface so that they are only shown once the application has been successfully installed.

Read Me pages are very similar to License Agreement pages—they just display an RTF file. The main difference is that users are not required to click on any button to indicate that they have read or agree to the file's contents.

The RTF file is chosen with the ReadmeFile property. As with the License Agreement, this must be a file added to one of the folders visible in the File System view. Again, the file may have its Exclude property set to true if you wish to display it at installation time, but not copy it to the target machine.

Register User page

If your application has an online registration system, you might wish to direct users to that at the end of the installation process. You can do this by adding a Register User page, which provides a button that users can click to register. They are not forced to register—they are allowed to click the Next button without first clicking the Register button.

 The Register User page is usually placed in the End phase so that registration only occurs after a successful installation. You are not prevented from putting it in the Start phase, but you would not normally want to do this.

If the user clicks the button in order to register, Windows Installer will launch the application of your choice. You should supply an executable, which should be in one of the folders in the File System view. You specify the executable with the Executable property. Windows Installer will pass the arguments listed in the Arguments property. Note that you can pass any installer properties by enclosing them in square brackets. For example, placing [EDITA1] in the parameter list will pass the text entered into the first text box on the Textboxes (A) page.

File System View

All applications need to copy one or more files onto the target computer. Visual Studio .NET's Setup project File System view lets you choose which files will be installed and where they will go. Figure 6-12 shows a typical File System view in a normal Setup project. (Web Setup projects have different defaults—they just have a single folder labeled Web Application Folder.)

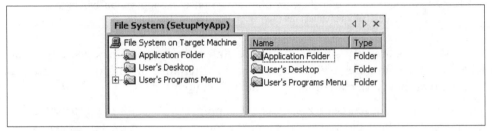

Figure 6-12. File System view

The tree on the left of the view represents various folders on the target machine. Folders are never referred to by their exact path, as hardcoding paths into installers is bad practice. System directories tend to be in different places from one machine to the next. (For example, the Windows directory might be *C:\WINNT* or *D:\WINDOWS*.) Forcing a particular installation path for the application is also bad practice—you should let users choose where to put the program. The exact path for all folders will therefore be determined during installation.

Visual Studio .NET therefore supports a number of predefined abstract folders. For example, the Application Folder shown in Figure 6-12 represents the folder chosen by the user when installing the application. (By default, this is typically, but not necessarily, *C:\Program Files\Company Name\Application Name*.) You would usually put your program's executable files in here. For Web Setup projects, you will instead see a Web Application Folder, which represents the virtual directory into which the application is installed.

You can add other folders by choosing from the Add Special Folder submenu of the "File system on target machine" node's context menu. Most of the standard system directories are supported. Table 6-3 describes each special folder.

Table 6-3. Special folders

Folder	Use
Common Files	Where components shared between applications can be installed. Usually *C:\Program Files\Common Files*.
Fonts	The system fonts directory. Typically *C:\Windows\Fonts*.
Program Files	Where applications are usually installed. This is typically *C:\Program Files*.

Table 6-3. *Special folders (continued)*

Folder	Use
System	The Windows system directory. Usually *C:\Windows\System32*.
User's Application Data	Per-user application-specific data in the user's profile. Typically *C:\Documents and Settings\ <username>\Application Data*.
User's Desktop	The user's desktop. This is usually *C:\Documents and Settings\<username>\Desktop*.
User's Favorites	The user's Favorites menu. Typically *C:\Documents and Settings\<username>\Favorites*.
User's Personal Data	Per-user My Documents directory. This is usually *C:\Documents and Settings\<username>\My Documents*.
User's Programs	The Programs section of the user's Start menu. Typically *C:\Documents and Settings\ <username>\Start Menu\Programs*.
User's Send To Menu	The Send To submenu on the Windows Explorer file context menu. This is usually *C:\Documents and Settings\<username>\SendTo*.
User's Start Menu	The user's start menu. Typically *C:\Documents and Settings\<username>\Start Menu*.
User's Startup Folder	Files to be executed when the user logs on. This is usually *C:\Documents and Settings\ <username>\Start Menu\Programs\Startup*.
User's Template Folder	Holds new document templates—used for the New submenu of Windows Explorer. Typically *C: \Documents and Settings\<username>\Templates*.
Windows Folder	The Windows directory. Usually *C:\Windows*.
Global Assembly Cache Folder	The .NET Global Assembly Cache. Files added to this directory should be strongly named .NET components. They will be added to the GAC at installation time.
Module Retargetable Folder (Merge Modules only)	A folder whose destination may be specified by any application that includes this merge module.
	Some merge modules don't care where their files are installed so long as they are installed somewhere. They allow the exact location to be chosen by the application that is using the merge module. If you want to allow the same flexibility for your own merge modules, put the files in this folder.
	When you use a module that has retargetable files in an installer, you can choose where to place the files with the Properties window. Select the merge module in the project and expand its `MergeModuleProperties` property. Modules with retargetable output will have a child `ModuleRetargetableFolder` property, allowing you to choose where to put the merge module's output.

Having decided which directories you wish to populate during installation, you must tell Visual Studio .NET what files it should place in those directories. You do this by selecting the folder and then selecting Add from the context menu.

As Figure 6-13 shows, you have several choices. You can add a new subdirectory with Folder. You can install any file you like. The Assembly item lets you install a . NET component and get Visual Studio .NET to automatically determine which other components it depends upon and install those too. Project Output lets you install components built by other projects in the same solution as your Setup project.

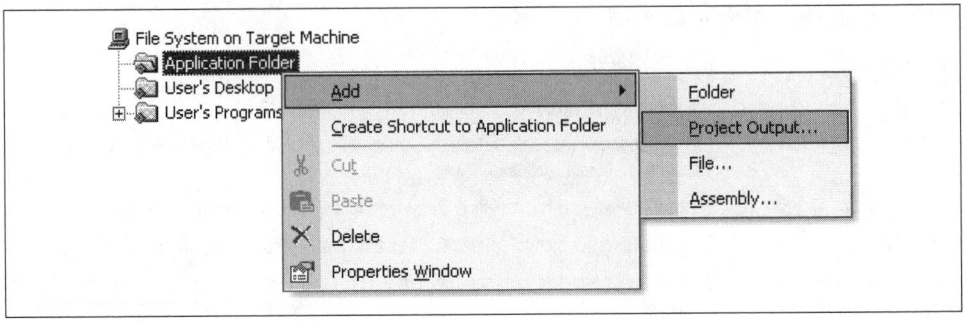

Figure 6-13. Populating folders

Adding Project Output

Whatever else you choose to install on the target machine, you will almost certainly want to copy your program's executable code. The way to do this is to add a Project Output item to the appropriate folder. (For a normal application, this will be the Application Folder. For a web application, it will usually be the Web Application Folder.)

> Do not place the Project Output of a web application in the Web Application Folder's *bin* subdirectory. Although this is where the DLL must be installed, the web project will create the *bin* directory as part of its output. So placing the output in the *bin* subdirectory would cause the DLL to end up in a *bin\bin* subdirectory. The correct (and the default) place for a web application's output group is therefore always the Web Application Folder.

When you select Add → Project Output... from a folder context menu (as shown in Figure 6-13) the Add Project Output Group dialog (Figure 6-14) will appear. This lets you choose the project whose output you would like to include (from the Project: combo box). It also allows you to select which particular items you would like to install—projects generate several outputs, but you don't necessarily want to install all of them.

For nonweb applications, you will normally want just the Primary Output group (see Table 6-4). The Primary Output is the main file that the project builds. This will usually be either a DLL or an EXE file, depending on the project type. For web applications, you will also want to select Content Files—this includes *.aspx* pages and any graphics.

>
> If you use either this dialog or the wizard to add both Primary Output and Content Files groups in one step, they will both end up in the same directory, and you will need to move one of them afterward.

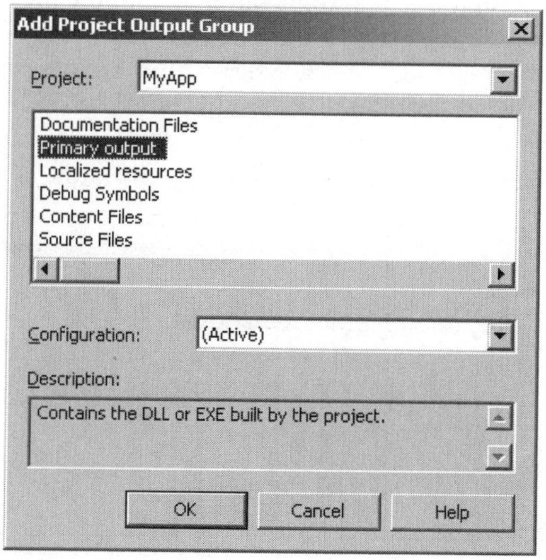

Figure 6-14. Adding project output

Table 6-4. Primary output groups

Output group	Usage
Documentation Files	C# source files can be annotated with special comments (starting with `///`). The C# compiler strips out this information to build an XML documentation file. Visual Studio .NET is able to use these files to provide documentation tooltips.
	You would include such output when building a Setup project whose purpose is to install software components on a developer's machine. You would not normally include this output group in anything intended to be installed on an end user's machine.
Primary Output	The Primary Output is the main file built by the project, usually a DLL or an EXE file. You would normally include this output group in any Setup project.
Localized Resources	Any satellite resources created for localized versions of an application will be in this output group. You would include this group for any project in which you have created localized resources.
Debug Symbols	When compiling with debugging enabled, the compiler produces a separate file containing the symbolic information required by the debugger (a *.pdb* file). This output group contains that information.
	You would not normally want to redistribute debug symbols. However, sometimes you will not be able to reproduce problems on a developer's machine, in which case it can be useful to install debug symbols on a target machine in order to try and diagnose problems. You would include this group when building a special debugging installation.
Content Files	Project files that do not get compiled will appear in this group. (This will include any project item with a `BuildAction` property of `Content`.)
	You usually want to include this output group for web applications because *.aspx* files and graphics are all classed as Content. For other applications, you usually wouldn't include this group.
Source Files	This group includes all of the source code in the project.
	You would very rarely include this group. However, if you are diagnosing a problem in situ, this, in conjunction with the Debug Symbols group, would provide a way of installing everything required to do source-level debugging on a machine without having to copy the entire solution across.

Sometimes, you may wish to include some but not all of the files in an output group. For example, a web application may contain pages that are for debugging purposes and that should not be deployed on a live server. Visual Studio .NET allows you to leave out certain files when installing an output group by setting the output item's `ExcludeFilter` property. You may add multiple filters with this property. Each filter can be either a specific file or a filename containing wildcards, as Figure 6-15 shows.

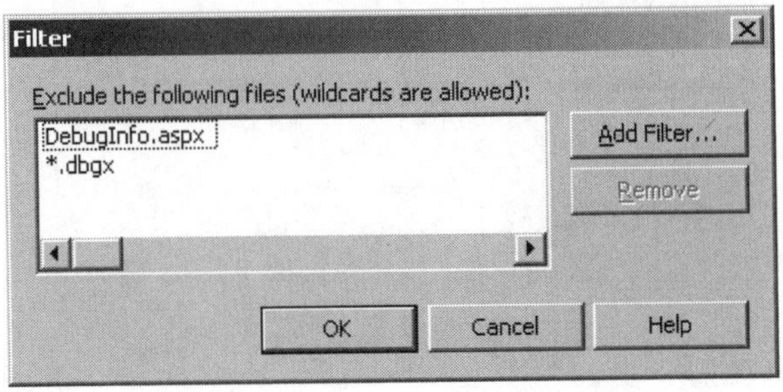

Figure 6-15. Setting an ExcludeFilter

COM registration

If you have a project that builds a COM component, you will need to make sure that the component is registered correctly when it is installed. You can ensure this by setting the project output's `Register` property. The Properties page allows you to select the `Register` property's value from a listbox; the available options are `vsdrpNoRegister`, `vsdrpCOM`, `vsdrpCOMRelativePath`, `vsdrpCOMSelfReg`, and `vsdrpFont`. (`vsdrpFont` is used for installing new fonts and is not used for COM registration.)

To install a COM component in the usual way, making it available to any application on the machine, select the `vsdrpCOM` option. Isolated registration is also supported—you can install the component in such a way that it will be accessible only to your application, and not to the whole system. For this, you should choose the `vsdrpCOMRelativePath` option. (This works only when the target system is Windows 2000 or later.)

`vsdrpCOM` and `vsdrpCOMRelativePath` allow Windows Installer to perform all registry updates. Visual Studio .NET will make sure that all of the appropriate registry configuration information is stored in the Windows Installer file. However, it is sometimes vitally important that a component be allowed to do its own registration. (For example, it may do more in its `DllRegisterServer` function than just updating the registry.) In this case, you should choose the `vsdrpCOMSelfReg` option. As a rule, though, it is better not to use `vsdrpCOMSelfReg` if possible—you should avoid creating COM components that require it, because Windows Installer cannot robustly repair or roll back installations that use this technique, as it doesn't know what configuration changes are made by the component.

Adding Files

If you wish to install a specific file that is not a part of a project, you can do this with the Add → File... option from the folder context menu. You would normally do this only with isolated files such as bitmaps or documents. You should avoid using this option to install binaries—you should instead add the merge module for the binary component to the project.

> If Visual Studio .NET detects that you are adding a file for which there is an associated merge module, it will allow you to add the merge module to the install instead. You should choose the merge module. But you should not let this lull you into a false sense of security—Microsoft does not ship all available merge modules with Visual Studio .NET. Some of them must be downloaded from Microsoft's web site. Don't get into the habit of relying on Visual Studio .NET to notice when you should be installing a merge module instead of a file—just because it doesn't prompt you doesn't mean there isn't a merge module. Adding individual files is usually the right thing to do only if those files are definitely not part of some larger component.
>
> There is no authoritative global list of merge modules, because anyone can produce a merge module. However, you can find a list of popular ones at *http://www.installsite.org/*.

Adding Assemblies

If you want to add a .NET assembly for which you don't have a merge module, you can at least get Visual Studio .NET to do automatic dependency analysis for the component. Instead of adding it as a file, select the Add → Assembly option from the folder context menu. Visual Studio will present the Component Selector dialog. (This is the same dialog used when adding a reference to a project, except it shows only the .NET tab.) You can select assemblies that your project requires from this list.

Most of the time you will not need to do this—if you add a project reference to the component in the usual way, Visual Studio .NET will detect the dependency automatically, and you will not need to add it manually. You would need to add it this way only if the reference was not automatically detectable (e.g., you are using the assembly entirely through the .NET Reflection API).

Adding Merge Modules

If your application depends on another component, you should include the merge module for that component in your installer. Strictly speaking, merge modules are not added to the File System view. This is because merge modules are self-contained—they know where the files they contain need to be installed.

You can add a merge module to the project explicitly with the Add → Merge Module... option of the Setup project's context menu. This displays a normal File Open dialog that lets you choose the merge module to include. By default, it will show you the contents of *C:\Program Files\Common\Merge Modules*, which is where Visual Studio .NET installs redistributable merge modules.

This option is not available in a Merge Module Setup project, because you cannot nest a merge module inside another. However, if your component does depend on another component, you can add a reference to its merge module with the project context menu's Add → Merge Module Reference... item. The result of this will be that when your merge module is added to an application, Visual Studio .NET will automatically add in all the other merge modules that yours depends on.

File Types View

If your application is able to edit or open certain kinds of documents, it is usually desirable to register the types of files it edits. This means that such files will integrate properly with Windows Explorer—it will use the icon of your choice, double-clicking will launch your application, and the context menu will show actions appropriate to the file type.

Registering a file type with Windows involves adding various entries in the appropriate places in the registry. Fortunately, with a Setup project, all this work is done for us. The File Types view provides a simple user interface for defining new file types to be registered at installation time.

Figure 6-16 shows a typical File Types view displaying two file types. Each file type is represented as a node underneath the "File types on target machine" tree. Each type shows its full name, as it will appear in the Windows Explorer details view and File Types list, followed by a semicolon-separated list of file extensions for this type. Underneath each type is a list of supported actions. These will appear on the context menu for files of this type in Windows Explorer, and the first action is the one that will be invoked if a user double-clicks on the file.

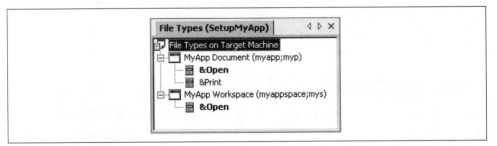

Figure 6-16. File Types view

To add a new file type, open the context menu for the "File types on target machine" item and select Add File Type.

File Type Properties

You are required to supply a certain amount of information for each file type. First, you must supply a full name for the type, either by editing the type's label in the view window or editing its (Name) property in the Properties window. You must also supply one or more file extensions with the Extensions property. If you specify multiple extensions for a single type, put a semicolon between the entries.

 You should not specify the leading period when adding a file extension. If the file always ends in *.foo*, then just set the Extension property to *foo*.

All file types are required to have an associated executable—this will be launched whenever any of the type's actions are invoked. This is set with the Command property and must refer to a file in one of the folders in the File System view. (When you edit this property, the dialog shown earlier in Figure 6-11 will be shown.) You would usually set this to be the primary output of one of the projects in the solution.

You will normally want to supply an icon for your file type. This is set with the Icon property, which lets you choose an icon from any *.ico*, *.dll*, or *.exe* file in the File System view.

You can also specify a MIME type for your file. This does not affect the way the file behaves in Windows Explorer—Windows uses file extensions to determine the type of a file, because the MIME type is not currently stored in the filesystem. However, when Internet Explorer retrieves a file from the web, it usually knows what its MIME type is, because the HTTP protocol provides this information. It will use this information in preference to the extension when deciding what the file's type is. So, if there is a MIME type defined for a file type that your application manages, you should register this with the type's MIME property.

File Type Actions

All file types must have at least one action—the one that will be invoked when the user double-clicks the file in Windows Explorer. Many have more, which will appear on the file's context menu. For each action your file types support, you must supply certain information.

All actions must have a name, specified either in the view window itself or with the (Name) property. This is the text that will appear in the file's context menu. You can support shortcut keys by placing an ampersand in front of the shortcut letter, as Figure 6-16 shows.

You must also supply a verb, using the Verb property. You should use one of the standard shell verbs whenever appropriate. The most common are open, edit, play, print, preview, and (to support drag-and-drop printing) printto.

You can specify which parameters will be passed to your executable when the verb is invoked. At a minimum, you will want to make sure that the full path of the file in question is passed—this will be substituted wherever you place the text %1. You should enclose this text in double quotes, so that your application can deal correctly with filenames with spaces. By default, the Arguments property for any action is "%1" which passes the quoted filename and nothing else.

Registry View

Some registry configuration has already been dealt with—COM component registration can be managed in the File System view; file types get their own special treatment. But if you want to add other registry entries, you can use the Setup project's Registry view.

As Figure 6-17 shows, the Registry view looks like a trimmed-down version of the Windows registry editor. The registry key hierarchy is presented in a tree view on the left, and values can be edited on the right. The most obvious difference is that only a small subset of the keys is shown—only the structure required by the application is present.

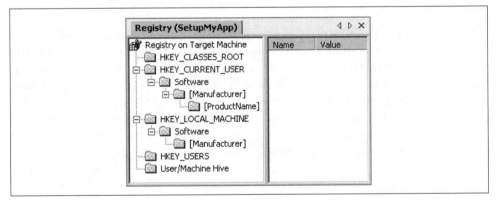

Figure 6-17. Registry view

By default, Setup projects contain a certain amount of structure but no data. Various HKEY_XXX roots are provided as a convenience. As Figure 6-17 shows, [Manufacturer] key will be added under HKCU\Software and HKLM\Software. (This is present only in non-web-based applications.)

 As with most text values in Setup projects, you can use any installer property as a name or value in the Registry view by placing it in square brackets. All values and keys also support the Condition property described earlier.

By default, the keys in this view will not be created at install time unless they need to be—keys will be created only if you specify values underneath them. (So, although a newly created Setup project contains several keys in the Registry view, it will not cause the registry to be modified unless you add some values.) If you want to create keys without values, simply select the key and set its AlwaysCreate property to true.

> If you choose to create registry entries underneath machine-wide keys such as HKLM, this will require the user who installs the program to have access to such keys. Machinewide keys are normally writable only by Administrators. So you should avoid writing into these areas of the registry if possible.

Registry keys have a DeleteAtUninstall property. By default, this property is false, but this is often the appropriate setting. The best way to understand this property is to think of it as meaning "Force delete at uninstall." If an installer has to create a key at installation time, it will usually delete it automatically when the program is uninstalled. There is only one exception: if you forced a key to be created by setting its AlwaysCreate property to true, then you must also force its removal by setting DeleteAtUninstall to true.

> The documentation for the DeleteAtUninstall property is wrong. It says that a registry key will be deleted only if this property is set to true and it says that to meet Windows Logo requirements this property must be true. This is not true—you need to set DeleteAtUninstall only on keys whose AlwaysCreate property is also true.

> Setting DeleteAtUninstall will delete the key and all of its children even if those keys were present before the program was installed, so it should be used with care. It is better to avoid using it, by making sure that all of your keys have their AlwaysCreate property value set to false (which is the default).

Registry settings can be imported into a Setup project. The context menu for the Registry on Target Machine node in the Registry view has an Import Node... item. This lets you open a *.reg* file and import its contents into the project.

Custom Actions

Although Visual Studio .NET Setup projects handle the most common installation requirement, some applications will need to perform some extra steps at installation time. For example, your application might install custom performance counters or create a message queue. To enable operations such as this, Windows Installer supports custom actions. A *custom action* is a piece of code supplied by you that will be invoked during the installation process.

As Figure 6-18 shows, the Custom Actions view presents four folders. These represent various stages of the installation phase. Remember that the user sees the installation progress through three phases: information collection, installation, and confirmation. The installation phase itself, however, can go through up to four different stages, described later. You can add a custom action to any or all of these stages.

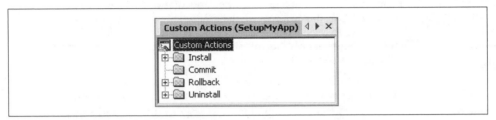

Figure 6-18. Custom Actions view

Items placed in the Install stage will be run after Windows Installer has completed all other installation work, which means that by the time your custom action runs, all files and registry settings will be in place. Custom actions in the Install stage are allowed to abort the installation (see details later). If you want to run a custom action only after it is certain that the installation has completed successfully, you can place it in the Commit stage. Of course, actions in the Commit stage are not able to abort the installation. Actions in the Rollback stage will be run if the application installation aborts before completing. Actions in the Uninstall stage will be run when the user uninstalls the application.

Windows Installer will not correlate the same item added to both the Install and the Rollback phases. If a rollback occurs, your Rollback custom action will always be called, regardless of whether the corresponding action in the Install phase ran successfully (or at all). So if you provide a Rollback custom action, it must work out whether the corresponding Install custom action had even begun and, if so, how far it had got.

You can add items to a stage with the context menu's Add Custom Action... item. If you select this item from the Custom Action item's context menu (instead of one of the four stages), the action will be added to all four phases.

When adding an action, you will be shown the usual item selection dialog shown in Figure 6-19. You can select any *.exe*, *.dll*, or script file in any of the folders from the File System view.

If you specify an *.exe* file, Windows Installer will run the program at the chosen stage. You can specify command-line parameters with the Arguments property. You can pass installer properties by putting them in square brackets (e.g., [EDITA1] will

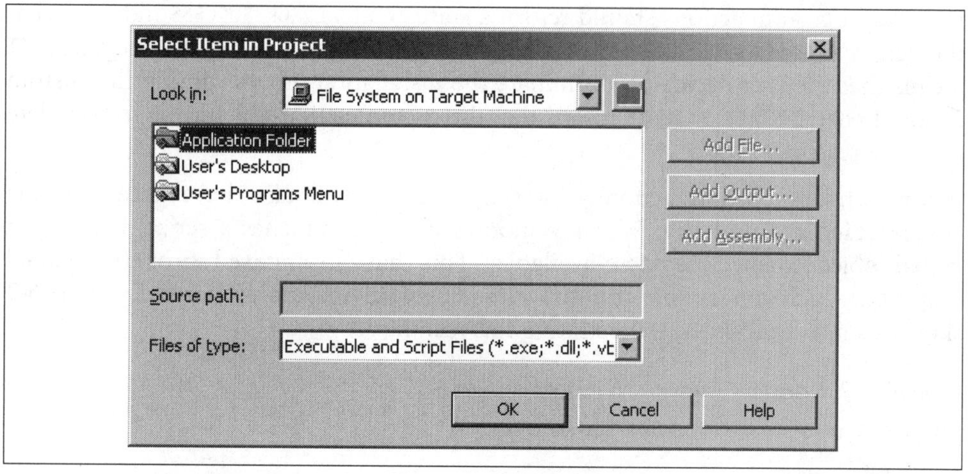

![Select Item in Project dialog box showing Look in: File System on Target Machine, with Application Folder, User's Desktop, User's Programs Menu listed; Add File, Add Output, Add Assembly buttons; Source path field; Files of type: Executable and Script Files (*.exe;*.dll;*.vb); OK, Cancel, Help buttons]

Figure 6-19. Adding a custom action

pass the contents of the first textbox on the Textboxes (A) screen). Remember to put quotes around any properties whose values might have spaces in them. If your custom action is in the Install phase, you can abort the installation by returning a non-zero exit code. This will cause the installation to go through the rollback procedure, undoing any work the installer has done so far.

If you specify a DLL, you must also tell Visual Studio .NET what entry point it should call, using the EntryPoint property. You can give the method whatever name you like, but it must use the __stdcall calling convention, and take an MSIHANDLE as its sole parameter. Example 6-1 shows a suitable function declaration. You should also set the custom action's InstallerClass property to false. (If you set it to true, Visual Studio .NET will presume that the DLL is a .NET assembly and will look for an installer class. See the later ".NET Installation Components" section for details on how to write a .NET custom action.)

Example 6-1. A custom action in a DLL

```
int __stdcall CustomAction(MSIHANDLE hInstall);
```

You can pass data to the action by setting the CustomActionData property in Visual Studio .NET. The DLL will be able to retrieve this using the MsiGetProperty API. Any installer properties passed in square brackets will be expanded by Windows Installer before being passed to the DLL via the CustomActionData property.

 Custom actions are given only limited access to the installation session and cannot access arbitrary installer properties with MsiGetProperty. You must therefore pass any necessary information through the CustomActionData property, since this is one of the few properties that will be available.

DLL-based custom actions should return a status code. ERROR_SUCCESS indicates that the action succeeded. It can indicate a failure in two ways: ERROR_INSTALL_USEREXIT means that the user decided to terminate the installation process during the custom action. ERROR_INSTALL_FAILURE means that the custom action was unable to complete for some reason.

If you write a custom action as a script file, it will also have access to the CustomActionData property. When Windows Installer launches a script, it makes a global object named Session available. This has an indexed property named Property, which you can use to retrieve the CustomActionData property. Example 6-2 shows a snippet of VBScript illustrating this technique.

Example 6-2. Retrieving CustomActionData in script

```
data = Session.Property("CustomActionData")
```

Custom actions in scripts cannot abort the installation process. This is a Visual Studio .NET limitation—although Windows Installer supports this functionality, it relies on the script being contained in a function so that it can have a return code. Unfortunately, Visual Studio .NET provides no way of specifying the name of the function, so only global code can be executed, which has no means of returning a value.

Scripts will be run inside a special scripting host supplied by the Windows Installer. This means that your script will not have access to the normal intrinsics that would be available in the WSH (Windows Scripting Host) host. However, it is easy enough to get hold of the standard WSH objects if you need them. Example 6-3 shows how to retrieve a registry setting using the WSH shell RegRead function from within an installer script.

Example 6-3. WSH functions from an installer script

```
Dim WSHShell, CLSIDRegPath, CLSID
Set WSHShell = CreateObject("WScript.Shell")
CLSIDRegPath = "HKCR\EvilCorp.Engine\CLSID\"
CLSID = WSHShell.RegRead(CLSIDRegPath)
```

If you have supplied an *.exe*, *.dll*, or script file for the sole purpose of providing a custom install action, it is not necessary to copy the file to the target machine as part of the installation. Although the file must be present in the File System view to be used as a custom action, you are allowed to set the item's Exclude property to true. This means the file will be present in the *.msi* file and can therefore be used as a custom action but will not be left in the application folder once installation is complete.

This option is not available if you have written a custom action based on the .NET installation component technique (described later). Components using this approach must have their Exclude properties set to false.

Example custom action

The code in Example 6-4 shows an example custom action DLL written in C++. It creates a text file containing the installation date of the application.

The location of the file created by this installer is determined by a GetInstallFilename function, not shown here. This could use the MsiGetProperty API to retrieve the CustomActionData property, allowing installer properties to be passed in. For example, if the custom action's CustomActionData property were set to [ProgramFilesFolder][Manufacturer]\[ProductName], the custom action could create the file in the program's installation directory.

Example 6-4. Custom action

```
extern "C" __declspec(dllexport)
    int __stdcall Install(MSIHANDLE hInstall)
{
    std::string fileName;

    if (!GetInstallFilename(hInstall, fileName))
        return ERROR_INSTALL_FAILURE;

    FILE* f = fopen(fileName.c_str(), ("w"));
    if (f == NULL)
    {
        return ERROR_INSTALL_FAILURE;
    }
    else
    {
        SYSTEMTIME sysTime;
        ::GetSystemTime(&sysTime);
        fprintf(f, "Installed on %d/%d/%d\n",
            (int) sysTime.wYear, (int) sysTime.wMonth,
            (int) sysTime.wDay);

        fclose(f);

    }

    return ERROR_SUCCESS;

}

static int RemoveFile(MSIHANDLE hInstall)
{
    std::string fileName;

    if (!GetInstallFilename(hInstall, fileName))
        return ERROR_INSTALL_FAILURE;

    // Silently ignore errors—it is possible that we might
    // not have successfully created the file during installation,
    // in which case deleting it won't work either...
```

Example 6-4. Custom action (continued)

```
        ::DeleteFile(fileName.c_str( ));

        return ERROR_SUCCESS;
}

extern "C" __declspec(dllexport)
    int __stdcall Rollback(MSIHANDLE hInstall)
{
    return RemoveFile(hInstall);
}

extern "C" __declspec(dllexport)
    int __stdcall Uninstall(MSIHANDLE hInstall)
{
    return RemoveFile(hInstall);
}
```

This particular custom action DLL provides `Install`, `Rollback`, and `Uninstall` methods. You would therefore add this DLL three times in the Custom Actions view, under the Install, Rollback, and Uninstall phases. (This particular code doesn't have anything useful to do at Commit time.) Each place the DLL appears in the Custom Actions view, you would set its `EntryPoint` property to be the name of the appropriate DLL entry point (i.e., Install, Rollback, or Uninstall).

.NET Installation Components

If you are writing a .NET project, automated support is available for certain operations that would normally require you to write code. If you need to configure a message queue, an event log source, or a performance counter on the target system, Visual Studio .NET can add installation components to your project that will do all of the necessary work for you.

All three of the supported installation component types use the same basic model. They assume that you will configure your development system so that it has whatever message queues, event log sources or performance counters your application requires. Visual Studio .NET is then able to examine the items you have created and add an installation component to your project that can create an identically configured item on a target machine.

You can add as many installation components as you like to a project, but they are all managed by a single `Installer` class. The `Installer` class will be invoked at installation time and will run each installation component in turn, in order to configure the target machine to your application's needs.

This mechanism relies on installer custom actions. You must add a project that uses .NET installation components as a custom action in the usual way, but you must set the custom action's `InstallerClass` property to true. This changes the way that

Windows Installer will use the component. Instead of executing the program (or calling a named entry point in the case of a DLL), it will search for the `Installer` class and allow that to control the custom action.

 You should always add this kind of custom action to all four stages of installation. The predefined installation components all expect to be able to run code for all four phases. The easiest way to do this is to use the Add Custom Action... item from the Custom Actions view's context menu.

You should also ensure that this custom action comes first in the Install stage; otherwise, errors can arise if a rollback occurs. When an `Installer` class is asked to roll back, it will look for a log file that it created during the Install phase in order to work out which operations need to be undone. If the `Installer` is not the first custom action, then a preceding action might cancel the installation, in which case the `Installer` will not have had a chance to create this log file. This causes it to display an error dialog during rollback. The error is harmless (if the log file doesn't exist, then there is no work to be undone) but will not inspire confidence in your users.

`Installer` classes live in the main application project. You can add an Installer class to your application with the usual Add Project Item dialog. Simply choose Installer Class from the Code category. This will add a new class that derives from the `Installer` class (which is defined in the `System.Configuration.Install` namespace). It also marks it with the `RunInstaller` custom attribute, which enables Windows Installer to locate the class at installation time.

A newly added `Installer` class will not do anything at installation time. If you want to add some code of your own, you can override any of the `Install`, `Commit`, `Rollback`, or `Uninstall` methods, which will get called at the relevant phases. But since the main point of using this mechanism is to automate the configuration of certain system resources, you will normally want to add installation components to the installer.

To add an installation component for a message queue, event log source, or performance counter, your main project must be using a component that represents the item in question. If you don't already have such a component in use in your project, you could drag the relevant item from the Visual Studio .NET Server Explorer onto, say, a Form. (Any design view will do.)

When you select an object, if it can have an associated installation component in the designer, the Properties window will show an Add Installer method in the verb panel. Figure 6-20 shows the Properties page for a `PerformanceCounter` component, with the Add Installer method visible in the middle.

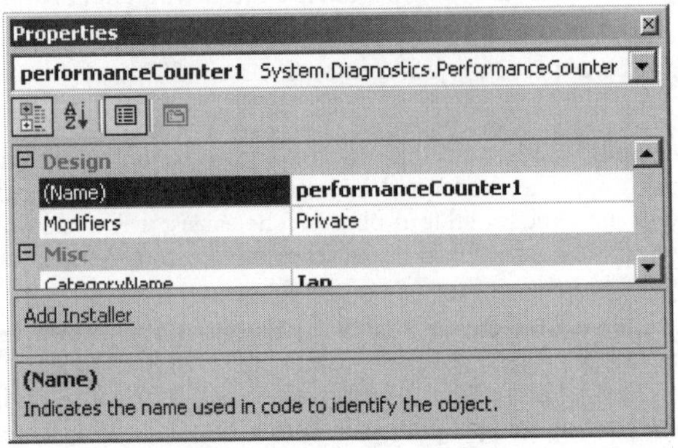

Figure 6-20. A component that supports installation components

If you have not yet added an Installer class to your project, clicking on Add Installer will create one for you, calling it ProjectInstaller. It will then add an installation component to the Installer and will show you the Installer class's design view. (The Installer's design view consists of just the component tray.)

The Installer will now contain an entry for the installation component you just added. This item's properties will contain enough information to create a new item on the target machine. (Either a message queue, event log source, or performance counter, depending on what type of component you added an Installer for.) The item it creates on the target will have all the same characteristics as the original, unless you edit its settings—installer components let you modify all of the information they contain, just like any other component, as Figure 6-21 shows.

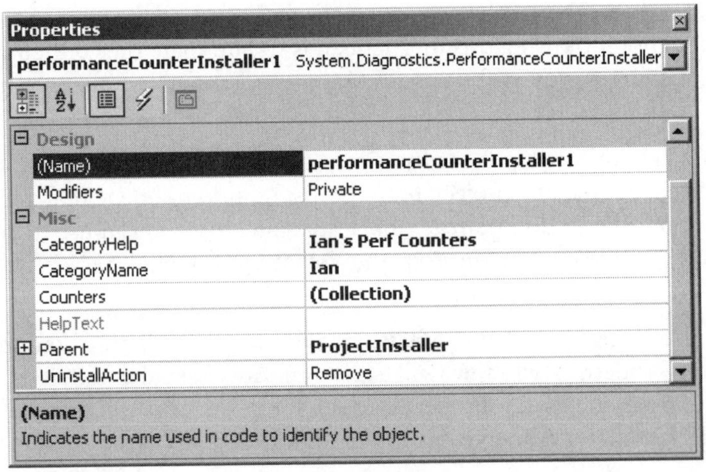

Figure 6-21. Installer properties for a performance counter

The `Installer` class will automatically install any components that you add in this fashion. You do not need to write any code; you simply need to make sure that the executable is added as a custom action for all installation phases and that its `InstallerClass` property is set to true. (When you add a custom action for a binary that contains an Installer class, Visual Studio .NET automatically sets the `InstallerClass` property to true, so you should find that the defaults are correct.)

If you want to add code of your own to the `Installer` class, you may want to pass information such as the value of properties selected by the user earlier in the installation. Once again, the `CustomActionData` property should be used. However, it must use a certain format, because it will be parsed by the `Installer` class. It should take the form of name-value pairs, specified as */name=value*. Pairs should be separated with a space. If the value contains a space, it should be enclosed in quotes.

These name-value pairs are available through the `Installer` class's `Context` property. The `Context` has a `Parameters` property, which is a dictionary of strings containing the name-value pairs passed in `CustomActionData`. The way that we pass user input to the custom action is to place it in the `CustomActionData` property. For example, if the installation user interface uses the Textboxes (A) page, the installer property `EDITA1` will contain the string the user entered in the first edit box on that page. Custom actions don't have access to most installer properties, so, by default, a custom action will not be able to retrieve this information. However, we can set the `CustomActionData` property to `/FavoriteColor=EDITA1`, enabling the custom action to retrieve this value using the code shown in Example 6-5. You can pass multiple values if necessary. For example, you might set the `CustomActionData` property to `/FavoriteColor=EDITA1 /Weapon=BUTTON4VALUE` to pass in a text field and a radio button setting.

Example 6-5. Retrieving CustomActionData properties

```
string somePropVal = Context.Parameters["FavoriteColor"];
```

Launch Conditions

It is often useful to be able to impose installation prerequisites. Many applications will not run unless the target system meets certain requirements. For example, an application might run only on particular versions of Windows, or it might need the .NET Framework to be installed.

Only applications can specify launch conditions. You cannot specify launch conditions for a merge module.

The Launch Conditions view lets you add and edit such requirements and prevent installation if they are not met. As Figure 6-22 shows, the view is divided into two sections. The first section, Search Target Machine, does not impose any conditions. It merely collects information about the target machine. For example, you can add entries to search for a particular file or registry entry or the presence of a particular component. Each search item stores its result in an installer property. The installation constraints are defined in the Launch Conditions section.

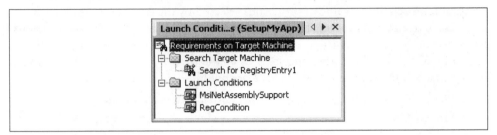

Figure 6-22. Launch Conditions view

The items in the Launch Conditions section are nothing more than items with a normal Condition property and an error message. The Condition property uses the usual syntax described earlier. If the condition does not evaluate to be true, the installation will not be allowed to proceed, and the user will be shown the error text in the Message property.

You will often, but not always, add searches and conditions in pairs. For example, if you want to test whether a particular product has been installed by checking for a certain registry key, you would add a registry key search and a condition based on the result of that search. You can add a search and condition pair with the context menu for the Requirements on Target Machine node—this will add a search and a condition that depends on the result of that search.

The .NET Framework Launch Conditions will just add a condition. (This is the `MsiNetAssemblySupport` condition, which is shown in Figure 6-22.) This condition does not need a corresponding search because Windows Installer provides an intrinsic property, `MsiNetAssemblySupport`, which indicates whether the .NET Framework is installed.

Visual Studio .NET will add this condition automatically if you add the project output from a .NET project. Note that the default behavior for installing .NET projects is therefore to fail the install if the .NET Framework is not present—it will not try to add the entire .NET Framework to your installer automatically. This usually is a good thing as the framework is large!

Although there is a series of merge modules for the .NET Framework, *dotnetfxredist_x86_<xxx>.msm*, where *xxx* is the language code, these merge modules do not install the .NET Framework. They are merely a complete list of all of the files in the framework. If an installer project has a reference to one of these merge modules, it will prevent Visual Studio .NET from listing dependencies for any framework assemblies that the project uses—it is present only to keep the development environment happy. The only way to install the .NET Framework is to use the redistributable package *Dotnetfx.exe*.

The MSDN Library contains an article entitled "Using Visual Studio .NET to Redistribute the .NET Framework." This describes in detail the various options available for shipping the .NET Framework redistributable with your application. The MSDN Library can be found at *http://msdn.microsoft.com/library/*.

You can also add searches and conditions individually. If you are testing properties provided by Windows Installer, such as those indicating which OS version is installed or whether the .NET Framework is installed, you will not need a corresponding search—you can just test the `VersionNT` or `Version9X` installer properties (see the following "Detecting Windows Versions" sidebar). Also, you may wish to express combinational constraints (e.g., install on Windows 98 only if component `Foo` is installed), in which case there will not be a straightforward mapping of searches to conditions.

You can perform three kinds of searches. You can search for the presence of a particular file, you can search for a registry entry, or you can test for the presence of a particular component. (A component search is added with the Add Windows Installer Search or Add Windows Installer Launch Condition context menu items.)

Detecting Windows Versions

Several intrinsic installer properties can be used to determine the exact version of Windows. The VersionNT and Version9X properties tell you the basic product version. Only one of these will be set on any given system. Windows 95, Windows 98, and Windows ME set the Version9X property to 400, 410, and 490, respectively. Windows NT 4.0, Windows 2000, and Windows XP set VersionNT to 400, 500, and 501, respectively. Windows Server 2003 also uses 501. (Windows Installer is not supported on older versions of Windows NT.)

If you need more specific information, the WindowsBuild property enables you to distinguish between certain flavors of Windows 9X. For example, early versions of Windows 95 were build 950, but Windows 95 OSR2.5 was build 1111. The original edition of Windows 98 was build 1998, but the second edition was 2222.

When installing on one of the Windows NT family (NT, 2000, XP, or Server 2003) the ServicePackLevel property is available, enabling you to find out which service packs (if any) are installed.

For example, the following condition:

```
(VersionNT=400 And ServicePackLevel>=6) Or VersionNT>=500
```

will allow installation on Windows NT 4.0 only if Service Pack 6 (or later) has been applied but will otherwise allow installation on Windows 2000, Windows XP, or subsequent members of the NT product family. It will not allow installation on any of the Windows 9x products.

File Search

A file search simply looks for a particular file in a given location, optionally searching subdirectories. You should avoid using this to test for the presence of a particular piece of software. If you need a component that is normally installed by Windows Installer (i.e., it has an *.msi* or *.msm* file), then you should use the Windows Installer search. Failing that, a registry search is often more appropriate, since registry keys for a specific product are usually always in the same place, while files have a tendency not to be in the same location on all machines.

However, sometimes neither a component search nor a registry search will work—some software doesn't register its presence with Windows Installer or the registry. In this case, the only way to test for its presence is to look for one or more of its files.

You can add a file search through the context menu for the Search Target Machine node. (You can also add one with the Requirements on Target Machine's menu, which will also add a condition that tests the result of the search.) Visual Studio .NET will create a unique name for the installer property that will hold the result and store the name in the search's Property property. You will probably want to change this name—you will use it in the corresponding condition, and it is easier for maintenance if these installer properties have meaningful names. Of course, you should also set the FileName property to indicate which file you are looking for.

 The FileName property does not support wildcards. You are expected to know precisely which file you are looking for.

You should also set the Folder property to indicate where you expect to find the file. By default, this will be [SystemFolder], which is typically *C:\Windows\System32*. The Folder property supports several standard folders—it presents a drop-down list of these in the Properties window. Most are for normal system locations— [ProgramFilesFolder], [WindowsFolder], and [FontsFolder] are all fairly self-explanatory, and [CommonFilesFolder] is usually *c:\Program Files\Common Files*. The list also has a [TARGETDIR] entry, which is the main application installation directory. As always, you can also use any other installer property here by enclosing it in square brackets.

If you want to search in subdirectories for the file, you can set the Depth property— this is a number indicating how many levels of subdirectories should be searched before Windows Installer gives up.

If the mere presence of a file is not sufficient to be sure that your application will run, you can also test various other file attributes. You can specify a range of acceptable versions with the MinVersion and MaxVersion properties. MinDate and MaxDate let you specify a range of acceptable dates. (This will check the Modified date. For read-only files, this will be the same as the Created date.) Finally, if all other indicators are unreliable, you can specify the size of file you expect to find with MinSize and MaxSize.

File tests are an intrinsically fragile way of testing for a component's presence. The file may well be in different places on different systems. And just because you find a file of the right name, that doesn't necessarily mean that it is really the file you require—it could be an entirely different product that happens to have chosen the same filename. Although you can mitigate this by specifying versions, sizes, or dates, this makes your test fragile in the face of later versions of the same component. You should therefore always prefer one of the other searches whenever you have the choice.

Registry Search

A registry search lets you test for the presence of a registry value. You must specify the root and path with the Root and RegKey properties. Root provides a drop-down list supporting all the standard registry starting points. For example, the default is vsdrrHKLM, the HKEY_LOCAL_MACHINE root. The RegKey is relative to this root. If you want to retrieve a value other than the default, set the Value property.

The value retrieved will be stored in the installer property named in the `Property` property. If the key or value is not found, this value will be empty.

If you specify a `RegKey` but no `Value`, the key's default value will be retrieved. If the key has no default value, the property will be empty.

This means that there is no way to detect the presence of a key that has no default value—the result will be the same whether the key is missing or it is present but has no default value. You should therefore always make sure that your registry searches either test for a named value or test a key that will have a default value.

If you really need to test for the presence of a key that has a default value, you will need to write your own code. Unfortunately, the only place Visual Studio .NET allows you to put your own code is in a custom action. Custom actions are run much later in the installation process. This is unsatisfactory, because it will allow the user to get all the way through the first phase of installation before discovering that there is a problem. The only way around this is to not use Visual Studio .NET to create the installer.

In a condition based on the results of a registry search, if you specify just the name of the installer property to which the result was assigned, the condition will succeed if a value was found and fail if it was not. However, if you need to, you can test for a particular value, because the property will be set to the value retrieved. For example, you might set the registry search to retrieve a `CurrentVersion` value of some application's key. You could then add a condition such as `EXTAPPVERSION>=200` to make sure that your application can be installed only if a sufficiently recent version of the dependent application has been installed.

Windows Installer Search

If your application depends on another piece of software, it is best to get Windows Installer to find out whether the software is already installed. All *.msi* files and merge modules have unique identifiers. These are always in the form of a GUID (globally unique identifier), a 128-bit number generated with an algorithm that guarantees uniqueness.

You can add a Windows Installer search, specifying the identifier in the `ComponentId` property. This property expects the usual text formatting for a GUID—the string of hexadecimal digits between braces.

If you do not know the component ID for a product that your application depends on, but you have either an *.msi* or *.msm* file for it, you can use the MSI Spy tool to discover the ID. Alternatively, you can discover component IDs programmatically with the `MsiEnumComponents` API.

MSI Spy used to ship with the Windows Installer SDK, which is a part of the Microsoft Platform SDK. For some reason, it has been removed from the Platform SDK but can still be downloaded from Microsoft's web site as a part of the Visual Studio 6 samples at the following URL:

http://msdn.microsoft.com/library/default.asp?url=/library/en-us/ vcsample98/html/vcsmpsampprod.asp

Cab Files

Cab files are used only in legacy web environments in which Windows Installer files cannot be used. They are much less flexible than Windows Installer files—Cab files are simply a collection of files and some dependency information. They are mostly used to deploy ActiveX controls to web browsers.

Visual Studio .NET does not present any views for a Cab File project. A Cab file's contents can be viewed only in the Solution Explorer. As Figure 6-23 shows, the Solution Explorer simply shows the files the Cab file will contain.

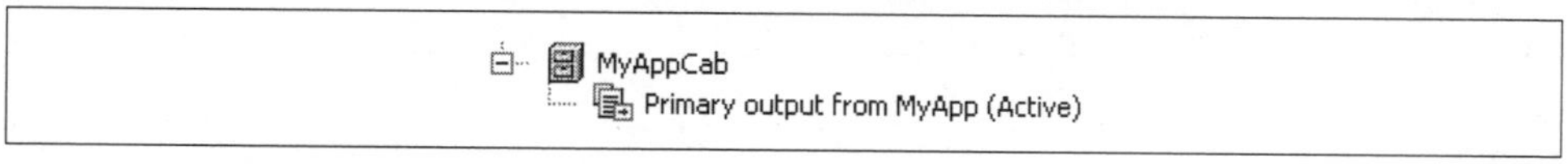

```
⊟ 📰 MyAppCab
    └ 📑 Primary output from MyApp (Active)
```

Figure 6-23. A Cab File project

You can add files to a Cab with the Add → Project Output... and Add → File... project context menu items. These work in much the same way as adding files to a Windows Installer Setup project, except Cab files don't have any notion of a destination directory.

The Cab project itself has three properties. FriendlyName is the public name that will be stored in the Cab file. This name can be displayed by applications that understand Cab files, such as Internet Explorer. A Version number may be set. Finally, the WebDependencies property allows a list of other Cab files that this file depends on to be specified.

If you edit the WebDependencies property, the dialog in Figure 6-24 will be shown. This lists the file's dependencies. For each dependency, you can specify the URL at which the dependent Cab file can be found, what its friendly name is expected to be, and the expected version number. This information will be processed by applications that understand Cab files. For example, Internet Explorer can use this information to work out what other files need to be downloaded when installing an ActiveX control from the Web.

Conclusion

Visual Studio .NET Setup and Deployment projects provide a straightforward way of building *.msi* files to install either normal executables or web applications. Although

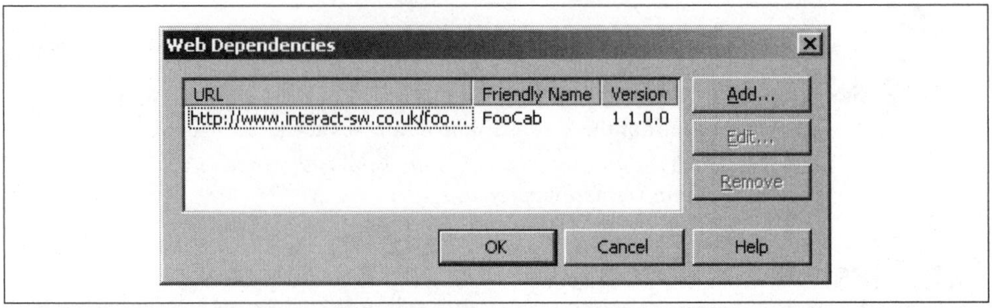

Figure 6-24. Cab file dependencies

these projects do not offer the full flexibility that Windows Installer can provide, they make it very easy to build simple installers. These projects have a set of standard UI pages, and a limited degree of intelligence can be built into the installer using conditional installation. These basic facilities can be extended by writing custom actions or .NET installer components.

CHAPTER 7

Integrating Components
with Visual Studio .NET

Visual Studio .NET presents a great deal of information about controls and other components you use in the development environment. When you drag a component from the toolbox into your project, VS.NET appears to know everything about it—the events and properties it supports are displayed in the property panel, neatly categorized, with a short description available for each member. Some controls have their own unique interactive editing features. Many add extra items to Visual Studio .NET's menus.

You might suspect that this level of extensive and often highly specialized support is something that is available only for the built-in controls, but that is not the case. Visual Studio .NET has a very open architecture for allowing components to customize the way in which they integrate with the environment.

Basic Integration

To build components that exploit Visual Studio .NET's integration facilities, you must understand the basic mechanisms involved. Component integration relies heavily on the .NET runtime's reflection mechanism—the facility that allows type information to be examined at runtime. VS.NET uses reflection to discover what properties and events your component provides.

> Strictly speaking, Visual Studio .NET doesn't use reflection directly. It uses the TypeDescriptor class and its friends in the System. ComponentModel namespace. These provide a virtualized view of type information, which allows a component's properties to be extended dynamically. The TypeDescriptor API is implemented using the reflection API however.

One of the advantages of this reflection-based approach is that components get a great deal for free. All of their public properties and events will be detected automatically. So a component as simple as that shown in Example 7-1 can participate fully in visual editing in a Visual Studio .NET project.

Example 7-1. A very simple component

```
using System.ComponentModel;

public class MyComponent : Component
{
    public string Title
    {
        get { return myTitle; }
        set { myTitle = value; }
    }
    private string myTitle;
}
```

If you compile the code in Example 7-1 into a class library, you can drag the compiled DLL from Windows Explorer onto a toolbox. (Alternatively, you can add it by right-clicking on the toolbox, selecting Customize Toolbox..., choosing the .NET Framework Components tab, clicking the Browse... button, and locating your component. This will have the same effect but is considerably more long-winded than the drag-and-drop approach.)

When you add a DLL to a toolbox, Visual Studio .NET searches it for classes that implement System.ComponentModel.IComponent and will add an entry to the toolbox for each such class that it finds. This includes all classes that derive from ComponentModel—it implements IComponent. If the DLL just contains the class shown in Example 7-1, the toolbox will grow one extra entry, as shown in Figure 7-1. (The cog icon is the default graphic used when a component does not provide its own bitmap. We will see how to supply a custom bitmap later.)

Figure 7-1. A newly added toolbox item

You will now be able to drag this component onto Visual Studio .NET design windows just like any other component. Because it derives directly from Component (and not the Windows Forms or Web Forms Control classes), it will appear in the component tray of any form you add it to, rather than on the form itself. This makes perfect sense—we didn't write a visual component, so it would have no business appearing on the form itself.

Once you have added an instance of your component to the component tray, you can select it and edit its properties by displaying the Properties window, just as you can for any built-in component. Figure 7-2 shows the Properties window for this component.

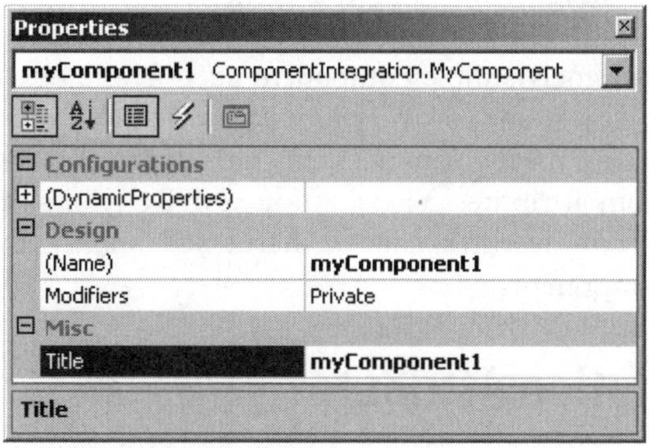

Figure 7-2. A custom component in the Properties window

Notice that the one public property defined by our class—Title—has appeared in the Properties window, along with the standard pseudo properties that the designer always adds. (The (Name) entry simply determines the name of the designer-generated field that will hold a reference to the component. Note that if you add a property called Name, this can lead to confusion, as VS.NET tends to want the Name property to be the same as the name of the field that holds the object. The Modifiers property determines that field's protection level.) If the component has any public events, and you are using it in a C# project, the lightning bolt button will appear at the top of the window, allowing us to browse the events instead of the properties. (For a Visual Basic .NET project, the events will instead be listed at the top of the source editor window.) Our property has appeared in the default Misc category, but we will see how to change that shortly.

> If you are trying things out as you read this, be aware that Visual Studio .NET appears to cache information about components. This is reasonable, since most of the time components do not change while you are using them, but it is slightly inconvenient if you are developing a component's design-time features. If you modify your component (e.g., you add an event), you may need to do the following steps to make changes visible in the client project::
>
> - Delete all instances of the component in the client project.
> - Remove the reference to the component from the client project (in the project's References section in the Solution Explorer).
> - Add the component back into the client project.
>
> These first three steps are usually sufficient, but if they do not work, try performing these extra steps before adding the component back to the project:
>
> - Delete the component from the toolbox.
> - Recompile the component.
> - Add the component back to the toolbox.

This reflection-based designer integration is great because it requires no effort to get a component working in Visual Studio .NET. However, this is all pretty bare-bones stuff. Even for an extremely simple component such as the one in Example 7-1, we are missing basic features, such as property categorization and description. Fortunately, .NET's reflection mechanism is extensible—types and their members can be annotated with custom attributes. Visual Studio .NET exploits this extensibility, and many of its integration features can be harnessed simply by adding the right attributes to your components.

Simple Integration Attributes

There are certain custom attributes that Visual Studio .NET will look for when you use a component. These allow you to improve your component's integration with the development environment, often without having to write any additional code at all. (Some of the more advanced integration features require both attributes and code, but we shall look at those later.)

Toolbox Bitmap

One of the first things you will want to do to your component is to change its toolbox bitmap. By default, all components get the cog icon shown in Figure 7-1, and there is no way for the end user to change it. It would be hard to locate specific items in a full toolbox if they all had the same bitmap, so it is best to supply a graphic for your component. You can specify a custom toolbox bitmap by applying the ToolboxBitmap attribute (defined, inexplicably, in the System.Drawing namespace) to your class.

The ToolboxBitmap attribute has three constructors. The first takes a string specifying the name of the file containing the bitmap. You will not normally use this, since it requires the bitmap to be stored in a separate file. It is much more convenient for a component to be a single self-contained file, so you will want to use one of the other constructors—both of these expect the bitmap to be an embedded resource in the component (see the "Embedded Resources" sidebar). The most commonly used constructor is the one that takes just a type object; its use is illustrated in Example 7-2.

Embedded Resources

Many applications and components require resources, such as bitmaps, icons, and mouse cursors. Although such items can be stored in separate files, this is inconvenient as it means that the component will no longer be self-contained: all of the associated resource files would need to be distributed along with the component in order to make it work.

Windows has long had a solution to this problem. The PE file format (the format used by all DLL and EXE files) allows arbitrary byte streams, as well as the usual executable code and data, to be embedded in the file. Most applications embed icons, bitmaps, and the like using this technique.

.NET provides its own solution, which is similar but different. *Assembly manifest resources* are conceptually similar to PE file resources—they are just byte streams stored within the file. The main difference is that, whereas PE file resources are identified by numbers, assembly manifest resources have names (e.g., *MyApplication. MyPicture.bmp*).

Because .NET components are compiled into DLL or EXE files, it is technically possible for a single file to contain both types of resources. However, because most .NET applications don't need to use PE file resources, Visual Studio .NET 2003 allows only a single PE file resource to be added to any given component—the one that will be used for the file icon. (This is the *App.ico* item that most .NET projects have. You can change which file will be used as the icon in the Project Property Pages—this property is in the Common Properties → General page, under the Application category.)

PE file resources, which are supported for only non-.NET projects, can be added using Add Resource... in the project context menu in the Solution Explorer.

Assembly manifest resources can be added to a component in a Visual Studio .NET project by selecting the item in the Solution Explorer and using the Properties window to set its Build Action to Embedded Resource.

In a Windows Forms application, each form will have its own *.resx* file containing resources associated with the form. Each *.resx* file can contain many resources, but it will be compiled into the component as a single assembly manifest resource. (The .NET ResourceManager class knows how to extract the individual resources from such a container.)

Example 7-2. The ToolboxBitmap attribute

```
using System.Drawing;
using System.ComponentModel;

[ToolboxBitmap(typeof(MyComponent))]
public class MyComponent : Component
{
. . . as before
```

By convention, the type object passed to the `ToolboxBitmap` attribute is the component's type, but this is not a requirement. The type object serves two roles here. First, Visual Studio .NET will look for the bitmap resource in the assembly in which the type is defined. (Although in principle you could use a bitmap defined in an external assembly by referring to a type defined in that assembly, in practice you will always want this to be the same assembly as the component itself.) Second, the resource name will be based on the fully qualified name of the type. So if `MyComponent` in Example 7-2 is defined in the `MyNamespace` namespace, Visual Studio .NET will look for an embedded resource called *MyNamespace.MyComponent.bmp*. (In other words, it takes the fully qualified name of the type and appends *.bmp*.)

For this to be of use, you must make sure that your component contains an embedded bitmap resource with the right name. To do this, first add a bitmap to the project. (Select Add New Item... from the project's context menu in the Solution Explorer and choose Bitmap File from the Resources category.) Your bitmap should have the same name as the component class. Visual Studio .NET automatically prepends the project default namespace to the bitmap when embedding it as a resource, so you do not need to supply the fully qualified name. In our example, the bitmap filename would be *MyComponent.bmp*. Your bitmap should be 16x16 pixels. Visual Studio .NET will look at the color of the bottom-left pixel and will draw all pixels with that color as transparent.

By default, bitmaps do not get compiled into projects, so simply adding a bitmap to the project is not enough. You must change the bitmap's Build Action to be Embedded Resource. You can do this from the bitmap project item's Properties page, shown in Figure 7-3. Note that bitmaps have two different property pages: the one that appears when you are editing the bitmap and the one that appears when you select the bitmap item in the Solution Explorer. The Build Action is located in the latter.

Note that the filenames are, somewhat unusually, case sensitive. This is because the mechanism by which the bitmap resource is retrieved from the component is case sensitive. (`Assembly.GetManifestResourceStream` is used.) So you must make sure that the bitmap name's case matches that of your class exactly and that the *.bmp* extension is all lowercase.

Visual Studio .NET always prepends the project's default namespace to an embedded resource. (The project's default namespace can be set in the project property pages. Right-click on the project in the Solution Explorer, and in the Properties window that appears, select the Common Properties → General tab. The Default Namespace property is in the Application category.) If the resource file is in a subdirectory within the project, VS.NET will also add the folder name between the namespace and the filename. So if a bitmap called *Picture.bmp* is in a folder called *SomeFolder*, the embedded resource will be named *MyNamespace.SomeFolder.Picture.bmp*.

There is no way to disable this behavior. This means that if you want to embed a resource whose name does not start with the default namespace, your only option is to give the project a blank default namespace.

There is a third constructor for the `ToolboxBitmap` attribute, which takes both a type reference and a string. The documentation is a little misleading here, as it suggests that the type reference is used only to determine which assembly the name is in and that you can specify the name of the resource with the string. This is not quite true—the type object is used in two ways. The embedded resource name is formed by taking the namespace of the type and appending the string supplied. So if you were to supply the following reasonable-looking parameters to the custom attribute:

```
[ToolboxBitmap(typeof(MyComponent), "MyNamespace.MyComponent.bmp")]
```

Visual Studio .NET would look for an embedded resource called *MyNamespace. MyNamespace.MyComponent.bmp*!

Sadly, just as there is no way to force Visual Studio .NET to compile in an embedded bitmap with the exact name that you require, there is also no way to specify the precise name of the embedded resource to use with the `ToolboxBitmap` attribute. In both cases, the namespace will be added, and there is nothing you can do about it. So you should stick to the following rules:

- Name the bitmap resource after the unqualified class name
- Define your component in the project default namespace

Since the Visual Studio .NET wizards will always add new components into the project default namespace, it is easy to stick to these rules in practice.

Categories and Descriptions

When Visual Studio .NET displays properties and events in the Properties window, it usually provides two hints as to their use: it groups members by category, and it provides a short textual description when an item is selected. By default, your components' members will appear in the Misc category and will have an empty description, but it is easy to fix this.

You can use the Category attribute (defined in the System.ComponentModel namespace) to determine the category in which members appear in the Properties window. The attribute just takes a string, which is the name of the category. You can use whatever you like as a string, but it is recommended that you use one of the standard categories if possible. (These are Action, Appearance, Behavior, Data, Design, DragDrop, Focus, Format, Key, Layout, Mouse, and WindowStyle.)

The Description attribute is also very simple to use. As with the Category attribute, it just takes a string. This string will be displayed in the Description pane of the Properties window when the property is selected.

Example 7-3 shows both the Category and the Description attributes in use on the Title property of our component. With these in place, the Properties window will look like Figure 7-4.

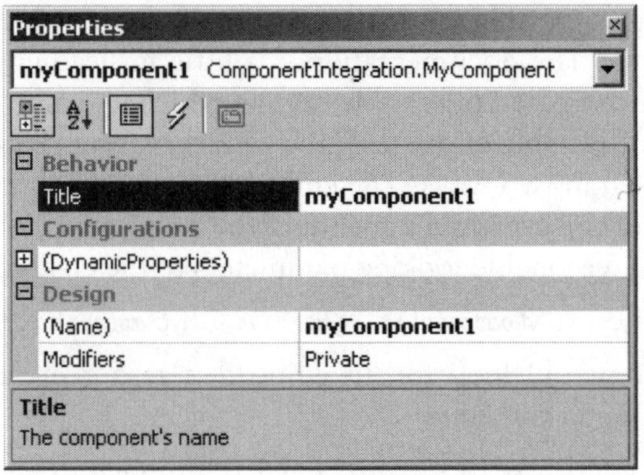

Figure 7-3. Category and description in the Properties window

Example 7-3. A property with a category and a description

```
using System.ComponentModel;

. . .

[Category("Behavior")]
[Description("The component's name")]
public string Title
{
. . . as before
```

Localization

Both the Category and the Description attributes cause text to be displayed in Visual Studio .NET's user interface. If your component might be used at design time in different countries, this presents a localization issue—how do you ensure that the category and description strings are appropriate to the locale?

With the Category attribute, life is very easy if you stick to the built-in category names (listed earlier). Visual Studio .NET recognizes these names and will translate them for you automatically. The Description attribute presents more of a challenge. (As does using nonstandard category names.)

If you want your description strings to be localized, you must create your own attribute class that derives from the Description attribute, overriding its Description property to perform the appropriate lookup. (You would normally use the ResourceManager class in the System.Resources namespace to look the name up in the appropriate satellite resource assembly.)

To make custom category names localizable, you use a similar technique—you create your own class that derives from the Category attribute. For some reason, instead of overriding the Description property, you are required to override a protected method called GetLocalizedString and look up the translated resource there; the Category attribute class will call this when translation is required.

Default Events and Properties

With most of the .NET Framework's built-in components, double-clicking on them will cause an event handler to be added to your code. (This is true of all components that raise events, not just controls.) With components that raise multiple events, Visual Studio .NET always seems to know which event handler to add—for a button it will handle the Click event, for a text box it will handle TextChanged, and so on. And likewise, if you drag a new component onto a form and just type in some data without first selecting a property in the grid, it will usually pick a sensible property to modify (e.g., Text for most controls).

For our own components, we can determine which event and property Visual Studio .NET will choose under these circumstances. There are attributes for choosing a default property and event. These are applied to the class and simply take the name of the relevant member as a construction parameter, as shown in Example 7-4.

Example 7-4. A component with a default event and property

```
[DefaultEvent("OnTitleChanged")]
[DefaultProperty("Title")]
public class MyComponent : Component
{
```

Property Visibility

Sometimes your components may have properties that you will not wish to be displayed in the Properties window. This is particularly common with controls—the base control classes in Windows Forms and Web Forms provide many standard properties, not all of which make sense in derived controls. (For example, the Panel control does not use the Text property.) Also, some properties are designed to be used only from code, such as the Windows Forms Control class's Created property, and it would be confusing and unhelpful for them to appear in the property grid.

To prevent such properties from appearing, you can mark them with the Browsable attribute. This takes a Boolean; specifying false prevents the property from appearing in the Properties window. (If you are using this to hide an unused property inherited from the base class, you will need to override that property in order to use this attribute. If the only reason you are overriding the property is to apply an attribute, you should just defer to the base class in the implementation, as Example 7-5 does.)

Example 7-5. A nonbrowsable property

```
[Browsable(false)]
public override string Text
{ get { return base.Text; } set { base.Text = value; } }
```

Although the property in Example 7-5 will not appear in the Properties window, it will still show up in IntelliSense in source editing windows. If you wish to prevent it from appearing even in source windows, you can apply the EditorBrowsable attribute. If you pass the EditorBrowsableState.Never enumeration value to the constructor, the member will not appear in IntelliSense lists. (Developers who know the property is there will still be able to use it however—the compiler itself ignores this attribute.) If you do not supply an EditorBrowsable attribute, the effective default is EditorBrowsable.Always. There is also an EditorBrowsable.Advanced setting, which is supposed to hide the property for all but advanced users. By default, this hides the property in Visual Basic .NET projects but does not hide it in C# projects. (See Appendix F for information on how to change this and other text editor settings.)

Designer Serialization

When users change your component's properties in the Properties window, Visual Studio .NET generates code that will set the property at runtime. (It does this in the autogenerated InitializeComponent method; it effectively serializes the properties as code.) Of course, you will want code to be generated only when the property has actually been changed. Visual Studio .NET relies on knowing what your property's default value is to work out whether the value has been changed. (It doesn't just remember what the value was before the user started making edits.)

You can tell Visual Studio .NET what a property's default value is by applying the DefaultValue attribute. This has a wide array of constructors—most of the intrinsic types get their own constructor, and there is also one that takes an object, allowing you to pass any value at all. When Visual Studio .NET generates the InitializeComponent method, it will compare your component's property's current value to the default value, and generate initialization code only if they differ.

Some properties' default values are determined at runtime. For example, a `Control` object's default `BackColor` property value is determined by its parent. Under these circumstances, a `DefaultValue` attribute cannot be used. Instead, the property should have an associated `ShouldSerialize` method. (For example, if the property in question is called `Title`, then there should be a `ShouldSerializeTitle` method.) This method should return a Boolean, indicating whether the property has been set, and the designer therefore needs to generate code to serialize this property. If you supply a `ShouldSerialize` method, you should also supply a corresponding `Reset` method (e.g., `ResetTitle`). Visual Studio .NET will use this when the user selects the Reset item from the property's context menu. This method should cause the property to return to its original state (i.e., the value should revert to the dynamically determined default, and the `ShouldSerialize` method should return false).

You can disable designer serialization entirely if necessary. (For example, it would not be worth serializing a property whose value is calculated from other properties at runtime.) The `DesignerSerializationVisibility` attribute allows you to control what code is generated at serialization time. If you construct the attribute with the `DesignerSerializationVisibility.Hidden` enumeration member, the property will never have any code generated for it in the `InitializeComponent` method. The default setting is the `Visible` enumeration member. There is also a `Content` member, which indicates that the designer should enumerate the property's contents, rather than trying to serialize the whole property in one step. You would normally do this only if the property's type does not serialize correctly, but each of its individual member properties can be serialized. (For example, if you have a custom type that has no corresponding `TypeConverter`, Visual Studio .NET will not know how to generate code to serialize properties of this type. But if this custom type's own properties are all of standard types, the `Content` setting would cause Visual Studio .NET to generate code to serialize each of these individually.)

Data Binding

If you are writing a control, you may wish for certain properties to be presented under the (`DataBindings`) section of the Properties window—this is where Visual Studio .NET allows data bindings to be configured interactively. Programmatically, any control property can be bound to a data source, but only those explicitly marked as bindable will appear under (`DataBindings`).

By default, the `Control` class's `Tag` and `Text` properties are bindable, but you can add your own with the `Bindable` attribute. Simply mark any property that you want to appear in the data binding section with this attribute, passing in true as a constructor parameter.

Custom Property Types

The Visual Studio .NET property grid (which, incidentally, is available for use in your own applications as the System.Windows.Forms.PropertyGrid control) is able to deal with a wide range of different property types. It can supply appropriately specialized user interfaces for the types commonly used for control properties, such as Color and Size. But what if your component has a property of some custom type?

Even with custom types, the property grid can display the value of your property. In the absence of other information, it will simple call the ToString method and display the results. However, the property will be grayed out, so users will not be able to edit it. Also, ToString may not produce the desired result—by default, this simply returns the name of the type.

You can enable editing of properties with custom types in two ways. Both involve writing special support classes—you cannot support custom types with attributes alone. You can enable full text-based editing by supplying a custom *type converter*. You can also provide a graphical user interface for editing the property by writing a custom *UI type editor*.

Type Converters

A type converter is a class derived from TypeConverter, which is defined in the System.ComponentModel namespace. (Despite the similar name, this class is in no way connected to the System.Convert class.) Its job is to convert between types, usually between a custom type and a string. If a custom type has an associated type converter, Visual Studio .NET will use that to convert properties of that type to strings in the property grid. And if the user modifies the properties in the grid, the type converter will be used to convert the modified strings back to property values. The framework class libraries supply type converters for many widely used types, such as Point and Rectangle. You will usually need to supply converters only for your own custom types.

We tell Visual Studio .NET that a custom type converter is available with the TypeConverter attribute. This attribute can be applied either to the custom type itself or to the property itself, shown respectively in Example 7-6 and Example 7-7. A converter specified for a property will take precedence over one specified for the type. So, although ThreeDPoint is associated with the MyThreeDPointConverter type converter in Example 7-6, the property in Example 7-7 has elected to use the ExpandableObjectConverter type converter instead.

Example 7-6. Associating a type converter with a type

```
[TypeConverter(typeof(MyThreeDPointConverter))]
public class ThreeDPoint
{
```

Example 7-6. Associating a type converter with a type (continued)

```
    public ThreeDPoint(int x, int y, int z)
    {
        this.x = x; this.y = y; this.z = z;
    }

    public ThreeDPoint( )
    {
    }

    public int X { get { return x; } set { x = value; } }
    public int Y { get { return y; } set { y = value; } }
    public int Z { get { return z; } set { z = value; } }
    private int x, y, z;
}
```

Example 7-7. Associating a type converter with a property

```
public class HasPoint
{
    [TypeConverter(typeof(ExpandableObjectConverter))]
    public ThreeDPoint P1 { get { return p1; } set { p1 = value; } }
    private ThreeDPoint p1;
}
```

The type converter itself is just a class derived from TypeConverter. We typically overload four methods. Visual Studio .NET uses two of these to discover which conversions we support. It will call CanConvertTo to discover if we can convert to a particular type and CanConvertFrom to see if we can transform a particular type into the custom type. These are called when a property is displayed in the property grid. In both cases, VS.NET asks about support for conversion to and from strings.

The other two methods we overload are ConvertTo and ConvertFrom. These are called when Visual Studio .NET needs to perform a conversion. ConvertTo will be called (with a target type of string) when the property grid is being displayed. ConvertFrom is called (with a source type of string) when the user edits a property in the grid.

Example 7-8 shows a sample type converter for the three-dimensional point class, shown in Example 7-6. Its CanConvertTo and CanConvertFrom methods support conversions to and from strings.

Example 7-8. A type converter

```
using System;
using System.ComponentModel;

public class MyThreeDPointConverter : TypeConverter
{
    public override bool CanConvertTo(ITypeDescriptorContext context,
        Type destinationType)
    {
        if (destinationType ==  typeof(string)) return true;
```

Example 7-8. A type converter (continued)

```
        return base.CanConvertTo(context, destinationType);
    }

    public override bool CanConvertFrom(ITypeDescriptorContext context,
        Type sourceType)
    {
        if (sourceType ==  typeof(string)) return true;
        return base.CanConvertFrom(context, sourceType);
    }

    public override object ConvertTo(ITypeDescriptorContext context,
        System.Globalization.CultureInfo culture, object value,
        Type destinationType)
    {
        if (destinationType ==  typeof(string))
        {
            ThreeDPoint point = (ThreeDPoint) value;
            return string.Format("{0},{1},{2}", point.X, point.Y, point.Z);
        }
        return base.ConvertTo(context, culture, value, destinationType);
    }

    public override object ConvertFrom(ITypeDescriptorContext context,
        System.Globalization.CultureInfo culture, object value)
    {
        if (value.GetType() ==  typeof(string))
        {
            string src = (string) value;
            string[ ] points = src.Split(',');
            if (points.Length != 3)
                throw new ArgumentException("String must be formatted as 'x,y,z'",
                    "value");

            return new ThreeDPoint(int.Parse(points[0]),
                int.Parse(points[1]), int.Parse(points[2]));
        }
        return base.ConvertFrom(context, culture, value);
    }
}
}
```

The actual conversions are done in `ConvertTo` and `ConvertFrom`. They convert the string to and from a comma-separated list of the three coordinate values. Figure 7-5 shows this type converter in action on a property grid. It displays a component with a single property, `Point`, of type `ThreeDPoint`. (The full source code for these types is shown in Example 7-6 and Example 7-7. If you compile this code into a Class Library project, you will then be able to add it to your toolbox using the toolbox context menu's Customize Toolbox item: select the .NET Framework Components tab and then Browse for your component. Alternatively, you can drag your compiled DLL from a Windows Explorer window onto the toolbox.)

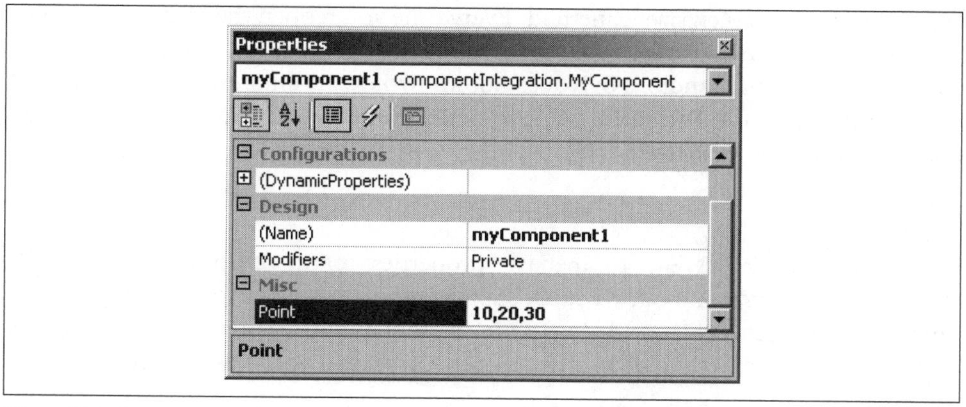

Figure 7-4. A type converter in action

If your type already has a suitable ToString method, you do not need to override CanConvertTo and ConvertTo simply to support string conversion. TypeConverter provides default implementations of these methods that support string conversion by calling ToString on the object. (As you will see shortly, you will normally want to override these methods to support code serialization. But even then, you can still defer to the base class for string conversions unless the type's ToString method does not provide appropriate behavior.)

We can go one better than this and provide the same expandable editing that built-in classes such as Size and Point have. If we change the type converter in Example 7-8 so that its base class is ExpandableObjectConverter, the property grid will display an expandable version of the property, as Figure 7-6 shows.

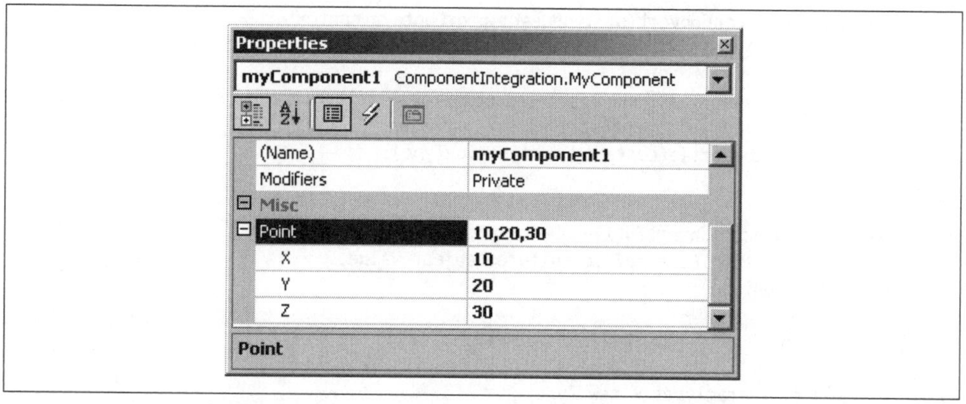

Figure 7-5. An expandable property

Unfortunately, if you try to use this type converter in Visual Studio .NET, you will discover that it has a serious shortcoming. The designer fails to save the edited values in the InitializeComponent method. Every time you reopen the form containing a component that uses this type, the property will have forgotten its value. The reason for this is that Visual Studio .NET does not know how to initialize new instances of our ThreeDPoint class. We must tell it how to do this by adding code serialization support to our type converter.

Code serialization

For Visual Studio .NET to persist properties of a custom type in the InitializeComponent method, we must support an extra conversion in our type converter. The CanConvertTo and ConvertTo methods must support conversion to InstanceDescriptor (defined in the System.ComponentModel.Design.Serialization namespace).

The InstanceDescriptor class encapsulates instructions on how to create an instance of a particular type. We can use it in our type converter to tell Visual Studio .NET how to generate code to create a ThreeDPoint object. (We need to supply conversion only *to* InstanceDescriptor. Converting *from* an InstanceDescriptor back to our type is not needed—Visual Studio .NET just constructs the object according to the instructions in InstanceDescriptor.)

Example 7-9 shows the modified CanConvertTo and ConvertTo methods. When asked to convert to an InstanceDescriptor, the converter builds one, supplying a ConstructorInfo object (from the System.Reflection namespace) to indicate which constructor to use. It also supplies the parameters required by this constructor. With the type converter thus modified, Visual Studio .NET can now generate code for properties of type ThreeDPoint.

Example 7-9. Type converter code serialization support

```
public override bool CanConvertTo(ITypeDescriptorContext context,
    Type destinationType)
{
    if (destinationType == typeof(InstanceDescriptor)) return true;
    if (destinationType == typeof(string)) return true;
    return base.CanConvertTo(context, destinationType);
}

public override object ConvertTo(ITypeDescriptorContext context,
    System.Globalization.CultureInfo culture, object value,
    Type destinationType)
{
    if (destinationType == typeof(InstanceDescriptor))
    {
        Type[ ] ctorParamTypes = new Type[ ]
            { typeof(int), typeof(int), typeof(int) };
        ConstructorInfo ctor = typeof(ThreeDPoint).GetConstructor(ctorParamTypes);

        ThreeDPoint p = (ThreeDPoint) value;
```

Example 7-9. Type converter code serialization support (continued)

```
        object[ ] ctorParams = { p.X, p.Y, p.Z };

        return new InstanceDescriptor(ctor, ctorParams);
    }
    if (destinationType == typeof(string))
    {
        ThreeDPoint point = (ThreeDPoint) value;
        return string.Format("{0},{1},{2}", point.X, point.Y, point.Z);
    }
    return base.ConvertTo(context, culture, value, destinationType);
}
```

Example 7-10 shows some generated code from an `InitializeComponent` method.

Example 7-10. Code generated based on an InstanceDescriptor

```
//
// componentWith3D1
//
this.componentWith3D1.Point = new ThreeDPoint(10, 20, 30);
```

Custom UI Type Editors

Visual Studio .NET will use type converters only for text-based property editing and code serialization. Some built-in types, such as `Color` or `DockStyle`, get a specialized user interface in the property grid as well as text support. If you would like to supply a graphical editing interface for your own property types, you can do so by supplying a UI type editor.

 Any type or property is allowed to have both a type converter and a UI type editor. Supplying both gives developers who use your controls a choice—they can edit properties either as text or using the custom UI.

A UI type editor is similar to a type converter—it is a class associated with a custom type via an attribute and used by Visual Studio .NET in the property grid. The attribute for a UI type editor is the `Editor` attribute, defined in the `System. ComponentModel` namespace. As with a type converter, you may apply this attribute either to the custom type or to a property itself. If you apply this attribute to a property, the property's type doesn't even need to be a custom type—you can supply a custom editing UI for a built-in type if you want, as Example 7-11 shows.

Example 7-11. A property with a custom UI type editor

```
[Editor(typeof(ContrastEditor), typeof(UITypeEditor))]
public int Contrast
{
    get { return myContrast; }
    set { myContrast = value; }
```

Example 7-11. A property with a custom UI type editor (continued)

```
}
private int myContrast;
```

As Example 7-11 shows, the Editor attribute requires you to indicate what sort of
editor you are specifying as well as the editor's class—it is designed to allow multiple different kinds of editors to be associated with a property or type. In this case, we
are specifying UITypeEditor. (In fact, with Visual Studio .NET 2003, custom UI type
editors are the only kind of editor supported.) UI type editors must derive from the
UITypeEditor class, which is defined in the System.Drawing.Design namespace. (The
ContrastEditor is a fictional editor. Two possible implementations are shown later in
Example 7-12 and Example 7-13.)

When we write the UI editor class itself, we have a choice as to the kind of user interface we can supply. We can either open a modal dialog or supply a pop-up user
interface that will appear in the property grid itself. We indicate this by overriding
the GetEditStyle method. This method returns a value from the
UITypeEditorEditStyle enumeration, either Modal or DropDown. For either type of user
interface, we must also override the EditValue method, which will be called when the
user tries to edit the value.

Example 7-12. A dialog custom UI type editor

```
using System.Drawing.Design;
using System.Windows.Forms;

public class ContrastEditor : UITypeEditor
{
    public override UITypeEditorEditStyle GetEditStyle(
        ITypeDescriptorContext context)
    {
        return UITypeEditorEditStyle.Modal;
    }

    public override object EditValue(ITypeDescriptorContext context,
        IServiceProvider provider, object value)
    {
        DialogResult rc = MessageBox.Show("Maximum contrast?",
            "Contrast", MessageBoxButtons.YesNoCancel);
        if (rc == DialogResult.Yes)
            return 100;
        if (rc == DialogResult.No)
            return 50;
        return value;
    }
}
```

Example 7-12 shows a custom UI type editor that displays a simple message box.
(Any modal dialog would do.) The value returned from EditValue will be written
back to the property. The property grid indicates that a modal editor is available for

---

the property by putting a button with a ... label on the grid when the property is selected, as Figure 7-7 shows. It will call EditValue when the button is clicked.

Figure 7-6. A property with a modal custom UI type editor

If you want to provide a drop-down editor user interface (such as the one supplied for the built-in Color type), the technique is slightly different. You must get Visual Studio .NET to open the window for you, so that it can be placed and sized correctly. The code for doing this is shown in Example 7-13.

Example 7-13. A drop-down custom UI type editor

```
using System.Drawing.Design;
using System.Windows.Forms;
using System.Windows.Forms.Design;

public class ContrastEditor : UITypeEditor
{
    public override UITypeEditorEditStyle GetEditStyle(
        ITypeDescriptorContext context)
    {
        return UITypeEditorEditStyle.DropDown;
    }

    public override object EditValue(ITypeDescriptorContext context,
        IServiceProvider provider, object value)
    {
        IWindowsFormsEditorService wfes = provider.GetService(
            typeof(IWindowsFormsEditorService)) as
            IWindowsFormsEditorService;
        if (wfes != null)
        {
            TrackBar tb = new TrackBar( );
            tb.Minimum = 0;
            tb.Maximum = 100;
            tb.Value = (int) value;
            tb.TickFrequency = 10;
            wfes.DropDownControl(tb);
            value = tb.Value;
        }
        return value;
    }
}
```

This code uses the IServiceProvider passed to EditValue. It asks it for the IWindowsFormsEditorService interface (which is defined in the System.Windows.Forms.Design namespace). This service provides the facility for opening a drop-down editor—we simply call the DropDownControl method on it, and it will open whichever control we pass. It sets the size and location of the control so that it appears directly below the property when the drop-down arrow is clicked, as Figure 7-8 shows. (It will modify the control's width to be the same as the property grid's value column, but it will use whatever height you specify. Since we have not set the height in this example, we are simply getting the TrackBar control's default height.)

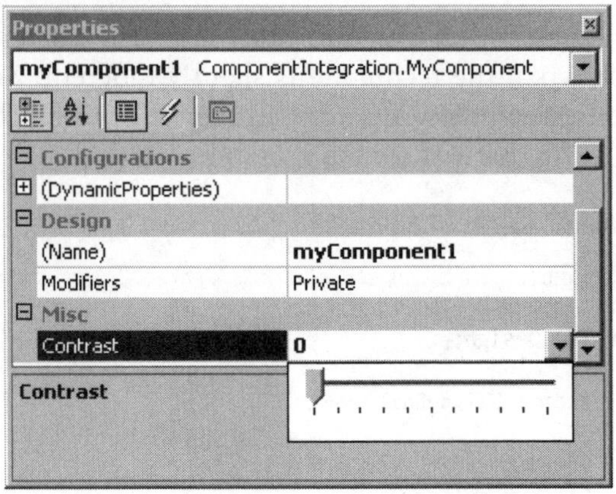

Figure 7-7. A drop-down UI type editor in action

> Although this example uses one of the built-in controls, the TrackBar, you are free to use any control, including controls of your own devising. It is common practice to create a UserControl (a custom control built by composing several other controls) for a drop-down editor.

Custom UI type editors can also add a small graphic to the property grid, which will be displayed in the value field whether the user opens the custom editor or not. Several of the built-in types use this facility. For example, properties of type Color always show a small rectangle of the currently selected color in the grid. To supply a similar graphic of your own, you must override two methods: GetPaintValueSupported and PaintValue.

As Example 7-14 shows, the GetPaintValueSupported method is very simple. This will be called when the property is shown in the property grid and we return true to indicate that we would like to supply a graphic for the property. Visual Studio .NET will then call the PaintValue method, in which we draw the graphical representation of the value. The PaintValueEventArgs object supplies a Graphics object into which we draw the representation and a Bounds rectangle indicating how large the drawing should be.

Example 7-14. Adding a value graphic

```
// Add these using statements to Example 7-13.
using System.Drawing;
```

Example 7-14. Adding a value graphic (continued)

```csharp
using System.Drawing.Drawing2D;

// Add these methods to the ContrastEditor class from Example 7-13.
//
public override bool GetPaintValueSupported(ITypeDescriptorContext context)
{
    return true;
}


public override void PaintValue(System.Drawing.Design.PaintValueEventArgs e)
{
    Graphics g = e.Graphics;
    int contrast = (int) e.Value;

    int darkValue = ((100-contrast) * 127) / 100;
    int lightValue = 255 - darkValue;
    Color darkColor = Color.FromArgb(darkValue, darkValue, darkValue);
    Color lightColor = Color.FromArgb(lightValue, lightValue, lightValue);

    using (Brush fill = new LinearGradientBrush(
                        e.Bounds, darkColor, lightColor,
                        LinearGradientMode.BackwardDiagonal))
    {
        g.FillRectangle(fill, e.Bounds);
    }
}
```

The Graphics object supplied to the PaintValue method is the same one that the property grid uses to paint itself. This means that you should take care to leave it in the state that you found it. If you change anything such as the transform, or smoothing mode, you should save the state at the start of your method by calling Save, and restore it at the end using Restore. If you fail to do this, the property grid's appearance may be adversely affected.

Also, note that clip rectangle for the Graphics object is not quite set correctly. It is possible to draw slightly outside of the region specified by the PaintValueEventArgs object's Bounds property. (With the current implementation, you can draw anywhere in the cell showing your property's value.) You should therefore be careful not to draw anything outside of the region specified by Bounds.

Example 7-14 simply fills the available space with a rectangle painted with a gradient fill. When the property (which in this case is the Contrast property from Example 7-11) is at 100%, the fill will be high-contrast, ranging from black to white, as Figure 7-9 shows. When the contrast is 0%, the fill will be a uniform shade of gray.

Figure 7-8. A property with a custom value graphic

Custom Component Designers

Type converters and custom UI editors enable us to provide specialized editing facilities for custom property types. But what if we are writing controls and want to be able to customize the way they are presented on forms? Visual Studio .NET even lets us provide custom editing facilities for controls hosted in the forms designer, by writing a *custom designer*.

A custom designer is a class that derives from `ComponentDesigner` (which is defined in the `System.ComponentModel.Design` namespace). Designers for nonvisual components derive directly from this class, but control designers derive from one of the two `ControlDesigner` classes. (The `System.Windows.Forms.Design` and `System.Web.UI.Design` namespaces each have a `ControlDesigner` class. These are used for Windows Forms and Web Forms designers, respectively.)

 This separation of runtime and design-time elements allows you to place all of the design-time code into a separate component. This will mean that, at runtime, your component will not be carrying any unnecessary design-time baggage, making it slightly more memory-efficient.

Whether for Web Forms Controls, Windows Forms Controls, or plain components, designer classes have certain commonalities. They are associated with their components by applying the `Designer` attribute (in the `System.ComponentModel` namespace) to the component class. And although most of the integration features are specific to either Windows Forms or Web Forms, all designer classes can add extra menu items to the Visual Studio .NET context menu.

Adding Menu Verbs

To add extra items to the context menu for a component in the forms designer, we must override the associated designer class's Verbs property. This property is of type `DesignerVerbCollection`, which is defined in the `System.ComponentModel.Design` namespace.

Example 7-15 shows a control designer with an example Verbs property.

Example 7-15. Adding custom menu verbs

```
public class MyComponentDesigner : ComponentDesigner
{
    public override DesignerVerbCollection Verbs
    {
```

Example 7-15. Adding custom menu verbs (continued)

```
    get
    {
        DesignerVerb[ ] verbs = new DesignerVerb[ ]
        {
            new DesignerVerb("Add Widget",
                new EventHandler(OnAddWidget)),
            new DesignerVerb("Remove Widget",
                new EventHandler(OnRemoveWidget))
        };
        return new DesignerVerbCollection(verbs);

    }
}

private void OnAddWidget (object sender, EventArgs e)
{
    MyComponent ctl = (MyComponent) this.Component;
    . . .
}

private void OnRemoveWidget(object sender, EventArgs e)
{
    MyComponent ctl = (MyComponent) this.Component;
    . . .
}
}
```

The easiest way to build a `DesignerVerbsCollection` is to construct one from an array of `DesignerVerb` objects. Each `DesignerVerb` is relatively simple—it simply needs the text that will appear on the menu and a delegate referring to the event handler that should be called when the relevant menu item is clicked. So when you right-click on an item with this custom designer, Visual Studio .NET will show a context menu with extra Add Widget and Remove Widget menu items, as Figure 7-10 shows. It will call our `OnAddWidget` or `OnRemoveWidget` method, respectively, when these menu items are selected. (The component being edited can be retrieved from the `ComponentDesigner` base class property `Component`, as Example 7-15 shows.)

Any menu verbs added like this will also appear in the property grid. Visual Studio .NET adds an extra panel to the grid and shows verbs there using a hyperlink style (a blue, underlined word), as Figure 7-11 shows.

Windows Forms Control Designers

Windows Forms custom control designers are essentially specialized component designers. They can provide extra menu items, just like a normal component designer. They can also modify how resizing and positioning are handled, paint adornments (such as extra handles) on your control, and manage mouse clicks in the Visual Studio .NET Windows Forms designer.

Figure 7-9. Visual Studio .NET context menu with custom items

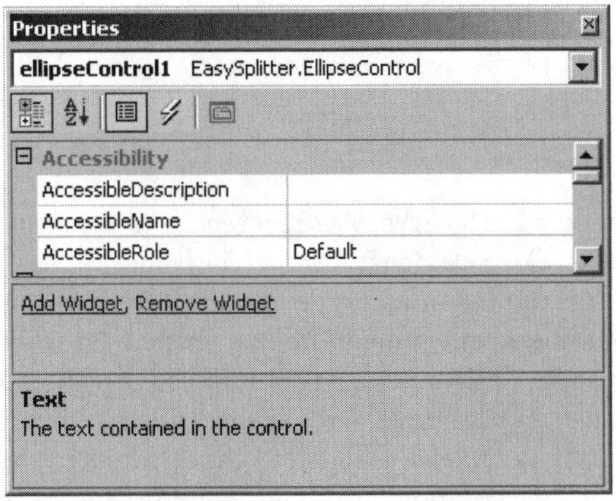

Figure 7-10. Custom verbs in the property grid

Example 7-16 shows a control with a custom designer, specified with the Designer attribute. The designer class itself must derive from the ControlDesigner class. (ControlDesigner itself derives from ComponentDesigner.) We choose which methods to override in the designer class based on which aspects of the control's design-time functionality we would like to customize.

Example 7-16. A Windows Forms control with a custom designer

```
[Designer(typeof(MyControlDesigner))]
public class MyControl :
   System.Windows.Forms.Control
{
   . . .
}
```

Resizing and moving

The forms designer will automatically provide all controls with an outline allowing them to be moved and resized. However, this is not always appropriate—some controls need to have a fixed size. (For example, the TabPage control's size and position are always determined by its parent TabControl.) Visual Studio .NET therefore lets us specify whether our control should be movable and which edges should be resizable. We simply override the SelectionRules property in our designer class, returning the required combination of bits from the SelectionRules enumeration (defined in the System.Windows.Forms.Design namespace).

Example 7-17 specifies SelectionRules.Visible, meaning that the resize/move outline should be displayed; it also indicates that the lefthand side of the outline should be resizable, with SelectionRules.LeftSizeable. (So, this particular control will not be vertically resizable. It cannot be moved either—you must specify SelectionRules. Moveable to enable that.) The default implementation of SelectionRules returns SelectionRules.AllSizable | SelectionRules.Moveable | SelectionRules.Visible.

Example 7-17. Modifying support for moving and resizing

```
public override SelectionRules SelectionRules
{
    get
    {
        return SelectionRules.Visible |
            SelectionRules.LeftSizeable;
    }
}
```

Figure 7-12 shows how the control with the designer class in Example 7-17 will look in the forms designer. Notice that all of the resize handles are gray, with the exception of the one halfway up the lefthand side, which is white. (Visual Studio .NET also uses the mouse cursor to indicate which edges can be resized. In this example, a resize cursor will appear only when the mouse is over the handle halfway up the lefthand side.) Resizing with all of the other handles has been disabled because we told Visual Studio .NET that the control cannot be moved, and only the lefthand side can be resized. VS.NET colors handles that cannot be moved gray.

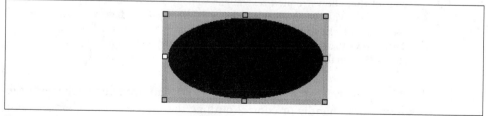

Figure 7-11. A control with one resizable edge

Adornments

Sometimes it is useful to add extra visual features to a control at design time, to allow developers to change properties visually. The outline and handles that Visual Studio .NET adds to controls to enable them to be moved and resized are an example of this. With a custom designer class, it is possible to add further such adornments of your own.

We could simply modify our control's OnPaint method to draw adornments at design time. (It is possible to detect that a control is hosted in a designer by examining the Control class's DesignMode property.) However, adornments are normally drawn only when the control is selected, and it is hard to detect this in OnPaint. Moreover, to do this would defeat the ability to separate runtime and design-time facets into separate components. Fortunately, Visual Studio .NET gives us an opportunity to paint adornments in our designer class. It will call the OnPaintAdornments method when the control is selected.

Example 7-18 illustrates the basic principle.

Example 7-18. Drawing custom adornments

```
protected override void OnPaintAdornments(PaintEventArgs pe)
{
    pe.Graphics.DrawString("Hello", Control.Font, Brushes.Red, 0, 0);
}
```

The results are shown in Figure 7-13. Normally, you would draw an adornment that reflected some aspect of the component's control, of course. But as this example shows, you draw adornments in just the same way that you draw in a normal OnPaint method—simply use the Graphics object supplied in the PaintEventArgs object.

Figure 7-12. A custom adornment

Many controls draw extra grab handles as adornments. For example, a control that shows rotated text might want to allow the angle to be controlled with a draggable handle. The System.Windows.Forms. ControlPaint class provides a method for doing this: DrawGrabHandle. This allows the size of the grab handles to be specified. To be consistent with Visual Studio .NET you should use 7x7.

Visual Studio .NET provides extra visual feedback for its adornments—whenever the mouse moves over a grab handle or control outline, the mouse cursor changes. You can do the same thing for your adornments. If the mouse pointer is over your control, Visual Studio .NET will call your designer class's OnSetCursor method every

---

time it moves. You can write code in here to detect whether the cursor is over any of your grab handles (or other adornments) and set the cursor. Just set the `Cursor` class's `Current` property. Unfortunately, `OnSetCursor` is not passed the cursor's current position, so you must retrieve that from the `Cursor` class and map the coordinates to your control's coordinate space, using the technique shown in Example 7-19.

Example 7-19. Modifying the cursor

```
protected override void OnSetCursor( )
{
    Point cp = Control.PointToClient(Cursor.Position);
    if (IsPointOverAnAdornment(cp))
    {
        Cursor.Current = Cursors.SizeWE;
    }
    else
        base.OnSetCursor( );
}

private bool IsPointOverAnAdornment(Point p)
{
    . . . Do hit testing
}
```

> You must call the base class's `OnSetCursor` method if you do not set the cursor yourself. Otherwise, the default cursor will not be restored when the mouse moves away from one of your adornments.

Most adornments are designed for clicking on and dragging. (Especially those drawn with `ControlPaint.DrawGrabHandle`.) You will, therefore, usually want to handle mouse input if you draw any adornments.

Handling mouse input

Visual Studio .NET will notify a designer class of certain types of mouse activity. It presumes that controls will typically be interested in drag operations—the three methods it calls to indicate mouse activity are `OnMouseDragBegin`, `OnMouseDragMove`, and `OnMouseDragEnd`. Override these to be notified when the mouse button is first pressed, when the mouse moves while the button is pressed, and when the button is released, respectively.

All three methods are passed the current mouse position as a pair of integers. However, despite what the documentation claims, these are screen coordinates, so, as with `OnSetCursor`, you must use `Control.PointToClient` to map them back into your control's coordinate space.

You should always call the base class implementations of these methods unless you handle them completely yourself. You should always call the base OnMouseDragEnd method in any case. If you fail to call the base class's OnMouseDragEnd, the forms designer will be left in a state in which the mouse stops working correctly, as shown in Example 7-2.

Example Windows Forms Control with Designer

This section presents a complete example of a custom Windows Forms control with an associated designer class to illustrate all of the points raised in the previous section. The control is a directional label control. It is similar to the built-in Label class, except it allows text to be displayed at any angle. Figure 7-14 shows an application using this control.

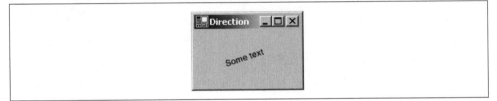

Figure 7-13. DirectionalLabel control

The source for the DirectionalLabel control is shown in Example 7-20. The structure of the class is fairly straightforward. It begins with a constructor. The OnPaint method follows—this contains the code that draws the rotated text. After the redraw code are two properties, Origin and Direction. These set the start position of the text and the direction in which it should be drawn. These properties have been annotated with the Category and Description attributes, to make sure that they are displayed correctly in the property grid. These properties also provide change notifications (through OnOriginChanged and OnDirectionChanged methods and associated events).

Because the Origin and Direction properties use the Point and Size types, respectively, it is not possible to use the DefaultValue attribute. (Attributes must be initialized with constant values. Here, the default values are new Point(0,0), and new Size(30,0). You cannot construct an attribute with these values.) These properties, therefore, have corresponding ShouldSerialize methods. This enables Visual Studio .NET to know whether the properties currently have their default values or not despite the absence of the DefaultValue attribute.

The control's appearance depends on several properties. As well as using the Origin and Direction properties, the redraw code in OnPaint uses the standard Text, Font, ForeColor, and BackColor properties. The control needs to be redrawn whenever any of these properties changes, so the control ends with a series of change handlers, all of which call Invalidate to redraw the control. Example 7-20 shows the source code for this control.

Example 7-20. DirectionalLabel control class

```csharp
using System;
using System.ComponentModel;
using System.Drawing;
using System.Drawing.Text;
using System.Windows.Forms;

[ToolboxBitmap(typeof(DirectionalLabel))]
[Designer(typeof(DirectionalLabelDesigner))]
public class DirectionalLabel : Control
{
    public DirectionalLabel()
    {
        // Enable double-buffering – reduces flicker when the
        // user adjusts the control in the designer.
        SetStyle(ControlStyles.AllPaintingInWmPaint |
            ControlStyles.DoubleBuffer | ControlStyles.UserPaint, true);
    }


    protected override void OnPaint(PaintEventArgs pe)
    {
        Graphics g = pe.Graphics;
        float angle = (float) (Math.Atan2(Direction.Height, Direction.Width) /
                               Math.PI * 180.0);

        g.TranslateTransform(Origin.X, Origin.Y);
        g.RotateTransform(angle);
        g.TextRenderingHint = TextRenderingHint.AntiAlias;
        using (Brush b = new SolidBrush(ForeColor))
        {
            g.DrawString(Text, Font, b, 0, 0);
        }

        base.OnPaint(pe);
    }



    [Category("Appearance")]
    [Description("The starting point (top left) of the label's text")]
    public Point Origin
    {
        get
        {
            return originVal;
        }
        set
        {
            if (value != originVal)
            {
                originVal = value;
                OnOriginChanged(EventArgs.Empty);
```

Example 7-20. DirectionalLabel control class (continued)

```csharp
            }
        }
    }
    private Point originVal = new Point(0, 0);

    public event EventHandler OriginChanged;
    protected virtual void OnOriginChanged(EventArgs e)
    {
        if (OriginChanged != null)
            OriginChanged(this, e);
        Invalidate( );
    }

    public bool ShouldSerializeOrigin( )
    {
        return Origin != new Point(0, 0);
    }


    [Category("Appearance")]
    [Description("The direction in which the text will be drawn")]
    public Size Direction
    {
        get
        {
            return directionVal;
        }
        set
        {
            if (value != directionVal)
            {
                directionVal = value;
                OnDirectionChanged(EventArgs.Empty);
            }
        }
    }
    private Size directionVal = new Size(30, 0);

    public event EventHandler DirectionChanged;
    protected virtual void OnDirectionChanged(EventArgs e)
    {
        if (DirectionChanged != null)
            DirectionChanged(this, e);
        Invalidate( );
    }

    public bool ShouldSerializeDirection( )
    {
        return Direction != new Size(30, 0);
    }
```

Example 7-20. DirectionalLabel control class (continued)

```
    protected override void OnForeColorChanged(System.EventArgs e)
    {
        Invalidate( );
        base.OnForeColorChanged(e);
    }

    protected override void OnBackColorChanged(System.EventArgs e)
    {
        Invalidate( );
        base.OnBackColorChanged(e);
    }

    protected override void OnFontChanged(System.EventArgs e)
    {
        Invalidate( );
        base.OnFontChanged(e);
    }

    protected override void OnTextChanged(System.EventArgs e)
    {
        Invalidate( );
        base.OnTextChanged(e);
    }
}
```

The control has had the ToolboxBitmap attribute applied. This means that the custom embedded bitmap will be used when the control is displayed in a Visual Studio .NET toolbox. (You can add a control to a toolbox either by dragging the DLL from a Windows Explorer window onto the toolbox or by using the toolbox's customization menu option.)

The control also has the Designer attribute, indicating that it has an associated designer class. The designer allows the position and direction of the text to be adjusted in the Visual Studio .NET Forms Editor using a pair of grab handles, as shown in Figure 7-15. These grab handles have an arrow drawn between them to make it clear in which direction the text will be displayed. Either grab handle can be moved with the mouse at design time. The designer class that supplies this editing facility, DirectionalLabelDesigner, is shown in Example 7-21.

Figure 7-14. The DirectionalLabel at design time

Example 7-21. The direction label control's designer class

```
using System;
using System.Drawing;
using System.Drawing.Drawing2D;
using System.Windows.Forms;
using System.Windows.Forms.Design;
using System.ComponentModel;
using System.ComponentModel.Design;

public class DirectionalLabelDesigner : ControlDesigner
{
    public override void Initialize(IComponent component)
    {
        base.Initialize(component);

        selectionService = GetService(typeof(ISelectionService))
                                as ISelectionService;
        if (selectionService != null)
        {
            selectionService.SelectionChanged +=
                    new EventHandler(OnSelectionChanged);
        }

    }
    private ISelectionService selectionService;

    private void OnSelectionChanged(object sender, EventArgs e)
    {
        Control.Invalidate();
    }

    protected override void OnPaintAdornments(PaintEventArgs pe)
    {
        DirectionalLabel label = (DirectionalLabel) Control;
        if (selectionService != null)
        {
            if (selectionService.GetComponentSelected(label))
            {
                // Paint grab handles.

                Graphics g = pe.Graphics;
                Rectangle handle = GetHandle(label.Origin);
                ControlPaint.DrawGrabHandle(g, handle, true, true);
                handle = GetHandle(label.Origin + label.Direction);
                ControlPaint.DrawGrabHandle(g, handle, true, true);

                // Paint a line with an arrow—this makes it
                // more clear which grab handle is which.
                //
                // The built-in line caps are a bit small, so we'll
                // draw our own arrow on the end.  The easiest way
                // to do this is to translate and rotate the transform.
```

Example 7-21. The direction label control's designer class (continued)

```
            float angle = (float) (Math.Atan2(label.Direction.Height,
                label.Direction.Width) / Math.PI * 180.0);
            g.TranslateTransform(label.Origin.X, label.Origin.Y);
            g.RotateTransform(angle);

            float distance = (float) Math.Sqrt(
                label.Direction.Width * label.Direction.Width +
                label.Direction.Height * label.Direction.Height);

            g.SmoothingMode = SmoothingMode.AntiAlias;
            using (Pen p = new Pen(Color.Blue))
            {
                g.DrawLine(p, 0, 0, distance, 0);
                g.DrawLine(p, distance, 0, distance - 5, -4);
                g.DrawLine(p, distance, 0, distance - 5, 4);
            }
        }
    }
}


// Get a standard-sized grab handle rectangle centered on
// the specified point.
private Rectangle GetHandle(Point pt)
{
    Rectangle handle = new Rectangle(pt, new Size(7, 7));
    handle.Offset(-3, -3);
    return handle;
}

protected override void OnSetCursor( )
{
    // Get mouse cursor position relative to
    // the control's coordinate space.

    DirectionalLabel label = (DirectionalLabel) Control;
    Point p = label.PointToClient(Cursor.Position);

    // Display a resize cursor if the mouse is
    // over a grab handle; otherwise show a
    // normal arrow.

    if (GetHandle(label.Origin).Contains(p) ||
        GetHandle(label.Origin + label.Direction).Contains(p))
    {
        Cursor.Current = Cursors.SizeAll;
    }
    else
    {
        Cursor.Current = Cursors.Default;
    }
}
```

Example 7-21. The direction label control's designer class (continued)

```csharp
// Drag handling state and methods.

private bool dragging = false;
private bool dragDirection;
private Point dragOffset;

protected override void OnMouseDragBegin(int x, int y)
{
    DirectionalLabel label = (DirectionalLabel) Control;
    Point p = label.PointToClient(new Point(x, y));

    bool overOrigin = GetHandle(label.Origin).Contains(p);
    bool overDirection = GetHandle(label.Origin + label.Direction).Contains(p);
    if (overOrigin || overDirection)
    {
        dragging = true;
        dragDirection = overDirection;
        Point current = dragDirection ?
            (label.Origin + label.Direction) :
            label.Origin;
        dragOffset = current - new Size(p);
    }
    else
    {
        dragging = false;
        base.OnMouseDragBegin(x, y);
    }

}

protected override void OnMouseDragMove(int x, int y)
{
    if (dragging)
    {
        DirectionalLabel label = (DirectionalLabel) Control;
        Point p = label.PointToClient(new Point(x, y));

        Point current = p + new Size(dragOffset);
        if (dragDirection)
        {
            label.Direction = new Size(current) - new Size(label.Origin);
        }
        else
        {
            label.Origin = current;
        }
    }
    else
    {
        base.OnMouseDragMove(x, y);
    }
}
```

Example 7-21. The direction label control's designer class (continued)

```
protected override void OnMouseDragEnd(bool cancel)
{
    if (dragging)
    {
        // Update property via PropertyDescriptor to
        // make sure that VS.NET notices.

        DirectionalLabel label = (DirectionalLabel) Control;
        if (dragDirection)
        {
            Size d = label.Direction;
            PropertyDescriptor pd =
                TypeDescriptor.GetProperties(label)["Direction"];
            pd.SetValue(label, d);
        }
        else
        {
            Point o = label.Origin;
            PropertyDescriptor pd =
                TypeDescriptor.GetProperties(label)["Origin"];
            pd.SetValue(label, o);
        }
        dragging = false;
    }

    // Always call base class.
    base.OnMouseDragEnd(cancel);
}
}
```

The grab handle and line adornments are drawn only when the control is selected, so the class starts with code that causes the control to be redrawn each time a selection change event occurs. This is followed by the OnPaintAdornments method, which renders the grab handles and the line.

The remaining code handles mouse input. OnSetCursor is used to display the resize cursor whenever the mouse is over one of the grab handles. The remaining three methods update the appropriate properties when a drag operation occurs. The only surprising code here is the use of the PropertyDescriptor class in OnMouseDragEnd. Without this code in place, Visual Studio .NET does not notice when a drag operation causes a control's property to change. However, if we update the property through a PropertyDescriptor, it will detect the change and save the modified property in the form's InitializeComponent method.

Web Forms Control Designers

A Web Forms Control custom designer is a class derived from the ControlDesigner class defined in the System.Web.UI.Design namespace. This class derives from

`ComponentDesigner` and inherits the standard designer features such as the ability to add extra context menu items. As Example 7-22 shows, a web control designer is associated with a control in exactly the same way as any other component designer. It can also control its resizability in the designer, and it can influence the way it appears in Visual Studio .NET's design-time HTML view.

Example 7-22. A Web Forms control with a custom designer

```
[Designer(typeof(MyControlDesigner))]
public class MyControl :
    System.Web.UI.Control
{
    . . .
}
```

Resizing

A Web Forms control has less power than a Windows Forms control over the way in which it can be resized. With Web Forms, it is a yes/no choice—we can override the `AllowResize` property and return a Boolean indicating whether we want the control to be resizable in the designer.

Design-time rendering

When your control is hosted in the designer, Visual Studio .NET will create an instance of it and ask it to render itself in the normal way. This means that the control will look the same at design time as it does at runtime. Most of the time, this will be the behavior that you require. However, sometimes you will want to provide a different appearance at design time. For example, your control may not be visible at runtime, in which case it is useful to be able to make something appear in the designer so that developers can see and select your control.

To modify the control's design-time appearance, override the `GetDesignTimeHtml` method in the designer class. This method returns a string, which should be HTML. Although you can return whatever you like here, the `ControlDesigner` class provides a protected method called `CreatePlaceHolderDesignTimeHtml` that will generate a placeholder for you. Example 7-23 shows how to use this. It just generates a gray box containing the specified text.

Example 7-23. Providing design-time HTML

```
public class WebControlDesigner : System.Web.UI.Design.ControlDesigner
{
    public override string GetDesignTimeHtml()
    {
        return CreatePlaceHolderDesignTimeHtml("My control");
    }
}
```

There is another popular use of the GetDesignTimeHtml method. Data-bound controls might be invisible unless they have some information to display. It is common practice for such controls to preload some fake data at design time so as to be visible. You can do this in the GetDesignTimeHtml method and then call the base class's implementation to get your control to render itself as usual.

Conclusion

Visual Studio .NET automates a great many of the design-time features of components—all public properties are intrinsically editable, well-known property types get special-purpose editing user interfaces, components derived from certain well-known base classes (e.g., Controls) get further special design-time support. However, VS.NET also allows component authors to enhance design-time behavior. This can range from simply adding attributes to categorize properties and events to providing full custom editing for controls or their properties.

CHAPTER 8

Automation, Macros, and Add-ins

Once you have been working with VS.NET for a while, you will discover that you often perform certain tasks over and over. The particular tasks you need to perform will be very dependent on how you are using the IDE, what language and project types you deploy, and your own development style (or the development guidelines under which you are working). This chapter is all about how to get the IDE to automate these activities, by writing either macros or add-ins.

A macro is a snippet of VB.NET code that automates some operation in VS.NET. Macros provide a quick and easy way to automate tasks. They are straightforward to create, because VS.NET has built-in macro creation and editing features.

Macros are fairly powerful, but they have their limits, so VS.NET supports a more flexible if somewhat more complex integration interface for building add-ins. Add-ins are COM components, which means that they take more effort to create—you must compile and install add-ins before you can use them. (Macros can be written and executed on a whim—VS.NET compiles them automatically, and they do not need to be installed.) However, as well as having access to a more powerful API than macros, add-ins offer some further advantages—add-ins are easier to redistribute than macros are, and there is also no danger that anyone using your add-in might inadvertently break it when using VS.NET's macro editor.

If you are writing functionality that you want to distribute outside of your organization, an add-in is the way to go. It allows tighter integration with the IDE, plus allows you to add information to the VS.NET About dialog. However, even add-ins are not the most powerful integration mechanism VS.NET has to offer—packages allow even deeper integration. See Chapter 10 for more details.

The VS.NET Automation Object Model

The IDE exposes an object model that allows you to automate many of the tasks that would normally be done manually. The same object model is used by macros, add-ins, and wizards. (Wizards are discussed in the next chapter.)

At the core of the object model is the DTE object. (DTE stands for Development Tools Extensibility. Technically the object's coclass is DTE, and it implements an interface named _DTE, with an underscore. However, this COM-level detail will be hidden from you if you are working with VB.NET.) This object is the gateway into all of the functionality of the IDE.

 The VS.NET object model is COM-based. A set of primary interop assemblies is provided to allow access to the object model from managed code.

The way in which you obtain a reference to the DTE object will depend on what type of code you are writing. Macros just use a global variable provided by the macro environment called DTE. Add-ins are passed a reference to this object when VS.NET initializes them. (Wizards, which are discussed in the next chapter, also have access to the DTE object in their script files through a global object called dte.) The best way to get a feel for what functionality is available from the DTE object model is to look at the properties available from the DTE object. Table 8-1 lists these properties and shows which sections of this chapter provide further information about the areas of functionality to which the various properties belong.

Table 8-1. DTE object properties

Property	Description
ActiveDocument	The Document object for the document with the input focus. (See the "Document Objects" section.)
ActiveSolutionProjects	A collection of Project objects, representing the projects currently selected in the Solution Explorer. (See the "Solution and Project Objects" section.)
ActiveWindow	A Window object representing the window with the input focus. (See the "User Interface Objects" section.)
AddIns	A collection of AddIn objects representing the add-ins listed under the VS.NET Add-in Manager. (See the "Add-ins" section.)
CommandBars	A collection of CommandBar objects representing all of the toolbars and menu bars in the VS.NET UI, including all those currently hidden. (See the "User Interface Objects" section.)
CommandLineArguments	A string containing everything on the command line after the program name itself. (Usually empty unless VS.NET was run as part of an automated build script.)
Commands	A collection of Command objects, representing actions that can be performed in VS.NET. (See the "Command Objects" section.)

Table 8-1. DTE object properties (continued)

Property	Description
ContextAttributes	A collection of ContextAttribute objects that allows extra items to be added to the Dynamic Help window.
CSharpProjects	A collection of Project objects containing all of the C# projects in the solution. (See the "Solution and Project Objects" section.)
Debugger	A Debugger object representing the VS.NET debugger. (See the "Debugger Object" section.)
DisplayMode	A member of the vsDisplay enumeration indicating whether the UI is in Multiple Document Interface (MDI) mode (vsDisplayMDI) or tabbed mode (vsDisplayTabs).
Documents	A collection of Document objects, representing all of the documents currently open in the UI. (See the "Document Objects" section.)
DTE	The DTE object. This may seem pointless—this property refers back to itself. However, all of the objects in the DTE object model have a property called DTE allowing you to get a reference back to the DTE object. For the sake of consistency, even the DTE object has this property.
Edition	A string indicating which edition of VS.NET is installed (e.g., "Enterprise Architect" for the VS.NET Enterprise Architect edition).
Events	The Events object, which provides access to a family of objects that raise event notifications. (See the "DTE Events" section.)
Find	The Find object, which can perform global search operations.
FullName	The full path of the *devenv.exe* (VS.NET) executable.
Globals	A Globals object, storing per-user configuration for add-ins or macros. (Note: there are three objects in the DTE hierarchy that provide a Globals property: the DTE object, Solution objects, and Project objects. They all work in the same way, the only difference being where the data is stored. The "Configuring add-ins" section shows the use of the Solution object's Globals property.)
ItemOperations	An ItemOperations object that allows common operations to be performed on the object currently selected in the Solution Explorer, such as adding a new or existing item.
LocaleID	The locale ID in which VS.NET is running.
Macros	A Macros object, representing the macros recorder. (See the "Recording and Running a Macro" section.)
MacrosIDE	Returns the DTE object for the macros IDE. (Macros have their own IDE, as described in the "Editing with the Macro IDE" section. This IDE has its own DTE object.)
MainWindow	A Window object representing the main VS.NET window. (See the "User Interface Objects" section.)
Mode	A value from the vsIDEMode enumeration indicating whether VS.NET is in design mode (vsIDEModeDesign) or debugging mode (vsIDEModeDebug).
Name	A string whose value is "Microsoft Development Environment" (unless this is the DTE object returned by the MacrosIDE property, in which case the string will be "Visual Studio Macros").

Table 8-1. DTE object properties (continued)

Property	Description
ObjectExtenders	An ObjectExtenders property that manages the installed automation extenders. This provides a mechanism by which third-party vendors can add their own objects into the VS.NET automation model.
Properties	A parameterized property that returns Properties objects representing a page of global settings configured in the VS.NET Options dialog. (See the "Properties collections" section.)
RegistryRoot	A string of the registry path VS.NET is using to retrieve its settings.
SelectedItems	A collection of currently selected items. (For treelike views such as the Solution Explorer, this will be an array of UIHierarchyItem objects—see the "User Interface Objects" section.)
Solution	The Solution object for the currently loaded solution. (See the "Solution and Project Objects" section.)
SourceControl	An object allowing simple source control operations to be performed. (See the "Source Control Object" section.)
StatusBar	A StatusBar object representing the status bar at the bottom of the main VS.NET window. Typically used by long-running macros or add-ins in order to present progress notifications.
SuppressUI	Flag indicating whether user interface elements should be suppressed—false when running VS.NET normally, but true when running a command-line build.
UndoContext	Allows sets of operations to be grouped so that they can be undone in a single step. (This is useful for macros that perform lots of individual steps—by default, everything done to documents through the automation model will be undoable one step at a time. This allows higher-level blocks of work to be undone in one step.)
UserControl	Flag returning true if the IDE is being used interactively, false if it is under automation control. (UserControl refers to the fact that VS.NET is under the control of the user—it has nothing to do with Windows Forms user controls.)
VBProjects	A collection of Project objects representing all of the VB.NET projects in the current solution. (See the "Solution and Project Objects" section.)
Version	A string containing VS.NET's version number ("7.10" for VS.NET 2003, "7.00" for VS.NET 2002).
WindowConfigurations	A collection of WindowConfiguration objects for each set of window layouts. VS.NET stores several different layouts for windows according to the mode—the set of tool windows and toolbars you require tends to be different according to whether you are debugging, editing code, or designing forms, so VS.NET stores each layout separately.
Windows	A collection of Window objects representing all of the open document or tool windows. (See the "User Interface Objects" section.)

The DTE model provides access to many different aspects of VS.NET—some of the objects deal with solutions and projects, some deal with the VS.NET user interface, some deal with source control, and some deal with settings. The most important groups of objects are described in the following sections.

This chapter is not a reference guide to the object model—the MSDN Library that ships with VS.NET already fulfills that role perfectly well. The goal of this chapter is to explain what features are available and how they are used. If you want a comprehensive list of the members available on each object, consult the MSDN documentation. To find the relevant section, open the Help Contents using Help → Contents... (Ctrl-Alt-F1) and look for the "Developing with Visual Studio .NET" section. Underneath this is a "Reference" topic, containing an "Automation and Extensibility Reference" section. This describes the whole DTE object model in full detail.

Solution and Project Objects

As Figure 8-1 illustrates, the DTE model provides an object hierarchy that mirrors the hierarchy of a solution and its projects in the IDE. The DTE object represents the IDE (VS.NET itself), and it has a Solution property, which is an object that represents the currently loaded solution. The Solution object contains a collection of Project objects, one for each project in the solution. Each Project contains a collection of ProjectItem objects that represent the files in the project. Each object in the hierarchy exposes methods and properties that allow you to carry out actions that you would normally perform interactively in the IDE. For example, the Solution object has a Remove method that allows you to remove a project from the solution. This method is the programmatic equivalent to right-clicking on the project in the Solution Explorer and selecting Remove.

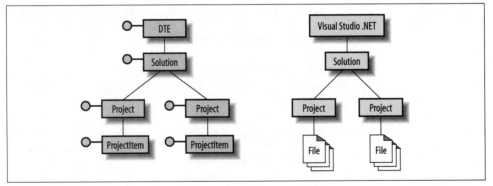

Figure 8-1. Solutions, projects, and files in the DTE object model

Example 8-1 shows how to iterate through all of the items in each project in a solution using C#. (This snippet presumes that there is a field or variable in scope called DTE that contains a reference to the DTE object. Macros have such a property available globally. Add-ins are passed the DTE object during initialization.)

Example 8-1. Iterating through project items

```
Solution s = DTE.Solution;
foreach(Project p in s.Projects)
{
    foreach(ProjectItem pi in p.ProjectItems)
    {
        MessageBox.Show("Item {0} in {1} Project of the {2} Solution",
            pi.Name, p.Name,s.FullName);
    }
}
```

Project objects and VSProject

Although all project types have a great deal in common, there are certain features found only in .NET projects. For example, a .NET project has a list of references to other .NET components, but a Database project would have no use for such settings. To accommodate project-specific functionality, the Project object has a property called Object through which extra features are exposed, when appropriate.

VS.NET uses this facility with .NET projects to provide an object of type VSProject. You can retrieve a VSProject object like this:

```
Imports EnvDTE
Imports VSLangProj


...


Dim project As Project
project = DTE.Solution.Projects.Item(1)
Dim vsProject As VSProject
vsProject = project.Object
```

Note the Import statements—most of the VS.NET object model is defined in the EnvDTE namespace, but here we also need to import the VSLangProj namespace, as this is where VSProject is defined.

 This VSProject object is also available on unmanaged (non-.NET) C++ projects. This may seem surprising, as you would think that an unmanaged C++ project would have no use for .NET-specific features. However, an unmanaged C++ project can be turned into a managed C++ project by changing a single flag in its project settings. (The 'Use Managed Extensions' flag in the General settings.) The only real difference between an unmanaged C++ project and a managed one is the setting of this switch, so the Project.Object property always supplies a VSProject object.

The VSProject object provides a References property, which is a collection of Reference objects, one for each reference the project has. It also has a WebReferencesFolder property for web service references. It provides a WorkOffline property, which allows you to work on web projects in a disconnected environment. It also provides a couple of utility methods for managing web service references.

Properties collections

Many of the entities you deal with in VS.NET have properties associated with them. Solutions, configurations, projects, and files all present property sets either in the Properties panel (F4) or the Property Pages dialog (Shift-F4).

Properties present a challenge because the exact set of properties available can vary—for example, a `Project` object's properties will depend on the type of project. Although in certain special cases this is dealt with by introducing an extra object such as the `VSProject` object described earlier, the DTE object model has a more extensible way of dealing with properties. All objects that represent items with property sets have a property called `Properties`. This is a collection of `Property` objects and is indexed by the name of the property.

The set of properties available depends on the type of object—the VS.NET documentation provides the full (and extensive) lists for each type. Example 8-2 shows how to use this feature to retrieve the `DefaultNamespace` property that is present on C#, J#, and VB.NET projects.

Example 8-2. Retrieving a project property

```
Public Function GetNamespace(proj As Project) As String
    Dim prop As [Property]
    prop = proj.Properties.Item("DefaultNamespace")
    Return prop.Value
End Function
```

 The full lists of the members of the various property collections are linked to from the help page entitled "Properties Property (General Extensibility)," which can be found here:

http://msdn.microsoft.com/library/default.asp?url=/library/en-us/ vsintro7/html/vxlrfPropertiesPropertyGeneralExtensibility.asp

The "See Also" section of this page contains links to pages that describe what can be found in the `Properties` collection for the various objects in the DTE model that support this property.

The `DTE` object itself also has a `Properties` property, but it works slightly differently. It contains systemwide settings, as configured in the Options dialog (Tools → Options). But unlike the other `Properties` properties, this one is not a collection object. Instead, it is a parameterized property that takes two strings, a `Category` and a `Page`. These mostly correspond to the Options dialog's categories and pages. For example, you can access the settings in the Environment category's General page with `DTE.Properties("Environment", "General")`. However, there are a few documented anomalies. For example, although the Fonts and Colors page is in the Environment category, you must use `DTE.Properties("FontsAndColors", "TextEditor")` to access these settings.

User Interface Objects

The DTE object model has two main kinds of objects that represent user interface elements: `Window` objects and `CommandBar` objects. `Window` objects represent windows, such as document editor windows, the Toolbox, the Solution Explorer, the Breakpoint window, and so on. `CommandBar` objects represent menu bars and toolbars, such as the main menu.

Window objects

For each visible window, whether it is the main VS.NET window, a document window, or a tool window, there is a corresponding `Window` object available in the DTE object hierarchy. You can obtain these objects in a number of ways.

The `DTE` object itself provides two properties that provide direct access to certain windows. Its `MainWindow` property refers to the main VS.NET window. The `ActiveWindow` property refers to whichever window currently has the input focus.

The DTE object also provides a `Windows` property. This is a collection of `Window` objects and allows access to every window in the VS.NET UI. The property is indexed by the *window kind*, which is a GUID that indicates the type of window. This GUID would normally be one of those listed in the DTE's `Constants` enumeration, which defines a series of `vsWindowKindXxx` values for the built-in window types. (The documentation page entitled "vsWindowKind constants" provides the full list of built-in windows and their corresponding vsWindowKind names.) Example 8-3 shows how to use this collection to obtain the `Window` object for the Solution Explorer.

Example 8-3. Obtaining a particular Window object

```
Dim wnd As Window
wnd = DTE.Windows.Item(Constants.vsWindowKindSolutionExplorer)
```

 If you enumerate through the `DTE.Windows` collection using a `For Each` construct, you may be surprised by the results. The collection will appear to contain only entries for windows that have either been made visible at some point or been explicitly requested from the `Windows` collection. This is because the `Windows` collection is populated on demand. (This is not a problem if you ask for a window by name, as Example 8-3 does—if the relevant window was not already in the collection, it will be added at that point.)

Once you have a `Window` object, you can perform various operations on it. As you would expect, anything that can be done interactively can also be done through code. The `AutoHides` property determines whether the window disappears when it loses the focus—this corresponds to the pushpin icon on the window. The `IsFloating` property determines whether the window is currently docked. The `Top`, `Left`, `Width`, and `Height` properties allow the window's size and position to be set when it is undocked.

The Visible property determines whether it is shown at all. The Activate method gives the window the focus.

If the window is an editor window, you can access the associated document through its Document property. Certain window types provide an extra programming interface, which is available from the Window object's Object property. All of the windows that show a tree view (e.g., the Solution Explorer or the class view) use this to provide an object of type UIHierarchy. UIHierarchy objects provide a GetItem method that allows access to any item in the tree. It also provides SelectUp and SelectDown methods for navigation and a DoDefaultAction method to allow a double-click to be simulated.

Example 8-4 shows the use of the UIHierarchy object. It obtains the Window object for the Solution Explorer and then retrieves the UIHierarchy object. It then calls GetItem on this to retrieve the item representing the *MyProject* project in the *MySolution* solution. It then calls Select on this, in order to make that the currently selected item.

Example 8-4. Using the UIHierarchy object

```
Dim wnd As Window
wnd = DTE.Windows.Item(Constants.vsWindowKindSolutionExplorer)

Dim uih As UIHierarchy
uih = wnd.Object

Dim uihItem as UIHierarchyItem
uihItem = uih.GetItem("MySolution\MyProject")
uihItem.Select(vsUISelectionType.vsUISelectionTypeSelect)
```

CommandBar objects

CommandBar objects represent menus or toolbars. There is no distinction between a menu bar and a toolbar—buttons can be dragged onto the menu bar, and menu items can be dragged onto button bars.

 VS.NET uses Microsoft Office toolbars, so the CommandBar type is defined in the Microsoft.Office.Core namespace in the *office.dll* component. Macro projects and VS.NET add-in projects have a reference to this component added automatically.

The DTE object has a CommandBars property. This is a collection that contains every command bar in the VS.NET UI. (It includes any that are currently invisible, as well as all the visible ones.) The collection is indexed by the name of the command bars. It also provides an Add method that allows you to create new command bars.

CommandBar objects provide various properties that let you control their appearance and contents. Example 8-5 shows how to locate the *Standard* command bar (one of the built-in VS.NET toolbars) from the DTE object's CommandBars collection. It then toggles the bar's position between being docked to the top of the screen and floating.

Example 8-5. Changing a command bar's position

```
Imports Microsoft.Office.Core

Public Module MyModule
    Public Sub AddToolbar()
        Dim cmdBar As CommandBar

        cmdBar = DTE.CommandBars.Item("Standard")
        If cmdBar.Position = MsoBarPosition.msoBarTop Then
            cmdBar.Position = MsoBarPosition.msoBarFloating
        Else
            cmdBar.Position = MsoBarPosition.msoBarTop
        End If
    End Sub
End Module
```

The most interesting property of any CommandBar object is the Controls property. This is a collection of CommandBarControl objects, one for each item on the bar. There are several different types of control. You can find out which type any particular control is from its Type property, which will return an item from the msoControlType enumeration. Menus have a type of msoControlPopup, and the objects that represent menus can be cast to the CommandBarPopup type. Leafs in a menu and buttons on a toolbar both have the type msoControlButton. Objects in the bar's Controls collection that have this type can be cast to the CommandBarButton type. Example 8-6 shows how to navigate through a tree of pop ups in a command bar—in this case we are using the main menu in VS.NET, which is a command bar called "MenuBar". Example 8-6 locates the File menu and then the Source Control submenu, before executing the Open from Source Control... menu item.

Example 8-6. Navigating through controls in a menu

```
Imports Microsoft.Office.Core

Public Module MyModule
    Public Sub UseCommandbar()
        Dim cmdBar As CommandBar
        Dim ctl As CommandBarControl
        Dim cmdPopup As CommandBarPopup
        Dim cmdButton As CommandBarButton

        cmdBar = DTE.CommandBars.Item("MenuBar")

        ctl = cmdBar.Controls("File")
        If ctl.Type = MsoControlType.msoControlPopup Then
            cmdPopup = ctl
            ctl = cmdPopup.Controls("Source Control")

            If ctl.Type = MsoControlType.msoControlPopup Then
                cmdPopup = ctl
                ctl = cmdPopup.Controls("Open From Source Control...")
```

Example 8-6. Navigating through controls in a menu (continued)

```
                    If ctl.Type = MsoControlType.msoControlButton Then
                        cmdButton = ctl

                        cmdButton.Execute( )
                    End If
                End If
            End If
        End Sub
End Module
```

In fact, this code is unnecessarily complex—navigating through toolbars is required only if you wish to modify them in some way. If you merely wish to execute the command they represent, you should just use the corresponding Command object. You also need to use a Command object if you want to add an item to a command bar that actually does something—a command bar button must be associated with the command that it invokes.

Command Objects

Most user actions in VS.NET are associated with a command. There are commands for every action in the editor, such as entering text or moving the cursor. Each dialog has a command that opens it. Every action accessible through toolbars and menus is associated with a command.

 Appendix C lists the names of all of the commands that have keyboard shortcuts.

Every command has a corresponding Command object, which can be obtained through the DTE object's Commands collection. Commands are identified by name, available from the Command object's Name property. This name can also be used to invoke a command with the DTE object's ExecuteCommand method. Example 8-7 shows the more succinct way of invoking the same command that Example 8-6 executes.

Example 8-7. Executing a command

```
DTE.ExecuteCommand("File.OpenFromSourceControl")
```

If you want to add an item to a toolbar menu that invokes a particular command, you simply obtain the relevant command object and call its AddControl method, passing in a reference to the command bar to which you would like to add a control. Example 8-8 shows how to add a button for the OpenFromSourceControl command as the fourth item in the Standard toolbar.

Example 8-8. Adding a command to a command bar

```
Dim cmd As Command
cmd = DTE.Commands.Item("File.OpenFromSourceControl")
cmd.AddControl(DTE.CommandBars("Standard"), 4)
```

You can create your own custom command objects, although you will need to write an add-in to provide code that will run when the command is executed. This is done with the DTE object's Commands collection, which has an AddNamedCommand method. This allows you to create a command, specifying the name, the text that should be used for this command on command bars, optional tooltip text, and the bitmap that should be used to represent the command on any command bar. The VS.NET Add-in Wizard described later in this chapter can generate code to add a new command and attach it to the Tools menu for you.

Document Objects

Every document open for editing in VS.NET has a corresponding Document object, which allows the document's contents to be manipulated. If the document is a text file, the Document object's Object property will return a TextDocument object, which provides operations specific to text files.

The DTE object provides two properties through which you can obtain a Document object. The ActiveDocument property returns the document that has the focus (or, if a tool window currently has the focus, the document that most recently had the focus). The Documents property is a collection of all open documents.

Most manipulation of a document is done through the document's Selection property. For a text document, this will be a TextSelection object. This represents the current selection, or, if there is no selection, the cursor location. It provides methods equivalent to the keystrokes for navigating around documents—for example, the LineUp, LineDown, CharLeft, CharRight, PageUp, PageDown, StartOfDocument, and EndOfDocument methods. Each of these takes a Boolean indicating whether the operation should extend the current selection or not. (This is equivalent to whether or not you hold down the Shift key when using the corresponding keystroke.) An Insert method inserts text at the current cursor location. Cut, Copy, and Paste methods correspond to the standard clipboard operations.

Debugger Object

The DTE object provides a property called Debugger. This is an object that allows the debugger to be controlled. This provides a Breakpoints collection, allowing breakpoints to be created, destroyed, or modified. For multiprocess and multithreaded debugging, it allows the current process and thread to be retrieved or set using the CurrentProcess and CurrentThread properties. It provides methods that correspond to each of the debugger actions. (See Chapter 3 for more information on debugging.)

Example 8-9 shows how to use the `Debugger` object to step into the current line of code.

Example 8-9. Using the Debugger object

```
Dim dbg As EnvDTE.Debugger
dbg = DTE.Debugger
dbg.StepInto( )
```

Source Control Object

The DTE object provides a `SourceControl` property. This is an object that allows certain source control operations to be performed. Unfortunately, it is fairly primitive. All operations use filenames—you cannot pass a `ProjectItem` object in, for example. And you cannot check items in—you can only perform four source control operations.

You can discover whether items are under source control at all with the `IsItemUnderSCC` method. You can call the `IsItemCheckedOut` method to discover whether an item is already checked out. You can exclude items from source control with `ExcludeItem` or `ExcludeItems`. And you can check items out with the `CheckoutItem` or `CheckoutItems` methods.

DTE Events

The DTE object model is able to notify us when certain events happen. These events are raised through the standard COM notification mechanism (connection points). Events are grouped into categories, and as Figure 8-2 shows, each category has a corresponding event source object. (The objects shown with bold names are event sources. The other objects indicate how to navigate through the DTE object hierarchy to find the event sources.) Most of these objects are accessed through the DTE object's `Events` property. For example, build events are raised by the `DTE.Events.BuildEvents` object.

`VSProject` objects supply extra events specific to .NET projects through their `VSProjectEvents` objects. (`VSProject` objects are available on .NET projects, and are accessed through the associated `Project` object's `Object` property. `Project` objects can be accessed through the `DTE.Solution.Projects` collection.) These projects also provide project-specific events for individual items through the `VSProjectItemEvents` objects.

Add-ins can use normal COM event handling to deal with events from these objects, but macros must use their own technique. This is discussed in the next section, "Macros"; see Example 8-13 for an illustration of the technique.

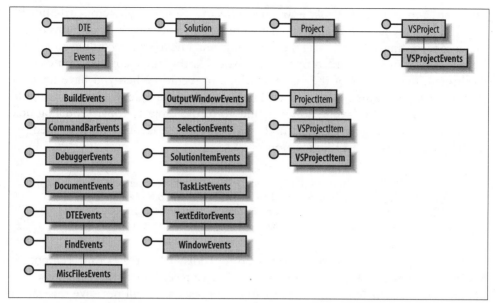

Figure 8-2. DTE event objects

Macros

VS.NET macros are small VB.NET functions that group together one or more actions that manipulate the development environment using the VS.NET automation object model. VS.NET makes it easy to create and use macros in a way that does not interfere with the way you develop your software—macro projects operate entirely independently of VS.NET solutions. Once you have created a macro, you can then make it available on a menu or toolbar for easy access.

Recording and Running a Macro

The easiest way to get started using macros is to use the macro recording functionality built into VS.NET. With macro recording, you use the IDE in the normal way, but VS.NET will record all of the actions you perform and save them in a macro.

As an example, consider the common task of changing a project's default HTML layout from Grid to Flow. (See Chapter 2 for information about the HTML designer and layout issues.) Since this is a common but slightly awkward task, it would be nice to have an automated way to set the value to Flow. This is a perfect job for a macro.

To record a macro, go to Tools → Macros → Record TemporaryMacro (Ctrl-Shift-R). Selecting this menu item brings up a small recorder toolbar with three buttons, one to pause recording, one to cancel the recording, and one to stop recording and generate a macro from the recorded operations. After starting the recording, you can just go through the motions of the task you'd like to record. When you have finished, press the Stop Recording button (Ctrl-Shift-R). (In this example, we are changing the project default HTML layout, so we would go to the Project Properties dialog box, go down to the Designer Defaults node, and change the layout. Once finished, we would press the Stop Recording button.)

> While you are recording a macro, VS.NET will still perform all of the actions you tell it to as well as recording them. So be careful if you are recording a sequence of operations that involves deletion—VS.NET really will delete whatever you tell it to even while recording a macro.

To execute your newly recorded macro, go to Tools → Macros → Run Temporary-Macro (Ctrl-Shift-P). Whenever you ask VS.NET to record a macro, it creates a temporary macro called TemporaryMacro to store the results. It will not save this macro unless you tell it to, so each time you record a new temporary macro, you will be destroying the previous one you recorded.

To store a recorded macro permanently, use Tools → Macros → Save Temporary-Macro. This will display the Macro Explorer window, which is shown in Figure 8-3, and will give you an opportunity to rename your macro. (You must rename it in order to save it—merely selecting the Save TemporaryMacro item is not enough.)

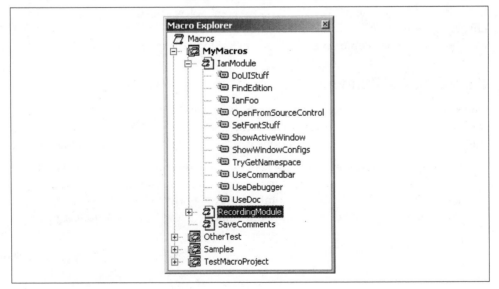

Figure 8-3. Macro Explorer

The Macro Explorer lets you see all the macros on your system. (You can display the Macro Explorer using View → Other Windows → Macro Explorer or with Alt-F8.) To run a macro from the Macro Explorer, you can either double-click it or right-click on it and select Run from the context menu. You can rename and delete macros from this menu. The menu also allows you to edit a macro, which is useful, because even when you create macros by recording them, you will often need to make a few modifications to the generated macro. When you choose to edit a macro, VS.NET will open the macro IDE.

You will often need to edit a recorded macro—as we shall see later, the macro we recorded for changing the HTML flow settings will need to be edited before it is useful.

Editing with the Macro IDE

The macro IDE can be invoked via Tools → Macros → Macros IDE (Alt-F11), or by choosing to edit a macro in the Macro Explorer. The macro IDE looks very much like a trimmed-down version of the VS.NET IDE, as Figure 8-4 shows.

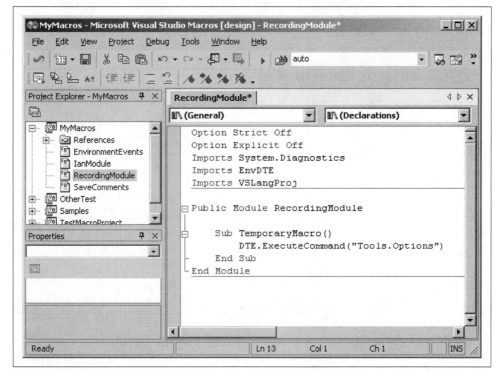

Figure 8-4. The macro IDE

The Project Explorer window (which is on the left side of the IDE by default) shows all of the macro projects that VS.NET is currently configured to use. (See the next section, "Managing Macro Files" for information on how VS.NET manages the files for these projects.) The editor is the normal VB.NET editor, so editing macros works in exactly the same way as writing VB.NET code in the main IDE.

Each macro project contains "files" (although in reality all of the "files" shown are typically contained in a single binary file). When you want to add a new macro, you can either edit an existing code file or add a new one (File → Add New Item). When you add a new file, you get three choices: a module, a class, or a source file. The only difference between the three is the declarations VS.NET places in the new file. A module contains a module declaration, a class file contains a class declaration, and the source file option creates an empty file.

 Because macros are simply VB.NET code that gets compiled and run, if you make a change to a macro that causes it not to compile, you will not be able to use *any* of the macros in that project. This should not be surprising—normal VS.NET projects are much the same in that the whole project must compile without errors before it can run. However, this is a change from how Microsoft's older macro systems used to work—they were based on script code rather than compiled code, which meant that macros would run in the presence of syntax errors so long as you didn't attempt to run the erroneous lines. Unfortunately, compiled code cannot offer this degree of latitude. This is not necessarily a disadvantage—it means that you get to find out about problems sooner rather than later. (And not only does compiled code offer much better compile-time type checking, it will also run faster once compiled.)

Managing Macro Files

VS.NET stores your macros in one or more macro project directories. There is one macro project directory for each item listed under the Macros node in the Macro Explorer (Figure 8-3). These are entirely unrelated to normal VS.NET projects and solutions.

By default, macro project directories will be in either a *VSMacros* or a *VSMacros71* directory underneath your *My Documents\Visual Studio Projects* directory. (You can place macro project directories wherever you like—these are just the default locations.) You will normally find two macro project directories here—*MyMacros*, which is intended for your own use, and *Samples*, which contains a set of example macros.

By default, VS.NET will put newly recorded macros in the *MyMacros* project. You can select a different project by right-clicking on the project in the Macro Explorer and selecting Set as Recording Project.

Macro project directories typically contain just one file, *ProjectName.vsmacro*, where *ProjectName* is the same as the containing directory name. The *.vsmacro* file is a COM structured storage file that contains all of the source files for the macro project.

You can have VS.NET store each of the source files for a project separately, instead of lumping them all into one structured storage file. (This would be a good idea if you wanted to place your macros into a source control system. However, you're on your own if you want to do that—VS.NET offers no integrated support for revision control of macros.) If you select the project in the Macro Explorer, the Properties panel (F4) will show a Storage Format property. By default, this is set to Binary (*.vsmacros*) but changing it to Text (UNICODE) will cause VS.NET to store the project as a collection of files instead of one single binary file.

 When you change the storage format of a macro project, the format you select becomes the default format for any new macro projects that you create.

Macro projects are not associated with VS.NET projects or solutions. VS.NET stores the list of macro projects in a per-user section of the registry:

```
HKCU\Software\Microsoft\VisualStudio\7.1\vsmacros
```

If you want to share your macro with someone else, you can export one of the individual files by right-clicking on it in the Project Explorer in the macro IDE, and selecting Export *Filename*.... This will export the macro file as a *.vb* file. Another developer can then import the macro on her copy of VS.NET using File → Add Existing Item, in the macro IDE. Or you can just email someone the text of the macro, and she can add it to her system using cut and paste.

Extending a Recorded Macro

Although many tasks can be recorded as macros, often you will want to edit a recorded macro to extend its functionality beyond what was initially recorded. For example, you may wish to add looping or conditional execution into your macro. Also, it is not uncommon for macro recording to miss steps—some actions, such as typing data into a dialog box, are not recordable,—so recorded macros often require a little tweaking.

Example 8-10 shows the macro that we recorded earlier to change a project's default HTML designer layout property from Grid to Flow. It is typical of recorded macros, in that it needs a little work before it will be useful.

Example 8-10. A recorded macro

```
Option Strict Off
Option Explicit Off
Imports EnvDTE
```

Example 8-10. A recorded macro (continued)

```
Imports System.Diagnostics

Public Module RecordingModule


Sub TemporaryMacro()
    DTE.Windows.Item(Constants.vsWindowKindSolutionExplorer).Activate()
    DTE.ActiveWindow.Object.GetItem("NSChange\NSChange").Select( _
            vsUISelectionType.vsUISelectionTypeSelect)
    DTE.Commands.Raise("{5EFC7975-14BC-11CF-9B2B-00AA00573819}", 397, _
            Customin, Customout)
    DTE.Windows.Item(Constants.vsWindowKindSolutionExplorer).Activate()
End Sub

End Module
```

The first problem with this macro that it is not very general purpose—it selects a particular project (`"NSChange\NSChange"`). Moreover, the part of the macro that does the actual work is hard to decipher: the `DTE.Commands.Raise` call is a generic method for invoking commands, and anybody who wanted to work out what this macro does by looking at it would have a hard time interpreting the command's GUID and ID. (See the sidebar, "Interpreting Command GUIDs and IDs" for notes on how to do this.) But worst of all, the macro didn't record the actual change we were trying to make in the properties—it just activated the properties dialog window. (This illustrates the problem with that impenetrable `Raise` method—it is wholly unobvious that the command being invoked happens to be the one that opens the Project Properties dialog.)

In all, this recorded macro is not very helpful. The success you will have with recorded macros depends on what you are trying to do. In general, they don't work at all well for anything involving dialogs. For most other kinds of user interface activity, they fare rather better though.

The best approach when using macro recording is usually to use the recorded macro as a starting point for a new macro. Your final macro will probably look quite different, but the recorded macro may provide a quick path to learning how the object model works for a particular action.

Setting project properties

So how do we fix the rather pointless macro in Example 8-10? The macro recorder leaves us in the lurch when it comes to project properties. To fix the code, we must use the `Project` object's `Properties` property, as we did in Example 8-2. This is a collection of `Property` objects that represent the project properties.

The exact set of properties that you will find in the `Properties` collection will depend on the project type. However, it is straightforward to write code that just ignores projects that do not have the property you are looking for. (As mentioned in the

Interpreting Command GUIDs and IDs

You may sometimes find yourself needing to work out what a command in a recorded macro actually does from the GUID and ID alone. The best way to deal with this is to write an experimental macro and single-step through it in the macro IDE, in order to observe the behavior. You can examine commands with the following code:

```
Public Sub DumpCommand(cmdGuid As String, _
                       cmdId As Integer)
    Dim cmd As Command
    cmd = DTE.Commands.Item(cmdGuid, cmdId)

    Debug.WriteLine(cmd.Name)

    Dim binding As Object
    For Each binding In cmd.Bindings
        Debug.WriteLine(binding)
    Next
End Sub
```

You would call this method with the GUID and ID of the command you are trying to decipher. In Example 8-10, these are "{5EFC7975-14BC-11CF-9B2B-00AA00573819}" and 397, respectively.)

If you single-step through this code in the macro IDE, it will print out the command's name and any key bindings to the Output window. (To show the Output window, use View → Other Windows → Command Window or Ctrl-Alt-A. This window will show any text that you print with Debug.WriteLine.) In this particular case, the command turned out not to have a name, which was not very helpful. Fortunately, this code revealed a key binding to "Alt+Enter". This just happens to be the shortcut for bringing up the properties window, thus showing what the command really does.

Of course, the other way of interpreting a command GUID and ID is just to execute the command and see what happens. However, this is potentially risky—some commands are destructive, and you may end up deleting something. Do you feel lucky?

"Properties collections" section earlier, the VS.NET documentation describes the set of properties available for each object that supports a Properties collection.) In our case, we are looking for the property called DefaultHTMLPageLayout. The code in Example 8-11 iterates through all of the projects currently selected in the Solution Explorer and looks for that property. When it finds it, it sets it to Flow layout.

Example 8-11. Setting the default HTML layout

```
Imports EnvDTE
Imports VSLangProj

Public Module FlowModule
    Public Sub FlowLayout()
        Dim proj As Project
```

Example 8-11. Setting the default HTML layout (continued)

```
        For Each proj In DTE.ActiveSolutionProjects
            Dim prop As [Property]
            For Each prop In proj.Properties
                If prop.Name = "DefaultHTMLPageLayout" Then
                    prop.Value = prjHTMLPageLayout.prjHTMLPageLayoutFlow
                End If
            Next
        Next
    End Sub
End Module
```

This code looks nothing like the code that the macro recorder generated for us. (It also behaves nothing like it—this code actually does what it is supposed to, unlike the recorded code.) Since we know that the macro recorder often doesn't do a good job of recording the setting of properties in dialogs, in retrospect this was a bad choice for the macro recorder—we would have done better to have started out from scratch with a custom macro.

Building a Custom Macro

You are not required to use a recorded macro as the starting point for all of your macros. After all, the macro recorder just ends up generating code that you could have written yourself. Sometimes it will be simpler to start from scratch.

We will now work through the creation of an example custom macro that could not reasonably have been created with the macro recorder: it will transfer the contents of the TaskList to a web page. Visual Studio .NET provides a TaskList that can keep track of outstanding development chores (see "TaskList Comments" in Chapter 2). Imagine a situation in which your team runs a daily build and you would like to make the resulting TaskList available in a web page so that management and other members of your team could see the remaining tasks. In this section, we will develop a custom macro that does just that.

Our macro will read the contents of the TaskList into a DataSet. It will then write the DataSet to disk as XML in a location accessible to the web page. The web page will load the XML back into another DataSet and bind it to a DataGrid control in order to present the results.

Example 8-12 shows the code for our macro. This example shows an entire source file, including all necessary Import statements, so you will need to add a new file to one of your macro projects if you plan to try this code out. Call the new file *BuildCommentDataSet*. Since this code uses the ADO.NET DataSet class, you will also need to add references to the *System.Data.dll* and *System.Xml.dll* components in your macro project.

Example 8-12. Example custom macro

```
Imports EnvDTE
Imports System.Data

Public Module BuildCommentDataSet
    Public Sub Build( )
        Dim tl As TaskList
        Dim ti As TaskItem

        ' Ask VS.NET for the Task List's Window object
        Dim win As Window = _
            DTE.Windows.Item(Constants.vsWindowKindTaskList)

        ' Get the TaskList object associated with the Window
        tl = win.Object

        ' Create a new DataSet and DataTable
        ' for holding the data
        '
        Dim ds As New DataSet("SolutionBuildDataSet")
        Dim dt As New DataTable( _
            DTE.Solution.Properties.Item("Name").Value.ToString( ) _
            & "Tasks")

        ' Need a column for each interesting property
        '
        dt.Columns.Add(New DataColumn("Category", GetType(String)))
        dt.Columns.Add(New DataColumn("Priority", GetType(String)))
        dt.Columns.Add(New DataColumn("Description", GetType(String)))
        dt.Columns.Add(New DataColumn("File", GetType(String)))
        dt.Columns.Add(New DataColumn("Line", GetType(String)))

        ' Add each task to the table
        '
        Dim dr As DataRow
        For Each ti In tl.TaskItems
            dr = dt.NewRow( )
            dr.Item("Category") = ti.Category
            dr.Item("Priority") = _
              ti.Priority.ToString( ).Replace("vsTaskPriority", "")
            dr.Item("Description") = ti.Description
            dr.Item("File") = ti.FileName
            dr.Item("Line") = ti.Line.ToString( )
            dt.Rows.Add(dr)

        Next

        ' Add the DataTable to the DataSet
        '
        ds.Tables.Add(dt)

        ' save the DataSet as an XML document
        '
```

Example 8-12. Example custom macro (continued)

```
        ds.WriteXml("c:\inetpub\wwwroot\tasklist.xml")
    End Sub

End Module
```

With this `DataSet` generation in place, building the ASP.NET page to display the data is quick and easy. Here is code in the *.aspx* file:

```
<%@ Page language="c#" Codebehind="SolutionTasks.aspx.cs"
    Inherits="Automate.SolutionTasks" %>
<!DOCTYPE HTML PUBLIC "-//W3C//DTD HTML 4.0 Transitional//EN" >
<HTML><HEAD></HEAD>
<body>
  <form id="SolutionTasks" method="post" runat="server">
    <asp:DataGrid id="DataGrid1" runat="server" BorderColor="#3366CC"
        BorderStyle="None" CellPadding="4">
      <HeaderStyle Font-Bold="True" ForeColor="#CCCCFF"
        BackColor="#003399"></HeaderStyle>
    </asp:DataGrid>
  </form>
</body>
</HTML>
```

If you are just copying these files into a web directory rather than adding them to a VS.NET web project, you will need to change the `Codebehind` attribute to an `Src` attribute, in order to get ASP.NET to compile the codebehind file. Here is the codebehind file:

```
using System;
using System.Data;
using System.Web.UI;
using System.Web.UI.WebControls;

namespace Automate
{
    public class SolutionTasks : System.Web.UI.Page
    {
        protected DataGrid DataGrid1;

        private void Page_Load(object sender, System.EventArgs e)
        {
            DataSet ds = new DataSet( );
            ds.ReadXml(MapPath("tasklist.xml"));
            DataView dv = new DataView(ds.Tables[0]);
            dv.Sort = "Priority, Category, File, Line DESC";
            DataGrid1.DataSource = dv;
            DataBind( );
        }
    }
}
```

You can see the result in Figure 8-5.

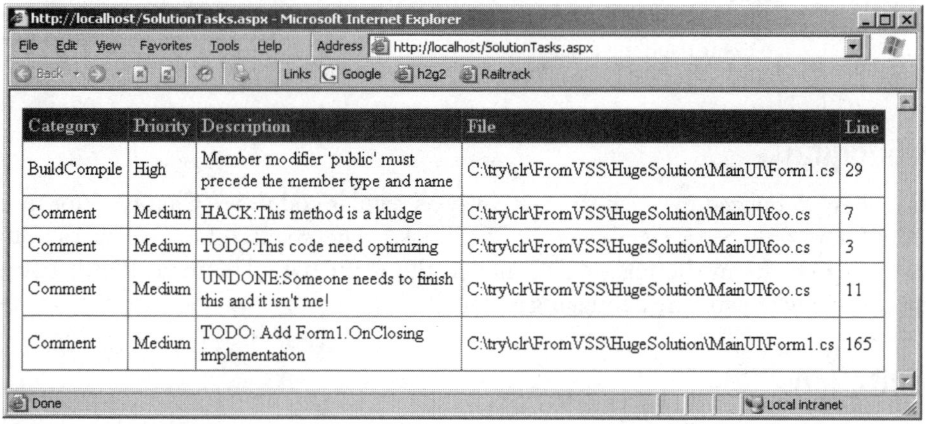

Category	Priority	Description	File	Line
BuildCompile	High	Member modifier 'public' must precede the member type and name	C:\try\clr\FromVSS\HugeSolution\MainUI\Form1.cs	29
Comment	Medium	HACK:This method is a kludge	C:\try\clr\FromVSS\HugeSolution\MainUI\foo.cs	7
Comment	Medium	TODO:This code need optimizing	C:\try\clr\FromVSS\HugeSolution\MainUI\foo.cs	3
Comment	Medium	UNDONE:Someone needs to finish this and it isn't me!	C:\try\clr\FromVSS\HugeSolution\MainUI\foo.cs	11
Comment	Medium	TODO: Add Form1.OnClosing implementation	C:\try\clr\FromVSS\HugeSolution\MainUI\Form1.cs	165

Figure 8-5. Tasklist displayed in an ASP.NET page

Handling Events in Macros

As described earlier in the section entitled "Properties collections," the VS.NET automation object model provides objects that raise events. Each category of events (e.g., build events, debugging events, text editor events) has a corresponding event source object. Writing macros that get called when these events are raised is very easy.

Whenever you create a new macro project, the macro IDE adds a module called `EnvironmentEvents`. The sole purpose of this module is to let you handle events raised by the IDE. If you open this file and click on the drop-down list at the top left of the editor window, you will see a list of event sources—`BuildEvents`, `DebuggerEvents`, `DocumentEvents`, and so forth. If you select one of these, the drop-down list at the top right will be populated with a list of events. If you select one of these, the IDE will add an event handler for you.

Example 8-13 shows a typical event handler. It handles the `OnBuildDone` event from the `BuildEvents` object. This example will display a message box every time a build completes.

Example 8-13. Handling a build event in a macro

```
Private Sub BuildEvents_OnBuildDone(ByVal Scope As EnvDTE.vsBuildScope, _
        ByVal Action As EnvDTE.vsBuildAction) _
       Handles BuildEvents.OnBuildDone

    MsgBox("Build complete!")

End Sub
```

Because macros are stored per-user and are not associated with any particular project or solution, this macro will be run any time any solution is built. You should, therefore, exercise caution when writing an event-handling macro—it will be run whenever the selected event is raised, regardless of context.

Debugging

Macros are debugged in much the same way as regular code. (See Chapter 3 for more information on VS.NET's debugging facilities.) The main difference is that the debugging occurs in the macro IDE, not in the main IDE. The main IDE becomes inaccessible when you are debugging a macro.

Limitations

Macros provide a powerful way to automate and customize the IDE, but they do have certain limitations. For example, you cannot invoke a macro as part of a command-line-based automated build, because VS.NET will display the IDE when it runs the macro.

Here are some other limitations on macros:

- Cannot create custom property pages for the Options dialog box on the Tools menu
- Cannot create custom tool windows
- Cannot dynamically enable and disable items on menus and toolbars
- Cannot add contact and descriptive information to the Visual Studio .NET Help About box
- Cannot build user interfaces for macros

Our TaskList DataSet macro would be much more useful if we could arrange for the DataSet to be created after a solution is built without user intervention. But we would need some way of allowing the user to configure which solutions require a DataSet to be generated and where each solution should write the XML file. This kind of configurability is difficult to achieve with a macro, because macros cannot display user interfaces. Fortunately, we can solve this problem by writing an add-in instead of a macro.

Add-ins

An add-in is a COM component that implements certain interfaces. These interfaces are used to connect the IDE and the add-in. It allows the IDE to notify the add-in about user input and other potentially interesting events, and it also allows the component to communicate with the IDE's object model.

Design Choices

An add-in can be developed in any language that can implement a COM class. It is easy enough to write an add-in from scratch, but you don't need to do that as VS.NET has a special project template for creating an add-in. The project is found in the New Project dialog under Other Projects → Extensibility Projects.

When you create a new Visual Studio .NET add-in project, you will be presented with a wizard that lets you choose how to build your add-in. It will first ask you which language you wish to use—VB.NET, C#, or C++. (J# is not supported by this wizard.) Our example will use C#.

 If you want to supply a custom tool window or a custom property page in the Options dialog, you are required to write an ActiveX control. Since C# and VB.NET do not support the authoring of ActiveX controls, you may want to choose C++ if you plan to use these features in your add-in. Alternatively, there is nothing stopping you writing the control in a separate component and using C# or VB.NET for the rest of the add-in.

Next you choose the IDEs in which you would like your add-in to be able to work. (You can choose VS.NET, the macro IDE, or both.) Then you will be asked to enter a name and description for your add-in. We will call our example the TaskList Data Gen Add-in.

The wizard presents many more options in the dialogs that follow, most of which are straightforward. For our example, the most important option is that we want our add-in to add an entry to the VS.NET Tools menu so that we can display a configuration user interface. (The wizard provides a checkbox to enable this.)

The Add-in Wizard creates two projects. One builds the actual add-in. The other is a Setup project—it builds a Microsoft Installer (*.msi* file) for the add-in. This makes it easy to distribute your add-in to other developers—the setup installer will put the component in a suitable folder and add all the necessary registry entries (more on that later).

In the main add-in project, the wizard creates a source file containing a class that implements IDTExtensibility2. IDTExtensibility2 has five methods, which are described in Table 8-2. (Older Microsoft development environments defined an interface called IDTExtensibility. This has been replaced entirely by IDTExtensibility2. Unlike certain I*Xxx*2 interfaces in COM, implementing IDTExtensibility2 does not require you to implement IDTExtensibility as well.)

Table 8-2. IDTExtensibility2

Method	Description
OnAddInsUpdate	Called when the add-in is loaded or unloaded in the environment.
OnBeginShutdown	Called when VS.NET is being shut down.

Table 8-2. IDTExtensibility2 (continued)

Method	Description
OnConnection	Called when the add-in is loaded by VS.NET.
OnDisconnection	Called when the add-in is unloaded by VS.NET.
OnStartupComplete	Called when VS.NET has completed starting.

The OnConnection method is particularly important—it is called by VS.NET when our add-in is first loaded. Among other things, VS.NET passes in references to a couple of objects in the automation object model. In the wizard-generated implementation of this method, the first thing this code does is to store these references in a couple of fields, so that they will be available later, as Example 8-14 shows.

Example 8-14. Storing the automation objects in an add-in

```
public void OnConnection(object application, ext_ConnectMode connectMode,
    object addInInst, ref System.Array custom)
{
    applicationObject = (_DTE)application;
    addInInstance = (AddIn)addInInst;

    . . .

}

. . .

private _DTE applicationObject;
private AddIn addInInstance;
```

If you told VS.NET to add an item to the Tools menu for your add-in, the OnConnection method will check to see if this is the first time the add-in has been called since being installed. (VS.NET will pass the value ext_cm_UISetup in as the connectMode parameter the very first time the add-in is loaded.) If this is the first time, the code creates a command object and a new entry for that command on the Tools menu.

Example 8-15 shows code that adds a command and a menu item. This has been modified slightly from the code generated by the wizard. By default, the wizard names the command after the add-in project name. However, as this menu item will be providing access to a configuration dialog, we have changed the command's name to Configure.

Example 8-15. Adding an item to the Tools menu

```
if(connectMode == ext_ConnectMode.ext_cm_UISetup)
{
    object[] contextGUIDS = new object[] { };
    Commands commands = applicationObject.Commands;
    _CommandBars commandBars = applicationObject.CommandBars;
```

Example 8-15. Adding an item to the Tools menu (continued)

```
try
{
    // Add the command object. (This is a persistent
    // operation, so we only need to do this the first
    // time we run.)

    Command command = commands.AddNamedCommand(addInInstance,
        "Configure",
        "Configure TaskList DataSet Generator...",
        "Configures the TaskList DataSet Generator",
        true, 59,
        ref contextGUIDS,
        (int)vsCommandStatus.vsCommandStatusSupported +
          (int)vsCommandStatus.vsCommandStatusEnabled);

    // Add an item to the Tools menu for the new
    // command object. (This is also a persistent
    // operation.)

    CommandBar commandBar = (CommandBar)commandBars["Tools"];
    CommandBarControl commandBarControl =
        command.AddControl(commandBar, 1);
}
catch(System.Exception /*e*/)
{
}
}
```

 The full name of the command will be *AddInProgID*.Configure, where *AddInProgID* is the ProgID of the AddIn class. By default, the wizard sets the ProgID to *ProjectName*.Connect. So if we called our add-in project TaskListAddin, the full name of the command would be:

> TaskListAddin.Connect.Configure

If you want to change the prefix from *ProjectName*.Connect, you must change the ProgID of your add-in. This is set with the ProgID attribute on the class that the wizard generates. If you change this, you must also modify the Setup and Deployment project to match—it refers to the ProgID in its registry configuration. See the later "Installation" section for details on how add-ins are configured in the registry. See Chapter 6 for information about how to modify Setup and Deployment projects.

The strings that follow in the AddNamedCommand parameter list determine the button/ menu item text and the tooltip text, so these have also been modified to be more appropriate than the generic defaults that the wizard provides.

Add-ins that add themselves to VS.NET menus or toolbars must implement the IDTCommand interface. This defines an Exec method, which VS.NET will call when the user clicks on the relevant items. Again, if you asked the wizard to add an entry to the toolbar, it helpfully provides an implementation that does the basic command handling. All you need to do is provide the functionality. In Example 8-16, we simply display a configuration dialog. (The configuration dialog is a Windows Forms form class called TaskListDataGenConfigDialog, which will be discussed later. Its constructor, which is shown in Example 8-20, takes a reference to the DTE object, so that it can store any configuration changes.)

Example 8-16. Handling commands in an add-in

```
public void Exec(string commandName,
    vsCommandExecOption executeOption,
    ref object varIn, ref object varOut, ref bool handled)
{
    handled = false;
    if(executeOption == vsCommandExecOption.vsCommandExecOptionDoDefault)
    {
        if(commandName == "TaskListAddin.Connect.Configure")
        {
            handled = true;

            using (TaskListDataGenConfigDialog dlg =
                    new TaskListDataGenConfigDialog(applicationObject))
            {
                dlg.ShowDialog( );
            }
            return;
        }
    }
}
```

IDTCommandTarget defines a second method, QueryStatus, which VS.NET calls to determine whether a particular command is available. This allows add-ins to gray out menu items or buttons. VS.NET will call Exec for a command only after it has checked its availability with QueryStatus. The Add-in Wizard provides an implementation of QueryStatus that looks very similar to Exec—it checks the command name and then sets the status. In our add-in, we never disable the command, so we can use a much simpler implementation, shown in Example 8-17. (We check the neededText parameter to see what kind of status query this is—this method also allows us to change the text dynamically. In this example we only care about making sure the command is enabled to ensure that we respond to only the appropriate kind of query.)

Example 8-17. Command status query handling

```
public void QueryStatus(string commandName,
    vsCommandStatusTextWanted neededText,
    ref vsCommandStatus status, ref object commandText)
{
    if(neededText ==
        vsCommandStatusTextWanted.vsCommandStatusTextWantedNone)
```

Example 8-17. Command status query handling (continued)

```
    {
        status = (vsCommandStatus)
            vsCommandStatus.vsCommandStatusSupported |
            vsCommandStatus.vsCommandStatusEnabled;
    }
}
```

We have not yet managed to implement our add-in's primary purpose: to generate a serialized DataSet containing the TaskList output. To do this, we need to port the VB.NET macro (from Example 8-12) to C#. However, since we want to be able to generate the DataSet automatically every time a build occurs, we need to do a little extra work—we cannot simply hook the ported code into the command handling that we have seen so far. Fortunately, the object model can notify us of build events through its BuildEvents object— Example 8-18 shows the code that adds a suitable event handler.

Example 8-18. Handling the OnBuildDone event

```
public void OnConnection(object application,
    ext_ConnectMode connectMode,
    object addInInst, ref System.Array custom)
{

    . . . as from Example 8-14 . . .


    // Handle OnBuildDone.
    // We don't want to do this the very first time
    // VS.NET loads us—it actually calls
    // OnConnection twice, once passing in
    // ext_ConnectMode.ext_cm_UISetup, then it calls
    // OnDisconnection, and then it calls OnConnection
    // again, passing ext_ConnectMode.ext_cm_Startup.
    // We ignore the exceptional first call.
    // (The buildEventConnected flag is used to make
    // sure we don't attach two event handlers — if the
    // user unloads and reloads the add-in using the
    // Add-in Manager, again we might see multiple
    // calls to OnConnection.)

    if ((connectMode != ext_ConnectMode.ext_cm_UISetup) &&
        !buildEventConnected)
    {
        applicationObject.Events.BuildEvents.OnBuildDone +=
            new _dispBuildEvents_OnBuildDoneEventHandler(
                                    BuildEvents_OnBuildDone);
        buildEventConnected = true;
    }


}
```

Example 8-18. Handling the OnBuildDone event (continued)

```csharp
private bool buildEventConnected = false;

public void OnDisconnection(ext_DisconnectMode disconnectMode,
    ref System.Array custom)
{
    // Disconnect the OnBuildDone event handler.
    if (buildEventConnected)
    {
        applicationObject.Events.BuildEvents.OnBuildDone -=
            new _dispBuildEvents_OnBuildDoneEventHandler(
                                    BuildEvents_OnBuildDone);
        buildEventConnected = false;
    }
}

private void BuildEvents_OnBuildDone(vsBuildScope Scope,
    vsBuildAction Action)
{
    TaskListGenerator.Build(applicationObject,
                @"c:\inetpub\wwwroot\tasklist.xml");
}
```

The OnConnection method is notified whenever the add-in is loaded, and in here we use the DTE object's Events property to locate the BuildEvents object. We hook up a handler for the OnBuildDone event called BuildEvents_OnBuildDone. This calls the code that generates the TaskList. (That code is just a C# version of the code shown in Example 8-12 and is not shown here.) The environment also notifies the add-in when it is about to be unloaded by calling OnDisconnection. In this function, we detach the event handler.

Configuring add-ins

Obviously, the user may not want the add-in to run every time any solution is built, so it would be prudent to add a way for the user to configure the add-in.

Add-ins have three ways of persisting configuration options. They can provide per-user settings, per-solution settings, or per-project settings. For per-user settings, an add-in can add an extra page to the Visual Studio .NET Options dialog (Tools → Options). To insert pages into the Options dialog, you must add some items to VS.NET's registry settings. The relevant registry key will be:

```
HKCU\SOFTWARE\Microsoft\VisualStudio\7.1\AddIns\<Addin ProgID>
```

where *<Addin ProgID>* is the COM ProgID of your add-in. If you are installing your add-in for all users in the machine instead of just the installing user, you will want to use the HKLM hive, not the HKCU hive. (For VS.NET 2002, you will require 7.0 instead of 7.1.) If you add an Options key underneath this key, you can add extra pages in the Options dialog.

The Options dialog presents option pages as a hierarchy—the pane on the lefthand side of the dialog presents a tree of folders and configuration pages. You can therefore add pages of your own in a hierarchical fashion. You do this by adding keys under your Options key in a hierarchy that reflects the structure you wish to see in the Options dialog. For example, if you create a Reporting key under your Options key and a Tasks DataSet key under Reporting, as illustrated in Figure 8-6, the Options dialog will show a Reporting folder containing a Tasks DataSet item, as illustrated in Figure 8-7.

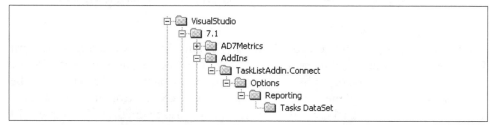

Figure 8-6. Options dialog registry configuration

Figure 8-7. A custom Options page

> You are allowed only two levels in this hierarchy. Add-ins cannot display a folder within a folder in the Options dialog.

Of course, you will need to provide a user interface to appear in the righthand side of the Options dialog box when the user clicks on your add-in's item on the left. VS.NET requires you to supply this user interface as an ActiveX control. Underneath the key for each page you must supply a text value called Control, containing either the GUID or the ProgID for the control.

 Because VS.NET requires you to provide an ActiveX control, you cannot use a Windows Forms control. This means you cannot use VB. NET, C#, or J# to write a custom property page for the Options dialog.

The site that hosts your ActiveX control in the Options dialog always seems to return an ambient background color property of black. This means you should ignore the ambient background color; otherwise, your property page's background will be black. If you are using the ATL to build the ActiveX control, it automatically retrieves the ambient background property in its Create method. Example 8-19 shows a suitable replacement Create method that you can add to your control class to disable this behavior.

Example 8-19. Ignoring the ambient background color

```
HWND Create(HWND hWndParent, RECT& rcPos, LPARAM dwInitParam = NULL)
{
    CComCompositeControl<COptionsDialog>::Create(hWndParent, rcPos,
                                                 dwInitParam);

    // The base class sets m_hbrBackground to be
    // whatever the container specifies as an
    // ambient property. Unfortunately, VS.NET
    // sets this to black, so we overrule that
    // here, selecting the normal dialog background
    // color.
    if (m_hbrBackground != NULL)
    {
        DeleteObject(m_hbrBackground);
        m_hbrBackground = NULL;
    }
    m_hbrBackground = ::GetSysColorBrush(COLOR_BTNFACE);

    return m_hWnd;
}
```

In order to be loaded into the Options dialog, the ActiveX control should implement the IDTToolsOptionsPage interface as well as the standard ActiveX control interfaces. The IDTToolsOptionsPage interface allows VS.NET to integrate your properties page into the Options dialog correctly. The interface has five methods. VS.NET will call OnAfterCreated after the options page is loaded, passing a reference to the DTE object. It calls either OnOK or OnCancel to indicate when and how the Options dialog is dismissed. It calls `OnHelp` if the user clicks the Help button. Finally, there is the `GetProperties` method. This should return a `Properties` collection—remember that global property collections are exposed through the DTE object's `Properties` property. The object you return through this method will also be available through the `DTE.Properties` collection. You are not obliged to support this—you may return a null reference—but you are advised to return a collection, in order that your settings may be controlled through automation.

The `IDTToolsOptionsPage` interface is defined in the Microsoft Development Environment type library, *dte.olb*. When you use the wizard to create an add-in project, this type library (or its equivalent primary interop assembly) will be referenced automatically. However, if you decided to write your add-in using C# or VB.NET and then added an extra ATL project to supply an ActiveX control for an Options page, the ATL project will not have a reference to this type library.

Fortunately, you can add a reference to this type library and also add a skeleton implementation of `IDTToolsOptionsPage` in one step using the Implement Interface Wizard. Open the class view, right-click on the control class and select Add → Implement Interface... In the dialog that appears, choose to implement an interface from the registry. The Microsoft Development Environment type library will be one of those offered in the Available Type Libraries list. If you select this library and then choose the `IDTToolsOptionsPage` interface from the list, the wizard will add most of the necessary settings to your project. However, you may find it necessary to add an auto_rename flag to the generated `#import` directive in the *stdafx.h* file, as the type library defines some symbols that clash with certain common include files.

The VS.NET Options dialog is intended for setting global options, not per-solution or per-project options. (These settings cannot be stored in a solution or a project file because the Options dialog is always available, even when no solution is loaded.) The Options dialog is therefore not a good choice for configuring which solutions our add-in will work for. So instead, we will use our add-in's entry on the Tools menu, to display a dialog for configuring whether the add-in should run when the currently loaded solution is built. Also, rather than hardcoding the path of the XML file to which the `DataSet` will be persisted, we will also allow this to be configured in the dialog. This dialog is shown in Figure 8-8, and it stores all of its settings in the loaded solution's *.sln* file, allowing per-solution configuration.

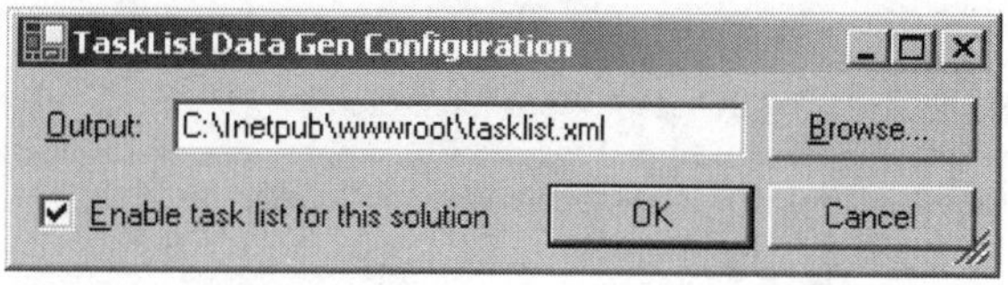

Figure 8-8. Add-in configuration dialog

The dialog is just a normal Windows Forms dialog. The two main interesting parts of the dialog's code are the initialization, where it reads settings out of the solution file, and the OK button click handler, where it writes them back in to the solution file.

Example 8-20 shows the form's constructor. It takes a reference to the DTE object as a parameter and stores it in a private field. It then uses the loaded Solution object's Globals property to see if the solution already has settings for this add-in—this is the mechanism by which VS.NET lets add-ins store configuration information in an .sln file (see Example 8-21). If settings are found, they are used to initialize the form. Otherwise, the form's fields are left in their default (blank) state.

Example 8-20. Add-in configuration dialog initialization

```
private _DTE dte;
public TaskListDataGenConfigDialog(_DTE dteObject)
{
    InitializeComponent();
    dte = dteObject;

    Globals g = dte.Solution.Globals;
    if (g.get_VariableExists("TaskDataSetAddinPath"))
    {
        txtOutputPath.Text = g["TaskDataSetAddinPath"].ToString();
        checkBoxEnable.Checked =
            bool.Parse(g["TaskDataSetAddinCmdBuild"].ToString());
    }
}
```

Example 8-21. Saving add-in settings in a solution

```
private void btnOK_Click(object sender, System.EventArgs e)
{
    Globals g = dte.Solution.Globals;

    bool save = checkBoxEnable.Checked;
    g["TaskDataSetAddinPath"] = save ? txtOutputPath.Text : "";
    g["TaskDataSetAddinCmdBuild"] = save.ToString();
    g.set_VariablePersists("TaskDataSetAddinPath", true);
    g.set_VariablePersists("TaskDataSetAddinCmdBuild", true);
}
```

This retrieves the user's settings from the controls on the configuration dialog and writes them into the Solution object's Globals collection. Then it tells the Globals object to persist the variables we are using, ensuring that they will be saved in the ExtensibilityGlobals section of the .sln file:

```
GlobalSection(ExtensibilityGlobals) = postSolution
        TaskDataSetAddinCmdBuild = True
        TaskDataSetAddinPath = C:\inetpub\wwwroot\taskdata.xml
    EndGlobalSection
```

Finally, for these settings to be of any use, we need to modify our `OnBuildDone` event handler from Example 8-18. This now needs to check the solution's settings to see if the TaskList DataSet generation facility is required for this particular project. A suitably modified handler is shown in Example 8-22.

Example 8-22. Checking the solution settings in OnBuildDone

```
private void BuildEvents_OnBuildDone(vsBuildScope Scope,
    vsBuildAction Action)
{
    seenBuildDoneEvent = true;
    Solution soln = applicationObject.Solution;
    Globals g = soln.Globals;

    string xmlPath = "";
    bool save = false;
    if (g.get_VariableExists("TaskDataSetAddinPath"))
    {
        xmlPath = g["TaskDataSetAddinPath"].ToString();
        save = bool.Parse(g["TaskDataSetAddinCmdBuild"].ToString());
    }
    if (save)
    {
        TaskListGenerator.Build(applicationObject, xmlPath);
    }
}
```

Installation

For your add-in to be loaded by VS.NET, you will need to add certain entries in the registry. The relevant registry key will be:

```
HKCU\SOFTWARE\Microsoft\VisualStudio\7.1\AddIns\<Addin ProgID>
```

where `<Addin ProgID>` is the COM ProgID of your add-in. And, of course, your add-in also needs to be properly registered as a COM object in the normal way. Fortunately, both of these requirements will be taken care of by the setup project that is created by the Add-in Wizard.

 The registry keys are specific to the version of VS.NET in which you wish to install the add-in. The key shown here is for VS.NET 2003, but for VS.NET 2002, you would need to change the 7.1 to 7.0. The simplest way of supporting both versions is to provide two installers.

In VS.NET you can select which of the currently installed add-ins is in use by selecting Tools → Add-in Manager. This brings up the dialog box shown in Figure 8-9.

This dialog lets you enable or disable add-ins. It also lets you control which add-ins are loaded at startup and whether they are available when VS.NET is invoked from the command line. Note that these settings are systemwide—they do not apply just to the currently loaded solution.

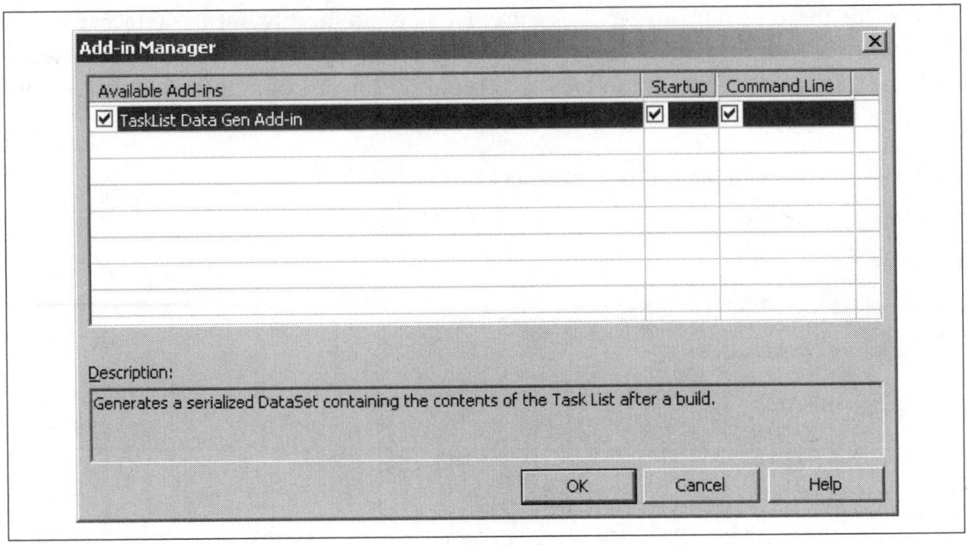

Figure 8-9. Add-in Manager dialog

Debugging

By default, VS.NET add-in projects are set up to launch another instance of VS.NET (*devenv.exe*) when you start debugging. Debugging is generally straightforward, but there is a minor complication when unhandled exceptions occur in your add-in. When this happens, VS.NET displays a dialog asking you whether you'd like to keep the add-in available. You should normally choose to keep the add-in—if the add-in gets disabled, you will have to reenable it before you can test it again.

Conclusion

Automation is one of VS.NET's greatest strengths. There is a wide gamut of options for using automation, ranging from recording a simple macro, through developing a custom macro, to building a COM component that loads as an add-in. In the next chapter we will look at another productivity-enhancing way of customizing VS.NET—custom wizards.

CHAPTER 9

Wizards

As you grow more familiar with VS.NET, you may become dissatisfied with some of the built-in project templates. Although the templates in the standard set are all useful, some of them may be almost but not quite right for your needs or you may want a new project item template based on an existing type of project you regularly need to create. VS.NET therefore lets you copy and customize existing project and item templates or even create whole new templates from scratch. And if the built-in template-based wizard mechanism doesn't meet your needs, you can write your own custom wizard components. This chapter describes the art of building templates and wizards in VS.NET.

Wizard Basics

Wizard is the generic name for the VS.NET facilities for creating new projects or items. Each of the project types listed in the New Project (Ctrl-Shift-N) and Add Project dialogs is a wizard, as are each of the items in the Add New Item dialog (Ctrl-Shift-A). Some wizards do nothing more complex than creating a new file, but the more advanced ones create several files and may even present a user interface to allow the user to configure the way in which the files are created. However, all wizards are based on the same underlying mechanisms.

Two main types of wizards are available in all languages: project wizards and item wizards. (C# and VC++ support a third wizard type: context wizards. However, unlike project and item wizards, you cannot write your own custom context wizard without writing a package, as only packages allow you to extend VS.NET context menus. See the next chapter for information on writing packages.) Each type of wizard uses the same underlying infrastructure, but each serves different purposes.

Project wizards

> VS.NET runs a project wizard when you select a project template from the New Project or Add Project dialog box. The wizard may present a UI to let you tailor the new project. The wizard then runs and copies a set of template files and adds

them to your project. When the wizard runs, it may dynamically alter the name and contents of these files based upon the name you gave the project and the input you provided to the UI. The wizard may choose to add certain files only if particular input conditions are met.

Some wizards, such as the ATL Project Wizard, display a user interface. Some, such as the C# Windows Application Wizard, do not.

Item wizards

An item wizard runs when you add a new item to your project. Some item wizards will display a UI, although this is less common than with project wizards.

Context wizards

C# and VC++ provide context wizards, which allow you to add files or to add text to an existing file. Context wizards are executed from the Class View window. For example, if you right-click on a C# or C++ class in the Class Viewer, the context menu will have an Add item, allowing you to add new class members.

Implementation Choices

VS.NET supports three main wizard implementation styles. You can write a one-file item wizard with no code, you can use the VS.NET wizard engine, or you can write your own custom wizard engine.

The simplest style is the one-file wizard, but this is the least flexible. You will not be able to display a user interface nor will you be able to customize the file.

The most popular approach is to use the VS.NET wizard engine. The majority of the built-in wizards use this technique. The wizard engine allows you to build a user interface for your wizard in HTML and to control its operation with script files. It also supplies a mechanism that lets your wizard modify parts of the files that it adds to the project. For example, if your wizard adds a class definition to a project, you can write a template file that contains the class definition but allows features such as the class name to be set dynamically.

Instead of using the built-in wizard engine, you can also write your own custom engine. This lets you use any language capable of implementing a COM component, rather than being limited to scripting languages. It also lets you use any UI technology, rather than having to use HTML. However, it does require more effort to implement than the other two techniques, since very little is automated for you.

Regardless of which of these implementation styles you use, the way in which you add new wizards to VS.NET is the same.

Adding Wizards

In order for a wizard to be available to the user, you must copy certain files into the correct directories. VS.NET also needs to know which language your wizard supports—for project wizards, this indicates the project type under which your wizard should appear in the New Project and Add Project dialogs. For item wizards, VS. NET must know which language the wizard supports in order to know when to make the wizard available—when the Add New Item dialog is displayed, it should contain only items appropriate to the current project's language. (This dialog must not offer to add C#-based items to a VB.NET project, for example.)

Each language uses a different set of directories for wizards and their configuration files. The VS.NET install directory (typically *C:\Program Files\Microsoft Visual Studio .NET 2003*) has four subfolders: *VC#, VB7, VC7,* and *VJ#,* and each of these in turn has subdirectories that contain the wizard files and wizard configuration information.

To indicate to VS.NET what kind of wizard yours is, and the language it is designed for, you copy one or more files into an appropriate directory. Table 9-1 shows which directories you should use for each language, according to whether you are creating a project wizard or an item wizard.

Table 9-1. Wizard type locations

	Project wizard	Item wizard
C#	VC#\CSharpProjects	VC#\CSharpProjectItems
VB	VB7\VBProjects	VB7\VBProjectItems
C++	VC7\vcprojects	VC7\vcprojectitems
J#	VJ#\VJSharpProjects	VJ#\VJSharpProjectItems

Each of the directories listed in Table 9-1 contains one or more *.vsdir* files. The *.vsdir* files contain lists of wizards. For example, the *.vsdir* files in the *VC#\CSharpProjects* folder contain entries for all of the items listed in the Visual C# Projects section of the New Projects dialog. If you are using the Professional edition (or better) of VS.NET, this particular directory will contain three *.vsdir* files—*CSharp.vsdir, CSharpEx.vsdir,* and *DevApp.vsdir,* which contain the basic, advanced, and Smart Device project types, respectively. There can be any number of *.vsdir* files in a particular directory—VS.NET will just concatenate them. To add new wizards, you can therefore simply add your own *.vsdir* files—there is no need to modify the existing ones.

For each wizard there must be a corresponding line in a *.vsdir* file. These entries consist of a series of fields separated by a | character, and they look like this:

```
Path|PackageID|Name|Order|Description|IconPath|IconID|Flags|BaseName
```

The first field, *Path*, is usually the relative path to the wizard's *.vsz* file, which contains the information needed to run the wizard (more on this in a minute). However, for item wizards, you can instead just specify the relative path of any file—if the specified file does not have the *.vsz* extension, VS.NET will automatically copy that file into the project when the item is selected. This is useful for simple item templates in which the contents of the new item are always the same. (This is how you implement the one-file wizards mentioned earlier.)

The second item in a *.vsdir* entry, *PackageID*, can be either 0 or the GUID of a VS.NET package. (See Chapter 10 for more information on VS.NET packages.) When a GUID is supplied, it is used for localization—the wizard's name and description can be stored as resources in the package. In this case, the third and fifth items in the *.vsdir* entry (*Name* and *Description*) are resource IDs. The *Name* will be displayed in the template list on the right of the relevant New/Add dialog, underneath the icon for the template. The *Description* will appear in the middle of the dialog when the template is selected. When these fields contain resource IDs, VS.NET will display appropriately localized strings in the dialog. Example 9-1 shows an entry that uses this technique—this is the entry for the C# Class Library project. (*.vsdir* entries are quite long, so this one has been split across multiple lines to make it fit. In the *.vsdir* file itself, each entry is on its own line.)

Example 9-1. .vsdir entry with package ID

```
CSharpDLL.vsz|{FAE04EC1-301F-11d3-BF4B-00C04F79EFBC}|
#2322|20|#2323|{FAE04EC1-301F-11d3-BF4B-00C04F79EFBC}|4547| |ClassLibrary
```

Localization of the name and description requires a package ID, so unless you are a Visual Studio Integration Partner (VSIP—see Chapter 10) and are writing your own package, you will not be able to use this feature for your own wizards. If you are not writing a package, you can just put strings in the *Name* and *Description* fields, specifying 0 for the package ID, as Example 9-2 shows.

Example 9-2. .vsdir entry with raw strings

```
MyWizard.vsz|0|My Project|0|My customized project|0|0|0|MyProject
```

The fourth field, *Order*, determines this item's position in the list in the relevant dialog. The lower the number, the earlier it will appear. Example 9-2 has specified an *Order* of 0. Since none of the built-in wizards have an *Order* lower than 1, this guarantees that the new wizard will appear first.

The sixth and seventh items, *IconPath* and *IconID*, indicate the icon to be used for this wizard in the New Project and Add New Item dialogs. The *IconPath* can be either another package ID or a string containing the relative path to the DLL. The *IconID* is the resource id of the icon in the DLL specified by *IconPath*.

You are not required to supply an icon. In Example 9-2, both *IconPath* and *IconID* are 0, which causes VS.NET to use a default icon.

The eighth field, *Flags*, controls certain features of the New/Add Project/Item dialogs when the template is selected. The supported flag values are:

VSDIRFLAG_NonLocalTemplate (1)

Used only in project wizards. This flag is set for all web projects—it will cause the New/Add Project dialog's Location field to require a URL rather than a file-system path. All the project files for such a template will be stored on a web server rather than on the filesystem. See Chapter 4 for more information about web projects.

VSDIRFLAG_BlankSolution (2)

Used only in project wizards. Indicates that VS.NET should just create a blank (empty) solution and not a new project. This flag is used to support the Blank Solution project type in the Visual Studio solutions category, and you would not normally use this in your own templates.

VSDIRFLAG_DisableBrowseButton (4)

Used only in project wizards. Disables the Browse button for this project/item.

VSDIRFLAG_DontAddDefExtension (8)

Used only in item wizards. Prevents a default extension from being appended to the name provided for the item.

VSDIRFLAG_DisableLocationField (32)

Disables the location field for this project or item.

VSDIRFLAG_DontInitNameField (4096)

Prevents VS.NET from initializing the Name field for the project or item with a valid default name.

VSDIRFLAG_DisableNameField (8192)

Disables the Name field for the project or item.

The flag names in this list are those given in the documentation. However, you cannot use these names in the *.vsdir* files—you must always use raw numbers. So, if your wizard is for a web project, you would specify the value 1, and not the string VSDIRFLAG_NonLocalTemplate.

The last item in the *.vsdir* entry, *BaseName*, is used by VS.NET to provide a default suggested name for the new item or project. As with all the other text fields, this can be either a resource ID or a string. (Again, to use a resource ID, you must supply a package ID, so only those signed up for VSIP will be able to use this. The rest of us must supply a raw text string, as Example 9-2 does.)

Item wizard .vsdir files

Item wizards are a little more complex than project wizards, because they are subdivided into multiple categories. If you look at the *.vsdir* file in one of the project item directories listed in Table 9-1, such as *CSharpItems.vsdir* in the *VC#\ CSharpProjectItems* directory (shown in Example 9-3), you will see that it doesn't actually hold references to wizards. It contains just two lines, both of which are references to folders: *WebProjectItems* and *LocalProjectItems*. This is because the set of project items available in the Add New Item dialog is different for local projects and web projects. Moreover, these two folders are divided into more folders, which correspond to the structure that the Add New Item dialog presents in its Categories tree on the left. This means that if you look in the *.vsdir* files in the *WebProjectItems* or *LocalProjectItems*, you will see that these too contain references to other directories.

Example 9-3. CSharpItems.vsdir

```
LocalProjectItems|{FAE04EC1-301F-11d3-BF4B-00C04F79EFBC}|#2339|10
WebProjectItems|{FAE04EC1-301F-11d3-BF4B-00C04F79EFBC}|#2340|20
```

In order for an item wizard to show in the appropriate folders in the Add New Item dialog, you will add *.vsdir* files in at least two places. Even if you want the item to appear only in local projects, you will still need to add a *.vsdir* entry in the *LocalProjectItems* subdirectory *and* the relevant subcategory (e.g., the *Utility* directory). If you add it to just the subcategory directory but not the *LocalProjectItems* subdirectory, your item will not appear when the user selects the top-level Local Project Items category. (All of the VS.NET item templates appear twice—once in the top-level category and once in the more specific category.)

Although you need to create or modify *.vsdir* files in at least two directories, everything else remains the same as it was for a project wizard.

Most of the information in the *.vsdir* file is concerned with how the template will be presented in the New/Add Project or Add Item dialog. However, when the user elects to run the wizard by clicking OK in the relevant dialog, VS.NET will refer to the first field in the *.vsdir* entry, Path. As already mentioned, for simple item wizards, this can be just the path of a source file that will get copied and added to the project. However, for project wizards or more sophisticated item wizards, Path will refer to a *.vsz* file that tells VS.NET what to do next.

.vsz Files

When the user creates a new project or adds a new item to a project, VS.NET loads the *.vsz* file for the corresponding wizard, as specified in a *.vsdir* file. The *.vsz* file it uses is determined by the first field in the wizard's *.vsdir* file entry. Example 9-1 specifies the *CSharpDLL.vsz* file, which is shown in Example 9-4.

Example 9-4. The C# class library .vsz file

```
VSWIZARD 7.0
Wizard=VsWizard.VsWizardEngine.7.1
Param="WIZARD_NAME = CSharpDLLWiz"
Param="WIZARD_UI = FALSE"
Param="PROJECT_TYPE = CSPROJ"
```

The first line of the *.vsz* file indicates what version of VS.NET this *.vsz* file is designed for. (VS.NET 2003 will accept Versions 6.0, 7.0, and 7.1. Although 7.1 is technically the version number for VS.NET 2003, in practice, all of the built-in templates specify 7.0, as this example does.)

The second line is the ProgID of the COM coclass that VS.NET will create in order to execute this wizard. Most wizards just specify the wizard engine that ships with VS.NET—VsWizard.VsWizardEngine.7.1. (In VS.NET 2002, the built-in wizards all specified just VsWizard.VsWizardEngine.) The wizard engine is described in the next section.

You are not required to use the built-in wizard engine. You may instead supply your own class, which must implement the IDTWizard interface. See the later section titled "Custom Wizard Engines" for more information.

The remainder of the file is used to supply parameters to the wizard class. If a custom wizard class were in use, you could pass whatever parameters you like here. However, since Example 9-4 is using the wizard engine, all of the parameters that it passes are standard wizard engine parameters.

The VS.NET Wizard Engine

All of the wizards installed with VS.NET are templates that are executed by the *wizard engine*, which is a COM class whose ProgID is VsWizard.VsWizardEngine.7.1. The wizard engine's job is to display a UI (if required), collect the input from that UI, execute a script, and (potentially) copy template files. The script's job is to take whatever data was entered into the UI and use this to modify the template files if necessary.

VS.NET knows to use the wizard engine because the wizard's *.vsz* file specifies that the VsWizard.VsWizardEngine.7.1 class should be used. Example 9-4 shows an example of this. The standard parameters you can place in a *.vsz* file that the wizard engine understands are listed in Table 9-2. Two of these—WIZARD_NAME and WIZARD_UI—are mandatory. WIZARD_NAME tells the wizard engine which wizard to run—it will look for a directory of the specified name in the language's wizard files directory, as specified in Table 9-3. The WIZARD_UI flag indicates whether the wizard will present a UI or just add the specified item straightaway.

Table 9-2. Standard wizard engine parameters for .vsz files

Parameter	Description
ABSOLUTE_PATH	An optional absolute path to the wizard. Not usually required, as VS.NET will look for the wizard in one of the directories listed in Table 9-3 , based on the WIZARD_NAME.
HTML_FILTER	File extensions that the wizard uses for HTML. Required only if something other than *.htm* is in use.

Parameter	Description
HTML_PATH	The path to the HTML files for this wizard. By default, VS.NET will look for an *HTML* folder under the main wizard folder.
IMAGES_PATH	The path of images to be used by the HTML. By default, VS.NET will look for an *Images* folder under the main wizard folder.
MISC_FILTER	Files that get copied into the *Misc* folder in the Solution Explorer. Specified as a semicolon-delimited list.
PRODUCT_INSTALLATION_DIR	The installation directory of the language for which the wizard is being executed. By default, this will be either the *VC#*, *VJ#*, *VB7*, or *VC7* subdirectory of the VS.NET installation directory.
PROJECT_TEMPLATE_NAME	Name of the template file used to create a project. This defaults to *template.inf*.
PROJECT_TEMPLATE_PATH	Path to the wizard files. This defaults to one of the folders listed in Table 9-3.
PROJECT_TYPE	The type of project. The default will be appropriate to the template's language (e.g., CSPROJ or VBPROJ).
RELATIVE_PATH	If no ABSOLUTE_PATH is specified, the RELATIVE_PATH can be used to specify from the location of the wizard files relative to PRODUCT_INSTALLATION_DIR. The WIZARD_NAME will be appended to this to form the actual directory. Not typically used, as wizards are normally directly beneath the PRODUCT_INSTALLATION_DIR.
SCRIPT_COMMON_PATH	The directory containing the common script files, relative to PRODUCT_INSTALLATION_DIR. You would not normally change this—you will usually want to have access to the standard common scripts.
SCRIPT_FILTER	File extension filter for files to be placed in the *Scripts* folder of the project (e.g., js and vbs.
SCRIPT_PATH	The path to the script file for this wizard. The default is START_PATH*Scripts*.
START_PATH	Never set in the *.vsz*—the wizard engine automatically sets this to the path it has determined as the location of the wizard.
TEMPLATE_FILTER	Any file extensions to be placed into the *Templates* directory.
TEMPLATES_PATH	Path to the wizard's template files. Usually START_PATH*Templates*.
WIZARD_NAME	Name of the wizard. This must be the name of the directory that contains the wizard.
WIZARD_UI	A Boolean that indicates whether or not this wizard shows a UI or not. TRUE means it shows a UI, FALSE means that it does not.

The script and HTML files that make up each wizard are placed underneath the directories listed in Table 9-3. For example, the built-in C# Class Library project template is in a folder named *VC#\VC#Wizards\CSharpDLLWiz*.

Table 9-3. Wizard file locations

Language	Wizard file location
C#	*VC#\VC#Wizards*
VB	*VB7\VBWizards*
C++	*VC7\VCWizards*
J#	*VJ#\vjsharpwizards*

Wizard Execution

All wizards that use the wizard engine follow the same execution sequence. First, the wizard's UI is shown if it has one. Then the wizard's script is executed.

Not all wizards need to present a UI, so the initial UI step is optional. When a UI is present, it is made up of any number of HTML files. The purpose of the UI is to collect input from the user and make it available to the script. The HTML files therefore contain special tags that indicate which fields contain values that represent user settings. Once the UI stage is complete, the wizard engine loads and executes the wizard's script. The script must be written in JScript in a file called *default.js*. The following sections describe how to write the UI and script files.

The UI

Wizards that use the wizard engine have HTML-based user interfaces. When the wizard runs, the wizard engine displays the first HTML page in a dialog. If the UI has multiple pages in its UI, the left side of the dialog will present a series of links allowing each individual page to be accessed. The main page is a file called *default.htm*. This must be in a subdirectory called *HTML\<Locale ID>*. If you are writing for the U.S. locale the ID is 1033.

> The MSDN Library provides a complete list of locale IDs on the "Locale ID (LCID) Chart" page in the Microsoft Scripting Technologies documentation. This can be found by typing `locale ID` into the VS.NET Help Index, which can be opened with Help → Index... (Ctrl-Alt-F2).

With multipage user interfaces, the user will not be forced to view every page—unlike some wizard UIs, VS.NET wizards are not sequential. (They behave more like an HTML frameset.) Since you cannot be sure that the user will even look at any page other than the first one, your wizard should supply reasonable defaults for all values.

When the user clicks the Finish button, the wizard engine will execute the script contained in the *default.js* file, where you will, of course, need to access the values that the user typed in. Fortunately, the wizard engine reads these for you and makes them available to your script and templates.

The VS.NET wizard engine provides a mechanism that deals with both setting default values in a wizard UI and retrieving user input. All such values are passed between the UI and the wizard engine using the <SYMBOL> tag. The <SYMBOL> tag is used to declare variables that represent input fields in the wizard. Example 9-5 is an extract from one of the ATL wizards, showing how this tag is used.

Example 9-5. SYMBOL tags from the ATL Wizard HTML

```
<SYMBOL NAME="SAFE_PROJECT_NAME" TYPE=text></SYMBOL>
<SYMBOL NAME="UPPER_CASE_PROJECT_NAME" TYPE=text></SYMBOL>
<SYMBOL NAME="LIB_NAME" TYPE=text></SYMBOL>

<SYMBOL NAME="DLL_APP" TYPE=checkbox VALUE=true></SYMBOL>
<SYMBOL NAME="EXE_APP" TYPE=checkbox VALUE=false></SYMBOL>
<SYMBOL NAME="SERVICE_APP" TYPE=checkbox VALUE=false></SYMBOL>

<SYMBOL NAME="MERGE_PROXY_STUB" TYPE=checkbox VALUE=false></SYMBOL>
<SYMBOL NAME="SUPPORT_MFC" TYPE=checkbox VALUE=false></SYMBOL>
<SYMBOL NAME="SUPPORT_COMPLUS" TYPE=checkbox VALUE=false></SYMBOL>
<SYMBOL NAME="SUPPORT_COMPONENT_REGISTRAR" TYPE=checkbox
        VALUE=false></SYMBOL>

<SYMBOL NAME="COMPREG_REGISTRY_FORMAT" TYPE=text></SYMBOL>
<SYMBOL NAME="LIBID_REGISTRY_FORMAT" TYPE=text></SYMBOL>
<SYMBOL NAME="APPID_REGISTRY_FORMAT" TYPE=text></SYMBOL>

<SYMBOL NAME="SOURCE_FILTER" TYPE=text></SYMBOL>
<SYMBOL NAME="INCLUDE_FILTER" TYPE=text></SYMBOL>
<SYMBOL NAME="RESOURCE_FILTER" TYPE=text></SYMBOL>

<SYMBOL NAME="CODE_PAGE" TYPE=text></SYMBOL>
<SYMBOL NAME="YEAR" TYPE=text></SYMBOL>

<SYMBOL NAME="ATTRIBUTED" TYPE=checkbox VALUE=true></SYMBOL>
```

Any symbol defined in this way can be used in any of the HTML files that make up the user interface. The usual way of doing this is to associate a control with the symbol. For example, the ATTRIBUTED symbol, which selects whether the generated ATL project will use attributes, has a corresponding checkbox in the UI. Such controls are associated with their symbols through the ID attribute. Example 9-6 shows an excerpt of the checkbox tag associated with the ATTRIBUTE symbol.

Example 9-6. Checkbox associated with a symbol

```
<INPUT CLASS="CheckBox" TYPE="checkbox" ID="ATTRIBUTED" ACCESSKEY="A">
```

Many of the SYMBOL tags in Example 9-5 have a VALUE attribute. This is used to specify default settings, although default values will not be populated automatically—a little manual intervention is required.

The wizard engine exposes symbols to the scripts on the UI pages. It does this through a series of objects called the *wizard engine helper object model*, which is accessible through the window.external script object. When an HTML UI is first loaded, the script in the HTML file typically uses the wizard engine object to load default values from the SYMBOL tags into the corresponding controls. This is done by calling the SetDefaults method, as shown in Example 9-7. (The <BODY> tag shown at the top of the example illustrates the usual way of ensuring that the InitDocument function is called when the page is first displayed.)

Example 9-7. Initializing field default values

```
<BODY ONLOAD="InitDocument(document);">
   . . .

<SCRIPT LANGUAGE="JSCRIPT">

function InitDocument(document)
{
   setDirection();

   if (window.external.FindSymbol("DOCUMENT_FIRST_LOAD"))
   {
      var L_WizardDialogTitle_Text = "My Wizard";
      window.external.AddSymbol("WIZARD_DIALOG_TITLE",
               L_WizardDialogTitle_Text);
      window.external.SetDefaults(document);
   }
   window.external.Load(document);
   InitControls();
}

</SCRIPT>
```

The initial call to setDirection sets text direction as left to right or right to left according to the locale. This function is supplied by the shared script files, *Script.js* and *Common.js*. To use these from script in your UI, you will need to include them explicitly, as shown in Example 9-8.

Example 9-8. Making standard script files accessible in HTML

```
<SCRIPT>
   var strPath = "../../../";
   strPath += window.external.GetHostLocale();
   var strScriptPath = strPath + "/Script.js";
   var strCommonPath = strPath + "/Common.js";
   document.scripts("INCLUDE_SCRIPT").src = strScriptPath;
   document.scripts("INCLUDE_COMMON").src = strCommonPath;
</SCRIPT>
```

The call to AddSymbol in Example 9-7 illustrates that script code can set symbol values at runtime without needing to declare them in the list of SYMBOL tags. This particular symbol, WIZARD_DIALOG_TITLE, has the side effect of setting the window title.

This code also calls both SetDefaults and Load. SetDefaults parses the document looking for SYMBOL tags and initializes the wizard engine's internal symbol tables with the specified default values. Load scans the HTML document looking for HTML controls with IDs that match the name of the SYMBOL tags and sets their values. (In other words, this is where the fields get set to their default locations.)

The script and the templates

Every wizard must have a script file called *default.js*. It contains the code that will be run once the UI stage of the wizard is complete. (For wizards that don't have a UI, this script will be run as soon as the wizard is launched.) This file must be in the *Scripts\<Locale ID>* subdirectory of the wizard's installation directory. (The Locale ID will be 1033 if you are using U.S. English.) Every wizard must also have a *templates.inf* file, located in the *Templates\<Locale ID>* subdirectory. This file contains a list of files that the wizard engine should copy to the project directory. The files that are to be copied must live in the same directory as the *templates.inf* file.

The wizard engine makes a common script file, *common.js*, available to all *default.js* files. Each of the languages supported by VS.NET (i.e., C#, J#, C++, and VB.NET) provides its own *common.js* file in its wizard folder's script directory. The wizard engine will expect your *default.js* script to contain an OnFinish function, which will be called when the user clicks the Finish button on the UI. (If your wizard has no UI, this function will be called as soon as the user decides to create a new project or item of your wizard's type.) The OnFinish function is responsible for instructing the wizard engine to munge and copy the appropriate template files into the project directory.

Your *template.inf* file must contain a list of template files to be copied into the project. Each filename appears on its own line. The listed files are text files that will be used as the basis for new files that are added to the project. However, files are not quite copied across verbatim—the wizard gets the opportunity to make modifications. These modifications are made using *template directives*. Template directives are markers in text files that indicate replaceable or optional sections. They can be applied to any of the files that are in the templates directory, including the *templates.inf* file itself. Example 9-9 shows a typical example.

Example 9-9. Template file with directives

```
using System;

namespace [!output SAFE_NAMESPACE_NAME]
{
    /// <summary>
    /// Summary description for [!output SAFE_CLASS_NAME].
    /// </summary>
    public class [!output SAFE_CLASS_NAME]
    {
        public [!output SAFE_CLASS_NAME]()
        {
            //
            // TODO: Add constructor logic here
            //
        }
    }
}
```

This is a fairly simple template that generates a C# source file containing a class definition. The template directives are the blocks enclosed with square brackets. In Example 9-9, all of the directives are of the form [! output SYMBOL]. When the wizard engine copies a template, it will replace all output directives with the value of the named symbol.

 The SAFE_NAMESPACE_NAME and SAFE_CLASS_NAME symbols are generated automatically by the wizard engine. They will typically be the project's default namespace and a default class name such as Class1.

So when the wizard that contains this template is run, the resulting file will look something like this:

```
using System;

namespace ClassLibrary1
{
    /// <summary>
    /// Summary description for Class1.
    /// </summary>
    public class Class1
    {
        public Class1()
        {
            //
            // TODO: Add constructor logic here
            //
        }
    }
}
```

Let's follow the execution of the *default.js* and the *templates.inf* files. The C# Class Library Wizard's *templates.inf* file has two files in it:

```
File1.cs
assemblyinfo.cs
```

When the user clicks OK in the New Project dialog or Open in the Add New Item dialog, the IDE passes control to the wizard engine. When the user clicks Finish on the UI, the wizard engine loads *default.js* and calls the OnFinish function. (With wizards that have no UI, this method will be run immediately.) Example 9-10 shows a typical wizard's OnFinish function.

Example 9-10. Example default.js OnFinish method

```
function OnFinish(selProj, selObj)
{
    try
    {
        var strProjectPath = wizard.FindSymbol("PROJECT_PATH");
        var strProjectName = wizard.FindSymbol("PROJECT_NAME");
```

Example 9-10. Example default.js OnFinish method (continued)

```
        var strSafeProjectName = CreateSafeName(strProjectName);
        wizard.AddSymbol("SAFE_PROJECT_NAME", strSafeProjectName);


        var proj = CreateCSharpProject(strProjectName, strProjectPath,
                     "defaultemplate directivel.csproj");

        var InfFile = CreateInfFile( );
        AddReferencesForClass(proj);
        AddFilesToCSharpProject(proj, strProjectName,
                strProjectPath, InfFile, false);
        proj.Save( );
    }
    catch(e)
    {
        if( e.description.length > 0 )
            SetErrorInfo(e);
        return e.number;
    }
    finally
    {
        if( InfFile )
            InfFile.Delete( );
    }
}
```

There are two parameters to the OnFinish function. These parameters change depending on the type of wizard, but generally the first parameter will be an object reference to the current project. The second parameter can be a reference to an object being added (e.g., a file object when the wizard being run is an item wizard). When running a project wizard, both parameters are null.

This code really does two things. First, it pulls a number of variable values from the wizard using wizard.FindSymbol. (The wizard variable is added to the script's context by the wizard engine so that the script can access the engine in order to do its job. The engine also makes a dte variable available, which refers to the VS.NET automation object.) The second thing it does is to use these values to create the new project by calling the utility function CreateCSharpProject. (This is defined in the shared C# *common.js*, as are all of the other utility functions used in this example.)

Having created the project, the next step is the call to CreateInfFile. This utility function parses the wizard's *template.inf*, processing any template directives, creating a temporary file containing the results. (This means that the *template.inf* file can contain template directives, which allows the set of files that a wizard creates to be determined dynamically. Without this step, a wizard would always end up adding the same set of files with the same names.)

Once the temporary *templates.inf* file is created, the script then needs to tell the wizard engine to process all of the files listed in this *.inf* file. C# wizards usually do this by calling the `AddFilesToCSharpProject` utility function. This parses the processed *.inf* file, and for each file listed there, it processes any template directives and adds a file containing the processed results to the project.

Template Directives

The template syntax is very simple: square brackets with an exclamation mark after the opening bracket—[! ...]—denote a template directive. The six keywords that you can use within a template directive are shown in Table 9-4.

Table 9-4. Template directive syntax

Keyword	Description/usage
`[!if SYMBOL_NAME]`	Checks the value of the Boolean symbol *SYMBOL_NAME*. If the value is true, the following block is included. If not, it is omitted.
`[!else]`	Part of the `[!if]` control structure. Allows an alternate block to be included when the condition is false.
`[!endif]`	End of the `[!if]` block.
`[!output SYMBOL_NAME]` or `[!output "string"]`	If a symbol name is provided, the value of the symbol will be sent to the output stream. If a literal string is supplied, the string will be sent instead.
`[!loop = SYMBOL_NAME]` or `[!loop = number]`	The block following this directive will be repeated as many times as specified by either the named numeric symbol's value or by the numeric constant.
`[!endloop]`	Marks the end of a loop block.

Copying and Modifying an Existing Wizard

If you want a wizard that is very similar to an existing wizard, it does not make sense to build a new wizard from scratch—it is much easier to adapt an existing wizard to your needs. We will now walk through the process of copying and modifying an existing wizard. In this example, we will define a modified C# Class Library project that creates an assembly with a strong name. (The default C# Class Library project does add the appropriate attributes to do this in the *AssemblyInfo.cs* file, but it leaves them blank.)

Since it is easy to build new wizards by copying the existing wizards, there is never any need to modify the built-in ones. You should avoid the temptation to change the built-in wizards, since your changes may be overwritten when you install a VS.NET service pack. (VS.NET does not expect you to change its files, so it reserves the right to replace them when a service pack is installed.)

Reusing the C# Class Library project template is a fairly simple task. First, we must make a copy of the wizard's files. You can find these in the *VC#\VC#Wizards\ CSharpDllWiz* folder in the Visual Studio .NET installation directory. Copy the files into a new directory called *CSharpSNDLLWiz* (SN for strong name), also under the *VC#\VC#Wizards* directory—this is where the VS.NET wizard engine expects all C# wizard directories to live.

We will need to modify the files in the *Templates* directory a little to make the template meet our needs. The project will have the same basic structure—it will contain an *AssemblyInfo.cs* file and an initial class file, so the *template.inf* file will not need modifying. The default class definition will also be just fine, so you can leave that as it is. Only the *AssemblyInfo.cs* template needs to be changed.

The *AssemblyInfo.cs* file is the usual place for all the assembly-level attributes. This is where the attribute that indicates the location of the strong name key file should go. This filename will be generated when the wizard is run—it will be placed in a variable that will be filled in by code in the *default.js* file. We need to modify the *AssemblyInfo.cs* to include an [!output] directive that will put this key file name into the source code. The *AssemblyInfo.cs* file already contains a line with an empty AssemblyKeyFile attribute, but we will modify it thus:

```
[assembly: AssemblyKeyFile("[!output KEY_FILE_NAME]")]
```

This is the only change we will make to the template files. But for this modified *AssemblyInfo.cs* template to work, we will need to change the *default.js* script file. It must do three things:

- Execute the *sn.exe* utility to create a strong name key file (*.snk*)
- Add a symbol called KEY_FILE_NAME containing the name of the key file, so that the *AssemblyInfo.cs* template will work correctly
- Add the *.snk* file to the project

Adding the *.snk* file to the project is not a strict requirement. We are doing it here for ease of use because it can then be added to source control. However, if you are relying on the secrecy of your strong name's private key to guarantee the authenticity of your code, you will probably want to use a more robust key management strategy than checking the key pair in to source control where everyone can see it. The technique shown here is appropriate only if you require the uniqueness offered by a strong name but don't care about its code signing capabilities.

Because *default.js* executes before the project directory is actually created, we must create the *.snk* file in a temporary directory, then tell the project object to add it to the project. This will cause VS.NET to copy the file to the appropriate place once the project directory has been created.

We can use the shell's `Tools.Shell` command to invoke the *sn.exe* command-line utility. (We pass *sn.exe* the -k switch to indicate that we would like it to generate a new key file. We also pass in the path and name of the file in which to create the key.) Because the dte object's ExecuteCommand method returns before the *sn.exe* command finishes executing, we have to poll to see if the file has been created before adding it to the project. The code for all this is shown in Example 9-11.

Example 9-11. Creating a strong name in a wizard

```
function CreateSNKeyFile(project, projectname)
{
    var fso;
    fso = new ActiveXObject("Scripting.FileSystemObject");
    var TemporaryFolder = 2;
    var tfolder = fso.GetSpecialFolder(TemporaryFolder);
    var strTempFolder = fso.GetAbsolutePathName(tfolder.Path);
    var keyfile = strTempFolder + "\\" + projectname + ".snk";
    var exestring = "sn -k " + keyfile;
    dte.ExecuteCommand("Tools.Shell",exestring);
    // Wait for the file to be created.
    while(!fso.FileExists(keyfile))
    {
    }
    // Add the symbol with the appropriate path onto the filename
    wizard.AddSymbol("KEY_FILE_NAME","..\\\\..\\\\" +
        projectname + ".snk");

    // Add the file to the project.
    var projfile = project.ProjectItems.AddFromTemplate(keyfile,
        projectname + ".snk");

}
```

We need to call this function from OnFinish, of course, but other than that, no further changes need to be made to the wizard files. However, every wizard must have a corresponding *.vsz* file. Because this is a C# project wizard, this file must go in the *VC#\CSharpProjects* folder. Fortunately, we can just copy the existing *CSharpDLL.vsz* file in that folder into a new file called *CSharpSNDLL.vsz*. The only change we need to make to this file is to set the name of the wizard to *CSharpSNDLL*:

```
VSWIZARD 7.0
Wizard=VsWizard.VsWizardEngine.7.1
Param="WIZARD_NAME = CSharpSNDLLWiz"
Param="WIZARD_UI = FALSE"
Param="PROJECT_TYPE = CSPROJ"
```

Finally, we must tell VS.NET how we would like this template to appear in the New Project dialog—remember that VS.NET looks for this information in *.vsdir* files. You could just open the *CSharp.vsdir* file in the *VC#\SharpProjects* directory and copy the CSharpDLL line and put it at the end of the file. However, since VS.NET is happy to load any number of *.vsdir* files, there is no need to go editing VS.NET's own files.

So, instead, we will create a new file called *MyProjects.vsdir*. This file will contain just one line—a copy of the CSharpDLL line from the *CSharp.vsdir* file, but with the first value changed to point to the new *.vsz* file and the third and fifth values changed from resource IDs to text to give our wizard a distinctive name and description, as shown in Example 9-12. (Note that this has been split across multiple lines to make it fit—the actual file contains just a single line.)

Example 9-12. The new wizard's .vsdir file

```
CSharpSNDLL.vsz|0|SN Class Library|20|
Strongly-named class library|
{FAE04EC1-301F-11d3-BF4B-00C04F79EFBC}|4547|0|IanProject
```

When you create a new SN Class Library project, the wizard will run, generating a new key file and adding the appropriate filename into the *AssemblyInfo.cs* file.

Custom Wizard Engines

We are not obliged to use the wizard engine in our custom wizards. Instead, we can write a COM server, implementing the IDTWizard interface (the same interface that the wizard engine implements) and have more control over the way the wizard looks and works.

There are two reasons you might choose to write a custom IDTWizard implementation instead of using the wizard engine infrastructure. One is that you can write your wizard in the language of your choice (either managed or unmanaged), rather than being forced to use JScript. The second reason is that, if your wizard has a UI, you get total control over it—you are not limited to using HTML.

The downside of writing the custom implementation is that you can no longer use the convenient template directive syntax—you are responsible for generating any files yourself. However, if you plan to support both VB.NET and C#, this may well not be a problem: if you use the classes in the System.CodeDom namespace, you can write a single code generator that can create source code in either language, removing the need to have two different sets of template files for each language.

 The CodeDom is currently supported for only C# and VB.NET, so you cannot use this technique to generate J# or C++ files.

As an example, let's build a wizard that creates a new file containing a class with a skeleton implementation of the IDTWizard interface. (So we will write a wizard wizard, so to speak.) We will use the CodeDom API to generate the necessary source files. The CodeDom is a .NET API, so we will write this wizard in C#. (But once we've written it, it will be able to generate new VB projects as well as new C# projects.)

Besides implementing the IDTWizard interface, the class that our wizard generates will need to support COM registration. For a .NET project, this means the containing assembly must be signed using a strong name, as well as have the appropriate attributes to support COM registration. This wizard is aiming only to add new classes to an existing project, so we can use the SN Class Library wizard we wrote earlier to create a project that will be signed with a strong name. This new wizard will just have to add a Guid attribute to the class it creates.

The IDTWizard interface has only one method, Execute. The first argument to Execute is a reference to the DTE object (the top-level object in the VS.NET object model). The ContextParams parameter is an array, the contents of which depend on whether this wizard is executing as a project wizard or an item wizard. Table 9-5 shows what is passed in each case.

Table 9-5. IDTWizard.Execute ContextParams argument

Index	Project wizard	Item wizard
[0]	WizardType enum	WizardType enum
[1]	Project name string	Project name string
[2]	Local directory	ProjectItems object
[3]	VS.NET install directory	Local directory
[4]	FExclusive (Boolean indicating whether the project should be created in a brand-new solution or be added to the current solution)	ItemName (name of the item to be added)
[5]	NA	VS.NET install directory

The third parameter, CustomParams, is a collection of the Param elements from the *.vsz* file. For each Param=<Value> line in the *.vsz* file of the wizard, there will be a string in the CustomParams array. These strings are in the same format as they appear in the *.vsz* file. So, with the *.vsz* file shown in Example 9-13, there would be two entries: "MY_ PARAM = Foo", and "This is another parameter".

Example 9-13. Custom parameters in a .vsz file

```
VSWIZARD 7.0
Wizard=MyWizard.CustomWizardEngine
Param="MY_PARAM = Foo"
Param="This is another parameter"
```

The last parameter of the Execute method is the logical return value—it indicates the outcome of the wizard. It must be set to one of the enumerated values listed in Table 9-6.

Table 9-6. wizardResult enum

Constant	Value	Description
wizardResultSuccess	-1	Wizard succeeded
wizardResultFailure	0	Wizard failed
wizardResultCancel	1	Wizard was canceled
wizardResultBackOut	2	Wizard was backed out of (i.e., Back button on UI was clicked, causing execution to stop)

Our Execute method must perform the following steps:

1. Determine the language of the project

2. Create a CodeDom object appropriate to the language

3. Display a Windows Forms-based UI, which asks the user for the class name, namespace, and ProgID of the class to be generated

4. Use the CodeDom to generate the source code file, which will contain a class that implements IDTWizard with a skeleton implementation of the Execute method

5. Add the ProgID and Guid attribute to the class

6. Add the file to the project

7. Add a reference to *envdte.dll* to the project references

Example 9-14 shows the implementation of Execute. It starts by caching the reference to the Project object in a member variable. Next, it switches code path based upon the language of the project. (If the project is a language other than VB.NET or C#, the wizard raises an error message.)

Example 9-14. IDTWizard implementation

```
public void Execute(object Application, int hwndOwner,
    ref object[ ] ContextParams, ref object[ ] CustomParams,
    ref EnvDTE.wizardResult retval)
{
    // The third item in ContextParams is the pProjectIitems object.
    ProjectItems pi = (ProjectItems)ContextParams[2];

    // Get the project from the ProjectItems reference.
    project = pi.ContainingProject;

    // We use the CodeModel to find out which language is in use.
    CodeModel cm = project.CodeModel;

    retval = EnvDTE.wizardResult.wizardResultSuccess;
    switch(cm.Language)
    {   // Switch based upon language of project.
        case CodeModelLanguageConstants.vsCMLanguageCSharp:
            DoCSharp( );
            break;
```

Example 9-14. IDTWizard implementation (continued)

```
        case CodeModelLanguageConstants.vsCMLanguageVB:
            DoVB( );
            break;

        default:
            MessageBox.Show("This wizard can only be used from "
                            "C# or VB.NET projects");
            retval = EnvDTE.wizardResult.wizardResultFailure;
            return;
    }
}
```

The CodeDom defines an abstract API for generating code. This means that the majority of our code generation will be common for the VB.NET and C# code paths. Our example wizard has a class called CodeGen that provides a generic implementation for generating the code file using any CodeDomProvider, shown in Example 9-15.

Example 9-15. Code generation with CodeDom

```
class CodeGen
{
    public static string Generate(string filename, string extension,
        string classname, string nspace, string progid,
        CodeDomProvider cdp)
    {
        // Create a code generator.
        ICodeGenerator cg = cdp.CreateGenerator( );

        // Need two namespaces so that the namespace imports appear
        // in the "outer" namespace that doesn't have a name.
        System.CodeDom.CodeNamespace cnamespace2 =
                new System.CodeDom.CodeNamespace( );
        System.CodeDom.CodeNamespace cnamespace =
                new System.CodeDom.CodeNamespace(nspace);

        // Add the approprate imports.
        cnamespace2.Imports.Add(new CodeNamespaceImport("System") );
        //  The vs.net object model.
        cnamespace2.Imports.Add(new CodeNamespaceImport("EnvDTE") );
        //  Needed for the COM interop attributes.
        cnamespace2.Imports.Add(
                new CodeNamespaceImport("System.Runtime.InteropServices"));
        //  If this is VB–add the VisualBasic namespace.
        if(cdp.GetType( )==typeof(VBCodeProvider))
                cnamespace2.Imports.Add(
                        new CodeNamespaceImport("Microsoft.VisualBasic"));

        // Create the new class.
        CodeTypeDeclaration co = new CodeTypeDeclaration (classname);

        // Add the Guid attribute.
        Guid g = Guid.NewGuid( );
```

Example 9-15. Code generation with CodeDom (continued)

```
co.CustomAttributes.Add(
        new CodeAttributeDeclaration("Guid",
                new CodeAttributeArgument(
                new CodePrimitiveExpression(g.ToString("D")))))) ;

// Implement IDTWizard. (Must also add Object base type
// for VB.NET, otherwise the VBCodeDom uses "Inherits IDTWizard"
// instead of "Implements IDTWizard".)
CodeTypeReference ctr =
        new CodeTypeReference(typeof (EnvDTE.IDTWizard));
co.BaseTypes.Add(typeof(object));
co.BaseTypes.Add( ctr);

// Add the type to the namespace.
cnamespace.Types.Add (co);

// Add the Execute method.
CodeMemberMethod cm = new CodeMemberMethod( );
cm.Name = "Execute";
cm.PrivateImplementationType = ctr;
cm.Attributes = MemberAttributes.Public | MemberAttributes.Final ;

// Add parameters.
cm.Parameters.Add (
        new CodeParameterDeclarationExpression(typeof(object),
                                                "Application"));
cm.Parameters.Add (
        new CodeParameterDeclarationExpression(typeof(int),
                                                "hwnd"));
CodeParameterDeclarationExpression cp =
        new CodeParameterDeclarationExpression(typeof(object[ ]),
                                                "ContextParams");
cp.Direction=FieldDirection.Ref;
cm.Parameters.Add (cp);
cp = new CodeParameterDeclarationExpression(typeof(object[ ]),
                                                "CustomParams");
cp.Direction = FieldDirection.Ref;
cm.Parameters.Add(cp);
cp = new CodeParameterDeclarationExpression(
                                typeof(EnvDTE.wizardResult),
                                "retval");
cp.Direction = FieldDirection.Ref;
cm.Parameters.Add(cp);

// Add the method to the type.
co.Members.Add (cm);

// Create the text file.
using (TextWriter w = new StreamWriter(fullFileName, false));
{
    //Generate the code.
    cg.GenerateCodeFromNamespace( cnamespace2,w,null);
```

Example 9-15. Code generation with CodeDom (continued)

```
            cg.GenerateCodeFromNamespace (cnamespace, w, null);
        }
        return fullFileName;
    }
}
```

Recall that our `IDTWizard` implementation in Example 9-14 called one of two functions depending on the project language. With the code generation class in Example 9-15 in place, all these two functions need to do is create an instance of the appropriate `CodeDomProvider`:

```
private void DoCSharp( )
{
    CSharpCodeProvider cdp = new CSharpCodeProvider( );
    InternalExecute(cdp, ".cs");
}
private void DoVB( )
{
    VBCodeProvider cdp = new VBCodeProvider( );
    InternalExecute(cdp, ".vb");
}
```

The rest of the wizard code is shown in Example 9-16. It is dedicated to displaying the UI, executing the CodeDom class, adding the file to the project, and adding a reference to *envdte.dll* to the project. (This UI is a simple Windows Forms dialog that asks the user for a class name and a namespace. It contains no code of direct relevance to writing wizards, so it is not shown here.)

Example 9-16. Finishing off the wizard

```
private void GetInputs( )
{
    // Display the form to retrieve user settings.
    wf = new WizardForm( );
    wf.ShowDialog( );
    wf.Dispose( );
}

private void InternalExecute(CodeDomProvider codeDom, string ext)
{
    GetInputs( );
    // Get a temp directory.
    TempFileCollection tfc = new TempFileCollection( );
    string cn = wf.classNameTextBox.Text;
    string ns = wf.namespaceTextBox.Text;
    string filepath = tfc.BasePath + wf.classNameTextBox.Text;
    string progid = wf.progIdTextBox.Text;

    // Execute the code generation method.
    string filefull = CodeGen.Generate(filepath, ext, cn, ns, progid,
                                        codeDom);
```

Example 9-16. Finishing off the wizard (continued)

```
    // Add generated file to project.
    AddFiletoProject(filefull,cn+ext);
}

private void AddFiletoProject(string filename,string realname)
{
    // Add a reference to envdte.dll.
    VSProject vsp = (VSProject)project.Object;
    vsp.References.Add("envdte");

    // Add the file to the project.
    project.ProjectItems.AddFromTemplate(filename,realname);
}
```

One last step is required to make this wizard work: we need to add an entry to the appropriate *.vsdir* file(s) and add the corresponding *.vsz* file to the appropriate directory.

Since this is an item wizard, the *.vsz* file will go the item directories for both VB and C#—*VC#\CSharpProjectItems* and *Vb7\VBProjectItems*, respectively. It may seem a bit wasteful to have two copies, and although we could try and use long relative paths in the *.vsdir* files, the *.vsz* is so simple that it's not really worth the effort. The *.vsz* just needs to have the correct ProgID for the class:

```
VSWIZARD 7.0
Wizard=CustomWizardWizard.Wizard
```

 Because this example does not use the wizard engine, the wizard files do not need to be installed in the *VC#\VC#Wizards* or *VB7\VBWizards* directories. However, the wizard will need to be installed somewhere on the system and registered with COM. (COM registration working as it does, however, it won't matter where you choose to install it.)

Conclusion

Visual Studio .NET has an extensible wizard architecture. You can plug into this at two levels—you can implement the IDTWizard interface directly, or you can use the wizard engine—VsWizard.VsWizardEngine–which implements this for you. If you use the engine, then you need to supply only template files and a script file. The templates are used as the basis for any new files that get created, and there is a directive mechanism that allows them to be modified at creation time. You can also supply an HTML-based user interface to collect settings from the user. All of the project and item types built in to VS.NET are built on this mechanism, making it very easy to create your own modified versions.

CHAPTER 10

Visual Studio Integration Program

In the previous few chapters, we've outlined various ways in which you can extend, customize, and automate the VS.NET environment. Macros provide a powerful way to automate routine tasks. Add-ins give you the power to integrate your code more deeply with the environment and to redistribute your customization. You can even write your own wizards and templates when the built-in project types don't quite provide the starting point you require. But there is one more way you can integrate your code into VS.NET, and it involves becoming a Visual Studio Integration Partner (VSIP). Once you become a VSIP licensee, you will have access to the documentation and samples required to build your own VS.NET packages. Packages are the most powerful way of extending VS.NET—with a package, you can go beyond adding new templates for the built in project types and add new types of your own, perhaps to provide support for different languages. This chapter will give you an overview of what is possible once you have joined the VSIP program. Since to use VSIP you will need the SDK (for the necessary interface definitions, documentation, etc.) and to get the SDK you need to be a VSIP licensee, we can't show you any sample code. Instead, this chapter will refer to the samples provided with the VSIP SDK. If you join the VSIP program, you will then have access to these samples.

Applying for VSIP

For the latest information about how to join the Visual Studio.NET Integration Program, see *http://msdn.microsoft.com/vstudio/vsip/vsi/default.asp*.

 VSIP appears to stand for two different things: a Visual Studio Integration Partner (VSIP) is an individual or organization who is on the Visual Studio Integration Program (also VSIP).

Why VSIP?

Since you can automate tasks, create custom commands, and even add wizards using the techniques shown in previous chapters, why would you ever need to use the VSIP extensibility model? The problem with macros, add-ins, and wizards is that they have their limits—there are many tasks that can be accomplished only by creating a VSIP package. Of course, just as add-ins are more complex to create than macros, the downside of building a package is that packages are much more complex (and therefore more time consuming) to develop than macros or add-ins. Also, while add-ins can be enabled and disabled at will by the end user, the only way to disable a package is to uninstall it, which may further complicate the development process. Table 10-1 shows which extensibility features are available to the various ways of extending VS.NET.

Table 10-1. Features of macros, add-ins, and packages

Feature	Can implement with macro	Can implement with add-in	Can implement with package
Manipulate the IDE object model (i.e., automate a task)	Yes	Yes	Yes
Create Tool windows	No	Yes	Yes
Insert a menu command	No	Yes	Yes
Create custom property pages on the Options dialog	No	Yes	Yes
Appear on the About box	No	Yes	Yes
Appear on the splash screen	No	No	Yes
Add a new project type	No	No	Yes
Be part of a build	No	No	Yes
Create a debugger	No	No	Yes
Create an editor	No	No	Yes
Create a designer	No	No	Yes
Add a new data source in the Server Explorer	No	No	Yes
Add a command-line switch to *devenv.exe*	No	No	Yes
Add IntelliSense or syntax coloring to an editor	No	No	Yes
Write using a managed language	Yes (VB.NET only)	Yes	No

Many of the features that can be implemented only with a package are already built into VS.NET for languages like C#; all of the project types and editors built into VS.NET are built using packages. If you build your own custom package, you will be using the same extensibility framework on which the majority of the functionality in VS.NET is built.

A package is a COM component, registered in a special way, which advertises services through various registry entries. VS.NET loads packages automatically when their services are required. Although all packages implement the same IVsPackage interface, individual packages may expose different sets of services to the environment. A package is effectively a factory object—it acts as a source of objects that implement services for the development environment.

 At this time it isn't feasible to implement a package in a managed language, so if you choose to write a package, you will be writing unmanaged code, unlike add-ins, which you can easily write in managed code. (It is technically possible to use a managed language, but there are some very tricky COM interop issues to deal with, meaning that it is more effort than it is worth. However, this is likely to improve with future versions of VS.NET.)

Table 10-2 shows the packages installed with VS.NET Enterprise Edition, organized by the kind of service that they provide. As you can see, Microsoft has not yet come up with a wholly consistent naming policy for its packages—the CSharp Project Package and the Visual J# Project Package seem to be using different conventions for representing language names, for example.

Table 10-2. Visual Studio .NET Enterprise Edition packages

Package type	Package name
Project	Visual Basic.NET Project System
	Visual C++ Package
	Solution Build Package
	Visual Basic .NET SDE Project System
	ATL Package
	Visual Studio Analyzer Package
	ACT Project Package
	CSharp Project Package
	Enterprise Templates Package
	Visual Studio Project Persistence Package
	Visual C++ Project System
	Visual J# Project Package
Language	Babel Language Package
	Visual Basic Common Compatibility Wrapper Package
	CPP Language Manager
	C# Language Service
Compiler	Microsoft Visual Basic Compiler
Debugging	Visual Studio Debugger
UI	Class Outline Package
	TaskList Package

Table 10-2. Visual Studio .NET Enterprise Edition packages (continued)

Package type	Package name
Editor/Designer	HtmEditorPackage
	Undo Package
	Visual Studio Deployment Editors
	Component Enumerator Package
	Visual Database Tools Package
	Binary Editor Package
	Visual Studio XML DataSet Designer
	VSDesignerPackage
	VsRptDesigner Package
	Text Management Package
	Crystal Reports Tools Package
	DesignerPackage
	Resource Editor Package
	VS7 CSS Editing Package
	CFDesignerPackage
Help	Help Package
Utility	Commands Definition Package
	Visual Studio Team Core Package
	DirListPackage
	Visual Studio Deployment Package
	Visual Basic Deploy Deployment Package
	DBServicesPackage Class
	PltPkg Package
	Device CAB Package
	Visual Studio .NET Converters Package
Shell	MS Environment Menu Package
	MS Help Package
	vsmacros
	Source Code Control Package
	WebBrowser Package
	MS Environment Package
	Complus Library Manager Package

The VS.NET environment is built around the idea of services. Packages provide interesting services to the environment and can also consume services provided by other packages. Packages do most of the heavy lifting by providing services for persistence, editing, building, and debugging—the shell mostly acts as a container for packages, although it also exposes a number of interesting services of its own. The shell and packages work together to provide all the services that we use in VS.NET.

When a package needs a service, either from the shell or from another package, it asks the shell for that service. The shell will attempt to locate the package that provides this service, on behalf of the requesting package. So in a way the shell is just a coordinator, obtaining services from packages and handing them back out again to other packages that request them.

Here are some of the services that the shell is responsible for:

- Drawing and maintaining the main UI windows
- Loading packages when needed (packages are loaded on demand)
- Routing of commands to the appropriate package
- Managing the solution files
- Maintaining a list of all the currently running documents in a running document table (RDT)

To enable packages to use one another's services, the shell acts as an intermediary— if a package needs another package's services, it can ask the shell. The shell therefore also offers these functions:

- Retrieving interface pointers to services or packages
- Registering a package's services with the environment
- Creating, hosting, and modifying windows in the UI

Typical Package Execution Path

Since the VS.NET architecture is built around packages, it is interesting to look at some typical usage scenarios to examine all the packages that come into play when creating, building, debugging, and persisting a project. Here is how packages are used as you work with a project in VS.NET:

Launching VS.NET
When you launch VS.NET, it loads a number of base packages, including the MS Environment Package and the MS Environment Menu Package, which are responsible for creating the basis of the VS.NET UI.

Loading or creating a project
When opening a project, VS.NET loads the package responsible for that particular kind of project. Each project type has a GUID, and these are all listed under VS.NET's Projects registry key. Each project type's key has a string value called Package, which contains the GUID of the package responsible for the project type.

For example, the GUID for the C# project type is {FAE04EC0-301F-11d3-BF4B-00C04F79EFBC}. Looking this up under the Projects key reveals that the package ID is {FAE04EC1-301F-11D3-BF4B-00C04F79EFBC}. VS.NET will then look up this ID in its Packages registry key, where it will find an entry for the CSharp Project Package.

Packages and the Registry

Although VS.NET packages are written as COM components, they are registered slightly differently. Instead of using the normal parts of the registry related to COM, VS.NET uses its own registry keys to hold information about the package coclasses. This is to allow multiple different versions of a VS.NET package to be installed simultaneously. This serves several purposes.

First, it is possible to install versions of your package that are specific to a particular version of VS.NET. Second, VS.NET is able to load the registration information from different parts of the registry, selected by a command-line switch. This means you can install packages that will be loaded only when you want them to be. This is very useful during development—if your package gets into a state in which it prevents VS.NET from loading, it is useful to be able to fire up a copy of VS.NET that won't try to load your package. This facility also allows you to override any of the built-in services with your own versions but still leave the original installation intact.

Figure 10-1 shows a VS.NET registry key with several different paths. The 6.0 key is for a previous version of Visual Studio, but the three keys starting with 7.1 are all for VS.NET 2003. (VS.NET 2002 used 7.0.) The key named 7.1 is the root key—it is the key from which VS.NET will normally load its configuration. The keys named 7.1Exp and 7.1Foo contain configuration settings that will only be loaded when you pass the appropriate command-line switch. To load the Exp settings, you would launch VS.NET thus:

```
devenv.exe /rootsuffix Exp
```

This 7.1Exp key is created when you install the VSIP SDK—it makes a copy of the settings in the main 7.1 key. When you are developing packages, you will normally install them under the 7.1Exp key during development. There is nothing magic about the 7.1Exp key—you can create as many more configuration keys as are useful to you. But as a general rule, you should never install packages that are still in development to your root key—if your package does something wrong, you may have to reinstall VS.NET to fix the problem.

In the rest of this chapter, registry keys are always named relative to the base registry path unless otherwise specified. So the Packages key means this key:

```
HKLM\SOFTWARE\Microsoft\VisualStudio\7.1\Packages
```

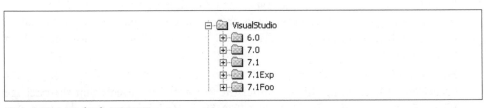

Figure 10-1. Multiple VS.NET registry sections

Putting the project under source control

When a project is added to source control, the project package asks the shell for the source control service. This service is provided by the Visual Studio Team Core Package.

Editing a file in design view

C# Windows Applications usually define one or more forms. These are C# source files containing a class derived from the Form class. When you double-click on a form in the Solution Explorer, the form will be shown in a *design* view, which displays the form more or less as it will appear at runtime and which allows you to edit the form using drag and drop.

When you open a file from the Solution Explorer, the CSharp Project Package asks the shell for the appropriate editor package. (By default, this will be the CSharp Project Package itself, although the user can choose a different editor by using the Open With dialog, as described in Chapter 2.) The CSharp Project Package then asks the editor package's Editor Factory class to open the design view if one is available. In the case of the CSharp editor, it actually looks at the *.cs* file to see if a designer is available for the class it contains. (There are built-in designers for all form classes.) If a designer class is found, the editor package will create and return the appropriate view. Otherwise, it will return a normal code view.

Editing a file in code view

A file may be opened in code view in several ways. The user can explicitly request this from the Solution Explorer's context menu. Files opened with the Open File dialog (Ctrl-O) are always opened with the code view. Or the user may have pressed F7 while looking at a file's design view. In all cases, the Editor Factory is located in the same way as it was for the design view. But this time, the factory will be asked for a *code* view. The factory will return an interface pointer to another view object, usually the VS.NET default text editor.

When the text editor first opens a file, it looks in the Language Services registry key and tries to find a language service for the relevant file extension. (See the "Language Services" section later in this chapter for detailed information about language services.) If it finds one, it loads that language service's package and sets up a bidirectional communication between the language service and the editor. The language service can then provide syntax highlighting, statement completion, and method tips. (The CSharp Language Service uses a language parser to provide highlighting and uses CLR metadata to provide statement completion and method tips.)

Building and debugging

When you build a project, the project package is responsible for loading and executing the appropriate compiler. If syntax errors are discovered during the build, the language service package can highlight the lines in the editor where the syntax errors occur.

After a successful build, you can debug your program. Loading the correct debugger is also the responsibility of the project package. All .NET projects compile to IL, so the .NET project packages just ask the shell for the IL debugger engine. VC++ projects compile to x86 machine code, so the VC++ project package asks for the standard Windows debugger engine. Both of these debug engine services are provided by the Visual Studio Debugger package.

Saving projects

When you save a project, the project package is responsible for persisting the project's settings. However, the shell provides services to aid that persistence. The shell is responsible for persistence of the solution files.

Creating Custom Packages

It is interesting to see how VS.NET uses packages, but since we can't change those packages, the most interesting thing we can do is create our own. In the Figures sample provided with the VSIP SDK, there are example packages that supply a design editor, a project package, and a language service. Once you obtain the VSIP license, this sample provides a good starting point if you decide to create your own packages.

Views

A *view* is a window that presents a project item such as a source code document to the user and allows him to edit it. (For example, the visual form designer for Windows Forms is a view, as is the code editor.) In VS.NET a document can have any number of views, although most only have two: Design and Code. For each view there is an object that is responsible for drawing the proper representation of the document. This object is known as the *DocView*. The document itself is represented by a *DocData* object, which is responsible for persistence and storing common information about the document.

Design views allow visual editing. In the most common scenario for building such an editor, you'd like to have a custom designer for some particular source file to allow visual editing and dragging and dropping of objects from the Toolbox, much like the built-in ASP.NET and Windows Forms design views. You can write such a visual editor in two ways:

Simple embedded editor

This type implements some VSIP-specific interfaces to coordinate the interaction between the editor and the shell (including UI elements such as menus and toolbars)

In-place activation editor

This type has a DocView object that implements a set of standard OLE interfaces. This type of editor is really just an ActiveX control that can host other

ActiveX controls. If you already have a visual editor that exposes the standard OLE interfaces for controls, this will be the preferable option.

If your project items are text files of some kind, you will want to supply a *code* view. However, you do not normally need to write this view yourself—the default VS.NET text editor (which is implemented as a package as well) will work fine. There is rarely a good reason to reinvent a text editor when VS.NET supplies one for you, so you can just reuse the existing "code" DocView rather than having to build your own.

 Remember, even if you use the existing code editor, you can still have total control over keyword highlighting and IntelliSense by implementing a language service.

The development environment keeps a table of documents that are currently open called the *running document table* or RDT. When a file is opened, the environment first checks the RDT to see if another editor already has the document open. If the file is not open, the environment asks the project package to open it. As already described, this finds the suitable editor package and uses its Editor Factory to open the correct DocView for the document being opened. By default, a design view will be opened if one is available, but the user can request a different view. The editor package controls the commands for switching between views and adds the commands necessary to support the exposed views. These may appear on the context menu or as tabs at the bottom of the editor pane, as they do in the HTML designer that you can see in Figure 10-2.

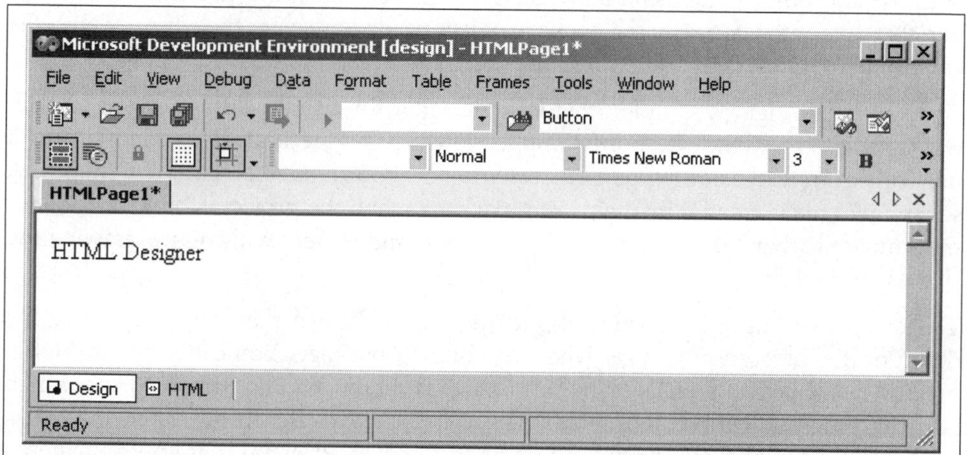

Figure 10-2. HTML designer commands

When the Factory gets a request to open a DocView, it is passed a string that tells it which view type is being requested. The Factory is then responsible for creating the correct DocView object. This could mean returning the current view if the document is already open. The Factory might also return a custom editor object (in the case of a custom designer), or it might ask the environment to return an instance of the default text editor. After the Factory returns an interface pointer to the correct object, its work is complete, and from then on the editor object talks directly to the environment.

Once you have built your package, you will need to add the necessary registry entries. Two entries come into play for an editor. The first is *HKLM\Software\Microsoft\Visual Studio\7.1\Packages\PackageGUID*. All packages require such a registry key, regardless of the services they provide. The *PackageGUID* is the CLSID for the coclass that implements the IVsPackage interface, which is the environment's entry point into the package for obtaining the necessary services. Remember, although packages are essentially COM components, they are not registered in the normal way. This entry takes the place of the normal COM registration, so it must also indicate where the package DLL resides. The *PackageGUID* key, therefore, has a string value called InprocServer32. This serves the same purpose as COM's InprocServer32 key in that it simply contains the path of the DLL (although for VS.NET packages, it's actually a registry value and not a key as it would be in COM).

The other registry entry needed is under *HKLM\Software\Microsoft\Visual Studio\7.1\Editors*. Here you need to add the necessary entries to tell VS.NET what file extensions you want to be an editor for and what views you support (as well as provide a pointer to your package GUID).

Once you have the registry entries taken care of, you can add a file to your project with the appropriate extension and VS.NET will load the editor package. During the initialization of the package, the package object needs to register the editor(s) with the environment. Once this is done, you can design and edit files with your new editor.

The VSIP SDK Figures sample provides a designer for visually designing shapes that will appear on a Windows Forms application. See Figure 10-3. This sample uses a file with a *.fig* extension to persist the type and coordinates of different shapes. A separate *.cs* file is created by the project package when the project is built. This file is the source file that will be compiled by the C# compiler and will end up drawing the shapes on the form.

There are a few things to notice about this project screen that help emphasize the depth of the integration you get when you build a package. You can see that the figure edit package has added a new tab to the Toolbox (FigPkg Sample) from which you can drag and drop the different figure objects onto the form designer. With a package you can also add command items to the context menu that appears when a user right-clicks on the form view. You can also see that the property window has specialized information about the *.fig* file.

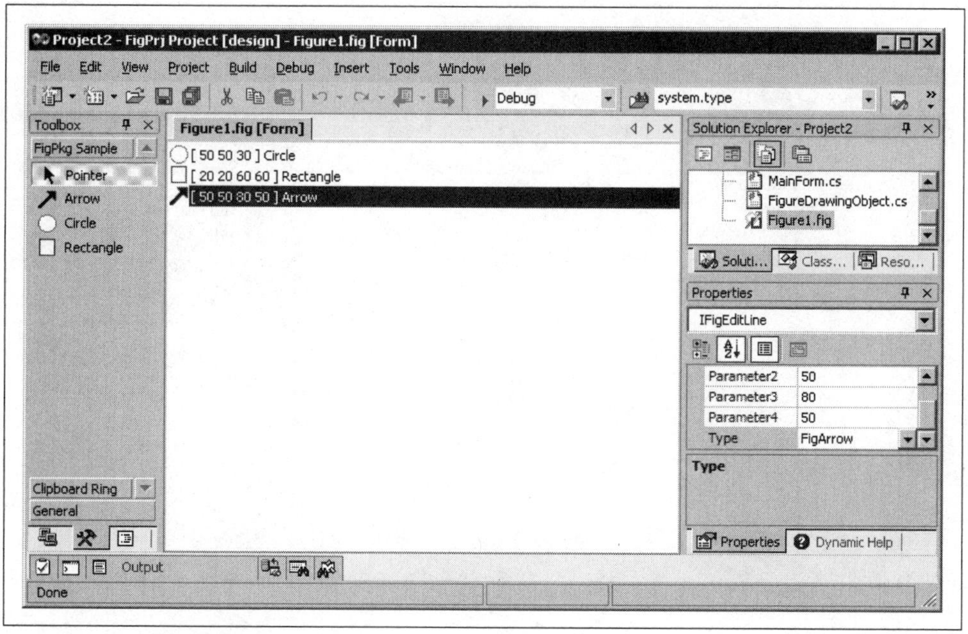

Figure 10-3. The Figures project screen

Language Services

If you switch to the code view of the *.fig* file, you will see that there is both syntax coloring and IntelliSense (see Figure 10-4).

As with most designer editors, the figure editor package relies on the VS.NET default text editor for the code DocView. In order to enhance this editor to provide all the cool stuff we expect when editing code files in VS.NET (e.g., syntax coloring, IntelliSense, statement completion, method tips, error markers) with a new language, you must provide a language service package.

Under the *HKLM\SOFTWARE\Microsoft\VisualStudio\7.1\Languages\File Extensions* key is a list of file extensions, each with a package GUID listed as the default value. This is the GUID of the language service for that particular file extension. This is not the package GUID—language services have their own GUID, which is typically not the same as the corresponding package GUID. VS.NET will locate the language service underneath the *HKLM\SOFTWARE\Microsoft\VisualStudio\7.1\Languages\ Language Services* key by looking for a key whose default value has the appropriate GUID. (The keys underneath the Language Services key all have textual names like Basic or CSharp, but each of these keys has a default value that is the language service's GUID.) The language service key has a value called Package, which is the GUID of the package that provides the language service.

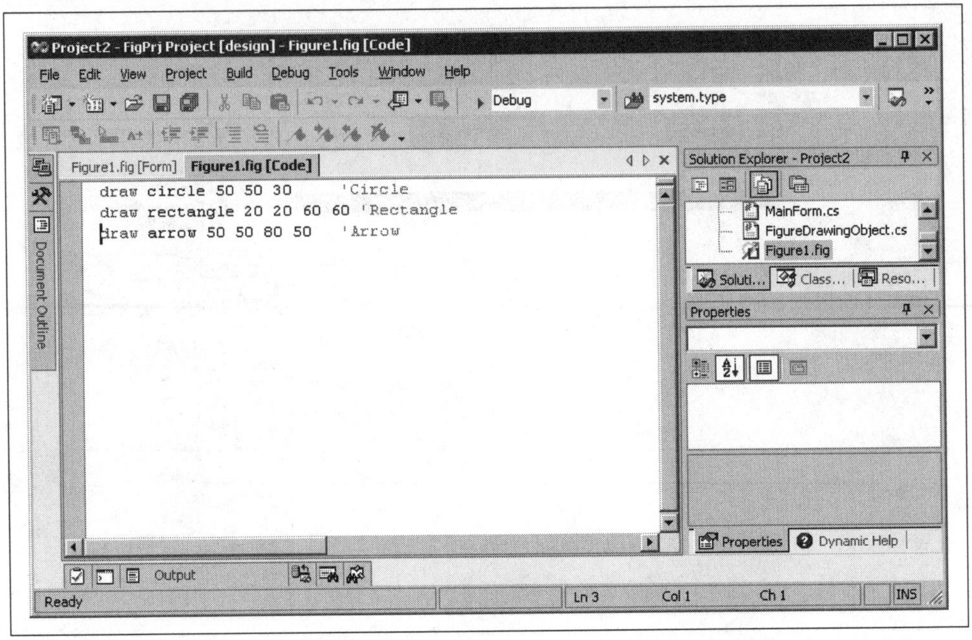

Figure 10-4. Code view enhancements

The language service works with the text editor and coordinates with it to provide enhancements such as syntax coloring and IntelliSense. As you type in the text editor, the editor and the language service have a constant bidirectional communication going on. So as you type in the editor, the editor passes the text you are typing to the service, and if the word you are typing needs to be colorized, the service will tell the editor. If you press Ctrl-spacebar to invoke statement completion, the editor calls the language service, which gives the editor a list of items appropriate for the current context.

Each different type of enhancement is implemented by providing an object that implements certain interfaces. When the document is being edited, the environment calls the appropriate interface for each enhancement, the interface pointers having been passed to the environment by the language service during initialization. (To obtain a list of these interfaces, you will need to become a VSIP licensee.)

For example, as text is typed into the *.fig* file, the text will be passed to an object that is responsible for colorization. As each token is passed into that object, it returns a flag attached to each token that should be colorized. (So the colorization object is really a lexical parser that tells the editor which words are language keywords.)

New Project Type

Editing the file with all the "extras" is nice, but in the end the file is useless if it cannot be compiled as part of the build process. The *.fig* file has to be converted

---

into a .cs file, so that when the project is compiled the correct shapes are drawn on the form. In order to be involved when the project is compiled, you need to create a project package (although in this case the .fig file could just have a custom tool associated with it—see Chapter 2). A project package is an object that implements a certain set of interfaces that allows it to interact with the IDE to coordinate project creation, persistence, and compilation. Unlike adding a New Project Wizard (which only allows you to create a custom set of project items for an existing project type), creating a new project type with a VSIP package give you total control over the whole project lifecycle.

You may need to create a project type package in order to:

- Be involved in building, debugging, file persistence, or source control
- Have control over items in the solution explorer
- Support project nesting (i.e., nesting one project below another)

If you need custom project items but don't need this type of control, you are much better off creating a new Project Wizard (see Chapter 9). In the case of the Figures project, the most interesting thing it does differently than any of the other project types is to take the .fig file and use an internal parser to generate a separate .cs file from the .fig file syntax. It adds this file to the project and compiles it when the project runs the C# compiler.

The project package architecture works much the same as other packages. The environment creates the package object, and passes in its interface pointer for the package to obtain services. The package object then registers its project factory interface with the environment. When a project that belongs to this package is opened (or created), the environment asks the factory to create (or hand back) an object that represents the project itself.

If the configuration of the project changes, the project object is called and is responsible for persisting that information. If a build command is issued, the project object must do whatever is appropriate to build the solution. When a new file is added, the project object is responsible for persisting that file and putting it in the appropriate place. When the project is added to source control, the project object is responsible for checking items in and out through the source control services exposed by the environment.

When a debug command is issued, the project object must work with a debugging package to start and manage the debugging process. If your compilation process generates machine code (generally x86) and you also output a .pdb file, there is a DE (debugging engine) for Windows code (that has an expression evaluator for C++), so you don't need to create any additional packages. Likewise, if your project builds a .NET component (i.e., it produces IL), you can use the IL debugger. If your project package implements a new language that doesn't compile into IL or x86 assembly, you need to create a new debugging engine package. In the case of the Figures project, since it is using C#, the project object can just use the existing DE built into

VS.NET for IL. However, it is useful to augment this by building an expression evaluator (EE) to work with the DE.

Debugging Engines and Expression Evaluators

If you implement a new language that does not emit either windows native code or the corresponding debug format files (.*pdb*), you will need to write a debugging engine (DE). The VSIP SDK includes information and a sample to show you how to build a DE.

A DE is a component that implements the services necessary to debug a particular architecture. (There are debugging engines for Windows code, IL, TSQL, and script built into VS.NET, so you need to provide a DE only if you are targeting some other architecture.) A DE works with an IDE (or the operating system) to provide execution control services (e.g., breakpoints and statement stepping).

Whether you write a DE or not, you may also wish to provide an expression evaluator (EE). An EE is a VS.NET package that coordinates with the IDE to evaluate language expressions at runtime. This can happen in both the immediate and watch windows while a program is being debugged.

When the VS.NET debugger loads and execution stops on a breakpoint, the DE in question creates an instance of the EE engine for the language in use and gives the EE a list of variables that need to be displayed in the locals window. The EE is responsible for parsing those variable (symbol) names and giving back to VS.NET the memory location of their values.

A similar process happens when a symbol is requested from the watch window. When a statement is typed into the immediate window, however, the EE must both parse the symbols and possibly return a result. (For example, the immediate window allows the evaluation of a valid language expression such as "4+5,") The VSIP SDK comes with a sample called MyCEE. This EE will evaluate locals and expressions in the watch window for the MyC language (which is a language whose compiler is also supplied as an example in the SDK of how to implement a language that compiles to IL).

Conclusion

The vast majority of functionality in VS.NET is implemented through packages. The Visual Studio Integration Program enables you to write your own packages, which means that your project types, editors, and designers effectively become peers of the built-in project types. VS.NET extensions built as packages are first-class citizens within the IDE. The main role of the IDE itself is to be a shell that hosts packages and enables them to exchange services. For more information on how to obtain the VSIP SDK, see *http://msdn.microsoft.com/vstudio/vsip/vsi/default.asp*.

Project Templates

This appendix lists all of the different project templates that are provided with Visual Studio .NET. As well as listing the names of the templates, a short description of the purpose of each template is provided. (See Chapter 9 for more information on how to add your own templates.)

Visual Basic, C#, and J# Projects

The following Visual Basic, Visual C#, and Visual J# projects are available in Visual Studio .NET:

Windows Application
> This template creates a .NET-based Windows application with a Windows Forms GUI.

Class Library
> This template creates a .NET class library (DLL).

Windows Control Library
> This template creates a .NET class library. There are only two differences between this and the Class Library template. First, newly created projects of this type have a reference to the Windows Forms components. Second, this template creates a project containing a Windows Forms user control by default.

ASP.NET Web Application
> This template creates an ASP.NET web application. VS.NET can create a new IIS web application on the web server, or it can just add the project files to an existing one. Since this template is designed for building web-based user interfaces, it includes a Web Form (*WebForm1.aspx*).

ASP.NET Web Service
> This template creates an ASP.NET web application. This is very similar to the ASP.NET Web Application template, the main difference being that instead of providing a Web Form as a starting point, it provides a skeleton web service (*Service1.asmx*).

ASP.NET Mobile Web Application

This template creates an ASP.NET web application. This is very similar to the ASP. NET Web Application template, except that it is intended for building web sites designed to be accessed from mobile devices such as phones and PDAs. It therefore provides a single Mobile Web Form (*MobileWebForm1.aspx*) by default.

Web Control Library

This template creates a .NET class library. It is very similar to the Class Library template, but it is intended for building libraries that contain controls that can be used in an ASP.NET application. It therefore has references to the ASP.NET components and provides a web user control.

Console Application

This template builds a .NET-based command-line application.

Windows Service

This template creates a .NET-based Windows Service. It creates a class that inherits from System.ServiceProcess.ServiceBase.

Empty Project

This template creates a project file with no source files. By selecting Output Type from the project property page, you can build a Windows Application, a Console Application, or a Class Library project. (All of the non-Web Application project templates are essentially fancy versions of this simple template.) The default output type is Console Application.

Empty Web Project

This template creates a project file for building a web application, but like the Empty Project, it does not add any files to the project. (All of the ASP.NET application templates are all effectively extended versions of this base template.)

New Project in existing folder

You can use this template instead of the Empty Project or Empty Web Project if you already have a folder that contains some or all of the source files you want to have in your project. If the folder is on the filesystem, the output type can be a Windows Application, a Console Application, or a Class Library project, the default being Windows Application. However, if you choose a web folder, the project will always build a Class Library, as ASP.NET applications can execute only DLLs.

Visual C++ Projects

There are five categories of Visual C++ projects: .NET, ATL, MFC, Win32, and General. The following sections describe each of these.

In VS.NET 2002, these projects were not divided into categories—all C++ projects were presented as a single category. Also, the .NET project types had slightly different names. In VS.NET 2003, these were changed to be more consistent with the project names used in VB, C#, and J# (although not entirely consistent, for some reason). The old names are given in parentheses after the new names.

Visual C++ .NET Projects

The following Visual C++ .NET projects (or managed C++ projects, as they are sometimes known) are available in Visual Studio .NET:

Windows Forms Application (.NET) (not available in VS.NET 2002)
    This template creates a .NET-based Windows application with a Windows Forms GUI.

Class Library (.NET) (was Managed C++ Class Library)
    This template creates a .NET class library (DLL).

Windows Control Library (.NET) (not available in VS.NET 2002)
    This template creates a .NET class library intended to contain Windows Forms controls.

ASP.NET Web Service (was Managed C++ Web Service)
    This template creates an ASP.NET web application that provides a web service.

Console Application (.NET) (was Managed C++ Application)
    This template builds a .NET-based command-line application.

Windows Service (.NET) (not available in VS.NET 2002)
    This template creates a .NET-based Windows Service. It creates a class that inherits from System.ServiceProcess.ServiceBase.

Empty Project (.NET) (was Managed C++ Empty Project)
    This template creates a Managed C++ project that initially contains no files.

Visual C++ ATL Projects

The following Visual C++ ATL projects are available in Visual Studio .NET:

ATL Project
    This template creates an ATL-based DLL, executable, or Windows Service that implements one or more COM classes. By default, this project template uses the new attributed version of ATL.

ATL Server Project
    This template creates an ATL Server ISAPI extension DLL that can be used to create a high-performance web-based UI.

ATL Server Web Service
> This template creates an ATL Server ISAPI extension DLL that can be used to create a high-performance web service.

Visual C++ MFC Projects

The following Visual C++ MFC projects are available in Visual Studio .NET:

MFC ActiveX Control
> This template creates an MFC-based ActiveX control. Its output will be an *.ocx* file.

MFC Application
> This template creates an MFC Windows Application.

MFC DLL
> This template creates a DLL that uses MFC.

MFC ISAPI Extension DLL
> This template creates an MFC ISAPI extension.

Visual C++ Win32 Projects

The following Visual C++ Win32 projects are available in Visual Studio .NET:

Win32 Console Project
> This template builds a command-line application. It creates a standard Win32 EXE file. This is essentially a specialized version of the Win32 Project template.

Win32 Project
> This template builds a Windows Application, a Console Application, a DLL, or a static library. By default, these projects have no access to technologies such as the MFC or the ATL. Only the standard C++ libraries and the raw Win32 API are available. (The wizard provides options to enable MFC support in console or static library applications. You can also enable the ATL in console applications. This will allow you to use the classes these libraries define, but this wizard will not generate all of the framework code you would get with the library-specific templates.)

Visual C++ General Projects

The following Visual C++ general projects are available in Visual Studio .NET:

Custom Wizard
> This template creates an MFC-based DLL project that can be integrated into VS.NET to create a custom wizard. (See Chapter 9 for information about other ways to create custom wizards for VS.NET.)

Extended Stored Procedure

This template creates a DLL that can be used in SQL Server as an extended stored procedure.

Makefile Project

This creates a project that will run *nmake* to build your application rather than using the normal VS.NET build mechanism. This can be useful if your existing project infrastructure relies heavily on traditional makefiles, and you do not want to introduce *devenv.exe* into your automated build process.

Setup and Deployment

The following Setup and Deployment projects are available in Visual Studio .NET:

Setup Project

This template creates a Microsoft Installer (*.msi*) file designed to install a normal Windows application and any associated components. This project type can install any of the non-web project types, whether you are using .NET, ATL, MFC, or just raw Win32.

Web Setup Project

This template creates a Microsoft Installer (*.msi*) file designed to install a web application. (This can be used to install any kind of application, not just web applications. For example, if you wanted to make a Windows Forms Application available for download from a web server, you could use this project type to build an installer that would put the application executable on a web server.)

Merge Module Project

This template creates a merge module (*.msm*) file. Merge modules can be integrated into MSI projects and are ideal for reusable components that might want to be installed as part of a larger application. (COM components and .NET class libraries are usually packaged as merge modules. Applications that use these components merge the MSM into their own MSI.)

Setup Wizard

This item runs a wizard, which will create a project using one of the other templates in this category. The template selected depends on the input you supply to the wizard.

Cab Project

This template creates a Cabinet (*.cab*) file.

Other Projects

Visual Studio .NET also supports a variety of other project types.

Database Projects

There is one kind of database project supported by Visual Studio .NET:

Database Project
> This project template is unusual in that projects of this type are never built and do not produce any output. Database projects just contain SQL scripts. (You can execute these scripts on a database if you choose to but would not usually do so as part of the normal build process of a solution.) These projects can contain creation scripts, which allow you to build new databases with a particular schema. They can also contain change scripts, which track changes you have made to a database, and let you apply these changes to another database. Note that you are not required to create a Database project just to use the visual Database tools (the interactive tools that let you add and edit tables and stored procedures). These tools can be used in any context. However, if you have a database project open while you use these tools, they are able to keep track of the changes you make. See Chapter 5 for more information on the visual database tools and database projects.

Enterprise Template Projects

Enterprise Template Projects are a special kind of project in VS.NET that are available only in the Enterprise editions. Software architects can use these to create a blueprint of the way in which a particular type of application should be built within their organization. Based upon these templates, programmers can create applications or components that will automatically conform to the prescribed architecture. (Most of the templates described next are prebuilt architectures that ship with VS. NET, but you can use the Enterprise Template Project to add your own.) See the VS. NET documentation for more information about how to use and make these types of projects.

Visual Basic Simple Distributed Application
> This creates a solution with seven different projects (each intended to be a different layer in a single distributed application):
> * Business Services
> * Business Façade
> * Business Rules
> * Data Access
> * System Frameworks
> * Web Service Projects
> * WebUI and WinUI

Visual C# Simple Distributed Application

This template creates the same set of projects as the Visual Basic Simple Distributed Application, but using C#.

Visual Basic Distributed Application

This template creates the same number of projects as the Visual Basic Simple Distributed Application (seven), but with each of those projects holding onto subprojects of each type (i.e., allowing multiple Data Access or Web Service projects in one distributed application).

Visual C# Distributed Application

This template creates the same set of projects as the Visual Basic Distributed Application, but using C#.

Distributed Application

This template creates the same set of projects as the Visual Basic or C# Distributed Application but allows each individual project to use either VB or C#.

Enterprise Template Project

This template creates a project that allows you to specify how you would like a distributed application built and generates a new project template that can be used in VS.NET.

Visual Basic/Visual C# Building Blocks

A building block project is a type of project that you can add to an Enterprise Template Project. The following types are included with VS.NET, but others can, of course, be added and customized to your own specification.

Business Façade

This type of project is used to create a shim layer to isolate the UI layer from the Business Rules layer in an application.

Business Rules

This project type is intended to hold the classes that implement the main business rules.

Data Access

This project type holds the classes that access the database for the Business Rules layer.

System

This project type holds the classes that perform system-level services (e.g., caching of HTML pages). Such projects may or may not be application-specific.

ASP.NET Web Service

This creates a web service project that is intended to be the shim layer between the web service-based client and the business layer (similar to the Business Façade layer, but accessible remotely).

WebUI

This creates a web application using ASP.NET that is used to expose the application (using the Business Façade layer) to HTML-based clients.

WinUI

This creates a Windows application that is used to create a UI for the application. (This would typically access the application logic via the ASP.NET Web Service layer.)

Visual Studio Analyzer Projects

Visual Studio Analyzer is a tool used for simple performance monitoring of the applications you create using VS.NET.

Analyzer Wizard

This steps you through a wizard to create a project that you can use to monitor your application.

Analyzer Project

This template creates an empty Analyzer Project to which you can add different parts of your application in order to monitor their performance using Visual Studio Analyzer.

Extensibility Projects

The following extensibility projects are available under Visual Studio .NET:

Visual Studio .NET Add-in

This template creates a VS.NET add-in. You can use C++ (unmanaged), C#, or Visual Basic. (This template does not support J#.) See Chapter 8 for more information about writing add-ins.

Shared Add-in

This template creates an add-in that can be loaded into multiple hosts (e.g., VS. NET, Office, etc.).

Application Center Test Projects

The following Application Center Test project is available under Visual Studio .NET:

ACT Project

This template creates a project for testing a web application with Application Center Test.

Visual Studio Solutions

This category contains one template, the Blank Solution template.

Blank Solution (unmanaged)

> This creates a new solution file with no projects in a new or existing directory. This type of solution allows the most control over setting up the file layout and naming of your solution/project hierarchy. It is also useful if you want to build a new solution that consists entirely of existing projects. See Chapter 1 for more information about solution and project structures.

Project Item Templates

Each project type has a number of associated item templates. (See Appendix A for a listing of project templates.) This appendix lists all of the item templates included in VS.NET. (See Chapter 9 for more information on how to add your own templates.)

VB.NET, C#, and J# Templates

Windows Form
> A source file that defines a class derived from System.Windows.Forms.Form.

Class
> A source file containing an empty class declaration.

Code File
> An empty source file.

Assembly Information File
> A source file containing general assembly information. This is where all assembly level attributes are placed.

Application Configuration File
> A .NET application configuration file. This file is named *app.config*, but at build time, VS.NET copies the file into the startup directory with the name *<exename>.exe.config*. (This is the name that the .NET Framework expects configuration files to have.)

Installer Class
> A source file containing a class to be invoked at setup time. This would be used in a project that implements a custom action for a Setup and Deployment project.

Component Class
> A source file containing a class that derives from System.ComponentModel. Component. (This enables integration with the VS.NET design-time environment. See Chapter 7 for more details.)

User Control

A source file containing a class derived from `System.Windows.Forms.UserControl`. User controls can be edited using the visual designer.

Data Form Wizard

A source file containing a Windows Forms form and also an associated type-safe `DataSet` to allow data binding to controls on the form.

DataSet

An XML schema and a generated strongly typed `DataSet` class.

Custom Control

A source file containing a class that derives directly from `System.Windows.Forms.Control`.

Inherited Form

A source file containing a Windows Forms form that derives from another form.

Web Custom Control

A source file containing a class that derives from `System.Web.UI.WebControl`.

Inherited User Control

A source file containing a Windows Forms control that derives from another control.

Windows Service

A source file containing a class for creating a Windows service.

Web Form

An *.aspx* file (an ASP.NET Web Form) and an associated codebehind file.

Web Service

An *.asmx* file and an associated codebehind file.

Dynamic Discovery File

A file used to publish information about a web service.

Static Discovery File

A file used to publish information about a web service.

Global Application Class

A class for handling web application events.

Web Configuration File

A *web.config* file used to configure ASP.NET web application settings.

VB.NET Templates

Module

A file for storing groups of functions.

COM Class

A class that can be exposed to COM.

Transactional Component
> A source file containing a class prepared for use with COM+. The class derives from `System.EnterpriseServices.ServicedComponent`.

C++ Templates

Generic C++ Class
> A generic C++ class. (This is not in the Add New Item dialog—it is in the Add Class dialog. The Add Class dialog can be opened by right-clicking on the project in the Solution Explorer and selecting Add → Add Class.)

C++ File (.cpp)
> A C++ source file.

Header File (.h)
> A C++ header file.

Midl File (.idl)
> A COM Interface Definition Language file.

Module-Definition File (.def)
> A file listing DLL entry points.

Windows Forms (.NET)
> A source file containing a class derived from `System.Windows.Forms.Form`.

Component Class (.NET)
> A source file containing a class that derives from `System.ComponentModel.Component`. (This enables integration with the VS.NET design-time environment. See Chapter 7 for more details.)

User Control (.NET)
> A source file containing a class that derives from `System.Windows.Forms.UserControl`. User controls can be edited using the visual designer.

DataSet
> An XML schema and a generated strongly typed `DataSet` class.

Configuration File (app.config)
> A .NET application configuration file. This file is named *app.config*, but at build time, VS.NET copies the file into the startup directory with the name *<exename>.exe.config*. (This is the name that the .NET Framework expects configuration files to have.)

Installer Class (.NET)
> A source file containing a class to be invoked at setup time. This would be used in a project that implements a custom action for a Setup and Deployment project.

ASP.NET Web Service
> An *.asmx* file and associated codebehind file.

ATL Templates

Add ATL Support To MFC
> Adds ATL support to an MFC project.

ATL Active Server Page Component
> An ATL Active Server Page component (also known as an ActiveX Server component).

ATL Control
> An ATL ActiveX control.

ATL Dialog
> An ATL dialog class.

ATL COM+ 1.0 Component
> An ATL COM+ 1.0 component.

ATL OLEDB Consumer
> An ATL OLEDB consumer class.

ATL OLEDB Provider
> An ATL OLEDB provider.

ATL Property Page
> An ATL property page object.

ATL Simple Object
> An ATL simple object.

ATL Performance Monitor Object
> A performance monitor object.

SRF File (.srf)
> A template file for creating an ATL Server dynamic web application.

WMI Instance Provider
> A WMI Instance Provider.

WMI Event Provider
> A WMI Event Provider.

MFC Templates

MFC Class
> An MFC class.

MFC ODBC Consumer
> An MFC ODBC consumer class.

MFC Class From TypeLib
> An MFC class based on a type library.

MFC Class From ActiveX Control
> An MFC class based on an ActiveX Control.

Text-Based Templates

Text File
> A blank text file.

VBScript File
> A script file containing VBScript code.

Windows Script Host
> A file containing script that is run as a Windows program.

JScript File
> A script file containing JScript code.

Database

Stored Procedure Script
> A script file defining a stored procedure.

View Script
> A script file defining a view.

Table Script
> A script file defining a table.

SQL Script
> A script file containing arbitrary SQL.

Trigger Script
> A script file defining a trigger.

Database Query
> A script file containing a query (will be edited in the query designer by default, rather than as raw SQL).

HTML (Web)

HTML Page
> An HTML page that can include client-side code.

Frameset
> An HTML file that hosts multiple HTML pages.

Style Sheet
> A cascading stylesheet containing HTML style definitions.

Active Server Page
> A web page that uses server-side script code.

JScript .NET Web Form
> A .NET web form containing JScript code.

XML

XML File
> A blank XML file.

XML Schema
> A file for creating an XML schema definition.

XSLT File
> A new XSL Transformations file.

Binary and Resource Templates

Bitmap File
> A blank Win32 bitmap file.

Icon File
> A blank icon file.

Cursor File
> A blank cursor file.

Resource Template
> A resource script file.

Assembly Resource File (.resx)
> A .NET resource file.

Resource File (.rc)
> A Win32 resource file.

Registration Script (.rgs)
> An ATL registration script file.

Resource Template File (.rct)
> A Resource template file.

Crystal Report (.rpt)
> A Crystal Report file that publishes data to a Windows or Web Form.

Shortcut Key Guide

This appendix describes keyboard shortcuts in the following categories:

- General
- Project related
- Window manipulation
- Text navigation
- Text manipulation
- Text selection
- Control editor (designer)
- Search and replace

- Help
- Debugging
- Object browser
- Tool window
- HTML designer
- Macro
- Dialog editor
- Accelerator and string editor

Table C-1. General

Command	Shortcut	Description
Edit.Copy	CTRL-C CTRL-INSERT	Copies the currently selected item to the system clipboard.
Edit.Cut	CTRL-X SHIFT-DELETE	Deletes the currently selected item and moves it to the system clipboard.
Edit.CycleClipboardRing	CTRL-SHIFT- INS CTRL-SHIFT-V	Pastes an item from the Clipboard Ring tab of the Toolbox at the cursor in the file and automatically selects the pasted item. You can cycle through the items on the clipboard by pressing the shortcut keys repeatedly.
Edit.GoToNextLocation	F8	Moves the cursor to the next item, such as a task in the TaskList window or a search match in the Find Results window.
Edit.GoToPreviousLocation	SHIFT-F8	Moves the cursor to the previous item in the TaskList window or Find Results window.
Edit.GoToReference	SHIFT-F12	Finds a reference to the selected item or the item under the cursor.

Table C-1. General (continued)

Command	Shortcut	Description
Edit.OpenFile	CTRL-SHIFT-G	Opens the file whose name is under the cursor or is currently selected (e.g., if you use this shortcut in a C++ file when the cursor is on a line with a #include statement, it will open the file being included).
Edit.Paste	CTRL-V SHIFT-INSERT	Inserts the item in the clipboard at the cursor.
Edit.Redo	CTRL-SHIFT-Z CTRL-Y SHIFT-ALT-BACK-SPACE	Redoes the previously undone action.
Edit.SelectionCancel	ESC	Closes a menu or dialog, cancels an operation in progress, or places focus in the current document window.
Edit.Undo	ALT-BACKSPACE CTRL-Z	Reverses the last editing action.
File.Print	CTRL-P	Displays the Print dialog.
File.SaveAll	CTRL-SHIFT-S	Saves all documents and projects.
File.SaveSelectedItems	CTRL-S	Saves the selected items in the current project (usually whichever source file is currently visible).
Tools.GoToCommandLine	CTRL-/	Switches focus to the Find/Command box on the Standard toolbar.
View.NextTask	CTRL-SHIFT-F12	Moves to the next task in the TaskList window.
View.PopBrowseContext	CTRL-SHIFT-8	Moves backward in the browse history. Available in the object browser or Class View window.
View.ViewCode	F7	Switches from a design view to a code view in the editor.
View.ViewDesigner	SHIFT-F7	Switches from a code view to a design view in the editor.
View.WebNavigateBack	ALT-LEFT ARROW	Goes back in the web browser history.
View.WebNavigateForward	ALT-RIGHT ARROW	Goes forward in the web browser history.

Table C-2. Project-related

Command	Shortcut	Description
Build.BuildSolution	CTRL-SHIFT-B	Builds the solution.
Build.Compile	CTRL-F7	Compiles the selected file. C++ projects only—.NET projects do not support compilation of individual files, only whole projects.
File.AddExistingItem	SHIFT-ALT-A	Displays the Add Existing Item dialog.
File.AddNewItem	CTRL-SHIFT-A	Displays the Add New Item dialog.
File.BuildandBrowse	CTRL-F8	Builds the current project and then displays the start page for the project in the browser. Available only for web projects.

Table C-2. Project-related (continued)

Command	Shortcut	Description
File.NewFile	CTRL-N	Displays the New File dialog. Files created in this way are not associated with any project. Use File.AddNewItem (Ctrl-Shift-A) to create a new file in a project.
File.NewProject	CTRL-SHIFT-N	Displays the New Project dialog.
File.OpenFile	CTRL-O	Displays the Open File dialog.
File.OpenProject	CTRL-SHIFT-O	Displays the Open Project dialog.
Project.Override	CTRL-ALT-INSERT	Allows you to override base class methods in a derived class when an overridable method is highlighted in the Class View pane.

Table C-3. Window manipulation

Command	Shortcut	Description
View.FullScreen	SHIFT-ALT-ENTER	Toggles full screen mode.
View.NavigateBackward	CTRL-+	Goes back to the previous location in the navigation history. (For example, if you press Ctrl-Home to go to the start of a document, this shortcut will take the cursor back to wherever it was before you pressed Ctrl-Home.)
View.NavigateForward	CTRL-SHIFT-+	Moves forward in the navigation history. This is effectively an undo for the View.NavigateBackward operation.
Window.ActivateDocumentWindow	ESC	Closes a menu or dialog, cancels an operation in progress, or places focus in the current document window.
Window.CloseDocumentWindow	CTRL-F4	Closes the current MDI child window.
Window.CloseToolWindow	SHIFT-ESC	Closes the current tool window.
Window.MoveToDropDownBar	CTRL-F2	Moves the cursor to the navigation bar at the top of a code view.
Window.NextDocumentWindow	CTRL-TAB CTRL-F6	Cycles through the MDI child windows one window at a time.
Window.PreviousDocumentWindow	CTRL-SHIFT-TAB CTRL-SHIFT-F6	Moves to the previous MDI child window.
Window.NextPane	ALT-F6	Moves to the next tool window.
Window.PreviousPane	SHIFT-ALT-F6	Moves to the previously selected window.
Window.NextSplitPane	F6	Moves to the next pane of a split pane view of a single document.
Window.PreviousSplitPane	SHIFT-F6	Moves to the previous pane of a document in split pane view.
Window.NextTab	CTRL-PAGEDOWN	Moves to the next tab in the document or window (e.g., you can use this to switch the HTML editor from its design view to its HTML view).
Window.PreviousTab	CTRL-PAGE UP	Moves to the previous tab in the document or window.

Table C-4. Text navigation

Command	Shortcut	Description
`Edit.CharLeft`	LEFT ARROW	Moves the cursor one character to the left.
`Edit.CharRight`	RIGHT ARROW	Moves the cursor one character to the right.
`Edit.DocumentEnd`	CTRL-END	Moves the cursor to the end of the document.
`Edit.DocumentStart`	CTRL-HOME	Moves the cursor to the start of the document.
`Edit.GoTo`	CTRL-G	Displays the Go to Line dialog. If the debugger is running, the dialog also lets you specify addresses or function names to go to.
`Edit.GoToBrace`	CTRL-]	Moves the cursor to the matching brace in the document. If the cursor is on an opening brace, this will move to the corresponding closing brace and vice versa.
`Edit.LineDown`	DOWN ARROW	Moves the cursor down one line.
`Edit.LineEnd`	END	Moves the cursor to the end of the current line.
`Edit.LineStart`	HOME	Moves the cursor to the beginning of the line. If you press Home when the cursor is already at the start of the line, it will toggle the cursor between the first non-whitespace character and the real start of the line.
`Edit.LineUp`	UP ARROW	Moves the cursor up one line.
`Edit.NextBookmark`	CTRL-K, CTRL-N	Moves to the next bookmark in the document.
`Edit.PageDown`	PAGE DOWN	Scrolls down one screen in the editor window.
`Edit.PageUp`	PAGE UP	Scrolls up one screen in the editor window.
`Edit.PreviousBookmark`	CTRL-K, CTRL-P	Moves to the previous bookmark.
`Edit.QuickInfo`	CTRL-K, CTRL-I	Displays Quick Info, based on the current language.
`Edit.ScrollLineDown`	CTRL-DOWN ARROW	Scrolls text down one line but does not move the cursor. This is useful for scrolling more text into view without losing your place. Available only in text editors.
`Edit.ScrollLineUp`	CTRL-UP ARROW	Scrolls text up one line but does not move the cursor. Available only in text editors.
`Edit.WordNext`	CTRL-RIGHT ARROW	Moves the cursor one word to the right.
`Edit.WordPrevious`	CTRL-LEFT ARROW	Moves the cursor one word to the left.
`View.BrowseNext`	CTRL-SHIFT-1	Navigates to the next definition, declaration, or reference of an item. Available in the object browser and Class View window. Also available in source editing windows if you have already used the Edit.GoToReference (Shift-F12) shortcut.
`View.BrowsePrevious`	CTRL-SHIFT-2	Navigates to the previous definition, declaration, or reference of an item.

Table C-5. Text manipulation

Command	Shortcut	Description
`Edit.BreakLine`	ENTER SHIFT-ENTER	Inserts a new line.

Table C-5. Text manipulation (continued)

Command	Shortcut	Description
Edit.CharTranspose	CTRL-T	Swaps the characters on either side of the cursor. (For example, AC|BD becomes AB|CD.) Available only in text editors.
Edit.ClearBookmarks	CTRL-K, CTRL-L	Removes all unnamed bookmarks in the current document.
Edit.CollapseToDefinitions	CTRL-M, CTRL-O	Automatically determines logical boundaries for creating regions in code, such as procedures, and then hides them. This collapses all such regions in the current document.
Edit.CommentSelection	CTRL-K, CTRL-C	Marks the current line or selected lines of code as a comment, using the correct comment syntax for the programming language.
Edit.CompleteWord	ALT-RIGHT ARROW CTRL-SPACEBAR	Displays statement completion based on the current language or autocompletes word if existing text unambiguously identifies a single symbol.
Edit.Delete	DELETE	Deletes one character to the right of the cursor.
Edit.DeleteBackwards	BACKSPACE SHIFT-BACKSPACE	Deletes one character to the left of the cursor.
Edit.Delete HorizontalWhitespace	CTRL-K, CTRL-\	Removes horizontal whitespace in the selection or deletes whitespace adjacent to the cursor if there is no selection.
Edit.FormatDocument	CTRL-K, CTRL-D	Applies the indenting and space formatting for the language as specified on the Formatting pane of the language in the Text Editor section of the Options dialog to the document. This shortcut is available only in VB.NET—in other languages you must first select the whole document with Ctrl-A and then format the selection with Ctrl-K, Ctrl-F.
Edit.FormatSelection	CTRL-K, CTRL-F	Applies the indenting and space formatting for the language as specified on the Formatting pane of the language in the Text Editor section of the Options dialog to the selected text.
Edit.HideSelection	CTRL-M, CTRL-H	Hides the selected text. A signal icon marks the location of the hidden text in the file. VB.NET only.
Edit.InsertTab	TAB	Indents the currently selected line or lines by one tab stop. If there is no selection, this inserts a tab stop.
Edit.LineCut	CTRL-L	Cuts all selected lines or the current line if nothing has been selected to the clipboard.
Edit.LineDelete	CTRL-SHIFT-L	Deletes all selected lines or the current line if no selection has been made.
Edit.LineOpenAbove	CTRL-ENTER	Inserts a blank line above the cursor.
Edit.LineOpenBelow	CTRL-SHIFT-ENTER	Inserts a blank line below the cursor.
Edit.LineTranspose	SHIFT-ALT-T	Moves the line containing the cursor below the next line.

Table C-5. Text manipulation (continued)

Command	Shortcut	Description
Edit.ListMembers	CTRL-J	Lists members for statement completion when editing code.
Edit.MakeLowercase	CTRL-U	Changes the selected text to lowercase characters.
Edit.MakeUppercase	CTRL-SHIFT-U	Changes the selected text to uppercase characters.
Edit.OverTypeMode	INSERT	Toggles between insert and overtype insertion modes.
Edit.ParameterInfo	CTRL-SHIFT-SPACEBAR	Displays a tooltip that contains information for the current parameter, based on the current language.
Edit.StopHidingCurrent	CTRL-M, CTRL-U	Removes the outlining information for the currently selected region.
Edit.StopOutlining	CTRL-M, CTRL-P	Removes all outlining information from the entire document.
Edit.SwapAnchor	CTRL-R, CTRL-P	Swaps the anchor and endpoint of the current selection.
Edit.TabLeft	SHIFT-TAB	Moves current line or selected lines one tab stop to the left.
Edit.ToggleAllOutlining	CTRL-M, CTRL-L	Toggles all previously marked hidden text sections between hidden and display states.
Edit.ToggleBookmark	CTRL-K, CTRL-K	Sets or removes a bookmark at the current line.
Edit.ToggleOutliningExpansion	CTRL-M, CTRL-M	Toggles the currently selected hidden text section or the section containing the cursor if there is no selection between the hidden and display states.
Edit.ToggleTaskListShortcut	CTRL-K, CTRL-H	Sets or removes a shortcut in the tasklist to the current line.
Edit.ToggleWordWrap	CTRL-R, CTRL-R	Enables or disables word wrap in an editor.
Edit.UncommentSelection	CTRL-K, CTRL-U	Removes the comment syntax from the current line or currently selected lines of code.
Edit.ViewWhiteSpace	CTRL-R, CTRL-W	Shows or hides spaces and tab marks.
Edit.WordDeleteToEnd	CTRL-DELETE	Deletes the word to the right of the cursor.
Edit.WordDeleteToStart	CTRL-BACKSPACE	Deletes the word to the left of the cursor.
Edit.WordTranspose	CTRL-SHIFT-T	Transposes the two words that follow the cursor. (For example, |End Sub would be changed to read Sub End|.)

Table C-6. Text selection

Command	Shortcut	Description
Edit.CharLeftExtend	SHIFT-LEFT ARROW	Moves the cursor to the left one character, extending the selection.
Edit.CharLeftExtendColumn	SHIFT-ALT-LEFT ARROW	Moves the cursor to the left one character, extending the column selection.
Edit.CharRightExtend	SHIFT-RIGHT ARROW	Moves the cursor to the right one character, extending the selection.

Table C-6. Text selection (continued)

Command	Shortcut	Description
Edit.CharRightExtendColumn	SHIFT-ALT-RIGHT ARROW	Moves the cursor to the right one character, extending the column selection.
Edit.DocumentEndExtend	CTRL-SHIFT-END	Moves the cursor to the end of the document, extending the selection.
Edit.DocumentStartExtend	CTRL-SHIFT-HOME	Moves the cursor to the start of the document, extending the selection.
Edit.GoToBraceExtend	CTRL-SHIFT-]	Moves the cursor to the next brace, extending the selection.
Edit.LineDownExtend	SHIFT-DOWN ARROW	Moves the cursor down one line, extending the selection.
Edit.LineDownExtendColumn	SHIFT-ALT-DOWN ARROW	Moves the cursor down one line, extending the column selection.
Edit.LineEndExtend	SHIFT-END	Moves the cursor to the end of the current line, extending the selection.
Edit.LineEndExtendColumn	SHIFT-ALT-END	Moves the cursor to the end of the line, extending the column selection.
Edit.LineStartExtend	SHIFT-HOME	Moves the cursor to the start of the line, extending the selection.
Edit.LineStartExtendColumn	SHIFT-ALT-HOME	Moves the cursor to the start of the line, extending the column selection.
Edit.LineUpExtend	SHIFT-UP ARROW	Moves the cursor up one line, extending the selection.
Edit.LineUpExtendColumn	SHIFT-ALT-UP ARROW	Moves the cursor up one line, extending the column selection.
Edit.PageDownExtend	SHIFT-PAGE DOWN	Extends selection down one page.
Edit.PageUpExtend	SHIFT-PAGE UP	Extends selection up one page.
Edit.SelectAll	CTRL-A	Selects everything in the current document.
Edit.SelectCurrentWord	CTRL-W	Selects the word containing the cursor or the word to the right of the cursor.
Edit.SelectToLastGoBack	CTRL-=	Selects from the current location in the editor back to the previous location in the navigation history.
Edit.ViewBottomExtend	CTRL-SHIFT-PAGE DOWN	Moves the cursor to the last line in view, extending the selection.
Edit.ViewTopExtend	CTRL-SHIFT-PAGE UP	Moves the cursor to the top of the current window, extending the selection.
Edit.WordNextExtend	CTRL-SHIFT-RIGHT ARROW	Moves the cursor one word to the right, extending the selection.
Edit.WordNextExtendColumn	CTRL-SHIFT-ALT-RIGHT ARROW	Moves the cursor to the right one word, extending the column selection.

Table C-6. Text selection (continued)

Command	Shortcut	Description
Edit.WordPreviousExtend	CTRL-SHIFT-LEFT ARROW	Moves the cursor one word to the left, extending the selection.
Edit. WordPreviousExtendColumn	CTRL-SHIFT-ALT-LEFT ARROW	Moves the cursor to the left one word, extending the column selection.

Table C-7. Control editor (designer)

Command	Shortcut	Description
Edit.MoveControlDown	CTRL-DOWN ARROW	Moves the selected control down in increments of one on the design surface.
Edit.MoveControlDownGrid	DOWN ARROW	Moves the selected control down to the next grid position on the design surface.
Edit.MoveControlLeft	CTRL-LEFT ARROW	Moves the control to the left in increments of one on the design surface.
Edit.MoveControlLeftGrid	LEFT ARROW	Moves the control to the left to the next grid position on the design surface.
Edit.MoveControlRight	CTRL-RIGHT ARROW	Moves the control to the right in increments of one on the design surface.
Edit.MoveControlRightGrid	RIGHT ARROW	Moves the control to the right into the next grid position on the design surface.
Edit.MoveControlUp	CTRL-UP ARROW	Moves the control up in increments of one on the design surface.
Edit.MoveControlUpGrid	UP ARROW	Moves the control up into the next grid position on the design surface.
Edit.SelectNextControl	TAB	Moves to the next control in the tab order.
Edit.SelectPreviousControl	SHIFT-TAB	Moves to the previous control in the tab order.
Edit.SizeControlDown	CTRL-SHIFT-DOWN ARROW	Increases the height of the control in increments of one on the design surface.
Edit.SizeControlDownGrid	SHIFT-DOWN ARROW	Increases the height of the control to the next grid position on the design surface.
Edit.SizeControlLeft	CTRL-SHIFT-LEFT ARROW	Reduces the width of the control in increments of one on the design surface.
Edit.SizeControlLeftGrid	SHIFT-LEFT ARROW	Reduces the width of the control to the next grid position on the design surface.
Edit.SizeControlRight	CTRL-SHIFT-RIGHT ARROW	Increases the width of the control in increments of one on the design surface.
Edit.SizeControlRightGrid	SHIFT-LEFT ARROW	Increases the width of the control to the next grid position on the design surface.
Edit.SizeControlUp	CTRL-SHIFT-UP ARROW	Decreases the height of the control in increments of one on the design surface.
Edit.SizeControlUpGrid	SHIFT-UP ARROW	Decreases the height of the control to the next grid position on the design surface.

Table C-8. Search and replace

Command	Shortcut	Description
Edit.Find	CTRL-F	Displays the Find dialog.
Edit.FindInFiles	CTRL-SHIFT-F	Displays the Find in Files dialog.
Edit.FindNext	F3	Finds the next occurrence of the previous search text.
Edit.FindNextSelected	CTRL-F3	Finds the next occurrence of the currently selected text or the word under the cursor if there is no selection.
Edit.FindPrevious	SHIFT-F3	Finds the previous occurrence of the search text.
Edit.FindPreviousSelected	CTRL-SHIFT-F3	Finds the previous occurrence of the currently selected text or the word under the cursor.
Edit.GoToFindCombo	CTRL-D	Places the cursor in the Find/Command line on the Standard toolbar.
Edit.HiddenText	ALT-F3, H	Selects or clears the Search Hidden Text option for the Find dialog.
Edit.IncrementalSearch	CTRL-I	Starts an incremental search—after pressing Ctrl-I, you can type in text, and for each letter you type, VS.NET will find the first occurrence of the sequence of letters you have typed so far. This is a very convenient facility, as it lets you find text by typing in exactly as many characters as are required to locate the text and no more.
		If you press Ctrl-I a second time without typing any characters, it recalls the previous pattern. If you press it a third time or you press it when an incremental search has already found a match, VS.NET searches for the next occurrence.
Edit.MatchCase	ALT-F3, C.	Selects or clears the Match Case option for Find and Replace operations.
Edit.RegularExpression	ALT-F3, R	Selects or clears the Regular Expression option so that special characters can be used in Find and Replace operations.
Edit.Replace	CTRL-H	Displays the Replace dialog.
Edit.ReplaceInFiles	CTRL-SHIFT-H	Displays the Replace in Files dialog.
Edit.ReverseIncrementalSearch	CTRL-SHIFT-I	Performs an incremental search in reverse direction.
Edit.StopSearch	ALT-F3, S	Halts the current Find in Files operation.
Edit.Up	ALT-F3, B	Selects or clears the Search Up option for Find and Replace operations.
Edit.WholeWord	ALT-F3, W	Selects or clears the Match Whole Word option for Find and Replace operations.
Edit.Wildcard	ALT-F3, P	Selects or clears the Wildcard option for Find and Replace operations.

Table C-9. Help

Command	Shortcut	Description
Help.Contents	CTRL-ALT-F1	Displays the Contents window for the documentation.

Table C-9. Help (continued)

Command	Shortcut	Description
Help.DynamicHelp	CTRL-F1	Displays the Dynamic Help window, which displays different topics depending on what items currently have focus. If the focus is in a source window, the Dynamic Help window will display help topics that are relevant to the text under the cursor.
Help.F1Help	F1	Displays a topic from Help that corresponds to the part of the user interface that currently has the focus. If the focus is in a source window, Help will try to display a topic relevant to the text under the cursor.
Help.Index	CTRL-ALT-F2	Displays the Help Index window.
Help.Indexresults	SHIFT-ALT-F2	Displays the Index Results window, which lists the topics that contain the keyword selected in the Index window.
Help.NextTopic	ALT-DOWN ARROW	Displays the next topic in the table of contents. Available only in the Help browser window.
Help.PreviousTopic	ALT-UP ARROW	Displays the previous topic in the table of contents. Available only in the Help browser window.
Help.Search	CTRL-ALT-F3	Displays the Search window, which allows you to search for words or phrases in the documentation.
Help.Searchresults	SHIFT-ALT-F3	Displays the Search Results window, which displays a list of topics that contain the string searched for from the Search window.
Help.WindowHelp	SHIFT-F1	Displays a topic from Help that corresponds to the user interface item that has the focus.

Table C-10. Debugging

Command	Shortcut	Description
Debug.ApplyCodeChanges	ALT-F10	Starts an edit and continue build to apply changes to code being debugged. Edit and continue is available only in C++ projects.
Debug.Autos	CTRL-ALT-V, A	Displays the Auto window to view the values of variables currently in the scope of the current line of execution within the current procedure.
Debug.BreakAll	CTRL-ALT-Break	Temporarily stops execution of all processes in a debugging session. Available only in run mode.
Debug.Breakpoints	CTRL-ALT-B	Displays the Breakpoints dialog, where you can add and modify breakpoints.
Debug.CallStack	CTRL-ALT-C	Displays the Call Stack window to display a list of all active procedures or stack frames for the current thread of execution. Available only in break mode.
Debug.ClearAllBreakpoints	CTRL-SHIFT-F9	Clears all of the breakpoints in the project.
Debug.Disassembly	CTRL-ALT-D	Displays the Disassembly window.
Debug.EnableBreakpoint	CTRL-F9	Enables or disables the breakpoint on the current line of code. The line must already have a breakpoint for this to work.

Table C-10. Debugging (continued)

Command	Shortcut	Description
Debug.Exceptions	CTRL-ALT-E	Displays the Exceptions dialog.
Debug.Immediate	CTRL-ALT-I	Displays the Immediate window, where you can evaluate expressions and execute individual commands.
Debug.Locals	CTRL-ALT-V, L	Displays the Locals window to view the variables and their values for the currently selected procedure in the stack frame.
Debug.Memory1	CTRL-ALT-M, 1	Displays the Memory 1 window to view memory in the process being debugged. This is particularly useful when you do not have debugging symbols available for the code you are looking at. It is also helpful for looking at large buffers, strings, and other data that does not display clearly in the Watch or Variables window.
Debug.Memory2	CTRL-ALT-M, 2	Displays the Memory 2 window.
Debug.Memory3	CTRL-ALT-M, 3	Displays the Memory 3 window.
Debug.Memory4	CTRL-ALT-M, 4	Displays the Memory 4 window.
Debug.Modules	CTRL-ALT-U	Displays the Modules window, which allows you to view the *.dll* or *.exe* files loaded by the program. In multiprocess debugging, you can right-click and select Show Modules for all programs.
Debug.NewBreakpoint	CTRL-B	Opens the New Breakpoint dialog.
Debug.QuickWatch	CTRL-ALT-Q	Displays the Quick Watch dialog with the current value of the selected expression. Available only in break mode. Use this command to check the current value of a variable, property, or other expression for which you have not defined a watch expression.
Debug.Registers	CTRL-ALT-G	Displays the Registers window, which displays CPU register contents.
Debug.Restart	CTRL-SHIFT-F5	Terminates the current debugging session, rebuilds if necessary, and then starts a new debugging session. Available in break and run modes.
Debug.RunningDocuments	CTRL-ALT-N	Displays the Running Documents window that displays the set of HTML documents that you are in the process of debugging. Available in break and run modes.
Debug.RunToCursor	CTRL-F10	Starts or resumes execution of your code and then halts execution when it reaches the selected statement. This starts the debugger if it is not already running.
Debug.SetNextStatement	CTRL-SHIFT-F10	Sets the execution point to the line of code you choose.
Debug.ShowNextStatement	ALT-NUM *	Highlights the next statement to be executed.

Table C-10. Debugging (continued)

Command	Shortcut	Description
Debug.Start	F5	If not currently debugging, this runs the startup project or projects and attaches the debugger. If in break mode, this allows execution to continue (i.e., it returns to run mode).
Debug.StartWithoutDebugging	CTRL-F5	Runs the code without invoking the debugger. For console applications, this also arranges for the console window to stay open with a "Press any key to continue" prompt when the program finishes.
Debug.StepInto	F11	Executes code one statement at a time, tracing execution into function calls.
Debug.StepOut	SHIFT-F11	Executes the remaining lines of a function in which the current execution point lies.
Debug.StepOver	F10	Executes the next line of code but does not step into any function calls.
Debug.StopDebugging	SHIFT-F5	Available in break and run modes, this terminates the debugging session.
Debug.This	CTRL-ALT-V, T	Displays the This window, which allows you to view the data members of the object associated with the current method.
Debug.Threads	CTRL-ALT-H	Displays the Threads window to view all of the threads for the current process.
Debug.ToggleBreakpoint	F9	Sets or removes a breakpoint at the current line.
Debug.ToggleDisassembly	CTRL-F11	Displays the disassembly information for the current source file. Available only in break mode.
Debug.Watch1	CTRL-ALT-W, 1	Displays the Watch 1 window to view the values of variables or watch expressions.
Debug.Watch2	CTRL-ALT-W, 2	Displays the Watch 2 window.
Debug.Watch3	CTRL-ALT-W, 3	Displays the Watch 3 window.
Debug.Watch4	CTRL-ALT-W, 4	Displays the Watch 4 window.
Tools.DebugProcesses	CTRL-ALT-P	Displays the Processes dialog, which allows you to attach or detach the debugger to one or more running processes.

Table C-11. Object browser

Command	Shortcut	Description
Edit.FindSymbol	ALT-F12	Displays the Find Symbol dialog.
Edit.GoToDeclaration	CTRL-F12	Displays the declaration of the selected symbol in the code.
Edit.GoToDefinition	F12	Displays the definition for the selected symbol in code.
View.FindSymbolResults	CTRL-ALT-F12	Displays the Find Symbol Results window.

Table C-11. Object browser (continued)

Command	Shortcut	Description
View.ObjectBrowser	CTRL-ALT-J	Displays the Object Browser to view the classes, properties, methods, events, and constants defined either in your project or by components and type libraries referenced by your project.
View.ObjectBrowserBack	ALT-+	Moves back to the previously selected object in the selection history of the object browser.
View.ObjectBrowserForward	SHIFT-ALT-+	Moves forward to the next object in the selection history of the object browser.

Table C-12. Tool window

Command	Shortcut	Description
Tools.CommandWindowMarkMode	CTRL-SHIFT-M	Toggles the Command window into or out of a mode allowing text within the window to be selected.
View.ClassView	CTRL-SHIFT-C	Displays the Class View window.
View.CommandWindow	CTRL-ALT-A	Displays the Command window, which allows you to type commands that manipulate the IDE.
View.DocumentOutline	CTRL-ALT-T	Displays the Document Outline window to view the flat or hierarchical outline of the current document.
View.Favorites	CTRL-ALT-F	Displays the Favorites window, which lists shortcuts to web pages.
View.Output	CTRL-ALT-O	Displays the Output window to view status messages at runtime.
View.PropertiesWindow	F4	Displays the Properties window, which lists the design-time properties and events for the currently selected item.
View.PropertyPages	SHIFT-F4	Displays the property pages for the item currently selected. (For example, use this to show a project's settings.)
View.ResourceView	CTRL-SHIFT-E	Displays the Resource View window.
View.ServerExplorer	CTRL-ALT-S	Displays the Server Explorer window, which allows you to view and manipulate database servers, event logs, message queues, web services, and many other operating system services.
View.ShowWebBrowser	CTRL-ALT-R	Displays the web browser window, which allows you to view pages on the Internet.
View.SolutionExplorer	CTRL-ALT-L	Displays the Solution Explorer, which lists the projects and files in the current solution.
View.TaskList	CTRL-ALT-K	Displays the TaskList window, which displays tasks, comments, shortcuts, warnings, and error messages.
View.Toolbox	CTRL-ALT-X	Displays the Toolbox, which contains controls and other items that can be dragged into editor and designer windows.

Table C-13. HTML Design view

Command	Shortcut	Description
Format.Bold	CTRL-B	Toggles the selected text between bold and normal.
Format.DecreaseIndent	CTRL-SHIFT-T	Decreases the selected paragraph by one indent unit.
Format.IncreaseIndent	CTRL-T	Indents the selected paragraph by one indent unit.
Format.Italic	CTRL-I	Toggles the selected text between italic and normal.
Format.LockElement	CTRL-SHIFT-K	Prevents an absolutely positioned element from being inadvertently moved. If the element is already locked, this unlocks it.
Format.ShowGrid	CTRL-G	Toggles the grid.
Format.SnapToGrid	CTRL-SHIFT-G	Specifies that elements be aligned using an invisible grid. You can set grid spacing on the Design pane of HTML designer options in the Options dialog, and the grid will be changed the next time you open a document.
Format.Underline	CTRL-U	Toggles the selected text between underlined and normal.
Insert.Bookmark	CTRL-SHIFT-L	Displays the Bookmark dialog.
Insert.DIV	CTRL-J	Inserts <div></div> in the current HTML document.
Insert.Hyperlink	CTRL-L	When text is selected, displays the Hyperlink dialog.
Insert.Image	CTRL-SHIFT-W	Displays the Insert Image dialog.
Table.InsertRowAbove	CTRL-ALT-UP ARROW	Adds one row above the current row in the table.
Table.InsertRowBelow	CTRL-ALT-DOWN ARROW	Adds one row below the current row in the table.
Table.InsertColumnstotheLeft	CTRL-ALT-LEFT ARROW	Adds one column to the left of the current column in the table.
Table.InsertColumnstotheRight	CTRL-ALT-RIGHT ARROW	Adds one column to the right of the current column in the table.
View.Details	CTRL-SHIFT-Q	Toggles display of marker icons for HTML elements that do not have a visual representation, such as comments, scripts, and anchors for absolutely positioned elements.
View.NextView	CTRL-PAGE DOWN	Switches from design view to HTML view and vice versa.
View.VisibleBorders	CTRL-Q	Displays a 1-pixel border around HTML elements that support a BORDER attribute and have it set to zero, such as tables, table cells, and divisions.

Table C-14. Macro

Command	Shortcut	Description
View.MacroExplorer	ALT-F8	Displays the Macro Explorer window, which lists all available macros.
Tools.MacrosIDE	ALT-F11	Launches the macros IDE.

Table C-14. Macro (continued)

Command	Shortcut	Description
Tools.RecordTemporaryMacro	CTRL-SHIFT-R	Places the environment in macro record mode or completes recording if already in record mode.
Tools.RunTemporaryMacro	CTRL-SHIFT-P	Plays back a recorded macro.

Table C-15. Dialog resource editor (but not the Windows Forms dialog Editor)

Command	Shortcut	Description
Format.AlignBottoms	CTRL-SHIFT-DOWN ARROW	Aligns the bottom edges of the selected controls with the dominant control. The dominant control is the last one to be selected.
Format.AlignCenters	SHIFT-F9	Aligns the vertical centers of the selected controls with the dominant control.
Format.AlignLefts	CTRL-SHIFT-LEFT ARROW	Aligns the left edges of the selected controls with the dominant control.
Format.AlignMiddles	F9	Aligns the horizontal centers of the selected controls with the dominant control.
Format.AlignRights	CTRL-SHIFT-RIGHT ARROW	Aligns the right edges of the selected controls with the dominant control.
Format.AlignTops	CTRL-SHIFT-UP ARROW	Aligns the top edges of the selected controls with the dominant control.
Format.ButtonBottom	CTRL-B	Places the selected buttons along the bottom center of the dialog.
Format.ButtonRight	CTRL-R	Places the selected buttons in the top-right corner of the dialog.
Format.CenterHorizontal	CTRL-SHIFT-F9	Centers the controls horizontally within the dialog.
Format.CenterVertical	CTRL-F9	Centers the controls vertically within the dialog.
Format.CheckMnemonics	CTRL-M	Checks uniqueness of accelerator mnemonics. If you have the same accelerator key assigned to two different controls, this will warn you of the problem.
Format.SizeToContent	SHIFT-F7	Resizes the selected control(s) to fit the caption text.
Format.SpaceAcross	ALT-LEFT ARROW	Evenly spaces the selected controls horizontally.
Format.SpaceDown	ALT-DOWN ARROW	Evenly spaces the selected controls vertically.
Format.TabOrder	CTRL-D	Sets the order of controls within the dialog.
Format.TestDialog	CTRL-T	Displays the dialog to allow you to check its appearance and behavior.
Format.ToggleGuides	CTRL-G	Cycles between no grid, guidelines, and grid for dialog editing.

Table C-16. Accelerator and string resource editor

Command	Shortcut	Description
Edit.NewAccelerator	INSERT	Adds a new entry for an accelerator key. Available only in the accelerator editor.
Edit.NewString	INSERT	Adds a new entry in the string table. Available only in the string editor.

Source Control Basics

Source control is a necessary part of any development project. VS.NET provides a basic user interface that can interact with any source control system that implements the Microsoft Source Code Control Interface (MSSCCI). The most common system is Visual Source Safe (VSS), so for this appendix, which will walk you through the basic operations of source control in VS.NET, we will assume you are using VSS Version 6.0d. (The d revision of Version 6.0 was released with VS.NET 2003. This is the only version of VSS that is supported with VS.NET 2003.)

Creating a VSS Database

When you install VSS, it sets itself to be the source control provider for VS.NET. Before you can add a solution to source control in VSS, you must have a VSS database. (VSS sets up a default database when you install it. If you are happy to use that, or if you have already created an appropriate database, you can skip this step.)

VSS databases are created using the VSS admin tool. This can usually be found in the Windows Start menu's Programs section, under Microsoft Visual Source Safe → Visual SourceSafe 6.0 Admin. From the main menu, select Tools → Create Database. This will display a dialog for entering the location in which you want to create the database (see Figure D-1). When you create a database, its name will be the same as the folder in which it resides.

The VSS admin tool can also be used to create VSS logins. In a multiuser project, you are likely to want to create a VSS login for each individual developer, so that VSS can track which check-outs and modifications have been performed by which developers. You can add new logins with the User → Add Users menu item.

Once you have created your database and added the necessary logins, you can connect to it through VS.NET.

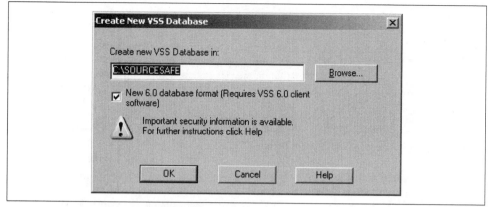

Figure D-1. Create New VSS Database dialog

Adding a Solution

If you would like to add a solution to a source control database, you can do so from within Visual Studio .NET using the File → Source Control menu. This menu presents two options with which you can add items to source control. "Add solution to source control" allows you to connect to a source control database and add the entire solution, including all the projects and files it contains, to that database. "Add selected projects to source control" allows you to add only projects that are currently selected in the Solution Explorer.

If you select either of these options, you will be presented with the Visual SourceSafe Login dialog box, as shown in Figure D-2.

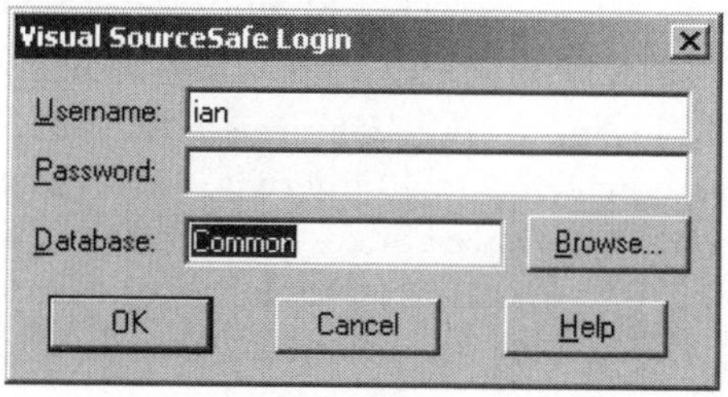

Figure D-2. SourceSafe Login dialog

If you wanted to connect to a different database than the one displayed, you can select the Browse button and browse to the directory that contains the database to which you would like to connect.

The first time you use source control in any VS.NET session, Source-Safe needs to log you in to the database. In general, it will try to do this automatically so that you don't need to see the login box—if there is a VSS account with the same name as your Windows account, it will normally log in with that name. (If you use this approach, do not make the passwords the same! VSS password security is weak to the point of being optional—for this style of automated login, you will never be prompted for your VSS password. You are better off leaving your VSS password blank and using Windows security to protect the database files, as described in VSS Help.)

However, in certain circumstances VS.NET will not log you in automatically, for example, when you add a solution to source control or use the File → Source Control → Open From Source Control... menu option. The reason for this is that the login dialog not only asks you for your credentials but also allows you to choose which VSS database to use. When adding new projects or retrieving projects for the first time on a given machine, it is important to be able to specify which database to use. VS.NET therefore always shows the login dialog in these circumstances. But when you open a local copy of a file that is source controlled, VS.NET logs in silently if it can. (Of course, if your VSS login name is different from your Windows name, you will always get the login prompt.)

Once you connect, a dialog allowing you to select where your solution will go in the SourceSafe database's hierarchy will appear. If you just press Enter, you will get a dialog asking if you want to create a *project* with the name of your solution. The term project means something quite different to SourceSafe than it does to VS.NET; in fact, a VSS project is most closely related to a solution in VS.NET (and VSS doesn't really have a direct equivalent of a VS.NET project). When you add a solution to a VSS database, it becomes a VSS project, and all of the VS.NET projects and files in the solution will be added to the new VSS project.

If you accept the default location, your VSS project will be created at the root of the VSS database you have connected to. (Otherwise, it will be created wherever you told VSS to create it.) Once you have added your solution, the nodes in the Solution Explorer add icons next to them to indicate their source control status. When you first add a solution, all of the files will be checked in, so every file will have a small lock icon, as Figure D-3 shows.

Files

There are two kinds of files that VS.NET will not add to source control. One is the *<projectname>.<language>proj.user* file. This contains per-user settings for each

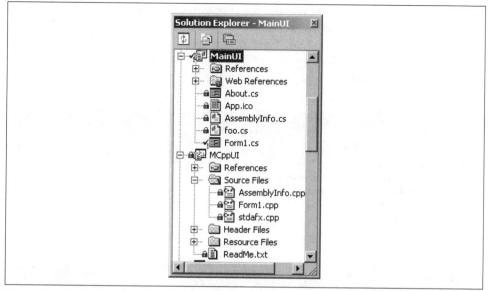

Figure D-3. Locked items in the Solution Explorer

project, as described in Chapter 1, so it would be inappropriate for all developers to use one central copy of such files. Since these files contain nothing that affects the build output, nothing is lost by omitting them from source control—it simply allows each member of the team to customize the way in which she works with the projects within VS.NET. The other type of file that is not added to source control is the *<solutionname>.suo* file. This file does much the same job as the *.user* files, except it stores per-user settings at the solution level rather than the project level.

Checking In and Out

Once your solution is in source control, you will not be allowed to modify it in any way without first *checking out* items you wish to change. This is to make sure that multiple developers don't work on the same file at the same time—a file can be checked out by only one developer at a time.

You can check an item out by selecting it in the Solution Explorer and then selecting File → Source Control → Check Out *Filename*. (The File menu will display the name of the selected file.) Alternatively, you can right-click on the file in Solution Explorer and select the Check Out... option from the context menu. Finally, if you attempt to modify a file that is not checked out (e.g., by typing in a source file or by changing a project's settings), VS.NET will offer to check the file out for you. (Of course, if some other developer has the file checked out, you will not be allowed to check it out until he checks it back in.)

Whichever of the mechanisms you use for checking out a file (or files, since you can check out multiple items at the same time), you will be shown the Check Out dialog, which is shown in Figure D-4. The Comments section allows you to specify the reason for checking the file out—this will be visible in the VSS browser, so you can let other users know why you have locked the file.

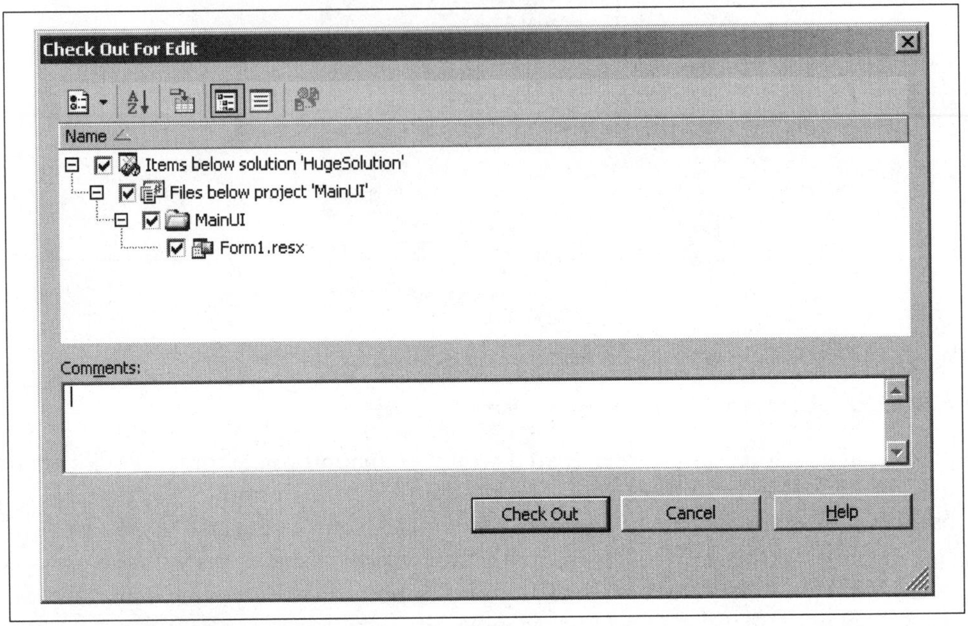

Figure D-4. Check Out dialog box

 When this dialog appears as a result of attempting to edit a file that is not checked out, in place of the Cancel button you will find an Edit button. If you click Edit, VS.NET will allow you to modify the file without checking it out, although it will warn you that this is likely to lead to loss of data. This can sometimes be useful for performing an experimental change without having to check the file out. But be aware that such changes are transient—the source control database contains the master copy, and any changes made outside of source control are liable to be overwritten whenever you update your local copy of the project.

Once you have made the changes you require, you will want to push those changes back to the source control database—VS.NET always edits local copies of files, and you need to tell it when to write those copies back. This process is known as *checking in*, and it is done in much the same way as checking out—select the file or files in the Solution Explorer and select Check In, either from the File → Source Control menu or from the Solution Explorer context menu.

Checking Out Versus Getting Latest Version

When you check out a file, VS.NET makes sure that your local copy is the most up-to-date version. So if the file has been changed by someone else recently, you may find that it looks different after you check it out—VS.NET has fetched a new version to make sure you are starting from the right place.

Checking a file out is not the only way of retrieving the latest version. If you right-click on a solution, project, or file in the Solution Explorer, you will find a Get Latest Version option. (For projects or solutions, this will usually have the text "(recursive)" appended, which indicates that it will retrieve the latest versions of everything in the solution and project, as opposed to just the *.sln* or project file.) This consults the source control database to see if any of the files have been modified by other developers, and if so, it copies the new versions to your system.

In a group project, you should get the latest version of any files in a solution you are working on regularly to make sure that your local copy of the project doesn't drift too far from the copy in the source control database. For the same reason, you should also regularly check in any files that you have checked out.

Check In Frequently

As a general rule, you should check in early and often. Automated builds typically work by retrieving the most recent version of the project from source control and building that. Changes you make to files will not be available in source control until you check those changes in, so your code will not become part of a nightly build until you check it in.

When multiple developers are involved, if files are not checked in regularly, the local copies of the project on the various developers' machines can become radically different—developer A may be writing code that works in conjunction with some class that is in the process of being modified by developer B. When they both eventually check their changes back in, the project may fail to work. These integration niggles are irritating, but in isolation they are usually fairly easy to fix. However, if you leave it for days or even weeks between checking files in, you are likely to have a huge integration mess to sort out before anything will work. If all the developers make a habit of trying not to go longer than a day or two between synchronizing their local copies with the database, these problems don't have the opportunity to grow.

Moreover, if you have a file checked out, nobody else can work with it. If you keep files checked out for long periods of time, you may end up holding other developers up. (Although if you really do have to work on a particular file for an extended period, it is usually best to check it in and back out every time you complete some meaningful unit of work, just to make sure that the copy in the source control database is kept up-to-date.)

Also, any sane development team will make sure that the server that contains the source control database is backed up on a regular basis (usually daily). However, it's not uncommon for developer machines not to be backed up at all. So checking in regularly reduces the potential for data loss.

For all these reasons, you should aim to keep as few files checked out as possible and to check files in as soon as you can.

Retrieving a Project

When you join a group project, you will usually need to retrieve a local copy of a project that is already in the source control database. (The only developer in a group project who doesn't have to do this is the one who created the project in the first place.) To do this, use the File → Source Control → Open from Source Control menu item. You will be presented with the login dialog (Figure D-2) to allow you to specify the database you want to use. Next, you will select the appropriate folder in the database. When you press OK, VS.NET will download the solution and all of its projects to the local folder that you specify.

 You have to do this only once for any particular solution on any given developer machine. If you simply want to refresh your local copy so that it is in sync with the version in source control, use the Get Latest Version technique described earlier.

File History

VSS keeps a log of all of the changes that have been made to a file since it was first added to source control. This *history* will contain one entry for every time the file was checked in. To see the history of a file, select it in the Solution Explorer and then choose the File → Source Control → History menu option. This will open the History Options dialog, which is shown in Figure D-5. This allows you to choose which aspects of the file's history will be displayed.

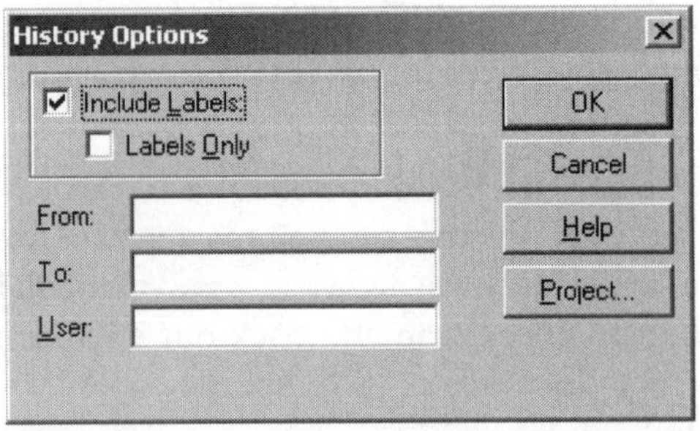

Figure D-5. VSS History dialog

As well as keeping track of changes to a file, VSS also lets you apply *labels*—these are additional markers in a file's history that are used to indicate versions of significance. For example, when a software product is released, it is common practice to apply a label to all of the files in a project. This way, all of the source file versions that correspond to the release are easy to identify. (This is important if you need to release a quick bug fix for an old version of a product.)

By default, VSS will show all labels in a file's history, but you can turn this off with the History Options dialog. (Alternatively, you can elect to see nothing but the labels.) The Options dialog also allows you to specify the range of dates in which you are interested—for aged files, the full history might be so extensive as to be overwhelming, so it is useful to be able to narrow it down a little. The From and To fields in the dialog can contain dates or times, with a D prefix (e.g., D01/01/02;13:15). You can also enter a label in these fields by prefixing them with an L (e.g., LMyLabel). Or they can contain a version range to show. (For example, you could specify From as 5, and To as 10.)

Finally, the User field allows you to restrict the history results to the changes made by a specific user. When you click OK, VS.NET will display the results in the dialog shown in Figure D-6.

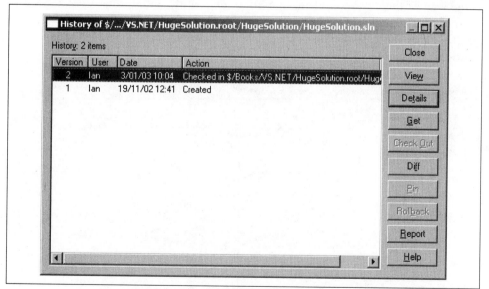

Figure D-6. VSS History search results

Diffs

It is often useful to be able to see at a glance what changes have been made to a file. If you have a history dialog (Figure D-6) showing more than one version, you can select two of these and then click the Diff button in order to find out what changed between the two versions. (Alternatively, you can select the File → Source Control → Compare Versions menu item.) You will be shown the dialog in Figure D-7, which allows you to choose exactly how the changes should be presented.

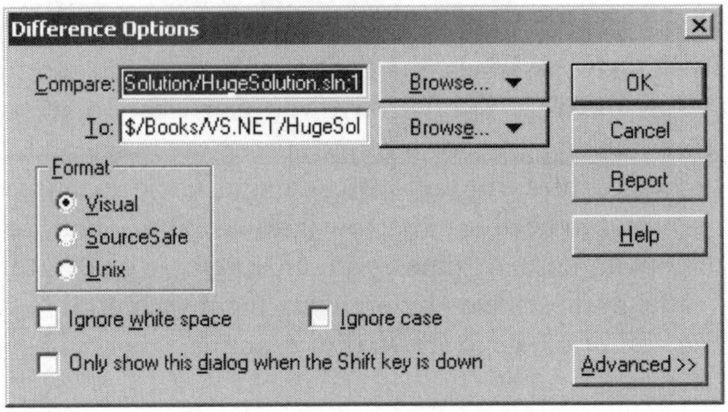

Figure D-7. The diff dialog

You can see the differences in three formats. Unix format presents the changes in the same way as the Unix command-line utility *diff*. SourceSafe format uses VSS's own textual format for presenting the changes. However, the easiest to use is the Visual format. This presents the two versions side by side in a window, highlighting the changes, as Figure D-8 shows.

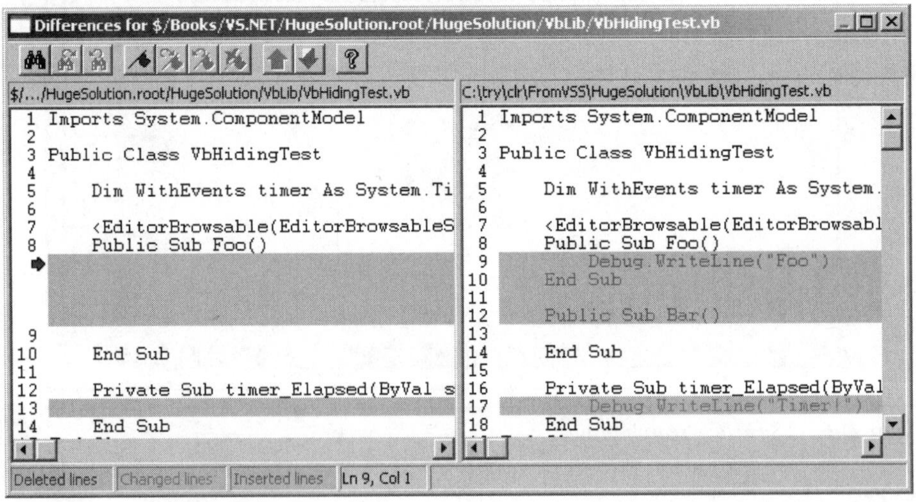

Figure D-8. VSS Differences dialog

Disconnected Operation

VSS allows you to work offline—this means that you can edit files without being connected to the server on which the VSS database resides. This is useful if you regularly work on the move with a laptop. To work offline, you must disconnect from the database. You can do this with the File → Change Source Control option, which presents the dialog shown in Figure D-9.

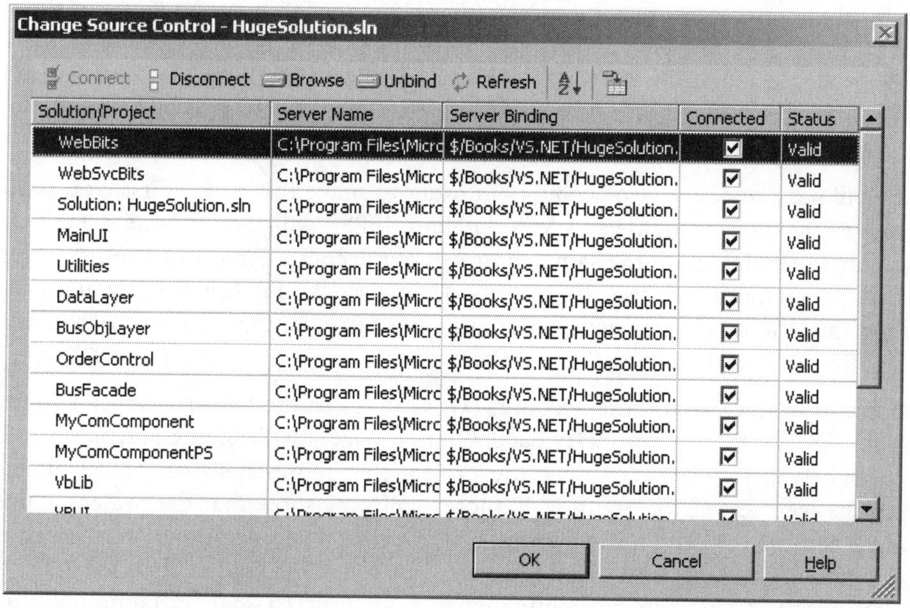

Figure D-9. Change Source Control dialog

To disconnect, select the projects with which you want to work offline and then press the Disconnect button at the top of the dialog. When you are ready to reconnect (e.g., when you get back to the office), open this dialog again (using File → Source Control → Change Source Control). This time, the Change Source Control dialog will have the Disconnect button grayed out, but the Connect button will be enabled. Click the Connect button to reconnect the solution to the VSS database. VS.NET will keep track of any changes that you made while disconnected and will attempt to check out the relevant files.

Web Projects

A web project can be placed in a source control database just as any other project can. If you want to use a web project in this way, see the discussion in Chapter 1 about setting up a solution with a web project for adding directly to a source control database.

Another way to use source control with a web project is to allow the FrontPage Server Extensions (FPSE) to interact with the source control database for you. There are two scenarios in which you would choose to allow FPSE to manage source control for you. The first is if you have multiple members of a development team working on the same copy of a web project and you are already using FPSE to access the shared project. If you require source control on that project, letting FPSE manage VSS will make development significantly easier than trying to coordinate check-ins and check-outs between multiple developer machines. The second scenario is if you are working on a web project in which there is a firewall between you and the web server. FPSE uses only HTTP over port 80 (or the port of the web server you are connecting to), so firewalls do not present a problem. In this situation, using VSS directly would fail, since it uses the SMB protocol, which does not usually work through firewalls.

You will need to create two accounts in order to make this work. First, you need to create an account in the default VSS database (FPSE will use only the default database on a machine) with the same name as your account name and another account for the anonymous web user (i.e., IUSR_<Machinename>). FPSE will use your account to log into the database when you change the FPSE settings and the IUSR account when FPSE is impersonating that user.

Once you have created these accounts, you can go to the Server Extensions tab on the IIS Virtual Directory property page. On that page, for Version Control, select Use External. When you next retrieve the project that represents that virtual directory from the web server, the Solution Explorer will now show that the project is under source control (i.e., the normal icons will appear). The operations are the same as when you are dealing with a local project, but it is FPSE, rather than the IDE, that calls into VSS. This can be helpful when you want to share a common project directly from a single web server.

Solution and Project File Formats

You will usually edit your solutions' and projects' properties with the IDE. However, at times you may want to look inside these files or write a tool that processes the contents of solution and project files. Fortunately, most of the properties of a solution and its projects are kept in simple text files, enabling you to edit these files directly if you so desire. Make sure you close the solution before editing any of these files, to avoid VS.NET overwriting your changes the next time it saves the solution.

 The structure of these files is not documented, and manual editing is not supported. We describe them here because it provides a useful insight into the inner workings of VS.NET projects and solutions. You will not normally need to edit these files and should exercise caution if you attempt to do so.

Solution Files

For every solution, VS.NET creates two files: *<solutionname>.sln* and *<solutionname>.suo*. The *.sln* file is a text file that contains all of the project and solution item information, as well as all of the properties that apply to all the projects in a solution.

The *.suo* file is a binary file that contains per-user information that has no effect on how projects are built. It keeps track of IDE settings such as the list of windows you currently have open, the locations of your breakpoints, and the project that will be launched when you start debugging the solution. Information in the *.suo* file is essentially dispensable, because it has precisely no effect on the build output. Since *.suo* files are not easily editable and contain nothing of lasting consequence, the *.suo* file format will not be documented here. However, the terminally curious may be interested to know that *.suo* files are based around COM structured storage and can be opened in the DocFile viewer that ships with the Windows Platform SDK.

.sln file

Each *.sln* file begins with the following header:

```
Microsoft Visual Studio Solution File, Format Version 8.00
```

(The version number will be higher for more recent versions—8.00 is the version used by Visual Studio .NET 2003. VS.NET 2002 used 7.00.) This is followed by the project sections:

```
Project("{FAE04EC0-301F-11D3-BF4B-00C04F79EFBC}") = "InBetween",
"InBetween.csproj", "{FF8A9B86-1B01-42A8-816B-A8EE2E8B2057}"
    ProjectSection(ProjectDependencies) = postProject
    EndProjectSectionEndProject
Project("{FAE04EC0-301F-11D3-BF4B-00C04F79EFBC}") = "CardLibrary", "..\CardLibrary\
CardLibrary.csproj", "{8E615625-7709-4677-A39B-C14C67089D3C}"
    ProjectSection(ProjectDependencies) = postProject
    EndProjectSectionEndProject
EndProject
```

Each project in the solution has its own `Project/EndProject` tag section. The `Project` tag's GUID indicates what kind of project—the GUID in this example signifies a C# project. (This GUID is used to work out which Project Package VS.NET should load in order to manage this type of project.[*] See Chapter 10 for more information on Project Packages.) After the equals sign is the name of the project, then the relative path from the solution file to the project file. The third item after the equals sign is the project GUID, which is a unique identifier for the project. (A project GUID is generated for each new project you create.)

All projects contain a `ProjectSection` called `ProjectDependencies`. This contains any explicit dependencies between the projects. (Implicit dependencies inferred from project references will not be stored here—project references are stored in the project files, not the solution.) A project with an explicit dependency on another looks like this:

```
Project("{FAE04EC0-301F-11D3-BF4B-00C04F79EFBC}") = "ConsoleApplication1",
"ConsoleApplication1\ConsoleApplication1.csproj",
"{4871AAA0-DE72-449B-A25D-B39B9A80FE1B}"
ProjectSection(ProjectDependencies) = postProject
  {89AC25CD-AA1D-4F08-8AAE-4ED052C716CA} = {89AC25CD-AA1D-4F08-8AAE-4ED052C716CA}
EndProjectSection
EndProject
```

 In VS.NET 2002, project dependencies were not stored as project sections—they were all listed in a global section.

---

[*] These GUIDS live in the registry at *HKEY_LOCAL_MACHINE\SOFTWARE\Microsoft\VisualStudio\7.1\ Projects*.

The next item in the file is a section marked with `Global` and `EndGlobal` markers. This section contains a series of `GlobalSection`/`EndGlobalSection` tags. The syntax of these sections is:

```
GlobalSection(<sectionname>) = <preSolution|postSolution>
    <settings go here>
EndGlobalSection
```

If one or more of your projects is under source control, a global section called `SourceCodeControl` will be present. This section contains the information that VS.NET requires to check projects in and out of the source control database. See Appendix D for more information about using source control in VS.NET.

All solution files contain a global section called `SolutionConfiguration`, which looks like this:

```
GlobalSection(SolutionConfiguration) = preSolution
    Debug = Debug
    Debug = Release
EndGlobalSection
```

This section simply contains a list of solution configurations. It is followed by the `ProjectConfiguration` global section, which determines which project configurations will be built in any particular solution configuration.

For VS.NET 2002 files, the `ProjectDependencies` global section is next. (As of VS.NET 2003, this information is stored in project sections instead, as described earlier.)

```
GlobalSection(ProjectDependencies) = postSolution
{3C3CF2F4-AD9A-42E0-82BA-32293ADC0756}.0 = {F068A500-1332-4918-9D78-A42FF13C7FC4}
EndGlobalSection
```

The final two sections are for the benefit of add-ins. (See Chapter 8 for more information about VS.NET add-ins.) The `ExtensibilityGlobals` section provides add-ins with a place to store solution-wide information. The `ExtensibilityAddins` section contains a list of add-ins that are in use with this solution.

```
GlobalSection(ExtensibilityGlobals) = postSolution
EndGlobalSection
GlobalSection(ExtensibilityAddIns) = postSolution
EndGlobalSection
```

Project Files

Each project's settings are stored in one or more project files. Different project types have their own file formats, and some even create many different files to store a single project's properties. The four language project types, C#, J#, VB.NET, and C++, each has its own file extension (*.csproj*, *.vjsproj*, *.vbproj*, and *.vcproj*, respectively). However, despite having different extensions, these files all use the same basic format—they are all XML files with a common schema.

As well as storing project properties, these files also contain the list of references to other assemblies. The following is an example of the XML for a references list:

```
<References>
    <Reference
        Name = "System"
        AssemblyName = "System"
        HintPath = "..\..\WINDOWS\Microsoft.NET\Framework\v1.0.3705\System.dll"
    />
    <Reference
        Name = "System.XML"
        AssemblyName = "System.Xml"
        HintPath = "..\..\WINDOWS\Microsoft.NET\Framework\v1.0.3705\System.XML.dll"
    />
    <Reference
        Name = "BusObj"
        Project = "{D045135B-9113-44CB-8E73-971DDF807358}"
        Package = "{FAE04EC0-301F-11D3-BF4B-00C04F79EFBC}"
    />
</References>
```

Although these references evidently contain relative paths to the system DLLs, VS. NET is robust in the face of relocated projects. If you change the location of a project on the filesystem, this will break the relative paths. However, when this happens, VS.NET searches to find the files again, using a heuristic that will find them quickly in most cases.

The final Reference element in this snippet is a project reference. Note how it uses the referenced project's GUID to identify the project rather than a path to the project file. This makes such references entirely location independent—if you move a project, VS.NET doesn't even have to rely on a heuristic to work out whether the project in the new location is the same one that used to be in the previous location. (Of course, you will have to update any solutions that contain this project so that they know the new location of the project file. But you will not have to re-create any project references.)

This file also saves the information about the project's files. See Chapter 2 for more information about managing files in projects.

User Files

C#, J#, and VB.NET projects also create a second project file. It will have the same name as the main project file, with .user added to the end (e.g., *MyProject,csproj. user*). This file keeps certain projectwide user-specific properties. Its relationship to the project settings file is similar to the .*suo* file's relationship to the .*sln* file—again, it contains settings that affect the IDE's operation but that have no impact on the build output. (These settings affect the way the program is executed and debugged, but not how it is built.) When you tell VS.NET to add a project to a source control database, it will omit this file, allowing each developer to have her own .*user* file.

This allows each of the developers working on the same project to modify the debug settings without affecting other members of the team.

Web Files

For web-based C# and VB.NET projects, there is an additional project file named *<projectname>.webinfo*. This file contains XML of the following form:

```
<VisualStudioUNCWeb>
    <Web URLPath = "http://localhost/WebUI/WebUI.vbproj" />
</VisualStudioUNCWeb>
```

The Web element has one attribute—URLPath—which points VS.NET to the correct URL for this web project.

Text Editor Settings

VS.NET provides a single text editor that is used by all languages. It has a very flexible scheme for configuring its operation. Some settings are applicable to all languages, such as the display of line numbers or the way that tabulation is performed. You can configure these settings either on a global basis or on a per-language basis. Other configuration options are unique to particular languages.

All of these settings are configured in the Options dialog (Tools → Options) under the Text Editor folder. This has subfolders for each language. It also has a folder called All Languages, which is where you can configure globally available features (such as tab management) in a global way. But the categories under the All Languages section (General and Tabs) are also available under each individual language if you would rather configure things on a per-language basis.

Global Settings

A few text editor settings are global (i.e., they cannot be changed per language). These can be edited by selecting the General item in the Text Editor category. The first four govern the editor's behavior:

Go to selection anchor after escape
Determines whether the Esc key causes the cursor to move to the start or end of the current selection. The default (off) behavior is for the cursor to move to the end of the selection.

Drag-and-drop text editing
Enables dragging and dropping chunks of text.

Include insertion point movements in undo list
Determines whether cursor movements (performed with either the mouse or the arrow keys) are included in the undo/redo history.

Automatic delimiter highlighting

> Controls whether matching pairs of delimiter characters are highlighted. (For example, if this option is enabled, when you close a bracket the editor will highlight the matching opening bracket.)

The next four settings change the appearance of the editor:

Selection margin

> Controls the display of a vertical margin on the left side of the text editor. When enabled, you can use this margin to select a whole line of text (rather than having to select the whole line manually). This margin also includes controls that you can use to collapse and expand classes, methods, and regions.

Indicator margin

> Controls the display of the indicator margin, which is the gray margin on the left side of the text editor where breakpoint and bookmark symbols appear.

Vertical scrollbar

> Determines whether a vertical scrollbar appears on the right side of the text editor pane. (You can still use documents larger than the screen even without a scrollbar of course—you just have to use the keyboard for navigation.)

Horizontal scrollbar

> Determines whether a horizontal scrollbar appears on the bottom of the text editor pane.

Fonts and Colors

The fonts and colors used by the text editor are configured globally—you cannot specify per-language settings. These settings live in a slightly different place from the other editor settings—they are in with all the other font and color selections for Visual Studio .NET. They are still in the Options dialog box, but you must select the Environment folder in the lefthand pane and then select Fonts and Colors.

To change the settings for the text editor, select Text Editor in the Show Settings For combo box. You can select only one font, but you can select the color for each different kind of text recognized by the editor. The different types of text are listed in the Display Items listbox. You may specify different foreground and background colors for each type of text.

Generic Settings

Two categories of settings—General and Tabs—are present in all languages.

The General item that appears under all of the languages is different from the General tab that appears directly under the Text Editor folder, despite having the same name.

Visual Studio .NET allows you to specify these settings on a per-language basis. However, if you want to use the same settings for these two categories in all languages, you can do so using the Text Editor → All Languages folder.

The General and Tabs categories contain settings for common editor services. However, some languages do not use all of these services. For example, the General setting lets you configure IntelliSense, but the Plain Text "language" (used for editing .txt files) cannot support this feature. In such cases, the relevant checkboxes will be grayed out.

General

The configuration panel for the General settings presents three groups of settings: Statement Completion, Settings, and Display.

Here is a summary of the General settings:

Autolist Members
　　IntelliSense will automatically show members of a type during code editing.

Hide Advanced Members
　　IntelliSense will hide advanced members of a type.

Parameter Information
　　IntelliSense will automatically show parameter information for function calls.

Enable Virtual Space
　　The insertion point can be placed anywhere in the editor window (whitespace padding will be inserted when necessary).

Word Wrap
　　Long lines of code will wrap within the text editor window.

Line Numbers
　　Line numbers will appear on the lefthand margin of the text editor.

Enable Single-click URL Navigation
　　URLs can be followed using a single-click.

Navigation Bar
　　A class/member navigation bar will appear at the top of the text editor window.

The first group, Statement Completion, contains three IntelliSense-related settings. The first (Autolist Members) determines whether Visual Studio .NET will display a pop-up list of members in appropriate scopes. With this option enabled, a member list will automatically appear in C# and VB.NET projects if you type a variable or class name followed by a period (.). (In C++ it will appear after typing in either a period, the → operator, or the :: operator, depending on the type of identifier.)

The second IntelliSense-related setting is Hide Advanced Members. This determines which members will be displayed on the member list. If this is enabled, certain items will be hidden when the member list is displayed. It is up to each individual language service to decide what constitutes an "advanced" member to be hidden. VB.NET is the most interesting language since it hides the most. Consider the following class definition:

```
Public Class TestHidden
        Public Sub Foo()
        End Sub
        Private Sub Quux()
        End Sub
    End Class
```

When Hide Advanced Members is turned on, the member list (see Figure F-1) shows only the Foo member function and the GetType function, which is defined by the base type (System.Object). If Hide Advanced Members is turned off, we will also see all of the functions that are inherited from the base class, as Figure F-2 shows. Note that in both cases, only the public members are shown—the member list will show only members that are in scope. (The private member Quux would have been visible if we had tried to display the member list from inside the TestHidden class itself.)

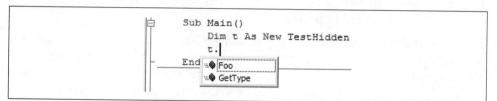

Figure F-1. Hide Advanced Members on

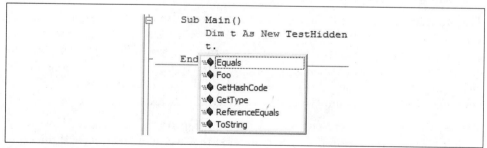

Figure F-2. Hide Advanced Members off

Although VB.NET makes its own decisions about which members of intrinsic types such as System.Object are advanced, we can influence its decisions with our own types. The .NET Framework Class Library defines a custom attribute called EditorBrowsable, which is defined in the System.ComponentModel namespace. We can use this to indicate that particular members of our classes are advanced. We can modify our TestHidden example to use this:

```
Imports System.ComponentModel
Public Class TestHidden
    <EditorBrowsable(EditorBrowsableState.Advanced)> _
    Public Sub Foo( )
    End Sub
    Private Sub Quux( )
    End Sub
End Class
```

This marks the Foo method as being advanced. VB.NET will no longer display this item in member lists if the Hide Advanced Members option is selected.

VB.NET and C# are the only languages that support the Hide Advanced Members setting—it is grayed out for all other languages. VB.NET has it turned on by default, while in C# it is turned off by default. Even if you turn it on for C#, the behavior you get is not quite the same as for VB.NET. C# considers a member to be advanced only if it has had the relevant EditorBrowsable attribute applied, so unlike VB.NET it will not hide members of the System.Object class. Also, C# honors the EditorBrowsable attribute only on classes defined in external components—it is ignored for classes in the same project.

Hide Advanced Members can be selected even if Autolist Members is deselected. This is because even though Autolist might be turned off, the list of members of a type can still be displayed by pressing Ctrl-J or Ctrl-Space.

The third IntelliSense-related setting is Parameter Information. When this option is selected, the parameter information for a particular function is automatically displayed when the function delimiter (in most cases the left parenthesis) has been typed in. The parameter information can be displayed at any time by using the Ctrl-Shift-spacebar shortcut while the cursor is inside a parameter list, regardless of whether this setting is enabled.

The second group of options in the General category is under the heading Settings. It contains two settings that affect the way you see and type text. The first, Enable Virtual Space, is off by default. If you turn this setting on, you will be able to place the cursor beyond the end of the line of code you are typing on. The space between the end of the line of code and the new placement of the cursor is automatically filled in with whitespace. This is similar to Microsoft Word's click-and-type feature.

The second option under Settings turns word wrap on or off. (Again, it is off by default.) When this option is enabled, any text that would appear beyond the right-hand side of the text editor window is automatically placed on the next line. VS.NET does not insert line-feed characters in the text to achieve this—this option merely changes how overly long lines are displayed.

The General category's third group of options is labeled Display. (It's not entirely clear what the distinction between Settings and Display is supposed to be. Word wrap is a display feature, despite appearing in Settings, and some of the items in Display modify the editor's behavior!) The first item, Line Numbers, determines whether numbers are shown on the lefthand side of the text editor pane (between the indicator margin and the selection margin). If Enable Single-click URL Navigation is on, a single-click on a URL in the text editor will follow the URL. If disabled, you have to right-click on the URL and select Navigate to URL. (The text editor supports this behavior for any text that looks plausible as a URL, regardless of context.) The last option, Navigation Bar, determines whether a class and member navigation bar is displayed at the top of the text editor. The navigation bar is described in Chapter 2.

Tabs

The second category of text editor settings available in all languages is the Tabs category. Here is a summary of the Tabs settings:

Indenting
> Controls whether and how automatic indenting is applied to source code

Tab Size
> The number of spaces between each tab stop

Indent Size
> The number of spaces inserted when you press the Tab key or when VS.NET indents your code

Insert Spaces/Keep Tabs
> Determines whether VS.NET will insert tab characters when it can

The first setting, Indenting, controls the behavior of the editor when you press the Enter key. It can be set to None, Block, or Smart. When set to None, the text editor never indents automatically. When set to Block, the text editor indents new lines by the same amount as the preceding line.

The most helpful indentation setting is Smart. This setting uses the current language service to provide context-sensitive indentation. For example, in a C# file, when you press Enter after an open brace ({), the language service tells the text editor to indent the new line by more than the preceding one. And when you type a closing brace, the editor (under the guidance of the C# Language Service) locates the line containing the corresponding opening brace and indents the closing brace by the same amount as the opening one. (It also reformats all of the code in between to fix its indentation if necessary.)

The next pair of settings (which are under the Tabs heading) allows you to control tab sizes. The first value, Tab Size determines the number of spaces between tab stops when a tab character is used. (Remember that a tab character does not insert a fixed number of spaces; it merely advances to the next tab stop.) By default, tab stops are 4 characters apart.

The default of 4 is an incongruous choice, since Windows itself favors 8-character tab stops, as do many other platforms. However, many years ago, the Visual C++ team decided to use 4-character tab stops in its editor, on the grounds that this is a much more useful width for tab stops than 8 characters.

Unfortunately, although 4-character tabs may well be more useful to software developers than 8-character tabs, most other software in Windows carries on using 8-character tab stops. This means that if you open text files containing tab characters in most other editors, they look completely different from how Visual Studio .NET shows them. (In fact, not even all of the development tools that ship with VS. NET follow suit—*WinDiff.exe* uses the more common 8-character convention.)

Changing this setting to 8 is not recommended either. Although this would be more consistent with other Windows software, a considerable amount of the source code that ships with VS.NET is formatted presuming 4-character tab stops, as is much of the wizard-generated code. This would all look wrong if you changed this setting to 8.

The only way to guarantee consistent display of your files in VS.NET and other tools is not to use tabs at all. (Fortunately, this is easy—use the Insert Spaces option described later.)

The second text box in the Tabs section of the Tabs category is Indent Size. This determines the spacing that Visual Studio .NET will use when you press the Tab key or when smart indenting decides to insert a tab in some code for you. (Again, the default is 4.) This setting is entirely independent of Tab Size. Tab Size controls how tab characters will be displayed; Indent Size controls how Visual Studio .NET will format your code. (Just because your system may be configured to display tabs as 4 characters wide, you are not required to format your code in 4-character columns.)

Visual Studio .NET will not necessarily insert a tab character when you press the Tab key or when it performs automatic indentation. For one thing, you may have chosen an Indent Size that is incompatible with the Tab Size. (For example, if you like to format your code with 3-space indentation, this style does not line up very well with either 4-character or 8-character tab stops.) But when use of tab characters is an option, VS.NET will insert them if you want it to.

The wizards ignore the tab settings. They always generate code with tab characters, because the code is based on a template file that contains tab characters. See Chapter 9 for details on how to add your own tab-free templates to VS.NET.

If you choose the Insert Spaces radio button, Visual Studio .NET will never generate any tab characters. All indentation will be done entirely with spaces. This has the advantage that your files will look the same in any text editor. It has the slight disadvantage of making your files larger. The alternative is to select Keep Tabs. This will cause Visual Studio .NET to generate tab characters whenever possible. If your Indent Size setting is not an exactly multiple of your Tab Size setting, VS.NET will use tab characters when possible and fall back to spaces otherwise. For example, suppose you use 3-space indentation with 4-character tab stops. If your current indentation level is 15 columns, VS.NET will insert 3 tabs to form the first 12 columns, followed by 3 spaces to make it up to 15.

We recommend that you choose the Insert Spaces setting. This is the only way to guarantee that the files you create with VS.NET will look the same in all text editors. The increase in file size is nominal and is a small price to pay for guaranteed consistency.

VB.NET

Visual Basic .NET provides one page of language-specific settings (the last two settings are not present in VS.NET 2002):

Automatic insertion of end constructs
If this setting is enabled, whenever you type in an opening construct, the VB. NET Language Service adds a corresponding end construct for you automatically. For example, when you type in Sub Foo and press Enter, the end construct End Sub is automatically added to your file.

Pretty listing (reformatting of code)
This setting enables automatic reformatting of code. When enabled, VB.NET will fix the case of keywords and identifiers (e.g., it will convert sub to Sub), add missing Then statements to If statements, add missing parentheses to function calls, and supply closing quotations for string constants.

Enter outlining mode on file open
Enables outlining in the text editor when a *.vb* file is opened.

Automatic insertion of interface and MustOverride *members*
When this option is enabled, if you add an Implements statement to your class, VS.NET will automatically add skeleton implementations for all of the members of the interface you choose to implement. Likewise, when you choose to derive from a base class using the Inherits statement, if that class has any MustOverride members, skeletons for those will be added.

Show procedure line separators
Shows horizontal lines between procedures in the source code.

C# and J#

C# and J# provide identical options. Each provides just one extra page, entitled Formatting:

Leave open braces on same line as construct
> When this is turned off, the language service will tell the text editor to move the opening brace ({) onto its own line whenever automatic formatting occurs. If this setting is on, automatic formatting will use the K&R style: the opening bracket appears on the same line as the construct to which it belongs. (Note that if the opening and closing braces are on the same line, this setting is ignored and the braces will not be moved.)

Indent case labels
> Controls indentation of case statements. When this setting is on, case statements will be indented from the switch statement. If it is off, case statements will be aligned with the switch statement.

Automatically format completed constructs and pasted source
> This setting tells the language service whether it should autoformat code constructs. With this setting on, code will be reformatted when it is pasted in from the clipboard. Also, when you type in a closing brace (}), VS.NET locates the matching opening brace and will format everything in between the two.

Smart comment editing
> If this is enabled, the editor will place an XML documentation skeleton when you type in three slashes to begin a comment block. (These comments enable the C# autogeneration of documentation from comments.)

Enter outlining mode on file open
> Enables outlining in the text editor when a *.cs* file is opened.

Collapse #region blocks when files open
> Tells the editor whether to have #region/#endregion sections closed or opened when a *.cs* file is opened.

IntelliSense preselects most frequently used members
> (This option is not available on Visual Studio .NET 2002.) With this option enabled, VS.NET will remember which items you select most often from IntelliSense member lists and will select them for you as a default first choice. This is particularly useful for classes that have several members that start with the same text. For example, the Debug, Trace, and Console classes all have both Write and WriteLine members. The WriteLine method tends to be used more frequently, but unfortunately it appears later in the list. If this option is off, typing in Debug. W will highlight the Write entry. However, if you have this option switched on, once you have selected WriteLine a few times, VS.NET will remember that this is your normal choice and will highlight that one first.

C/C++

C++ provides one extra page, entitled Formatting:

Enable automatic Quick Info ToolTips
Enables or disables the descriptive tooltip that will appear if you hover the mouse over a variable or declaration.

Enter outlining mode on file open
Enables outlining in the text editor when a *.cpp*, *.c*, or *.h* file is opened. (If you turn this off, you will not be able to turn outlining back on for individual files.)

Indent braces
Controls indentation of braces. When this is off, braces will be aligned with their corresponding construct (e.g., a function declaration or If statement). When this setting is on, the braces will be indented from the construct and aligned with the code that they contain.

HTML/XML

The HTML/XML Language Service has three pages for its custom settings. First is a Format page that contains settings that apply to both HTML and XML:

Apply automatic formatting when saving document
If enabled, the document will be autoformatted when saved.

Apply automatic formatting when switching from design to HTML/XML view
If enabled, the language service autoformats the document when you switch to the HTML/XML view from the design view. (See Chapter 2 for more information about the XML/HTML designers.)

Apply line breaks
Applies line breaks after certain HTML elements when enabled. This generates physical line breaks in the file (unlike the word wrap feature discussed earlier). However, this will not affect the way your HTML appears in a browser. (It doesn't generate line-break elements such as <p> or <br>.)

Insert attribute value quotes
This setting causes the editor to put quotes around the values of attributes of elements added using the design view. (This applies only to the design view. To control automatic insertion of quotes in the raw HTML/XML view, see the Attribute Value Quotes setting on the HTML-specific and XML-specific pages.)

Capitalization: tags/attributes
The capitalization setting tells the editor whether to change the case of the tags or attribute names you are entering. There are three options. As Entered tells the editor not to modify case. Uppercase and Lowercase are self-explanatory.

Next is a page containing settings specific to HTML:

Enable HTML validation
> If enabled, the editor will validate the document. (See Chapter 2 for details on how to use validation.)

Auto pop-up HTML statement completion
> Enables tag and attribute completion. The *targetSchema* document property is used to locate the type information for providing the statement completion. (See Chapter 2 for more information on the use of the *targetSchema* property.)

Auto pop-up scripting statement completion
> Enables statement completion for client-side scripting. Again, the *targetSchema* document property is used to determine which methods and members are available in script.

Autoinsert close tag
> If enabled, the editor will automatically put in the closing tag for an element. So entering the element <foo> will cause the editor to enter the ending tag </foo>.

Autoinsert attribute value quotes
> Enabling this setting causes the editor to put quotes around the value of attributes. This setting should not be confused with the setting of the same name in the Format page—that controls the behavior in the design view, whereas this setting controls the behavior in the text view.

Instantiate live value quotes
> If enabled (the default), ActiveX controls embedded in the HTML document are instantiated at design time and will appear in the design view of the HTML editor.

Finally, there is a page containing settings unique to XML:

Enable XML validation
> If enabled, the editor will validate the document. (See Chapter 2 for details on how to use validation.)

Auto pop-up XML statement completion
> Enables tag and attribute completion. The *targetSchema* document property is used to locate the type information for providing the statement completion. (See Chapter 2 for more information on the use of the *targetSchema* property.)

Autoinsert close tag
> If enabled, the editor will automatically put in the closing tag for an element. So entering the element <foo> will cause the editor to enter the ending tag </foo>.

Autoinsert attribute
> Enabling this setting causes the editor to put quotes around the values of attributes.

CSS

The CSS Language Service provides two extra property pages. The first is called CSS Specific:

Show statement completion pop ups
> If enabled, the editor will display a list of available properties and property values for the CSS style that you are editing.

Show property description tooltips
> Shows a tooltip description of the property you are editing.

Detect errors
> This property enables the next two settings to be used.

Detect unknown properties
> Causes unknown properties to be highlighted with a red wavy line drawn underneath the text of the property.

Detect invalid values
> Causes invalid property values to be highlighted with a red wavy line drawn underneath the text of the property value.

The second page contains CSS Format settings:

Style
> This can be one of three values. If Compact Rules is selected, all CSS declarations appear on a single line. If Semiexpanded is selected, the name of the rule and the opening bracket appear on a single line, and each of the attributes appears on its own line. Expanded (which is the default) is similar to Semiexpanded, but it also causes the beginning bracket to appear on its own line,

Capitalization
> If you select Lowercase (the default), the CSS editor will force all text to be lowercase. The other options—Uppercase and As Entered—are equally self-explanatory.

Plain Text and SQL Settings

The plain text language does not offer any settings beyond the standard General and Tabs pages. Nor do any of the supported SQL dialects.

Index

A

accelerator and string resource editor
    keyboard shortcuts, 355
ACT Project template, 332
Active Server page, 338
Add ATL Support to MFC template, 337
add-ins, 250, 274–286
    configuration dialog, 283
    configuring, 280–285
    custom Options page, 281
    debugging, 286
    defined, 250
    design choices, 275–285
    features of, 312
    installing, 285
    Manager dialog, 286
    Options dialog registry
        configuration, 281
administrative installation, 176
adornment, custom, 238
advanced debugging techniques, 101–109
alternative debugging protocols, 105
Analyzer Project template, 332
Analyzer Wizard, 332
app.config file, 334, 336
Application Center Test project, 332
application configuration file
    (app.config), 336
application configuration source file, 334
Apply automatic formatting when saving
    document setting, 381

Apply automatic formatting when switching
    from design to HTML/XML view
    setting, 381
Apply line breaks setting, 381
.asmx files, 124, 335, 336
ASP.NET
    debugging, 70
    web forms, 335
    Web Forms controls, 56
    web service file, 336
    web services, 56, 123
ASP.NET Mobile Web Application
    template, 326
ASP.NET Web Application template, 110,
    325
ASP.NET Web Service project, 331
ASP.NET Web Service template, 110, 325,
    327
aspnet_regiis utility, 114
.aspx files, 335
assemblies, adding, 193
assembly information source file, 334
assembly manifest resources, 217
assembly resource file (.resx), 339
ATL
    control, 337
    dialog class, 337
    performance monitor object, 337
    property page, 337
    server, 123
    simple object, 337
    templates, 337
ATL Active Server page component, 337
ATL COM+ 1.0 component, 337

We'd like to hear your suggestions for improving our indexes. Send email to *index@oreilly.com*.

ATL OLEDB
  consumer class, 337
  provider, 337
ATL Project template, 327
ATL Server
  Project template, 327
  template, 110
  Web Service template, 110, 328
Auto pop-up
  HTML statement completion setting, 382
  scripting statement completion
    setting, 382
  XML statement completion setting, 382
autocompletion, 38, 40
Autoinsert
  attribute setting, 382
  close tag setting, 382
Autolist Members text editor setting, 374
automated building, 28
Automatic insertion of
  end constructs setting, 379
  interface and MustOverride members
    setting, 379
Automatically format completed constructs
    and pasted source setting, 380
automation, 250–286
  object model, 251–262
  summary, 286
Autos windows, 91

B

Beautifier reformatting, 41
behavior changes and debugging, 64
bitmap file, 339
Blank Solution template, 333
bookmarks and navigation, 43
boundaries, language and technology, 101
breakpoints, 73–80
  Breakpoints window, 79
  conditional, 76
  data, 78
  halting on errors, 80–84
  memory leaks in C++, 76
build events, 29
build tools, custom, 58–62
building
  block project, 331
  project, 317
  web projects, 120
builds (see solutions, building)
Business Façade project, 331
Business Rules project, 331

C

C++
  memory leaks, 76
  projects
    differences from C# and J#
      projects, 30
    managed, 327
  templates, 336
C++ file (.cpp), 336
C#
  documentation, 40
  item templates, 334
  language service options, 380
C#, J#, and VB.NET managed local project
    templates, 8
.cab (Cabinet) files, 329
  installation and, 211
Cab project, 171
Cab Project template, 329
call stack, debugging, 93
Call Stack window, 94
Capitalization (CSS Format setting), 383
Capitalization: tags/attributes setting, 381
cascading stylesheet (.css), and solution
    items, 16
change scripts, 154–156
changing editors, 56
Check Constraints tab, 138
Checkboxes pages, 181
checking files in and out (VSS), 359–362
checking files in frequently (VSS), 361
checking files out versus getting latest version
    (VSS), 361
Class Library (.NET) template, 327
Class Library template, 325
class source file, 334
class view pane, 42
client-side script debugging, 71
clipboard ring, 46
CLR (Common Language Runtime)
  defined, 101
code serialization, 228
code source file, 334
code view
  editing a file, 317
codebehind file, 118
CodeDom, 304–310
Collapse #region blocks when files open
    setting, 380
colors in text editor, 373
Columns tab, 134
COM class, 335

COM components, adding references to, 21
COM registration, 192
command objects, 260
common.js file, 298
compiler packages, 313
component class (.NET) source file, 336
component class source file, 334
components
    adding menu verbs, 234
    basic integration, 213–216
    categories and descriptions, 220
    code serialization, 228
    COM, adding references to, 21
    custom component designers, 234–249
    custom designer, 234
    custom property types, 224–233
    custom UI type editors, 229–233
    data binding, 223
    default events and properties, 221
    designer serialization, 222
    embedded resources, 217
    integrating, 213–249
        summary, 249
    localization, 221
    property visibility, 222
    simple integration attributes, 216–224
    Toolbox bitmap, 216–219
    type converters, 224–229
    web forms control designers, 247–249
        design-time rendering, 248
        resizing, 248
    Windows forms control
        designers, 235–249
        adornments, 238
        example, 240–247
        handling mouse input, 239
        resizing and moving, 237
Configuration Manager, 24–26
Configure Data Adapter Wizard, 161
Confirm Installation page, 179
connection credentials, 128
connections, 148
Console Application (.NET) template, 327
Console Application template, 326
context wizards, 288
control editor keyboard shortcuts, 347
control with one resizable edge, 237
Copy Local property, 19
.cpp files, 336
create scripts, 149–154
    options, 152

crossing language and technology
        boundaries, 101
cross-machine debugging, 104
Crystal Report (.rpt), 339
CSS editor, 51–56
    design views, 52–56
CSS language service options, 383
cursor file, 339
custom
    actions, 197–205
        example, 201
    adornment, 238
    build tools, 58–62
    component designers, 234–249
    control source file, 335
    designer, 234
    Options page, 281
    parameters in a .vsz file, 305
    UI type editors, 229–233
custom build tools
    building your own, 60
    defined, 58
Custom tool COM interface definitions, 60
Custom Wizard template, 328
Customer Installation page, 182

D

Data Access project, 331
data adapters, 125, 156–162
    Configuration Wizard, 157
    defined, 156
data binding, of components, 223
Data Connections list in Server Explorer, 128
data form wizard, 335
database diagram designer, 130–132
Database Project template, 330
database projects, 125–166
    Check Constraints tab, 138
    Columns tab, 134
    connections and references, 148
    creating, 148
    data adapters, 156–162
    database diagram designer, 130–132
    datasets, 160
    diagram pane, 140–143
    Foreign Key table, 136
    grid pane, 143–145
    Indexes/Keys tab, 137
    multiuser issues, 156
    .NET projects and, 156–166
    Primary Key table, 136
    query and view designer, 139–146

database projects (*continued*)
  query files, 156
  Relationships tab, 136
  results pane, 146
  scripts, 149–156
  Server Explorer, 126–130
  SQL editor, 146
  SQL pane, 145
  summary, 166
  table designer, 138
  table property pages (see table property
    pages)
  Tables tab, 134
database query, 338
database references, 148
database support in Visual Studio .NET
    editions, 125
DataSet schema, 335, 336
datasets
  adapters, 160
  optimistic concurrency, 160
  XSD Designer, 162–166
debugger object, 261
debugging, 63–109
  add-ins, 286
  advanced techniques, 101–109
  alternative protocols, 105
  ASP.NET, 70
  attaching to a running process, 65
  autos, locals, and this windows, 91
  behavior changes, 64
  breakpoints (see breakpoints)
  call stack, 93
  choosing modes, 100
  client-side script, 71
  controlling execution, 72–88
  cross-machine, 104
  displaying variables and
    expressions, 88–91
  halting on errors, 80–84
  just-in-time, 67–70
  keyboard shortcuts, 349–351
  language and technology boundaries, 101
  launching, 64
  macros, 274
  memory windows, 94
  modules window, 97
  multiple processes, 103
  multiple threads, 102
  observing state, 88–97
  output window, 95
  packages, 313

  project settings, 97–101
  projects, 317
  registers, 92
  release-only bugs, 99
  single-stepping (see single-stepping)
  starting, 63–72
  summary, 109
  symbol servers, 106
  symbol store
    creating and maintaining, 108
    using, 107
  T-SQL, 105
  VSIP packages, 324
  watch windows, 88
  web projects, 120
.def files, 336
default.js file, 298
dependencies, defined, 22
design view, editing a file in, 317
design views, 52–56
  nonvisual components, 53
  Toolbox, 52
  web forms, 54
  windows forms, 54
designer packages, 314
designer serialization of components, 222
Detect errors setting, 383
Detect invalid values setting, 383
Detect unknown properties setting, 383
diagram pane, 140–143
  Bind to Schema option, 143
  Encrypt view, 143
  joins, 141
  Update Using View Rules checkbox, 143
dialog resource editor keyboard
    shortcuts, 354
DirectionalLabel control, 240
Distributed Application template, 331
Distributed Component Object Model
    (DCOM), 123
document objects, 261
Document Type Definition (DTD), 49
Draco website, 29
DTE (Development Tools Extensibility), 251
  object, 251
    events, 263
    properties, 251
    solutions, projects, and files in the
      DTE object model, 254
.dtq files, 156
dynamic discovery file, 335

E

editing a file
    in code view, 317
    in design view, 317
editor packages, 314
editors
    changing, 56
    miscellaneous, 56
    simple (see simple editors)
    summary, 62
    text (see text editor)
embedded resources, 217
Empty Project (.NET) template, 327
Empty Project template, 326
Empty Web Project template, 110, 326
Enable automatic Quick Info ToolTips
    setting, 381
Enable HTML validation setting, 382
Enable Single-click URL Navigation text
    editor setting, 377
Enable Virtual Space text editor setting, 376
Enable XML validation setting, 382
Enter outlining mode on file open
    setting, 379, 380, 381
Enterprise Template Project, 331
Enterprise Template Project template, 331
event handlers, adding, 41
exceptions, 80
ExcludeFilter property, 192
Execute method, IDTWizard
    interface, 305–306
existing web projects, 120
expandable property, 227
expression evaluators, 324
expressions, displaying, 88–91
Extended Stored Procedure template, 329
extensibility projects, 332
ExtensibilityAddins section, 369
ExtensibilityGlobals section, 369
external build tools, 29

F

file management, 15
file properties, 16
file references versus project references, 33
file search and installation, 208
file sharing
    versus FrontPage, 121
    VS.NET and, 121
File System view, 188–194
file type actions, 195

File Types view, 194–196
files, 37–62
    adding during installation, 193
    summary, 62
Finished page, 180
fonts in text editor, 373
Foreign Key table, 136
Formatting page
    C# and J#, 380
    C/C++, 381
frameset, 338
Framework, 114
FrontPage Server Extensions (FPSE), 121
    complicating use of source control, 122
    source control and, 366
FrontPage, versus file sharing, 121

G

generic C++ class, 336
Global and EndGlobal markers, 369
global application class, 335
Global Assembly Cache (GAC), 20
grid pane, 143–145
GUID, 269

H

.h files, 336
halting on errors, 80–84
handling events in macros, 273
header file (.h), 336
heisenbug, 64
help keyboard shortcuts, 349
Help packages, 314
Hide Advanced Members text editor
    setting, 375
HTML
    design view, keyboard
        shortcuts, 353–355
    language service options, 381
    page, 338
    script-only view, 48
    views, 48
HTML/XML editor, 48–50
    HTML script-only view, 48
    HTML views, 48
    IntelliSense, 48
    schemas, 48
    XML data view, 50
    XML schema, 50

I

icon file, 339
.idl files, 336
IDTExtensibility2 methods, 275
IDTWizard implementation, 306
IDTWizard interface, Execute
       method, 305–306
IIS virtual directories, 111
Indent braces setting, 381
Indent case labels setting, 380
Indent Size text editor setting, 377
Indenting text editor setting, 377
Indexes/Keys tab, 137
inherited form source file, 335
inherited user control source file, 335
Insert attribute value quotes setting, 381
Insert Spaces/Keep Tabs text editor
       setting, 377
INSERT stored procedure example, 162
installation
    adding assemblies, 193
    adding files, 193
    adding merge modules, 193
    adding project output, 190–192
    administrative, 176
    Cab files, 211
    COM registration, 192
    custom actions, 197–205
    file search, 208
    folders
        Common Files, 188
        Fonts, 188
        Global Assembly Cache Folder, 189
        Module Retargetable Folder, 189
        Program Files, 188
        System, 189
        User's Application Data, 189
        User's Desktop, 189
        User's Favorites, 189
        User's Personal Data, 189
        User's Programs, 189
        User's Send To Menu, 189
        User's Start Menu, 189
        User's Startup Folder, 189
        User's Template Folder, 189
        Windows Folder, 189
    launch conditions, 205–210
    .NET installation components, 202–205
    process, 172
    project output
        Content Files, 191
        Debug Symbols, 191
        Documentation Files, 191
        Localized Resources, 191
        Primary Output, 191
        Source Files, 191
    registry search, 209
    UI phases, 174
    Windows Installer search, 210
Installation Address page, 179
Installation Folder page, 178
Installer, 167–170
Installer class (.NET) source file, 336
Installer class source file, 334
Installer UI pages, 176–187
    Checkboxes pages, 181
    Confirm Installation page, 179
    Customer Installation page, 182
    Finished page, 180
    Installation Address page, 179
    Installation Folder page, 178
    License agreement page, 185
    Progress page, 180
    Radiobuttons pages, 180
    Read Me page, 187
    Register User page, 187
    Splash page, 186
    Textboxes pages, 182
    Welcome page, 178
Instantiate live setting, 382
integrating components (see components,
       integrating)
integrating components with Visual Studio
       .NET, 213–249
IntelliSense, 38–40, 48
    commands
        Complete Word, 39
        List Members, 38
        Parameter Info, 39
        Quick Info, 39
IntelliSense preselects most frequently used
       members setting, 380
item templates, 334–339
item wizards, 288

J

J# item templates, 334
J# language service options, 380
Join property page, 143
JScript file, 338
JScript .NET web form, 338
just-in-time debugging, 67

K

keyboard shortcuts, 340–355
  accelerator and string resource
      editor, 355
  control editor, 347
  debugging, 349–351
  dialog resource editor, 354
  general, 340
  help, 349
  HTML design view, 353–355
  macro, 354
  object browser, 351
  search and replace, 348
  text manipulation, 344–345
  text navigation, 343
  text selection, 345
  tool window, 352
  window manipulation, 342

L

language packages, 313
language service options, C/C++, 381
language-specific settings, 379
launch conditions, 205–210
launching VS.NET, 315
Leave open braces on same line as construct
      setting, 380
License agreement page, 185
Line Numbers text editor setting, 376
localization of components, 221
locals windows, 91

M

machine configuration file
      (machine.config), 118
Macro Explorer, 264
macro IDE, 265
macros, 250, 263–274
  building a custom macro, 270
  debugging, 274
  defined, 250
  editing with the macro IDE, 265
  extending a recorded macro, 267
  features of, 312
  handling events, 273
  IDE, 265
  interpreting command GUIDs and
      IDs, 269
  keyboard shortcuts, 354
  limitations, 274
  Macro Explorer, 264
  managing macro files, 266
  recorded macros project properties, 268
  recording and running macros, 263
Makefile Project template, 329
Managed C++ Application, 327
Managed C++ Class Library, 327
Managed C++ Empty Project, 327
Managed C++ project templates, 9
Managed C++ projects, 327
Managed C++ Web Service, 327
managed web projects, 113–122
managed web-based project, 9
manual building, 27
memory leaks in C++, 76
memory windows, 94, 95
menu verbs, adding, 234
Merge Module Project template, 329
Merge Module projects, 171
  User Interface view and, 174
merge modules, 169
  adding during installation, 193
  and shared components, 169
MFC ActiveX Control template, 328
MFC Application template, 328
MFC class, 337
  from ActiveX control, 337
  from TypeLib, 337
MFC DLL template, 328
MFC ISAPI Extension DLL template, 328
MFC ODBC consumer class, 337
MFC templates, 337
Microsoft Source Code Control Interface
      (MSSCCI), 356
Microsoft.VSDesigner.dll, 60
Midl file (.idl), 336
miscellaneous editors, 56
miscellaneous files, 17
module file, 335
module-definition file (.def), 336
Modules window, 97
  debugging, 97
moving files between projects, 15
MSI projects, 329
multiple solution files with a master, 32–34
multiple solution files with no project
      references, 34
multiuser issues for database projects, 156

N

NAnt website, 29
navigation and bookmarks, 43
navigation bar, 41
Navigation Bar text editor setting, 377
.NET assembly, 8
.NET Framework, 114
.NET installation components, 202–205
.NET projects, and database
        projects, 156–166
New Project
   dialog box, 115
     for a web application, 115
     in existing folder template, 326
nonvisual components, 53

O

object browser, keyboard shortcuts, 351
object model, documentation, 254
one-file wizards, 288
opening files not belonging to any
        project, 17
optimistic concurrency, 160
Optimize Code setting, 99
Options dialog registry configuration, 281
organizational methods, 35
organizing projects, 30–35
outlining and regions, 44–46
   commands, 45
   sections, 44
Output window, 96
   debugging, 95

P

packages
   defined, 313
   features of, 312
Parameter Information text editor
       setting, 376
point of execution, changing, 87
predefined abstract folders, 188
Pretty listing (reformatting of code)
       setting, 379
Primary Key table, 136
processes, multiple, 103
program execution, watching
       progress, 88–97

program types
   CLR .NET, 66
   native (Win32), 66
   script, 66
   T-SQL, 66
Progress page, 180
Project Build Order, 22
project file formats, 369–371
project files
   managing, 13–16
   storing, 118
project item templates (see item templates)
Project Location dialog box, 116
project objects, 254–256
   properties collections, 256
   VSProject, 255
project packages, 313
project references (see references)
project settings and debugging, 97–101
project templates, 325–333
project types, 7–12
   C++, 8
   Cab, 171
   managed local, 7, 8
   managed web-based, 7, 9
   Merge Module, 171
   setup, 171
   setup and deployment, 8, 12
   setup wizard, 171
   Smart Device, 8, 11
   unmanaged local, 11
   unmanaged web-based, 12
   Web Setup, 171
project wizards, 287
ProjectDependencies section, 368
Project/EndProject tag section, 368
projects, 1–36
   adding, 12
   adding references, 18–22
     Add Reference dialog box, 19
     purposes, 18
   administrative installation, 176
   building, 317
   creating, 287–310
   debugging, 317
   dependencies, 17–23
     build order, 22
   File System view (see File System view)
   File Types view, 194–196
   installation process, 172
   loading or creating, 315

managing files, 13–16
  adding an existing file, 13
  file properties, 16
  moving files between projects, 15
  removing or deleting files, 15
organizing, 30–35
  choosing method, 35
  multiple solution files with
    master, 32–34
  multiple solution files with no project
    references, 34
  single solution file, 31
output, 190–192
properties and conditions, 173
putting under source control, 317
Registry view, 196–197
saving, 318
  web-based, 5
setup and deployment, 167–212
setup, types, 170
summary, 36
types (see project types)
User Interface view (see User Interface
  views)
views, 172
web (see web projects)
Windows Installer, 167–170
proj.user file, 358
properties and conditions, 173
properties collections, 256
property visibility, of components, 222

Q

query and view designer, 139–146
query files, 156

R

Radiobuttons pages, 180
.rc files, 339
.rct files, 339
Read Me page, 187
recording and running macros, 263
references, 17–22
  adding to COM components, 21
  adding to other projects, 21
    COM, 22
    .NET, Copy Local=False, 22
    .NET, Copy Local=True, 22
    project, 22

adding to projects (see projects, adding
  references)
dependencies and, 22
file versus project, 33
references list (project file), 370
regions and outlining, 44–46
Register User page, 187
registers, debugging, 92
Registers window, 92
registration script (.rgs), 339
registry
  6.0 key, 316
  7.1 key, 316
  packages and, 316
registry search and installation, 209
Registry view, 196–197
Relationships tab, 136
release-mode, bugs, 99
release-only bugs, 99
Remote Debug Monitor, 106
removing or deleting a file, 15
resource file (.rc), 339
resource template, 339
resource template file (.rct), 339
results pane, 146
.resx files, 339
.rgs files, 339
.rpt files, 339
running process, 65

S

schemas, 48
script files, 298, 338
scripts, 149–156
search and replace keyboard shortcuts, 348
sections, 44
serial number template, 183
Server Explorer, 126–130
  Data Connections list, 128
server-side HTML elements, 56
setting a conditional breakpoint, 76
setup and deployment, 167–212
  summary, 211
Setup and Deployment projects, 12, 329
Setup Project
  template, 329
  types, 170
Setup project, 171
Setup wizard, 171
Setup Wizard template, 329
Shared Add-in template, 332

shell packages, 314
shell, services, 315
Show procedure line separators setting, 379
Show property description tooltips
  setting, 383
Show statement completion pop ups
  setting, 383
side-by-side support, 114
simple editors
    embedded editor, 318
    in-place activation editor, 318
single solution file, 31
single-stepping, 84–88
    and the IL assembler, 86
    changing point of execution, 87
    edit and continue feature, 88
    through multiple lines, 87
SLiNgshoT build utility, 29
.sln files, 367–369
Smart comment editing setting, 380
Smart Device projects, 11
sn.exe (strong name) utility, 303
.snk files, 302
solution file formats, 367–369
solution items, 16
solution objects, 254–256
solution organizational choices
    multiple solution files with master
        solution, 36
    multiple solution files with no project
        references, 36
    single solution file, 36
SolutionConfiguration section, 369
solutions, 1–36
    build events, 29
    building, 22–30
        automated, 28
        Configuration Manager, 24–26
        external build tools, 29
        manual, 27
    compared with IDE, 2
    creating, 2–4
    defined, 1
    navigating within, 42
    summary, 36
source code
    and outlining, 44
    contained in a hidden section, 44
    navigating through, 43
    outlining information, 44

source control
    basics, 356–366
    object, 262
    putting projects under, 317
SourceCodeControl section, 369
Splash page, 186
SQL
    editor, 146
    pane, 145
SQL script, 338
SRF file (.srf) template, 337
.srf files, 337
static discovery file, 335
stored procedure script, 338
strong name in a wizard, 303
Style (CSS Format setting), 383
stylesheet, 338
summaries
    automation, macros, and add-ins, 286
    database projects, 166
    debugging, 109
    files and editors, 62
    integrating components, 249
    project setup and deployment, 211
    projects and solutions, 36
    VSIP, 324
    web projects, 124
    wizards, 310
.suo files, 359, 367
symbol servers, 106
symbol store
    creating and maintaining, 108
    using, 107
System project, 331

T
Tab Size text editor setting, 377
table designer, 138
table property pages, 133–138
    Check Constraints tab, 138
    Columns tab, 134
    Indexes/Keys tab, 137
    Relationships tab, 136
    Tables tab, 134
table script, 338
Tables tab, 134
tabs text editor setting, 377
tasklist comments, 46
TaskList window, 47
team projects, debugging, 121
template directives, 301
template files, 298

templates, web projects, 110–113
templates.inf file, 298
text and the Toolbox, 46
text editor, 37–47
    Beautifier, 41
    C# documentation, 40
    class view pane, 42
    clipboard ring, 46
    CSS editor, 51–56
    HTML/XML editor, 48–50
    IntelliSense, 38–40
    navigation and bookmarks, 43
    navigation bar, 41
    outlining and regions, 44–46
    tasklist comments, 46
    Toolbox, 46
text editor settings, 372–383
    fonts and colors, 373
    General settings, 374–377
    global, 372
    tabs, 377
text file, 338
text manipulation keyboard
        shortcuts, 344–345
text navigation keyboard shortcuts, 343
text selection keyboard shortcuts, 345
text-based templates, 338
Textboxes pages, 182
this windows, 91
threads, multiple, 102
Threads window, 103
tool window, keyboard shortcuts, 352
Toolbox, 46
Toolbox bitmap, 216–219
transactional component source file, 336
trigger script, 338
T-SQL debugging, 105
type converters, 224–229
type-safe datasets, 125

U

UI packages, 313
unmanaged local projects, 11
    ActiveX control, 11
    application, 11
    ATL project, 11
    DLL, 11
    ISAPI extension, 11
    Win32 project, 11
unmanaged web-based projects, 12
user control (.NET) source file, 336
user control source file, 335

.user files, 370
user interface objects, 257–260
    CommandBar objects, 258
    window objects, 257
User Interface views, 174–187
    Merge Module projects and, 174
utility packages, 314

V

validation, 48
variables, displaying, 88–91
VB.Net item templates, 334
VB.NET, J#, and C# web-based projects, 10
VB.NET Language Service, 379
VB.Net templates, 335
VBScript file, 338
view script, 338
views
    File System (see File System view)
    File Types, 194–196
    project, 172
    Registry, 196–197
    User Interface (see User Interface views)
virtual directories (IIS), 111
Visual Basic Distributed Application
        template, 331
Visual Basic projects, 325
Visual Basic Simple Distributed Application
        template, 330
Visual C#
    Distributed Application template, 331
    projects, 325
    Simple Distributed Application
        template, 331
Visual C++
    ASP.NET web service, 123
    ATL projects, 327
    ATL server, 123
    building and debugging, 124
    creating, 123
    general projects, 328
    MFC projects, 328
    .NET projects, 327
    project files, 123
    projects, 326
    web projects, 122–124
    Win32 projects, 328
Visual J# projects, 325
Visual Source Safe (see VSS)
Visual Studio Analyzer projects, 332
Visual Studio Integration Partner (see VSIP)
Visual Studio Integration Program (see VSIP)

Visual Studio .NET Add-in template, 332
Visual Studio .NET Enterprise Edition
        packages, 313
Visual Studio Solutions, 333
.vsdir files, 289–292
VSDIRFLAG_BlankSolution, 291
VSDIRFLAG_DisableBrowseButton, 291
VSDIRFLAG_DisableLocationField, 291
VSDIRFLAG_DisableNameField, 291
VSDIRFLAG_DontAddDefExtension, 291
VSDIRFLAG_DontInitNameField, 291
VSDIRFLAG_NonLocalTemplate, 291
VSIP, 311–324
    applying for, 311
    justification for, 312–318
    SDK, 316
        Figures sample, 320
    SDK and, 311
    summary, 324
VSIP packages
    custom, 318–324
    debugging engines and expression
        evaluators, 324
    language services, 321–322
    new project type, 322
    typical, 315
        building and debugging, 317
        editing file in code view, 317
        editing file in design view, 317
        launching VS.NET, 315
        loading or creating projects, 315
        putting projects under source
            control, 317
        saving projects, 318
    views, 318–320
        code view, 319
        defined, 318
        in-place activation editor, 318
        simple embedded editor, 318
VS.NET, launching, 315
VS.NET packages
    registry and, 316
VSProject, 255
VSS (Visual Source Safe), 356
    adding solutions, 357–358
    checking files in and out, 359–362
    checking files in frequently, 361
    checking files out versus getting latest
        version, 361
    creating a database, 356
    diffing files, 363
    file history, 362

retrieving a project, 362
web projects, 365
working offline, 365
VsWebCache, 118
.vsz files
    custom parameters in, 305
    wizard engine parameters for, 293
    wizards and, 292

W
watch windows, 88
    format specifiers, 90
web applications, 113
    defined, 111
web configuration file, 335
Web Control Library template, 326
web custom control source file, 335
web form file, 335
web forms, 54
    HTML layout, 55
    server-side HTML elements, 56
    web services, 56
web forms control designers, 247–249
Web Forms designer, 54
web projects, 110–124
    building and debugging, 120
    codebehind file, 118
    creating, 115–117
    debugging, team projects, 121
    FrontPage versus file sharing, 121
    IIS virtual directories, 111
    managed, 113–122
    opening existing, 120
    storing project files, 118
    summary, 124
    templates, 110–113
    Visual C++, 122–124
    web applications, 113
web Service file, 335
web services, 56
Web Setup Project, 171
Web Setup Project template, 329
web-based projects, saving, 5
web.config file, 335
.webinfo files, 371
WebUI project, 332
Welcome page, 178
Win32 Console Project template, 328
Win32 Project template, 328
window manipulation keyboard
        shortcuts, 342
Windows Application template, 325

Windows Control Library (.NET)
  template, 327
Windows Control Library template, 325
Windows form source file, 334
windows forms, 54
Windows Forms Application (.NET)
  template, 327
Windows forms control designers, 235–249
Windows forms designer, 54
Windows forms (.NET) source file, 336
Windows Installer, 167–170
Windows Installer search, 210
Windows script host file, 338
Windows Service (.NET) template, 327
Windows service source file, 335
Windows Service template, 326
Windows versions, detecting, 208
WinUI project, 332
wizard engine, 288, 293–304
    custom, 304–310
    defined, 293
    execution, 295–301
    parameters for .vsz files, 293
    script and templates, 298–301
    script files, 298
    template directives, 301
    template files, 298
    user interface, 295–297
wizards, 287–310
    adding, 288–292
    basics, 287

context wizards, 288
copying and modifying, 301–304
custom engine, 288
defined, 287
flag values, 290
implementation, choices, 288
item wizards, 288
    .vsdir files and, 291
one-file, 288
project wizards, 287
strong name in, 303
summary, 310
type locations, 289
.vsdir files, 289–292
.vsz files, 292
WMI event provider, 337
WMI instance provider, 337
word wrap test editor setting, 376

X

XML data view, 50
XML editor (see HTML/XML editor)
XML file, 339
XML language service options, 381
XML schema, 50, 339
XML Schema Definition, 164
XML Schema Definition files, 49
XSD Designer, 162–166
.xsd file, defined, 164
XSD file, editing, 50
XSLT file, 339

About the Authors

Ian Griffiths is an independent consultant specializing in medical imaging applications and digital video. He also works as an instructor, teaching courses on .NET for DevelopMentor. Ian holds a degree in computer science from Cambridge University.

Jon Flanders is most at home spelunking, trying to figure out exactly how .NET (specifically ASP.NET and Visual Studio .NET) works. Although Jon spent the first few years of his professional life as an attorney, he quickly found chasing bits more interesting than chasing ambulances. Deducing the details and disseminating that information to other developers is his passion.

Chris Sells is an independent consultant, speaker, and author specializing in distributed applications in .NET and COM. He's written several books and is currently working on *Windows Forms for C#* and *VB.NET Programming*. In his free time, Chris hosts various conferences, directs the Genghis source-available project, plays with Rotor and, in general, makes a pest of himself at Microsoft design reviews.

Colophon

Our look is the result of reader comments, our own experimentation, and feedback from distribution channels. Distinctive covers complement our distinctive approach to technical topics, breathing personality and life into potentially dry subjects.

The animal on the cover of *Mastering Visual Studio .NET* is an Egyptian goose. It is common everywhere (except deep forests and desert) but is found usually in freshwater and grassy parkland; it feeds on crops and young grass. The Egyptian goose is at home in trees, regularly perching and even roosting there; cavities and holes in trees and abandoned nests of other birds may be selected to nest in.

Both sexes look alike, although the female is slightly smaller than the male. Its wing coverts are white with black primaries, and green and brown secondaries; its most distinctive feature is a chestnut-colored bandit's mask. The Egyptian goose draws attention to itself with noisy displays and fierce territorial fighting. Rivals stand or swim, breast to breast, attempting to seize each other's backs near the base of the neck while beating with their wings.

Sarah Sherman was the production editor and proofreader, and Norma Emory was the copyeditor for *Mastering Visual Studio .NET*. Jane Ellin and Claire Cloutier provided quality control. John Bickelhaupt wrote the index.

Emma Colby designed the cover of this book, based on a series design by Edie Freedman. The cover image is a 19th-century engraving from the Dover Pictorial Archive. Emma Colby produced the cover layout with QuarkXPress 4.1 using Adobe's ITC Garamond font.

Bret Kerr designed the interior layout, based on a series design by David Futato. This book was converted by Joe Wizda to FrameMaker 5.5.6 with a format conversion tool created by Erik Ray, Jason McIntosh, Neil Walls, and Mike Sierra that uses Perl and XML technologies. The text font is Linotype Birka; the heading font is Adobe Myriad Condensed; and the code font is LucasFont's TheSans Mono Condensed. The illustrations that appear in the book were produced by Robert Romano and Jessamyn Read using Macromedia FreeHand 9 and Adobe Photoshop 6. The tip and warning icons were drawn by Christopher Bing. This colophon was written by Sarah Sherman.

Other Titles Available from O'Reilly

Microsoft .NET Programming

VB.NET Language in a Nutshell, 2nd Edition

*By Steven Roman, Ron Petrusha &
Paul Lomax
2nd Edition May 2002
682 pages, ISBN 0-596-00308-0*

The documentation that comes with
VB typically provides only the bare
details for each language element; left
out is the valuable inside information
that a programmer really needs to know in order to solve
programming problems or to use a particular language
element effectively. *VB .NET Language in a Nutshell*, 2nd
Edition documents the undocumented and presents the
kind of wisdom that comes from the authors' many years
of experience with the language. Bonus CD integrates
the book's reference section with Visual Studio .NET.

Programming C#, 2nd Edition

*By Jesse Liberty
2nd Edition February 2002
650 pages, ISBN 0-596-00309-9*

The first part of *Programming C#*, 2nd
Edition introduces C# fundamentals,
then goes on to explain the development of desktop and Internet applications, including Windows Forms, ADO.NET, ASP.NET
(including Web Forms), and Web Services. Next, this
book gets to the heart of the .NET Framework, focusing
on attributes and reflection, remoting, threads and syn-
chronization, streams, and finally, it illustrates how to
interoperate with COM objects.

Learning Visual Basic .NET

*By Jesse Liberty
1st edition October 2002
320 pages, ISBN 0-596-00386-2*

Learning Visual Basic .NET is a complete introduction to VB.NET and
object-oriented programming. By
using hundreds of examples, this book
demonstrates how to develop various kinds of applications—including those that work with databases—and
web services. *Learning Visual Basic .NET* will help you
build a solid foundation in .NET.

Programming ASP.NET

*By Jesse Liberty & Dan Hurwitz
1st Edition February 2002
960 pages, ISBN 0-596-00171-1*

The ASP.NET technologies are so complete and flexible; your main difficulty
may lie simply in weaving the pieces
together for maximum efficiency.
Programming ASP.NET shows you how to do just that.
Jesse Liberty and Dan Hurwitz teach everything you
need to know to write web applications and web services
using both C# and Visual Basic .NET.

C# in a Nutshell

*By Peter Drayton & Ben Albarhari
1st Edition March 2002
856 pages, ISBN 0-596-00181-9*

C# is likely to become one of the
most widely used languages for building .NET applications. *C# in a Nutshell* contains a concise introduction
to the language and its syntax, plus
brief tutorials used to accomplish common programming tasks. It also includes O'Reilly's classic-style, quick-
reference material for all the types and members in core
.NET namespaces, including System, System.Text, Sys-
tem.IO, and System.Collections.

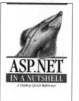

ASP.NET in a Nutshell

*By G. Andrew Duthie &
Matthew MacDonald
1st Edition June 2002
816 pages, ISBN 0-596-00116-9*

As a quick reference and tutorial in
one, *ASP.NET in a Nutshell* goes
beyond the published documentation
to highlight little-known details, stress
practical uses for particular features, and provide real-
world examples that show how features can be used in a
working application. This book covers application and
web service development, custom controls, data access,
security, deployment, and error handling. There is also
an overview of web-related class libraries.

Microsoft .NET Programming

.NET Framework Essentials, 2nd Edition

By Thuan L. Thai, Hoang Lam
2nd Edition February 2002
320 pages, 0-596-00302-1

.NET Framework Essentials, 2nd Edition is a concise and technical overview of the Microsoft .NET Framework. Covered here are all of the most important topics—from the underlying Common Language Runtime (CLR) to its specialized packages for ASP.NET, Web Forms, Windows Forms, XML and data access (ADO.NET). The authors survey each of the major .NET languages, including Visual Basic .NET, C# and Managed C++.

Learning C#

By Jesse Liberty
1st Edition September 2002
368 pages, ISBN 0-596-00376-5

With *Learning C#*, best-selling author Jesse Liberty will help you build a solid foundation in .NET and show how to apply your skills by using dozens of tested examples. You will learn how to develop various kinds of applications—including those that work with databases—and web services. Whether you have a little object-oriented programming experience or you are new to programming altogether, *Learning C#* will set you firmly on your way.

COM and .NET Component Services

By Juval Löwy
1st Edition September 2001
384 pages, 0-596-00103-7

COM & .NET Component Services provides both traditional COM programmers and new .NET component developers with the information they need to begin developing applications that take full advantage of COM+ services. This book focuses on COM+ services, including support for transactions, queued components, events, concurrency management, and security.

VB.NET Core Classes in a Nutshell

By Budi Kurniawan
1st Edition May 2002
576 pages, ISBN 0-596-00257-2

VB.NET Core Classes in a Nutshell, provides a concise and thorough reference to the types found in the core namespaces of the .NET Framework Class Library. A companion to *VB.NET Language in a Nutshell*, this is a reference that VB.NET programmers will turn to repeatedly. Due to a special partnership between O'Reilly and Microsoft, this book also includes a CD that integrates the book's reference into Visual Studio .NET.

Programming .NET Web Services

By Alex Ferrara & Matthew MacDonald
1st Edition October 2002
414 pages, ISBN 0-596-00250-5

This comprehensive tutorial teaches programmers the skills they need to develop XML web services hosted on the Microsoft .NET platform. *Programming .NET Web Services* also shows you how to consume these services on both Microsoft and non-Windows clients, and how to weave them into well-designed and scalable applications. For those interested in building industrial-strength web services, this book is full of practical information and good old-fashioned advice.

Object-Oriented Programming with Visual Basic .NET

By J.P. Hamilton
1st Edition September 2002
308 pages, ISBN 0-596-00146-0

Visual Basic .NET is a language that facilitates object-oriented programming, but does not guarantee good code. That's where *Object-Oriented Programming with Visual Basic .NET* comes in. It will show you how to think about similarities in your application logic and how to design and create objects that maximize the benefit and power of .NET. Packed with examples that will guide you through every step, *Object-Oriented Programming with Visual Basic .NET* is for those with some programming experience.

1325

O'REILLY®

To order: 800-998-9938 • order@oreilly.com • www.oreilly.com
Online editions of most O'Reilly titles are available by subscription at *safari.oreilly.com*
Also available at most retail and online bookstores.

How to stay in touch with O'Reilly

1.   Visit our award-winning web site

http://www.oreilly.com/

★ "Top 100 Sites on the Web"—PC Magazine
★ CIO Magazine's Web Business 50 Awards

Our web site contains a library of comprehensive product information (including book excerpts and tables of contents), downloadable software, background articles, interviews with technology leaders, links to relevant sites, book cover art, and more. File us in your bookmarks or favorites!

2.   Join our email mailing lists

Sign up to get email announcements of new books and conferences, special offers, and O'Reilly Network technology newsletters at:

http://elists.oreilly.com

It's easy to customize your free elists subscription so you'll get exactly the O'Reilly news you want.

3.   Get examples from our books

To find example files for a book, go to:

http://www.oreilly.com/catalog

select the book, and follow the "Examples" link.

4.   Work with us

Check out our web site for current employment opportunities:

http://jobs.oreilly.com/

5.   Register your book

Register your book at:

http://register.oreilly.com

6.   Contact us

O'Reilly & Associates, Inc.
1005 Gravenstein Hwy North
Sebastopol, CA 95472 USA
TEL: 707-827-7000 or 800-998-9938
       (6am to 5pm PST)
FAX: 707-829-0104

order@oreilly.com
For answers to problems regarding your order or our products. To place a book order online visit:

http://www.oreilly.com/order_new/

catalog@oreilly.com
To request a copy of our latest catalog.

booktech@oreilly.com
For book content technical questions or corrections.

corporate@oreilly.com
For educational, library, government, and corporate sales.

proposals@oreilly.com
To submit new book proposals to our editors and product managers.

international@oreilly.com
For information about our international distributors or translation queries. For a list of our distributors outside of North America check out:

http://international.oreilly.com/distributors.html

adoption@oreilly.com
For information about academic use of O'Reilly books, visit:

http://academic.oreilly.com